Hiking Intown Atlanta's Hidden Forests

Hiking Intown Atlanta's Hidden Forests

INSIDE AND ON THE PERIMETER

Jonah McDonald
and Zana Pouncey

MILESTONE PRESS
AN IMPRINT OF
THE UNIVERSITY OF GEORGIA PRESS
ATHENS

Published by Milestone Press,
an imprint of the University of Georgia Press
Athens, GA 30602
www.ugapress.org

Designed by Kaelin Chappell Broaddus
Set in 9.5/12 Bodoni Egyptian Pro
by Kaelin Chappell Broaddus
Maps by Jon Davies, Nicole Marie Greaux,
Rebecca A. Norton, and Ally Smith.
Printed and bound by Sheridan Books, Inc.
The paper in this book meets the guidelines for
permanence and durability of the Committee on
Production Guidelines for Book Longevity of the
Council on Library Resources.

Most University of Georgia Press titles are
available from popular e-book vendors.

Printed in the United States of America
28 27 26 25 24 P 5 4 3 2 1

Library of Congress Cataloging-in-Publication Data
Names: McDonald, Jonah, 1979– author. |
Pouncey, Zana, author.
Title: Hiking intown Atlanta's hidden forests :
inside and on the perimeter / Jonah McDonald
and Zana Pouncey.
Other titles: Hiking Atlanta's hidden forests intown and out
Description: Athens : Milestone Press, an imprint of the
University of Georgia Press, 2024. | Revised edition of:
Hiking Atlanta's hidden forests intown and out.
Almond, NC : Milestone Press, 2014.
Identifiers: LCCN 2024011382 |
ISBN 9781889596433 (paperback)
Subjects: LCSH: Hiking—Georgia—Atlanta Region—
Guidebooks. | Trails—Georgia—Atlanta Region—
Guidebooks. | Atlanta Region (Ga)—Guidebooks.
Classification: LCC GV199.42.G462 A856 2024 |
DDC 917.58/231—dc23/eng/20240401
LC record available at https://lccn.loc.gov/2024011382

For Zena Pouncey

CONTENTS

ON THE PERIMETER–WESTSIDE

BELTLINE CONNECTIONS–WESTSIDE

NORTHSIDE + MAP

ON THE PERIMETER–NORTHSIDE

BELTLINE CONNECTIONS–NORTHSIDE

CHATTAHOOCHEE RIVER NATIONAL RECREATION AREA

PREFACE

Jonah McDonald

Over 20 years ago, I arrived in Atlanta by way of the Appalachian Trail. After hiking this rugged 2,000-mile path from Maine to Georgia and establishing my new home in the city, I spent weekends driving hundreds of miles away from Atlanta in search of the peace and beauty that nature offers. On weekday afternoons, I sought out trails in the forests of Atlanta and wandered beside creeks, over ridges, and through some of the most impressive old-growth forests I've found anywhere. I have come to believe that short hikes close to home can be as life-changing as extended backpacking trips. And I have found that Atlanta is the perfect city for hiking.

In the decade since the original *Hiking Atlanta's Hidden Forests: Intown and Out* was published, Atlanta has reclaimed its identity as "The City in the Forest," and Atlantans have hiked countless miles, opened beautiful new parks, and built many miles of new trails. There are now twice as many hikes to experience inside and near the I-285 perimeter as there were in the original guidebook.

My hiking style and companions have changed over the years as well. My wife, Dana, has been my constant hiking partner, and the publication of *Hiking Atlanta's Hidden Forests* also coincided with the birth of our daughter, Annie Mae. Now I try to keep up with my energetic kid, who leads our family on hikes. I now experience these trails—and our city—through the eyes of my child.

This guidebook was written to inspire you as well to see our city through a new lens. Atlanta may be known throughout the world as a city of sports, traffic jams, civil rights, music, and culture, but it is also a haven for nature. I hope these trails change your life as they have changed mine.

Finally, I am honored to introduce you to my coauthor, Zana Pouncey, who is a delight to work with, a great hiking partner, and a fantastic trail guide. Her experience, passion, and knowledge have helped make this book even more thorough, accurate, and inclusive than it would have been if I had been on this writing journey alone.

Zana Pouncey

I grew up in Georgia, and when I was a kid, exploring the outdoors was my favorite pastime. I earned a degree in environmental science from Emory University and have had the opportunity to study and hike in some of the world's most beautiful and remote wildernesses, from the Rockies to the rainforest. But my love of hiking formed while I was traversing the trails no more than 30 minutes from my house. My appreciation for Atlanta's eclectic neighborhood trails was solidified while I worked at an after-school program that traveled to a new hiking destination every week. It was there that I first encountered Jonah's work: We used the original *Hiking Atlanta's Hidden Forests* as a guide to plan hikes.

I got to know Jonah almost 10 years later at an environmental education conference. We then became professional colleagues. It has been a deep honor and pleasure to join him in creating this resource for the community.

Environmental advocacy and accessibility are driving forces in my career and a motivation for writing this guidebook. When I was younger some part of me always understood that it wasn't typical for black women to go hiking alone, but it never crossed my mind that I (or anyone else) didn't belong on the trails or in the woods. Spending time in nature has always been a spiritual experience for me. Scientific data support my experience that being in nature is good for our mental and physical health. I want the trails and woods of Atlanta to reflect the city's diversity of people and cultures.

My hope is that this guidebook can help people of all levels of hiking experience to find a moment of peace and serenity on a trail. I hope to also bring a bit of love and awareness to some of the lesser-known parks and trails around the city. Atlanta is one of my favorite places not just because I call it home but also because of its endless options for amazing food, diverse cultural experiences, local music and art, civil rights history, grassroots advocacy, and ample greenspaces. I hope the hikes in this book help you fall a bit more in love with our city too.

ACKNOWLEDGMENTS

Writing this hiking guidebook was a giant undertaking and was only possible because of the patience, support, and encouragement of our families. So thank you, Dana, Annie Mae, and Matthew. You are our favorite hiking partners, collaborators, and cheerleaders.

Our extended families also accompanied us on this project, offering suggestions, edits, hike tests, and listening ears. Even in the midst of work, health, and personal challenges, you supported us in this project. Thank you, Ron, Susan, Jesse, Cindy, Marie, David, Mark, Marlene, Andrea, and Todd. Thank you, Winfred, Zena, and Tate.

We couldn't have even started writing this guidebook if the trails weren't cared for by the community. We've found that every hidden forest has a steward, a group or an individual who knows the trails best and goes above and beyond to protect and maintain the land. We lovingly call you the Lorax of your forest, and without your guidance and knowledge, this book wouldn't have become what it is. Thanks to Gwen, Jim, Michael, Sally, Joel, Steve, Amy, Betsy, Josh, Beth, Heather, Stephen, Margo, and many, many others.

Every hike route in this book has been tested and edited by volunteers who are passionate about hiking in Atlanta: Carolyn Hartfield, Theresa Hall, Eddas Bennett, Stacey Adams, Eli Dickerson, Robby Astrove, Dana Goldman, Annie Mae McDonald, Mark Goldman, Marlene Goldman, Marty Levine, Katie Hendrickson, Ben Fowler, Dean Leeper, Molly Samuels, Mike Harkin, Darleen Jarman, Andrew Tsivoglou, Jim Price, Maggie Akstin, Ron McDonald, Jesse McDonald, Sam Mugavero, Jessica Thompson, Paul Stevens, Kelsie Khalili, Shahid Khalili, and others tested hikes, took photos, and helped us hone the routes and our descriptions of them.

Finally, we are grateful for Jim Parham and Mary Ellen Hammond of Milestone Press, who first shared the vision for this guidebook and believed in Jonah enough to help make *Hiking Atlanta's Hidden Forests: Intown and Out* a reality. And to our editors at the University of Georgia Press, Nathaniel Holly, Laura Price Yoder, and Jon Davies, we appreciate your guidance and advocacy for us and for this book.

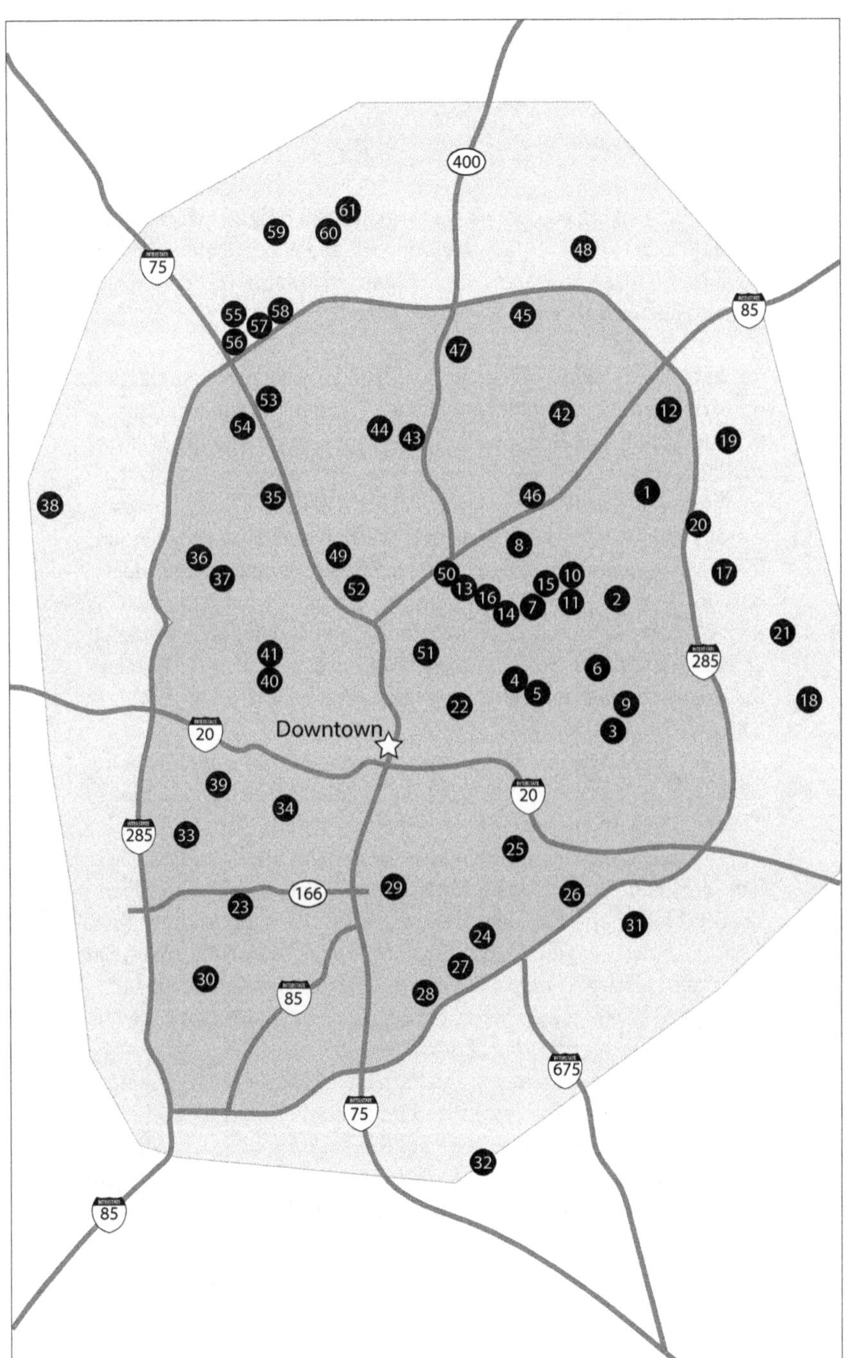

400
75
85
285
20
Downtown
166
675

1. Briarlake Forest Park
2. Clyde Shepherd Nature Preserve
3. Dearborn Park
4. Fernbank Forest
5. Frazer Forest & Deepdene Park
6. Glenlake Park & Decatur Cemetery
7. Hahn Woods & Lullwater Preserve
8. Kittredge Park
9. Legacy Park
10. Mason Mill Park–Burnt Fork Trails
11. Mason Mill Park–South Fork Trails
12. Mercer University Nature Trail
13. Morningside Nature Preserve
14. Peavine Trail
15. W.D. Thomson Park
16. Zonolite Park & Herbert Taylor Park
17. Friendship Forest Wildlife Sanctuary
18. Hairston Park
19. Henderson Park
20. Johns Homestead Park
21. Pine Lake
22. Freedom Park Trail
23. Connally Nature Park
24. Constitution Lakes Park
25. Glen Emerald Park
26. Gresham Park & South River Trail
27. Lake Charlotte Nature Preserve
28. Southside Park
29. Southtowne Trail & South Bend Park
30. Sykes Park
31. Michelle Obama Trail
32. Reynolds Nature Preserve
33. Cascade Springs Nature Preserve
34. Outdoor Activity Center
35. Paul Koshewa Trail
36. Riverwalk Atlanta & Whittier Mill Park
37. Spink Collins Park
38. Heritage Park
39. Lionel Hampton Park & Beecher Hills Park
40. Proctor Creek Greenway
41. Westside Park
42. Ashford Forest Preserve
43. Blue Heron Nature Preserve
44. Chastain Memorial Park
45. Murphey Candler Park
46. Peachtree Creek Greenway
47. Ridgeview Park
48. Brook Run Park & Pernoshal Park
49. Atlanta Memorial Park
50. Confluence Trail & Cheshire Farm Trail
51. Piedmont Park & Eastside Beltline
52. Tanyard Creek Park & Northside Beltline
53. East Palisades
54. West Palisades
55. Bob Callan Trail
56. Rottenwood Creek Trail
57. Cochran Shoals
58. Powers Island
59. Sope Creek
60. Johnson Ferry South
61. Johnson Ferry North & Hyde Farm

HIKES AT A GLANCE

	Hike distance	Miles from downtown	Difficulty	Popularity
EASTSIDE				
Briarlake Forest Park	1	12	Easy	★★★★☆
Clyde Shepherd Nature Preserve	2	9	Easy	★★★★☆
Dearborn Park	1.3	7	Easy	★★★☆☆
Fernbank Forest	2	5	Easy to moderate	★★★★★
Frazer Forest & Deepdene Park	2.5	5	Easy to moderate	★★★★☆
Glenlake Park & Decatur Cemetery	1.5	7	Easy	★★★★★
Hahn Woods & Lullwater Preserve	3	7	Easy to moderate	★★★★☆
Kittredge Park	1.5	8	Easy to moderate	★★★☆☆
Legacy Park	2.2	7	Easy to moderate	★★★★☆
Mason Mill Park—Burnt Fork Trails	2	9	Easy to moderate	★★★★★
Mason Mill Park—South Fork Trails	3.3	9	Moderate	★★★★☆
Mercer University Nature Trail	1	14	Easy	★★★☆☆
Morningside Nature Preserve	2	6	Easy to moderate	★★★★☆
Peavine Trail	1.5	6	Easy to moderate	★★☆☆☆
W.D. Thomson Park	1.25	8	Easy to moderate	★★★★☆
Zonolite Park & Herbert Taylor Park	2.75	7	Moderate	★★★★☆

Facilities	Primary trail surface	Champion tree	Views	Water	History
	Dirt		Ravine		Historic farmhouse
	Dirt			Pond & creek	
	Dirt Boardwalk Paved			Creek & sliding rock	
	Paved Boardwalk Dirt			Pond	Historic home
	Dirt Paved			Creek	Historic trolley stop
	Paved Dirt		Decatur	Creek	Cemetery
	Dirt Paved			Creek & two waterfalls	Houston Mill dam + Lullwater powerhouse
	Dirt			Creek & cascade	
	Dirt		Lake	Ponds	Historic dairy barn
	Boardwalk Dirt		Woodland cove	Wetland	
	Dirt Paved			Creek	Old Decatur Waterworks
	Dirt				Homesite ruins
	Dirt Boardwalk		Pencil Tower	Creek	
	Dirt			Creek	
	Dirt			Creek & small cascade	
	Dirt			Creeks & small cascade	

	Hike distance	Miles from downtown	Difficulty	Popularity
ON THE PERIMETER–EASTSIDE				
Friendship Forest Wildlife Sanctuary	1.2	13	Easy	★★★★☆
Hairston Park	1.25	13	Easy	★★★☆☆
Henderson Park	2.4	16	Moderate	★★★☆☆
Johns Homestead Park	1.5	14	Easy to moderate	★★★☆☆
Pine Lake	1.5	12	Easy	★★★★☆
BELTLINE CONNECTIONS–EASTSIDE				
Freedom Park Trail	3.5	3	Easy to moderate	★★★★☆
SOUTHSIDE				
Connally Nature Park	1.3	8	Easy	★★★☆☆
Constitution Lakes Park	2	6	Easy to moderate	★★★☆☆
Glen Emerald Park	1.2	6	Easy	★★★★☆
Gresham Park & South River Trail	3	8	Easy to moderate	★★★★☆
Lake Charlotte Nature Preserve	2	9	Easy to moderate	★★☆☆☆
Southside Park	4	9	Easy to moderate	★★★★☆
Southtowne Trail & South Bend Park	3	5	Easy to moderate	★★★☆☆
Sykes Park	1.5	9	Easy to moderate	★☆☆☆☆

Facilities	Primary trail surface	Champion tree	Views	Water	History
	Paved Dirt			Wetland & creek	
	Dirt Paved			Lakes	
	Dirt			Lake & waterfalls	
	Dirt			Wetland & lakes	Historic homestead
	Dirt Paved			Lake, creek, & wetland	
	Paved		Skyline		Site of Sherman's Civil War headquarters
	Dirt			Creek	Former plantation land
	Paved Dirt		Lake	Lake, wetland, & river	Former brick factory & industrial site
	Dirt Paved		Lake	Lake	Historic rock garden
	Paved			Creek	
	Dirt		Landfill		Former homesteads
	Dirt			Creek	
	Paved			River	
	Dirt			Creek	

	Hike distance	Miles from downtown	Difficulty	Popularity
ON THE PERIMETER–SOUTHSIDE				
Michelle Obama Trail	4	10	Moderate to strenuous based on length	★★★★☆
Reynolds Nature Preserve	2	14	Easy to moderate	★★★★☆
WESTSIDE				
Cascade Springs Nature Preserve	2	7	Easy to moderate	★★★★☆
Outdoor Activity Center	1	4	Easy to moderate	★★★☆☆
Paul Koshewa Trail	2	10	Moderate	★★★★☆
Riverwalk Atlanta & Whittier Mill Park	3	10	Moderate	★☆☆☆☆
Spink Collins Park	1	11	Easy to moderate	★★☆☆☆
ON THE PERIMETER–WESTSIDE				
Heritage Park	4	16	Easy to moderate	★★★★☆
BELTLINE CONNECTIONS–WESTSIDE				
Lionel Hampton Park & Beecher Hills Park	3	6	Moderate	★★★★☆
Proctor Creek Greenway	3	7	Easy to moderate	★★★★☆
Westside Park	2	7	Moderate	★★★★★
NORTHSIDE				
Ashford Forest Preserve	1.5	12	Easy to moderate	★★★☆☆
Blue Heron Nature Preserve	2	11	Easy	★★★★☆
Chastain Memorial Park	3.25	11	Easy to moderate	★★★★★

Facilities	Primary trail surface	Champion tree	Views	Water	History
	Paved			River & wetland	
	Dirt Boardwalk			Ponds & creeks	Former homestead
	Dirt		Turkeyfoot Falls	Waterfall & creeks	Former inn & resort
	Dirt			Creek	Negro League practice field
	Dirt		Corso Atlanta	Creek	
	Dirt		Chattahoochee River	River	Historic mill tower at Whittier Mill Park
	Dirt			Creek	Former Boy Scout lodge
	Dirt Boardwalk			Creek	Historic mill
	Paved Dirt			Creek	Union army trench line
	Paved			Creek	
	Paved		Reservoir & skyline	Reservoir	Former quarry site
	Dirt			Creek & small cascade	Runway lights
	Dirt Boardwalk			Waterfalls, wetland, & creek	Historic dams
	Paved			Creek	

	Hike distance	Miles from downtown	Difficulty	Popularity
Murphey Candler Park	2	16	Easy	★★★★★
Peachtree Creek Greenway	2.5	11	Easy	★★★★☆
Ridgeview Park	1	14	Moderate	★★★☆☆
ON THE PERIMETER–NORTHSIDE				
Brook Run Park & Pernoshal Park	2.8	19	Easy	★★★★★
BELTLINE CONNECTIONS–NORTHSIDE				
Atlanta Memorial Park	2	6	Easy to moderate	★★★★☆
Confluence Trail & Cheshire Farm Trail	3.2	8	Easy	★★☆☆☆
Piedmont Park & Eastside Beltline	2.5	3	Easy to moderate	★★★★★
Tanyard Creek Park & Northside Beltline	2	6	Easy	★★★★☆
CHATTAHOOCHEE RIVER NATIONAL RECREATION AREA				
East Palisades	4	11	Moderate to strenuous	★★★★☆
West Palisades	4.5	11	Moderate to strenuous	★★★★☆
Bob Callan Trail	2	13	Easy to moderate	★★★★☆
Rottenwood Creek Trail	4	12	Moderate	★★★★☆
Cochran Shoals	5.5	13	Moderate to strenuous	★★★★☆
Powers Island	2	7	Easy to moderate	★★★★☆
Sope Creek	4	18	Moderate	★★★★☆
Johnson Ferry South	2	19	Easy	★★★☆☆
Johnson Ferry North & Hyde Farm	1.5–5.5	19	Easy to strenuous	★★★★☆

Facilities	Primary trail surface	Champion tree	Views	Water	History
	Dirt Boardwalk Paved		Lake	Lake & creek	
	Paved			Creek	
	Dirt		Ridge	Creek	
	Paved			Creek	
	Dirt			Creek	Civil War battle site
	Dirt Paved			Creek	
	Paved Gravel		Skyline	Lake	
	Paved			Creek	Civil War battle site
	Dirt		River & bamboo forest	River	
	Dirt Paved		River	River	
	Paved		Creek	Creek	
	Paved		Waterfall	Creek, waterfall, & river	
	Dirt		River	River	1800s gravesite
	Dirt		River	River	
	Dirt Gravel		Creek	Lake & creek	Historic Civil War mill
	Dirt		River	River	
	Dirt Gravel		Morgan Falls Dam	River, cascade	Historic Hyde Farm

Hiking Intown Atlanta's Hidden Forests

AN INTRODUCTION TO URBAN HIKING

Why Urban Hiking?

As you hike the woodland coves, creekside trails, and wooded hilltops described in this guide, it's easy to forget that every trail in this book is truly urban—surrounded by neighborhoods, skyscrapers, businesses, highways, and industry. Each hike is less than a 20-mile drive from downtown, but these hidden forests transport you so much farther away. This guidebook can help you integrate hiking into your everyday life. If you want to walk your dog after work or are in search of a Sunday afternoon excursion for your family, you can find a trail close to home to explore. And if you want a full day of hiking without spending half the day in your car, you will discover that Atlanta's hidden forests are the perfect place to go.

HIKING FOR EXERCISE

Hiking on forest trails is one of the best physical activities available. Walking is cardiovascular exercise that promotes overall fitness, tones muscle, burns fat, strengthens joints, and develops balance. The uneven surface of hiking trails provides a more thorough workout than a walk on flat pavement. Dirt, grass, wood chips, and even gravel trail surfaces are also easier on joints than sidewalks.

HIKING FOR NATURE

Do you love big trees? Wildflowers? Bird-watching? Waterfalls? Atlanta may be one of the 10 largest metropolitan areas in the United States, but it is also a haven for nature. Our creeks and urban sprawl have left ample space between neighborhoods in which animals and plants thrive. The trails in this book are the perfect way to commune with nature without leaving the city.

HIKING FOR HISTORY

In the past, Atlanta has bulldozed historic structures to make way for new development. But in the city's hidden forests, you can still find relics of history: million-year-old geological formations, century-old trees, and human ruins, including old homesteads, dams, and Civil War battlefields. Using this book, you can hike to one of the oldest standing structures in DeKalb County, past a ruined paper mill, through an abandoned Scout camp, across a Negro League practice field, or around a defunct water treatment plant. What a fun way to learn Atlanta's history!

HIKING FOR CONNECTION

Hiking trails across the metro Atlanta area can help build connections across boundaries of geography, race, and ethnicity. We Atlantans are often siloed in our neighborhoods or areas of town. A Buckhead resident may never visit East Point. A Grove Park homeowner may not have a reason to explore Clarkston. When we welcome new hikers to the trails near our home or when we explore a park nestled in a neighborhood we've never visited, we take a literal step to break down barriers and build connections.

Safety, Ethics, and Etiquette

WHAT TO WEAR

Though many hikers swear by high-tech boots and specialized clothing, the hikes in this guidebook don't require a shopping spree at an upscale outdoor retailer. Wear what you have around the house and follow these general guidelines:

Dress for the season and weather. In warm weather, wear short sleeves, a sun hat or baseball cap, and breathable clothing that allows airflow. Though shorts are cooler, wearing lightweight pants in the summer can help you avoid annoyances such as ticks, chiggers, and poison ivy. In the winter, long sleeves and long pants are a good idea, but layering is key. It's good to be able to peel off a layer as you warm up from the exercise, and it's wonderful to put that warm layer back on when you begin cooling down afterward. Much body heat is lost through the head, and fingers can chill quickly, so a warm hat and gloves are especially effective means of staying warm in cold weather. A rain jacket, a poncho, or even an umbrella is important to bring in case of rain.

Choose appropriate footwear. Wearing the right shoes can make or break a hike. Unless you have ankle sensitivities, athletic shoes work as well as hiking boots for any of the hikes in this book. If you seek more hiking-specific footwear, look for trail runners or light hikers that combine the lightweight materials of sneakers with the ankle support and rugged soles of boots. Socks are an important factor in avoiding blisters. Choose athletic or hiking socks that fit well and come up over your ankle. Most walkers prefer woolen and synthetic-blend socks because they wick away moisture, keeping your feet cool and dry.

WHAT TO BRING

The following checklist can help you leave the house prepared for your hike in any weather:

- Backpack or waist pack
- Water (one liter per person, at least)
    - For hot summer hikes, electrolyte powder or tablets can help keep you hydrated. You can find these at most grocery stores.
- Food (lunch or snacks such as energy bars, trail mix, fruit, etc.)
- Navigation (guidebook, map)
- Clothes
    - Waterproof jacket, poncho, and/or umbrella
    - Fleece, sweatshirt, coat, warm hat if the weather is cold
- Sun protection (sunscreen, sun hat, sunglasses)
- Insect repellent
- First-aid kit (bandages, blister pads, insect-bite remedy, etc.)
- Plastic bag (to pack out trash)
- Cell phone (in waterproof case or bag)

DOGS

Nearly all the hikes in this book are dog-friendly destinations (and the few that prohibit dogs are noted as such). Hiking with your pet can add to your enjoyment and safety. Bringing your dog does decrease your likelihood of seeing birds and other wildlife, but hikers with dogs often connect and strike up friendships more easily than solo hikers.

Leashing your pet is both required by law and important for making everyone feel welcome on these trails. Some people are afraid of dogs (yes, even afraid of your sweet pooch). Some dogs are reactive when approached by an off-leash canine. Even if your pet is friendly and responds immediately to voice commands, please be a good neighbor and leash your canine companion. Nearby off-leash dog parks are noted throughout this book.

Despite the law and etiquette, you will likely come across hikers who are walking with loose dogs. Use common sense when approaching (or being approached by) an unleashed dog and politely ask the owner to leash the pet.

Following leash laws also can help protect our waterways. Pet waste is a significant cause of creek pollution in metro areas. Dog waste left in the woods is washed into streams by rainstorms and adds foreign bacteria and other pollutants. Bring waste bags and carry your dog's waste to an appropriate trash receptacle.

SAFETY

Preparation, vigilance, and common sense are the foundation of safe hiking. You are in charge of your own safety while exploring the trails in this guidebook. Below are some tips that may help you as you go.

Poison ivy is common in the Atlanta area. The uncomfortable effects of exposure make it important to learn how to identify its three leaflets and hairy roots and vines. Wear long pants when hiking, and avoid touching the plant. If you think you have touched poison ivy, wash your skin thoroughly. Over-the-counter products can help avoid the rash caused by poison ivy, but they must be used soon after you make contact.

Snakes live throughout the metro Atlanta area. Most are harmless and nonvenomous, but venomous copperheads may be seen in spring, summer, and fall. Though it's rare to have close encounters with snakes, vigilance is the key to avoiding them. Stay on the trail and look where you're putting your feet—do not step blindly over a large log or rock. Pay special attention when walking through marshy or open areas where snakes may choose to sun themselves. If a snake bites you, take a photo of the animal and call 911 immediately.

Insects you may encounter while hiking in Atlanta are primarily an annoyance, not a danger. Spiders, bees, hornets, wasps, and yellow jackets can best be avoided by not disturbing their homes—and staying on the trail. Mosquitoes, ticks, and chiggers can be the biggest annoyance in the forests of Atlanta. After your hike, check your body for ticks, especially in warm dark places on your body such as armpits and along waistbands and sock lines. Not all ticks carry Lyme disease, and ticks do not transmit the disease until at least 24 hours after biting you. So search for and remove ticks quickly and put your mind at ease. Chiggers are very small insects that cause itchy bumps that last for days. It is rare to get chigger bites when walking on maintained trails. If you walk through tall grasses or brush, wear long pants and shower soon after hiking to wash away any chiggers that might have found you. Though mosquitos are found everywhere in Atlanta, insect repellent is the best way to avoid their itchy bites.

Injuries most common to hiking are minor ankle sprains, blisters, weather-induced conditions such as heat exhaustion, and cuts caused by a fall. Watch where you are stepping, choose appropriate footwear, and use hiking sticks to lessen the likelihood of falls, sprains, and blisters. Most of these can be treated on-site with a small first-aid kit, but some injuries might need professional attention. And remember not to push yourself past your physical limits or take unnecessary risks for the perfect selfie. All of the hikes in this guidebook are in areas with mobile phone coverage. Call 911 if you need help.

Hiking alone on urban trails is not so different from walking alone on city streets. Pay attention to your surroundings, walk and speak with confidence, and trust your gut. Staying in any metro Atlanta park after dark is not recommended. If you're feeling particularly anxious about hiking alone, bring a dog, carry pepper spray, or invite a friend along.

Mobile phone reception is generally good throughout the metro Atlanta area, so carrying your phone can provide peace of mind and a direct connection to law enforcement. Always tell someone where you are going, and consider using a mobile phone app to share your location with a friend or family member. Call 911 if you need help while hiking, and pay attention to trail markers and other landmarks that can help you share your location to the emergency operator.

LEAVE NO TRACE PRINCIPLES

"Take only photos, leave only footprints" is an excellent motto for hikers. Urban hikers often add "and pack out trash." The Center for Outdoor Ethics promotes a philosophy that asks hikers to consider their impact on our natural places and take steps to actively leave no trace of their presence on a trail. While hiking through the urban greenspaces in this guidebook, you will often see signs of humans—old tires, beer bottles and cans, shopping bags, and other trash. As a visitor to these trails, you can also be a steward of the land by carrying a plastic bag and packing out any trash you find. The seven principles of Leave No Trace are:

1. Plan ahead and prepare
2. Travel on durable surfaces
3. Dispose of waste properly
4. Leave what you find
5. Minimize campfire impacts
6. Respect wildlife
7. Be considerate of others

For more information about Leave No Trace, visit www.lnt.org.

HOW TO USE THIS BOOK

This guidebook was written to break down the barriers that might stop you from enjoying Atlanta's trails:

Not enough time: In the pages that follow, you'll find hikes that don't require a full-day commitment or multihour drive. These hikes range from one-mile walks to six-mile treks.

Not enough information: This book provides all the pertinent information you'll need to plan for and enjoy your hike. You can follow the recommended route exactly or use the maps and landmarks to design your own adventure.

No guidance: We have designed, tested, and refined every hike route in this book. Both of us are seasoned outdoor guides and naturalists. Web searches and crowd-sourced apps can overwhelm you with options and still leave you unsure about trail conditions. We have taken the guesswork out of choosing a hike.

Lack of accessibility: Not every hiking trail is right for every person. Are you a wheelchair user? Are you bringing a baby along? Are you a first-time hiker? Do you deal with balance issues? This book offers a wide variety of hiking trails with options suitable for the needs of just about any hiker. Each chapter details what you can expect in terms of elevation, difficulty, and trail surface.

How to Get There

Each chapter includes a section that provides—at a glance—the information you need to get to each trailhead. The distance from downtown Atlanta is the actual driving distance from the Georgia Capitol, not an "as the crow flies" straight line. For your reference, we have also included the neighborhood and interstate highway that are closest to the trailhead. You can plug the address into your favorite map app and navigate to the trailhead. Once you get to the park, you can refer to this book's specific directions for parking and finding the trailhead.

Public Transit

Are you visiting Atlanta without a vehicle? Do you live in Atlanta car-free? Want to reduce your carbon footprint? Or are you just looking to avoid the city's traffic? Most hikes in this book are accessible via MARTA, Atlanta's system of trains and buses. Find the right bus or train route in this book, then use MARTA's website (itsmarta.com) or Google Maps' Transit function (maps.google.com) to plan your route. Bicycles are welcome on MARTA trains and buses and can make these hikes even more easily accessible via public transit. CobbLinc buses can help you access trails in Cobb County. Remember that the distance you'll walk or ride to and from the trailhead will increase your mileage, so plan accordingly. Bike racks at trailheads are noted throughout the book.

Hike Distance and Type

The hike distance listed is for the route recommended in this book. Remember, there are almost always more trails available at each greenspace, so you can add mileage by designing your own route or by hiking the recommended route more than once. Most hikes start and end at the same trailhead and are described as loop (one nonintersecting loop), figure-8 loop (a double loop that intersects), triple loop (three intersecting loops), lollipop loop (a loop with an out-and-back portion), or out-and-back (one linear trail with mileage that includes both the hike out and the hike back).

Difficulty Rating

Hike difficulty is subjective and is also based on many variables. We have provided an overall difficulty rating for each hike along with specific information to help you gauge how challenging a hike might be for you. These factors include but are not limited to how experienced you are with hiking, your level of fitness, the weather, how easy or difficult navigation is on a trail, the type of terrain and trail surface, how long or short the hike is, and the amount of elevation change.

Safety Rating

How comfortable you feel on these trails is also subjective, but we have analyzed each hike to provide a 1-5 scale rating for four aspects related to our feeling of safety. One star is the least sense of safety, five stars represent a high sense of safety.

- Usage
    - How common is it to pass other people on this trail?
    - Do women hike alone in this park? With or without dogs?
    - Are people using the park for activities other than hiking?
- Visibility
    - How open or secluded is the trail?
    - How close or far is the trail from the road?
    - How far ahead or behind can you see?
- Upkeep
    - Is the trail receiving regular maintenance? Are trails overgrown?
    - Are trails well marked?
- Parking
    - Is the parking area visible from the road? Is it in an open area?
    - Are there many cars or few cars in the parking area?
    - Are there cameras or staff on-site?

Dogs

Be sure to refer to this section of each chapter if you enjoy hiking with your pup. We've included information on whether leashed dogs are welcome on each trail and if there are nearby off-leash dog parks you can visit afterward.

Land Manager, Facilities, Hours, Fees

The hike route is not the only information you need to prepare for a hike. We've included information about the hours each trail is open and if there are any fees for use. A list of facilities can help you plan for bathroom breaks, water, picnicking, or pre- or posthiking activities such as fitness stations, sports fields, tennis courts, and playgrounds. If you need more information or clarification of the rules of each park, you can reach out to the entity that manages the trail, park, or facility.

Landmarks

What's better than a hike that's close to home? A hike that includes a scavenger hunt! The three landmarks listed for each hike give you a tip about what interesting and unique features you'll encounter along the trail. See if you can locate all three landmarks on every hike. These landmarks include historical ruins, unique ecological areas, waterfalls, overlooks, and other interesting features. In particular, we've identified unique and special trees on just about every trail:

Champion tree: One of the largest trees of its species within the I-285 perimeter as recorded by Trees Atlanta (treesatlanta.org).

Sentinel tree: This term, coined by author Jonah McDonald, describes a tree that is especially notable by virtue of its size, age, rarity, or other memorable characteristic.

Hike Description and Map

How you use the hike description will depend on your past hiking experience, confidence, and personality. Will you follow our directions to the letter? Will you wing it and use a map only as needed? Will you create your own route based on our recommendations? No matter your hiking style, reading the full hike description and reviewing the map before your hike will give you important information about trail conditions, landmarks, and possible impediments.

The hike description is written in narrative form, as if you were talking with the authors themselves. But even though the style is conversational, the content is precise. Still, changes occur in nature all the time, so you might encounter a newly fallen tree, a broken bridge, or even a brand new trail.

Each map is simple in design but includes a great deal of information. In addition to our recommended route, we have included all other trails in each greenspace, as well as connecting roads. You'll also find bridges, boardwalks, and other landmarks noted. These maps are just about the most thorough and accurate ones you can find anywhere.

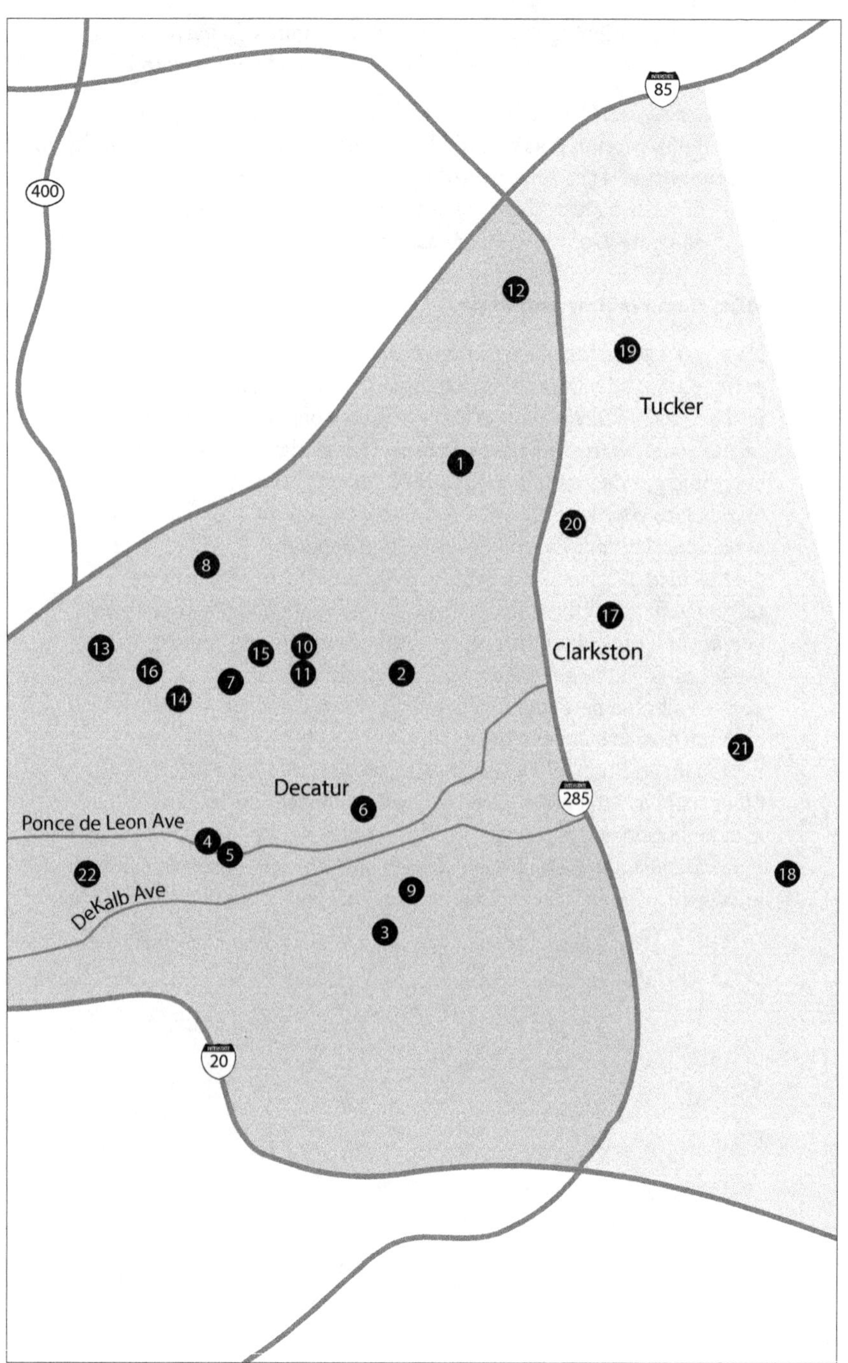

85
400
12
19
Tucker
1
20
8
17
13
15
10
Clarkston
16
11
2
7
14
21
Decatur
285
6
Ponce de Leon Ave
4
5
22
18
9
DeKalb Ave
3
20

EASTSIDE

1. Briarlake Forest Park
2. Clyde Shepherd Nature Preserve
3. Dearborn Park
4. Fernbank Forest
5. Frazer Forest & Deepdene Park
6. Glenlake Park & Decatur Cemetery
7. Hahn Woods & Lullwater Preserve
8. Kittredge Park
9. Legacy Park
10. Mason Mill Park—Burnt Fork Trails
11. Mason Mill Park—South Fork Trails
12. Mercer University Nature Trail
13. Morningside Nature Preserve
14. Peavine Trail
15. W.D. Thomson Park
16. Zonolite Park & Herbert Taylor Park
17. Friendship Forest Wildlife Sanctuary
18. Hairston Park
19. Henderson Park
20. Johns Homestead Park
21. Pine Lake
22. Freedom Park Trail

This bathtub wedged between two trees is a reminder of the past human impact on this nature park.

Briarlake Forest Park

One of DeKalb County's newest nature parks, Briarlake Forest is beloved by locals. Monthly work days and hours of loving care by volunteers have transformed an old family homestead into a natural gem. Along the peaceful trails beneath giant trees you can zigzag from trail to trail, building your own unique route, or follow the loop outlined here to visit some of the best spots in the park. This is a great hike for all ages, and you might be inspired to stay for a picnic or even come back to volunteer.

HOW TO GET THERE

Driving Distance from Downtown Atlanta: 12 miles
Address: 3330 Briarlake Road, Atlanta, GA 30345
Closest Interstate: I-85
Neighborhood: Briarlake / North Decatur
Public Transit: MARTA 30 or 133 bus + 0.5-mile walk
Parking: Small gravel parking area near park's entrance

HIKE DISTANCE

1-mile loop

DIFFICULTY

Overall: Easy
Navigation: Trail map posted at trailhead information boards; no other trail markers
Terrain: Mulched and hard-packed dirt trails, plus a short section on a sidewalk and two road crossings without crosswalks
Elevation Change: Mostly flat with a few minor hills

SAFETY

Usage ★★★★☆
Visibility ★★★★☆
Upkeep ★★★★★
Parking ★★★★★

HOURS

7:00 am to sunset

DOGS

Leashed dogs allowed

FACILITIES

- Toilets
- Water fountain, historic home converted to a pavilion, picnic area, volleyball net, benches

FEES & PERMITS None

LAND MANAGER DeKalb County Recreation, Parks & Cultural Affairs

Landmarks

AMERICAN CHESTNUT GROVE

A fungal blight decimated the American chestnut population in the early 1900s, but scientists have been breeding blight-resistant Chinese chestnuts with American chestnuts in the hopes of producing a blight-resistant hybrid. Under a canopy of oak, tulip tree, hickory, and beech, a small grove of hybrid chestnuts and pure American chestnuts have been planted as part of this nationwide restoration project.

AVENUE OF THE GIANTS

Back when this property was a farm, it's likely this area of giant beech and oak trees was grazed by cattle, which would feast on the beechnuts and acorns. The Avenue of the Giants is also on the historic route of the original Briarlake Road.

RAVINE OVERLOOK

This ravine is unusual because of the significant height at which you stand overlooking a tributary of North Fork Peachtree Creek. Some locals have speculated that the dramatic elevation change is caused by a fault line at this location.

Hike Route

Start on the patio in the center of what once was the historic Briarlake Forest Homestead and is now a pavilion with restrooms. Begin your hike through the open front doorway and across the porch to reach a crushed gravel path near the water fountain. Turn right on the stone-lined path, passing a trail on the left. Stay straight on a wide mulched path into the forest near a bike rack and picnic area. Don't curve to the right on the gravel path.

Pass a shed that is built to look like a tree stump. Many of the benches and picnic tables in this park are molded from concrete to seem like natural materials. Just after the tree shed, pass an old bathtub wedged between two trees and stay straight at a nearby junction with a trail that leads to the right.

In less than 100 yards, reach another junction near an old metal tank and a bench. Stay straight to continue on the main trail (not the

The Avenue of the Giants is an apt nickname for this park's amazing grove of beech and oak trees.

hard left turn that curves back to the park's entrance). This trail leads to the rear park boundary. Just after passing a bench on your right, stay straight past a trail on the right and then past a trail on the left. At the next junction where the trail splits, take the left fork. This trail leads to Castleway Lane and a trailhead. Facing the trailhead information board, turn right into the woods, take an immediate left, then hike downhill and across a bridge. Walk straight up a set of stairs.

The trail widens after ascending the stairs. In 0.1 mile turn left at a junction with a bench modeled after loblolly pine bark. Stay straight at the next junction where a trail on the left leads downhill to Amberwood Drive. The trail curves right, and in 0.1 mile you will reach the next junction, where you'll turn left and hike downhill. At the bench at the bottom of the hill, hike uphill to the left of a fallen tree and stay left at a junction just past the tree. This trail leads 100 yards to another junction, where you'll turn left and cross Amberwood Drive. At the other side of the road, look for a small trail that reenters the woods and hike uphill to a junction near a flat area where a building once stood. To the left is a grove of small American chestnut trees

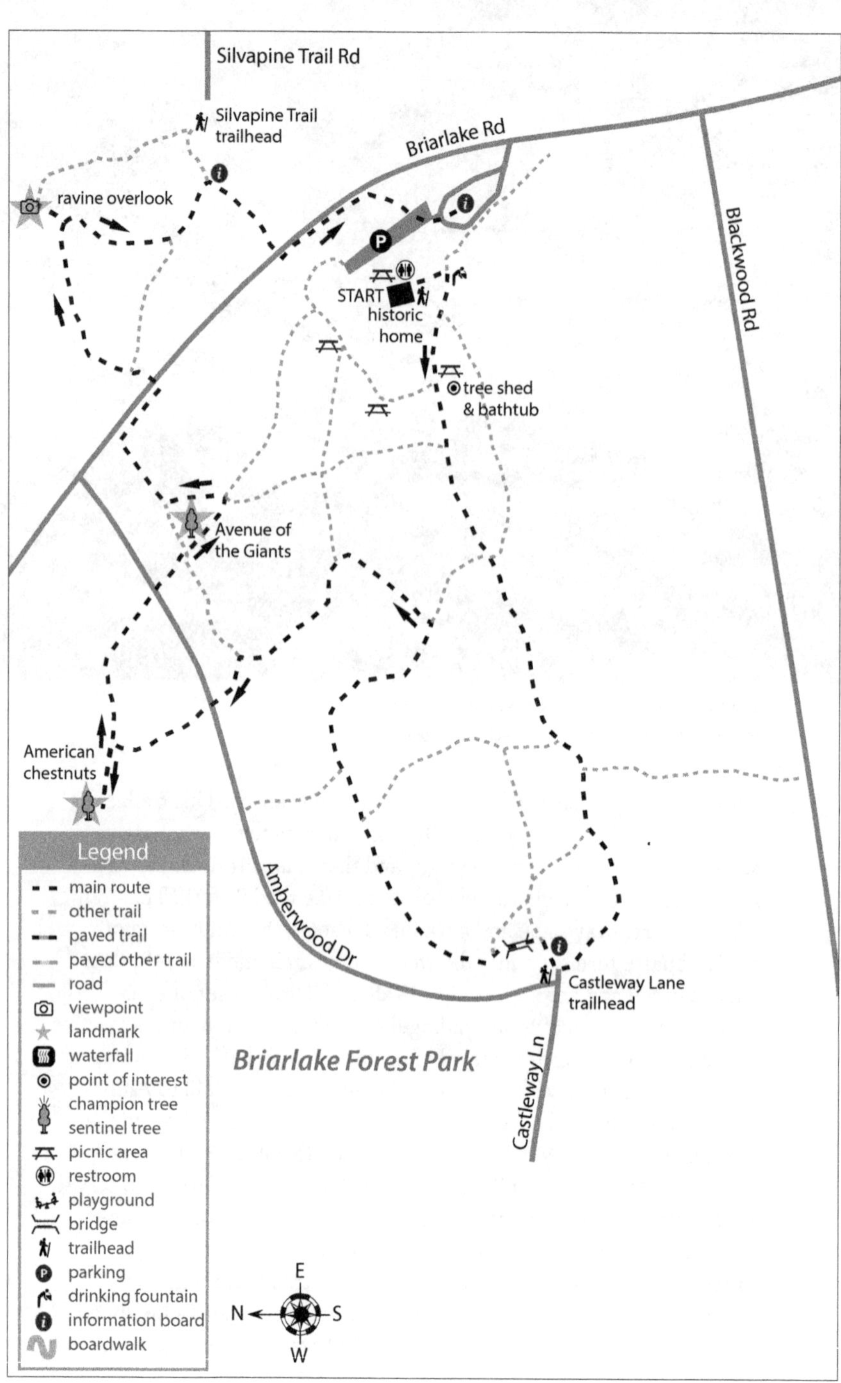
Silvapine Trail Rd
Silvapine Trail trailhead
ravine overlook
Briarlake Rd
Blackwood Rd
START
historic home
tree shed & bathtub
Avenue of the Giants
American chestnuts
Amberwood Dr
Castleway Lane trailhead
Castleway Ln
Briarlake Forest Park
Legend
main route
other trail
paved trail
paved other trail
road
viewpoint
landmark
waterfall
point of interest
champion tree
sentinel tree
picnic area
restroom
playground
bridge
trailhead
parking
drinking fountain
information board
boardwalk
E
N
S
W

that are part of an experimental restoration project. These trees are a collection of hybrid chestnuts and American chestnuts. After visiting the chestnuts, turn around, stay straight at the junction, and hike to another crossing of Amberwood Drive.

Cross Amberwood Drive, walk up the stairs, and enter the Avenue of the Giants. This spot used to be grazed by cows, and you'll see four white oaks and three American beech trees. Circle this area, then walk down to the sidewalk that's visible along Briarlake Road.

Turn right on the sidewalk, then carefully cross Briarlake Road to enter the forest on the far side through an opening in the split-rail fence. Turn immediately left at a junction and hike down four steps. At a bench in 100 yards, go left to a beautiful ravine overlook. After checking out the viewpoint, backtrack to the bench and, facing it, turn left. Stay left at the next junction to reach an information board at the Silvapine Trail trailhead. Turn right and hike slightly uphill back to Briarlake Road.

Carefully cross the road again, then head left on the sidewalk for 50 yards before turning right into the parking lot to end your hike near an information board where you can read about the human and natural history of this park.

Two unique rocks rise from the edge of the preserve's floodplain.

Clyde Shepherd Nature Preserve

This private nature preserve owes its existence to a generous donor, a group of dedicated volunteers, and the geography of South Fork Peachtree Creek. Because the county prohibits construction on floodplains, these 28 acres along South Fork Peachtree Creek have been preserved by the Shepherd family and many hours of volunteer labor. The result is a wonderful hiking destination and a sanctuary for many species of animals. Over 170 species of birds have been observed in the preserve, and this land is home to many species of frogs and salamanders and a wide variety of mammals. So walk lightly in this wildlife sanctuary and enjoy the beauty of this suburban oasis.

HOW TO GET THERE

Driving Distance from Downtown Atlanta: 9 miles
Address: 2580 Pine Bluff Drive, Decatur, GA 30033
Neighborhood: Medlock Park / North Decatur
Nearest Interstate: I-285
Public Transit: MARTA 36 bus + 1-mile walk
Parking: Street parking on Pine Bluff Drive

HIKE DISTANCE

2-mile figure-8 loop

DIFFICULTY

Overall: Easy
Navigation: Maps at trailheads; some trail signs at junctions and a few blazes
Terrain: Hard-packed dirt, mulch, and boardwalk trails; trails can be muddy after rain
Elevation Change: Mostly flat with a few minor hills

SAFETY

Usage ★★★★☆
Visibility ★★★☆☆
Upkeep ★★★★☆
Parking ★★★★☆

HOURS

Sunrise to sunset

DOGS

Leashed dogs allowed

FACILITIES

- No toilets
- Picnic tables, outdoor classrooms, bird feeders, benches, information boards, interpretive signage, and bike rack

FEES & PERMITS	None
LAND MANAGER	South Peachtree Creek Nature Preserves, Inc.

Landmarks

HARDWOOD FOREST

An interpretive sign along the Hardwood Forest Trail tells about the ecology of mature forests. Because the land here is a few feet above the floodplain, you can see a whole grove of relict hardwood trees, including tulip tree (commonly known as tulip poplar), sweetgum, beech, northern red oak, and red maple.

BEAVER POND

This seasonal pond is the centerpiece of this preserve and a mecca for Atlanta-area birders. It also provides a habitat for all kinds of creatures. What birds, turtles, or mammals might you see today?

RACCOON ROCK AND INDIAN ROCK

For generations, humans have marveled at these two geological formations at the edge of South Fork Peachtree Creek's floodplain. Erosion has unearthed these gneiss boulders, but we don't know much more about their origin.

Hike Route

Facing the pavilion, picnic table, and information sign at the preserve entrance, turn right and hike into the woods on Hardwood Forest Trail, near the bike rack and intersection of Wood Trail Lane and Pine Bluff Drive. Walk down the wooden stairs and turn right. This trail winds through a mature hardwood forest, which is the first landmark on this hike. You'll see large beech, sweetgum, oak, and tulip trees. After 0.15 mile, pass an interpretive sign near a giant oak tree and then reach a junction with Sheep Ridge Trail.

Hike left and then stay left past two more immediate junctions. Pass another interpretive sign, and you'll reach an outdoor classroom and junction with Pine Forest Trail and Beaver Pond Trail. Hike left on Beaver Pond Trail; a boardwalk begins in 100 yards. At the first junction on the boardwalk, turn right and walk a short spur trail to a photo blind that conceals you for photographing or viewing wildlife in the seasonal pond. Then turn back to the junction and turn right. Cross a small bridge and continue to walk along the boardwalk,

A hummingbird feeder hangs near the beaver pond.

which offers more views of the pond. At the end of the boardwalk, visit the elevated observation deck to the right. Climb down the stairs from the observation deck and turn right on a dirt trail.

In 100 yards you'll reach a junction near a pollinator garden and bird feeders. Look for a short wooden footbridge on the opposite side of the trail from the bird feeders and turn right to begin Outer Loop / Creek Trail. In 0.1 mile you'll reach a boardwalk and short spur to a trailhead at the intersection of Harrington Drive and Pine Bluff Drive. Continue straight on the boardwalk until it ends, and then follow the dirt trail as it curves slightly right and begins to parallel South Fork Peachtree Creek. On your left you'll pass a seating area and sandbar at the creek's edge. There are plans to install a paved multiuse trail along this route, which will eventually connect to the development that was once the North DeKalb Mall.

Continue on Outer Loop Trail, passing another photo blind on the right in 0.1 mile. Stay straight. In 0.15 mile stay straight at a junction with the Pine Forest Trail boardwalk. Then pass another junction with Pine Forest Trail in another 100 yards. Hike almost 0.2 mile farther to

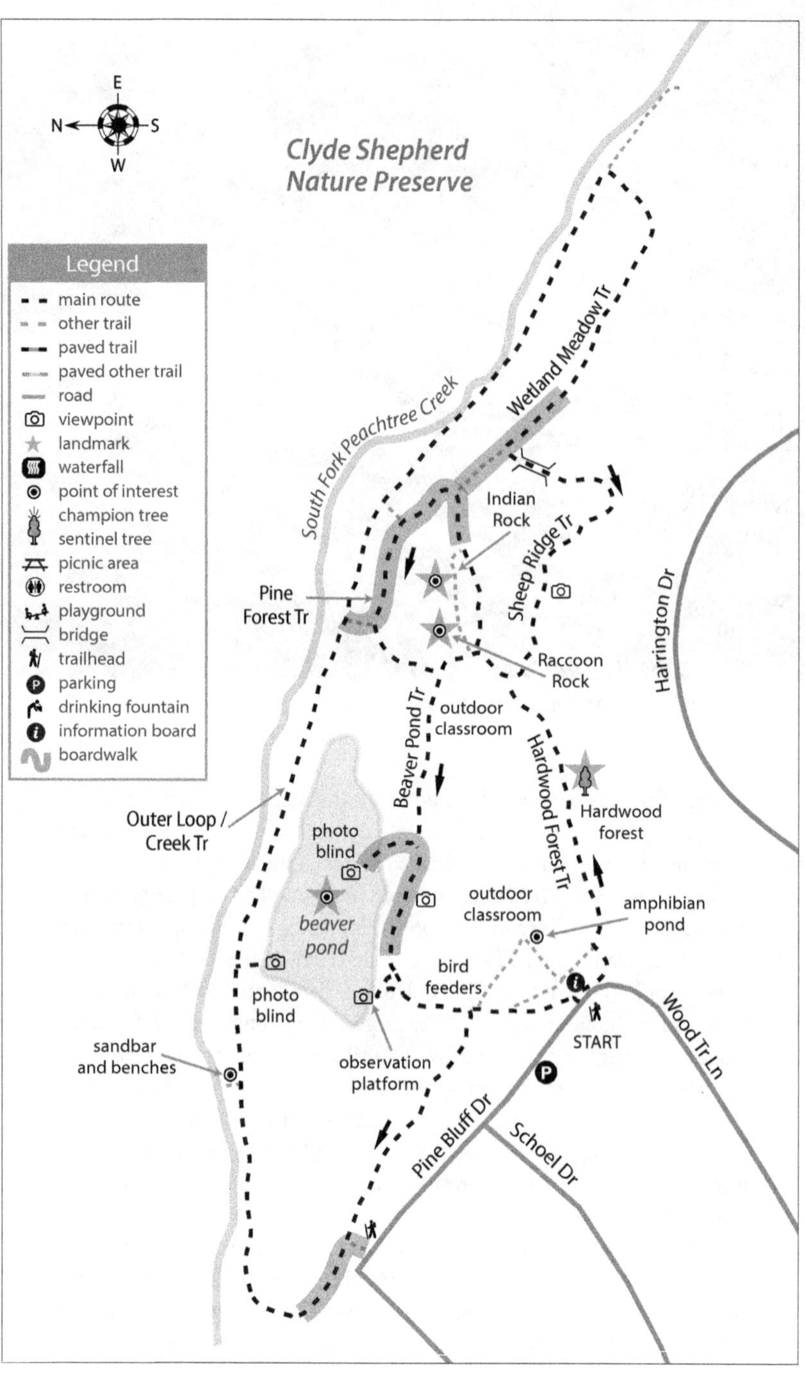
E
N
S
W
Clyde Shepherd
Nature Preserve
Legend
main route
other trail
paved trail
paved other trail
road
viewpoint
landmark
waterfall
point of interest
champion tree
sentinel tree
picnic area
restroom
playground
bridge
trailhead
parking
drinking fountain
information board
boardwalk
South Fork Peachtree Creek
Wetland Meadow Tr
Indian
Rock
Sheep Ridge Tr
Pine
Forest Tr
Raccoon
Rock
Harrington Dr
Beaver Pond Tr
outdoor
classroom
Hardwood Forest Tr
Hardwood
forest
Outer Loop /
Creek Tr
photo
blind
beaver
pond
outdoor
classroom
amphibian
pond
bird
feeders
photo
blind
Wood Tr Ln
START
sandbar
and benches
observation
platform
Pine Bluff Dr
Schoel Dr

a junction near the Stivers Subaru car dealership. Turn right to hike Wetland Meadow Trail.

A boardwalk begins in 0.1 mile. After 100 yards of boardwalk, keep your eye out on the left for a junction with Sheep Ridge Trail. The sign faces the opposite direction, so it is easy to miss. Turn left and hike Sheep Ridge Trail uphill for 0.1 mile to reach a glider bench, forest overlook, and passion vine trellis. Pass through the arched trellis and descend the ridge for 0.1 mile to reach a junction with the unmarked Hardwood Forest Trail. Turn right and then almost immediately take a right onto Wetland Meadow Trail, which passes Raccoon Rock and Indian Rock on your left. Just before a boardwalk begins, there is an unofficial trail on the left that will allow you to explore the unique boulders.

Stay straight on the Wetland Meadow Trail boardwalk and then turn left at the first junction you reach, with a Pine Trail sign. Hike Pine Forest Trail to the end of the boardwalk near a boardwalk spur that leads to Outer Loop Trail. Stay straight and hike the dirt trail, staying left at a junction with an unofficial trail, to reach a junction with Beaver Pond Trail near an outdoor classroom.

Turn right and hike Beaver Pond Trail, first on a dirt trail, then on a boardwalk until it ends. Turn left and hike to the bird feeders, then stay straight to return to the nature preserve entrance and end your hike. If you feel like you've been hiking in circles, it's because you have been!

American beech trees abound at Dearborn Park.

Dearborn Park

This small linear park between neighborhoods has a huge amount to offer to a nature lover. You'll be charmed by the gurgling of the creek, a mature canopy of hardwood trees, and a network of wide, flat paths, plus some more adventurous, winding, narrow trails. Even the developed area of the park—complete with a small playground, basketball court, fitness stations, and picnic areas—feels like you're in a deep forest. It's no wonder this neighborhood is called Midway Woods.

HOW TO GET THERE

Driving Distance from Downtown Atlanta: 7 miles
Address: 1300 Deerwood Drive, Decatur, GA 30030
Nearest Interstate: I-20
Neighborhood: Midway Woods / Decatur
Public Transit: MARTA 15 bus + 0.3-mile walk
Parking: Street parking on Deerwood Drive, just past the intersection with Creekwood Terrace

HIKE DISTANCE

1.3-mile loop

DIFFICULTY

Overall: Easy
Navigation: No trail markers, and some of the dirt trails can be overgrown and confusing
Terrain: Trails include hard-packed dirt, pavement, hard-packed gravel, boardwalk, and asphalt; dirt trails can be muddy
Elevation Change: Minimal elevation change

SAFETY

Usage ★★★☆☆
Visibility ★★☆☆☆
Upkeep ★★☆☆☆
Parking ★★★★☆

HOURS

7:00 am to sunset

DOGS

Leashed dogs allowed

FACILITIES

- No toilets
- Several picnic pavilions, basketball court, fitness stations, water fountain, playground, benches, and dog waste stations

FEES & PERMITS	None
LAND MANAGER	DeKalb County Recreation, Parks & Cultural Affairs

Landmarks

SLIDING ROCK

This rock formation of gneiss in Shoal Creek is more beloved by children than the playground itself.

SENTINEL TULIP TREE

It's hard not to stop and marvel at the size of this mature tulip tree (commonly known as tulip poplar) on the left of the trail. Though this

This linear park between Decatur neighborhoods is a great place to hike.

one isn't even the largest of its species in Atlanta, it's an impressive and massive specimen. Give it a hug!

SENTINEL BEECH GROVE

Large beech trees, identified by their smooth gray bark, are a sign of mature forest and an undisturbed ecosystem. Look for this grove on the hill above the trail. Notice that the trees keep their dry, brown leaves on all winter long, waiting to drop them in the springtime.

Hike Route

Start your hike on a paved sidewalk-width path on the left of the stone Dearborn Park sign. Walk downhill, passing a dirt trail to the left that leads to a small picnic area, before crossing a wooden bridge over Shoal Creek. After the bridge there is a short trail on the right to the Shoal Creek sliding rock, which is both a scenic cascade and a favorite play area for children.

Turn left and leave the paved path toward a Pedestrians Only sign and fitness station. The dirt trail enters the forest, and you'll soon see a small side trail to the left that leads to a series of boulders along Shoal Creek and a mature bamboo grove. Continue straight for another 0.1 mile before the trail passes a giant sentinel tulip tree, one of the biggest in the city. Keep straight for 0.3 mile, staying on the main trail, past several side trails on the right. Pay attention to when the main trail begins to curve right and a side trail leads off to the left. Here you can choose to follow the trail to the right to loop back on the main trail, or you can follow this route into the more wild part of Dearborn Park.

Take the left trail for 100 yards, and you'll arrive at a small tributary creek crossing. Hop on rocks across the water and go right on the main trail when you crest the creek's steep bank. This area of forest has many serpentine trails, so get your bearings and then explore. After 0.1 mile on this trail you'll reach a gate in an overgrown fence that was once part of a baseball field. Everything past this point is private property. Turn back and follow the trail you came on or explore the twisting side trails to the right; they can also lead you to the creek crossing.

Cross the tributary creek and turn left at the next junction. This short and often muddy trail leads to the Chevelle Lane trailhead and the park's wide main trail. Turn right and pass a grove of at least six mature American beech trees on the hillside to your left.

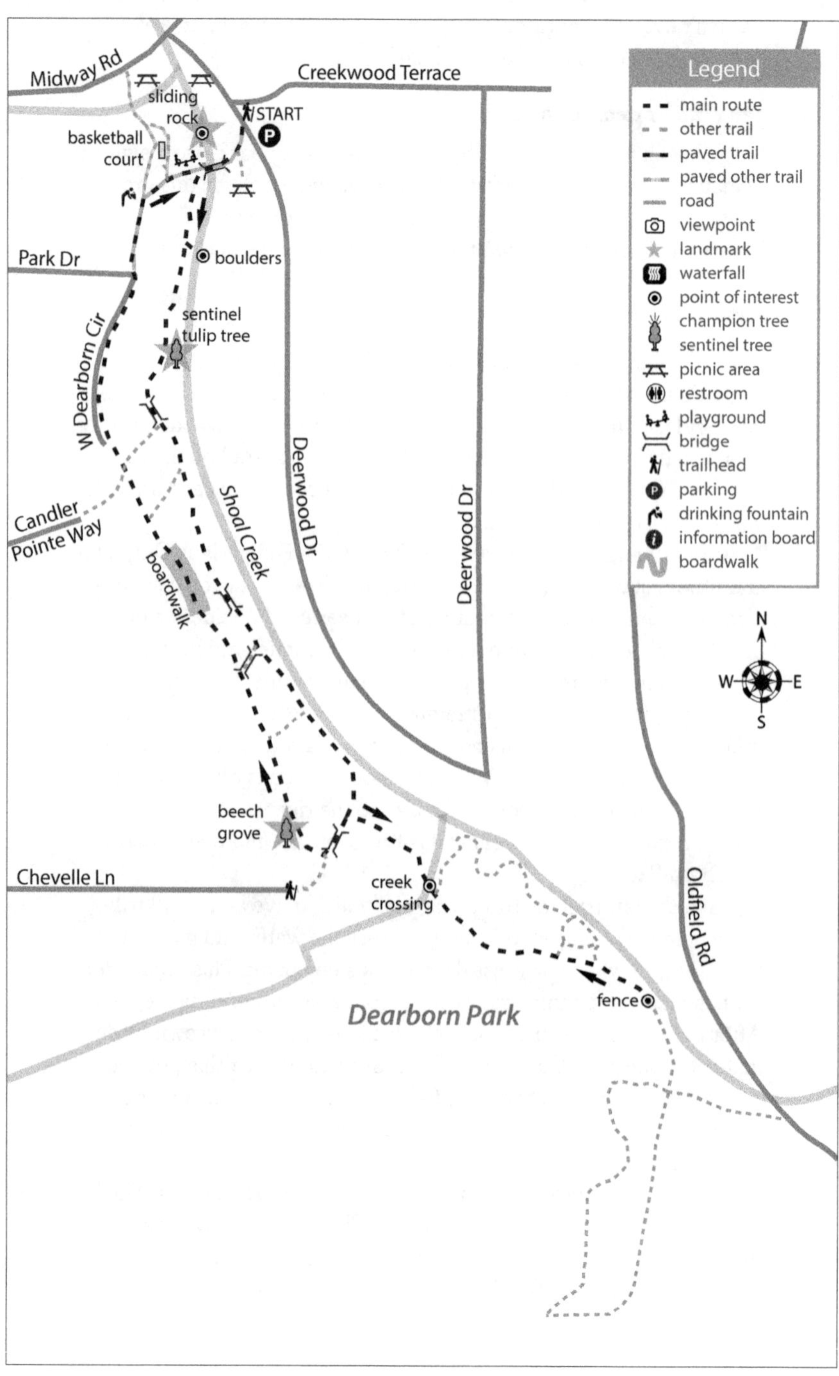

Midway Rd
Creekwood Terrace
sliding rock
basketball court
START
boulders
Park Dr
sentinel tulip tree
W Dearborn Cir
Candler Pointe Way
boardwalk
Shoal Creek
Deerwood Dr
Deerwood Dr
beech grove
Chevelle Ln
creek crossing
fence
Dearborn Park
Oldfield Rd
Legend
main route
other trail
paved trail
paved other trail
road
viewpoint
landmark
waterfall
point of interest
champion tree
sentinel tree
picnic area
restroom
playground
bridge
trailhead
parking
drinking fountain
information board
boardwalk
N
W
E
S

Hike this crushed-gravel trail 0.2 mile, cross a short boardwalk, and then hike another 0.1 mile to reach a trailhead at West Dearborn Circle. Continue straight on West Dearborn Circle. (If you prefer to stay on dirt trails, follow the trail to the right back to the sliding rock.) On the paved road, walk 0.1 mile to reach the park entrance at the corner of Park Drive and West Dearborn Circle. Enter the park and pass a bench and water fountain, then turn right to walk downhill past the playground and fitness station to end your hike at the sliding rock, bridge, and street parking.

Fernbank's old-growth forest has deep roots—literally and figuratively.

Fernbank Forest

FERNBANK MUSEUM OF NATURAL HISTORY

This fantastic trail through one of the city's largest intact old-growth forests is absolutely worth the price of admission. To anyone's knowledge, this 65-acre forest has never been logged or cleared. The resulting biodiversity is stunning—over 200 bird species have been observed here, 17 amphibian species, 13 reptile species, and 13 mammal species. And once you walk along the cool forest floor with trees towering 16 stories above you, you won't be surprised to learn that Fernbank Forest also contains over 30 city champion trees. Under the stewardship of the Fernbank Museum of Natural History, invasive plants are being removed, and native flora and fauna are thriving.

HOW TO GET THERE

Driving Distance from Downtown Atlanta: 5 miles
Address: 767 Clifton Road, Atlanta, GA 30307
Nearest Interstate: I-75/I-85
Neighborhood: Druid Hills
Public Transit: MARTA 2 bus + 0.2-mile walk
Parking: Multiple museum parking lots, which can be full on busy weekends

HIKE DISTANCE

2-mile figure-8 loop

DIFFICULTY

Overall: Easy to moderate
Navigation: Several trail maps are posted, and map brochures are available at museum entrance
Terrain: Many of these trails are paved or hard-packed gravel, and the WildWoods section of this hike is ADA accessible; there are also short sections of hard-packed dirt trail, a boardwalk, and a stone staircase
Elevation Change: Several extended ascents and descents

SAFETY

Usage ★★★★★
Visibility ★★★★☆
Upkeep ★★★★★
Parking ★★★★★

HOURS	Museum open 10:00 am to 5:00 pm every day except Thanksgiving and Christmas; forest closes at 4:30 pm
DOGS	Dogs are not allowed; leave your pups at home
FACILITIES	• Toilets in museum and in WildWoods but not in Fernbank Forest • Museum exhibits, two nature-themed playgrounds, water fountains, interpretive signs, benches, pavilions
FEES & PERMITS	Museum pass or membership required for trail access: \$23.95 (child, ages 3-12); \$25.95 (adult, ages 13-64); \$24.95 (senior, ages 65+)
LAND MANAGER	Fernbank Museum of Natural History

Landmarks

CITY CHAMPION EASTERN HEMLOCK

- 98" circumference, 99' tall, 56' crown spread
- Find the city's largest hemlock tree on your left just before you reach Perimeter Path, across from a mulched path and pawpaw grove on the right. This specimen is over 8 feet around and 100 feet tall. North Georgia hemlock trees are dying from the woolly adelgid blight, but the hemlocks in Fernbank Forest are safe because of the museum's care.

ELEPHANT ROCK

This giant rock across the creek from the pavilion is a marvel that has captivated forest visitors for decades. Why is it called Elephant Rock? Some claim that you can see a trunk, tusks, and ears from a certain angle. What do you see?

HUNTEMANN POND

This pond has some of the cleanest water in metro Atlanta, according to the Fernbank ecologist. Its spring source is right here in Fernbank Forest, and the old-growth trees and deep soil help filter rainwater. Salamanders, frogs, turtles, snakes, and even river otters have been seen here.

Hike Route

Start your hike at the rear doors of the museum's ground floor, past the large atrium filled with dinosaur skeletons. Just outside the

Where else in Atlanta can you meet a stegosaurus on a hike?

museum doors, there is a metal stegosaurus statue on your right. Hike straight under the WildWoods entry arch and onto a boardwalk, curving past wooden sculptures modeled after tulip tree flowers and fern fronds. The boardwalk curves right to reach the main WildWoods path, where you'll stay straight and walk past the Adventure Outpost Playground and then past the Ranger Pavilion on the right. This is your last opportunity for a restroom.

Continue straight on the path past a stone wall where you might see lizards such as anoles and skinks. At a junction on the left with Nature Gallery Trail, stay straight and then straight again at another junction on the right. In 100 yards cross a bridge over a tributary of Lullwater Creek. Here you can see a small human-made waterfall as well as live oak trees that were planted here by the former landowners.

In another 100 yards cross two bridges and look for maidenhair ferns growing below. Then you will arrive at the gate to Fernbank Forest. Hike uphill into the forest, and in 0.1 mile reach a small trail on the right and the city champion eastern hemlock tree on the left.

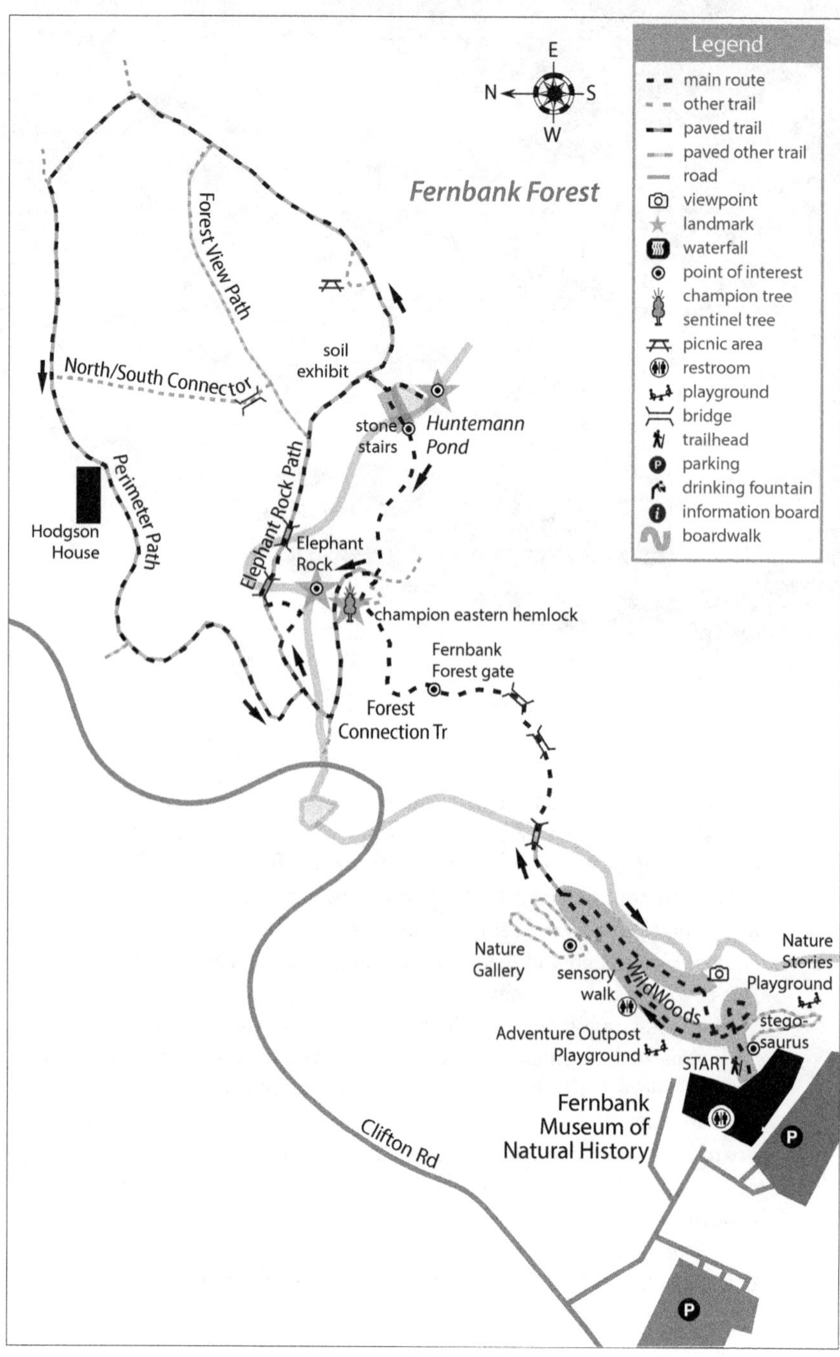
Legend
main route
other trail
paved trail
paved other trail
road
viewpoint
landmark
waterfall
point of interest
champion tree
sentinel tree
picnic area
restroom
playground
bridge
trailhead
parking
drinking fountain
information board
boardwalk
E
N
S
W
Fernbank Forest
Forest View Path
North/South Connector
soil exhibit
Huntemann Pond
stone stairs
Elephant Rock Path
Perimeter Path
Hodgson House
Elephant Rock
champion eastern hemlock
Fernbank Forest gate
Forest Connection Tr
Nature Gallery
sensory walk
WildWoods
Nature Stories Playground
stego-saurus
Adventure Outpost Playground
START
Fernbank Museum of Natural History
Clifton Rd
P

Just past this landmark you'll come to Fernbank Forest's paved Perimeter Path. Turn left and hike steeply downhill. In 0.1 mile the trail curves right, past a service gate on your left. Stay right at an immediate junction to hike Elephant Rock Path. In 100 yards you'll see a trail on the right leading to a pavilion. Follow this trail to view Elephant Rock and then return to the main trail on the other side of the pavilion. Turn right to continue on Elephant Rock Path.

Hike 0.2 mile, crossing two bridges, then stay right at a junction with Forest View Path. There is a soil exhibit 100 yards farther in which you can lift rubber flaps to see what's going on beneath the ground's surface.

Just beyond the soil exhibit is a junction with a trail that leads to the pond. Go right, then take the left spur to visit the pond and pavilion. Then backtrack to the junction near the soil exhibit and turn right to continue this hike on Perimeter Path. The trail ascends slowly, passing a pavilion on the left. In 0.1 mile stay straight at a junction and continue climbing the hill. Over the next 0.3 mile stay on the main trail, passing service roads on the right and North/South Connector on the left before reaching the Hodgson House on the right.

From here, Perimeter Path descends for 0.25 mile past another service entrance on the right before arriving at a T-junction at the bottom of the hill. You can turn right and hike up the steep incline on the paved Perimeter Path, or to continue your adventure, turn left and follow these instructions.

Pass the Elephant Rock pavilion on the right in 0.1 mile and hike the Elephant Rock Path another 0.2 mile to reach the soil exhibit again. This time, turn right on the trail to the pond and then take another immediate right to walk the boardwalk to a set of stone stairs built into the rock. After the stairs, a dirt trail leads to the top of the hill. Cross the pavement and hike straight on Forest Connection Trail, which leads back to the museum.

After passing through the Fernbank Forest gate and hiking another 0.15 mile across three bridges, reach a junction near the Animal Tracks exhibit. Go left toward the Isdell Wildlife Sanctuary and follow a boardwalk 0.1 mile down to the creek's floodplain, stopping at the overlook for views of the wetland area. Then hike up the stairs behind you to reach the main path near a tree bark exhibit. To your right is a trail to the Nature Stories Playground. Turn left and curve back up the boardwalk to finish your hike at the museum doors.

The lush forest of Deepdene sometimes looks like the entry to a magical world.

Frazer Forest & Deepdene Park

If you love the old-growth trees of the Joyce Kilmer Memorial Forest in North Carolina, you'll find one of Atlanta's closest equivalents in these two small adjoining forests. Tulip and oak trees in Frazer Forest and Deepdene Park stretch their branches skyward on massive ancient trunks. Hidden just beyond the eastern boundary of Atlanta, this area is a treasure reminiscent of the majesty of the great Piedmont forests that existed here before Atlanta.

HOW TO GET THERE

Driving Distance from Downtown Atlanta: 5 miles

Address: 1815 South Ponce de Leon Avenue NE, Atlanta, GA 30307

Nearest Interstate: I-75/I-85

Neighborhood: Druid Hills

Public Transit: MARTA 2 bus + 0.4-mile walk

Parking: Paved parking area near the main Frazer Center buildings at the top of the driveway

HIKE DISTANCE

2.5-mile figure-8 loop

DIFFICULTY

Overall: Easy to moderate

Navigation: Maps and information signs posted throughout Deepdene Park; no other trail markers

Terrain: Mostly wide, hard-packed dirt trails with some bridges, stone stairs, and several rock creek crossings

Elevation Change: Rolling hills with no major ascents or descents

SAFETY

Usage ★★★★☆

Visibility ★★★☆☆

Upkeep ★★★★☆

Parking ★★★★★

HOURS

7:00 am to sunset

DOGS

Leashed dogs allowed

FACILITIES

- No toilets
- Benches and information signs in Deepdene Park

FEES & PERMITS	None
LAND MANAGER	Frazer Center and DeKalb County Recreation, Parks & Cultural Affairs

Landmarks

SENTINEL TWIN TULIP TREES

These twin tulip trees (commonly known as tulip poplars) grow just beside the trail near the creek in Frazer Forest. Both of them have thick trunks and soar over 140 feet into the sky; being rooted in a low part of the forest and drawing from the constant water source of the creek have helped them grow big and tall. The twin on the right is 13 feet in circumference. It's big!

TALLEST TREE IN DEEPDENE

Just after entering the trail on the west side of Deepdene Park, you'll pass a tree labeled as the tallest in the park. Unfortunately, the height listed is incorrect. This tree is actually 158½ feet tall, not 185½. The tallest tree in Atlanta is also a tulip tree, but it's almost 10 feet taller than this one.

SENTINEL WHITE OAK

Look for this large tree on the right as you walk down stone steps toward a bridge. This is the largest white oak in Deepdene Park (12 feet 8 inches in circumference) and is also the oldest dated tree in Atlanta. Researchers from Fernbank Museum and Kennesaw State University cored the tree in 2011 to retrieve a sample of wood. They counted approximately 240 annual growth rings. This tree predates the signing of the Declaration of Independence.

HIKE ROUTE

This forest is laced with trails, so there are many possible hike routes. This route generally sticks to the most well-traveled trails, but we recommend you also explore the many additional trails. Use the map to guide your exploration.

Enter Frazer Forest from the upper parking lot, across from the Frazer Center buildings and near the upper gate. Look for a Little Free Library and chain-link fence on the west side of the parking lot, and, facing the Little Free Library, start your hike on the trail to the left. In 100 feet turn left at a trail junction. Hike another 100 yards to a junction near a ravine and turn right. Hike along the ravine,

The trees in this old-growth forest make us feel small.

then head downhill. Turn left at the first junction you come to and hike downhill until you are near the creek. At a junction at the bottom of the hill, turn left. The trail follows a bend in the creek near white sandbags to reach giant twin tulip trees. The trail curves right past these sentinel trees and then ascends the hill to the wide main trail. Turn left and hike to a small overflow parking lot. Walk through the parking lot, then turn left onto the Frazer Center driveway. Follow the driveway 0.2 mile to the exit gate, then turn right onto the sidewalk.

It's only 0.2 mile along this busy road to Deepdene Park at the intersection of Ponce de Leon Avenue and Lakeshore Drive. Cross Ponce de Leon Avenue at the crosswalk and circle the small grassy area to enter the forest of Deepdene Park near a trail map sign.

Once in the forest, you'll pass several very large tulip poplar trees on the left. Look for one with a sign at its base that identifies it as the tallest tree in Deepdene. When you are 100 yards past the tallest tree, you'll arrive at a junction with a sign pointing left to Creekside Path and right to Lower-Dene Bridge. Turn left and cross the creek on stone steps. This trail is only 0.15 mile long, but it will lead you

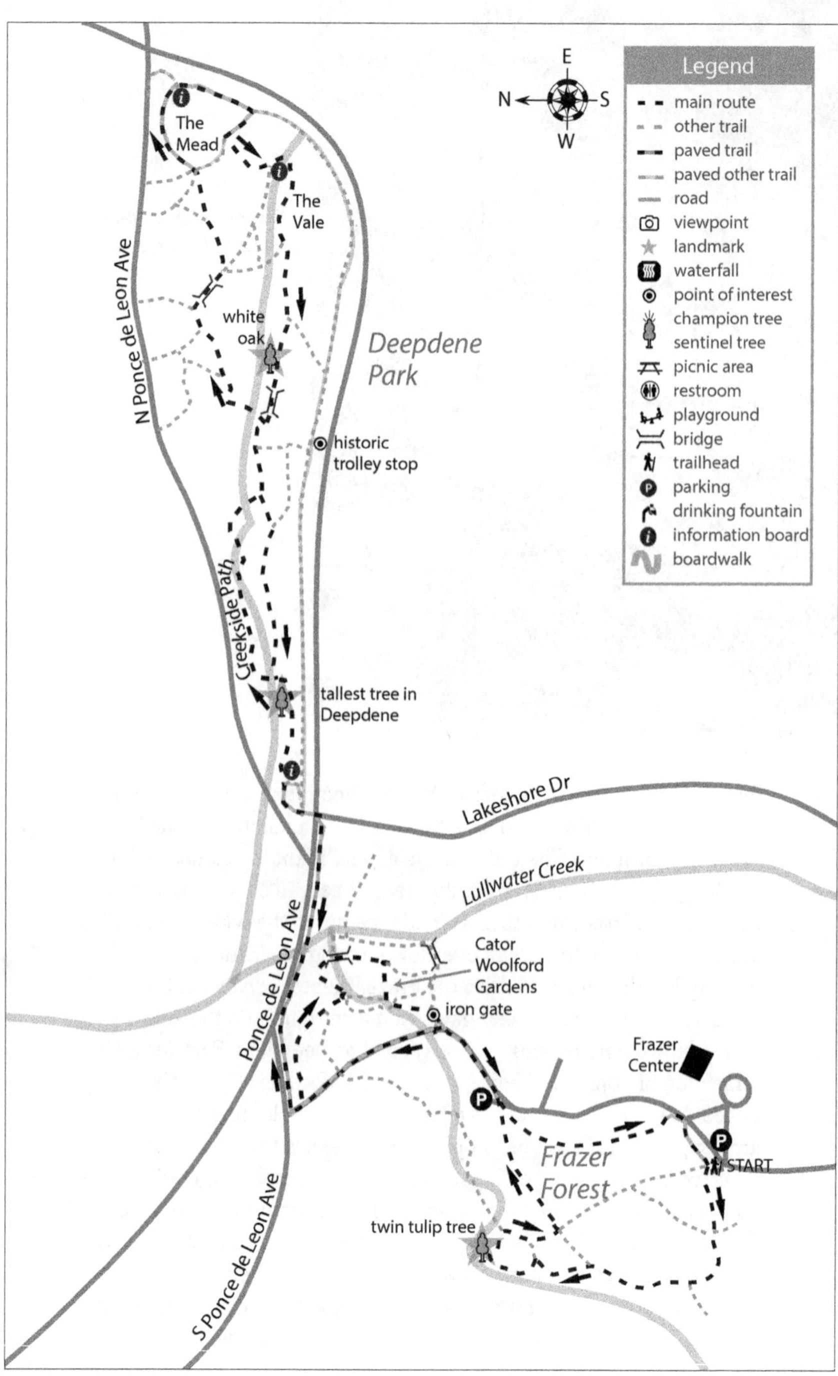
Legend
main route
other trail
paved trail
paved other trail
road
viewpoint
landmark
waterfall
point of interest
champion tree
sentinel tree
picnic area
restroom
playground
bridge
trailhead
parking
drinking fountain
information board
boardwalk
E
N
S
W
The Mead
The Vale
white oak
Deepdene Park
N Ponce de Leon Ave
historic trolley stop
Creekside Path
tallest tree in Deepdene
Lakeshore Dr
Lullwater Creek
Cator Woolford Gardens
iron gate
Ponce de Leon Ave
Frazer Center
START
Frazer Forest
twin tulip tree
S Ponce de Leon Ave

across the creek three more times on stone stairs, some of which are eroded and slippery and require good balance and sure footing. (To avoid these stairs, turn right at the junction and follow the arrow toward Lower-Dene Bridge.)

When Creekside Path meets up with the main trail near a small stone bridge, turn left and continue straight past a side trail on the right. Just before arriving at the arched Lower-Dene Bridge and an information sign, turn left and walk down the steps, over the creek, and then steeply uphill.

As you hike uphill, turn right at the first junction (across a stone bridge), then right again at the next junction to arrive at a park map next to the large Upper-Dene Bridge. Turn right and go across. Stay left after the bridge, then head right toward an open field called the Mead.

Circle the Mead to the left (clockwise) on the paved path, staying to the right when the paved path branches off to the left. After a sign that displays a description of the Mead, turn left and hike downhill on a gravel trail, then turn left at a junction with two signs (a map of the park and an information sign about the Vale).

At a junction just after a bench, go straight, then left and uphill at the next junction. Follow this trail, staying right at the next fork. As you hike down stone steps toward Lower-Dene Bridge, a sentinel white oak that predates the Revolutionary War is on the right.

After crossing the bridge, stay straight on the main trail for 0.25 mile to reach the west end of Deepdene Park. Cross Ponce de Leon Avenue and retrace your steps along the sidewalk to the Frazer Center driveway entrance. This time, immediately after entering the gates, turn left on a dirt trail that leads you into the Cator Woolford Gardens. Turn left, then left again past some large tulip trees. When you reach a small stone bridge, turn right (not across the bridge) to walk a path through the grassy central area of the gardens. Turn right at the first trail and then left, just past a statue of a girl reading. This will lead you to the garden parking area. Pass the iron gate and turn left on the driveway.

Walking up the hill, you'll pass a small hemlock grove on your left. Hemlock trees in Georgia are being destroyed by the woolly adelgid, so this secluded grove may someday be a relict of the great hemlock forests of the southern Appalachians. Continue uphill for 0.1 mile to reach the small overflow parking area. To the left of the parking entrance, a crushed slate trail leads uphill. Hike this trail up the hill for 0.1 mile to reach the driveway, across from the main Frazer Center building. Turn right and walk through the parking lot to end your hike.

There is something for everyone in the family on this hike.

Glenlake Park & Decatur Cemetery

This hike leads you through a popular park with a playground, to an urban forest along a small stream, and into a historic cemetery full of large trees and historic gravestones. The last leg winds along the manicured paths of a newer cemetery. The route will never bore you, and there's something for everyone here—even a dog park along the way.

HOW TO GET THERE	**Driving Distance from Downtown Atlanta:** 7 miles **Address:** 1121 Church Street, Decatur, GA 30030 **Nearest Interstate:** I-285 **Neighborhood:** Decatur **Public Transit:** MARTA 123 bus stops at Glenlake Park entrance **Parking:** Paved parking lot next to the tennis center in Glenlake Park; overflow parking in the cemetery on Bell Street
HIKE DISTANCE	1.5-mile loop
DIFFICULTY	**Overall:** Easy **Navigation:** Park and cemetery maps are posted in a few locations, but no other trail markers **Terrain:** Mostly asphalt or gravel trails with a short section of hard-packed dirt trails; several bridges and sets of stairs **Elevation Change:** This hike is quite hilly, but no major ascents or descents; the route is rarely flat
SAFETY	**Usage** ★★★★★ **Visibility** ★★★★★ **Upkeep** ★★★☆☆ **Parking** ★★★★★
HOURS	Dawn to dusk
DOGS	Leashed dogs allowed; off-leash dog park in Glenlake Park

FACILITIES	• Toilets near tennis courts • Water fountains, playground, sports fields, dog park, swimming pool, tennis courts, and covered picnic areas in Glenlake Park
FEES & PERMITS	None
LAND MANAGER	City of Decatur Parks & Recreation

Landmarks

CITY CHAMPION PIGNUT HICKORY

- 114" circumference, 116' tall, 78' crown spread
- The most impressive feature of this tree is its girth. Hickories grow notoriously slowly, adding very little new wood each year. But this one is 10 feet in circumference! The nuts contain edible meat but are hard to get to before the forest animals find them.

CITY CHAMPION EASTERN RED CEDAR

- 84" circumference, 72' tall, 33' crown spread
- This tree is in the historic portion of Decatur Cemetery. Easily identified by their shredding/peeling, lighter-colored bark and scaly, needle-like leaves, eastern red cedar make great cemetery trees because they thrive in full sun. The trunk of this one has engulfed a granite gravestone at its base.

GRAVES OF EDWARD COX AND ROBERT ALSTON

At cemetery marker #45, just past the gazebo, you'll find the grave of Robert Alston, who was murdered in the Georgia State Capitol by Edward Cox, who is his neighbor here in this cemetery. Read their story in *Secret Atlanta* by Jonah McDonald or in a free cemetery walking tour brochure available online.

Hike Route

Facing the restrooms near the tennis courts, start your hike on the paved path to the right of the restrooms. Cross the bridge over Glenn Creek and stay left at a junction where the path on the right leads to a playground and basketball court. Pass another junction on your left and hike uphill for another 0.1 mile. You'll cross a gravel drive and then take a slight left to continue onto a gravel path that becomes paved and curves around the outfield of a baseball field.

The historic section of the Decatur Cemetery is a great combination of history and nature.

Pass a junction leading out of the park on your left and continue to circle the baseball diamond. Descend the hill and pass a side trail on the right and the dog park. At the bottom of the hill near an open field, turn left and cross a bridge. Just after a bench, the champion pignut hickory is on your left in a small forest with many mature trees.

In another 0.1 mile, cross a bridge just before the path meets a larger paved, multiuse path. Make a right and then an immediate left onto a dirt path on the right bank of the creek. This trail starts faint but becomes more obvious in 50 feet and leads through a mature forest of tulip and sweetgum trees. Cross a long bridge over Glenn Creek, then stay straight and hike through a meadow. (The small trail on the right crosses and then parallels the creek.) At the end of the meadow, turn right and cross another bridge, following the gravel path into the cemetery. (Just after crossing the bridge, there is a spur trail on the left that leads to a small but scenic cascade.)

When the line of trees on the left ends, look for a small cobblestone path through the graves to the left, then cross the grass and

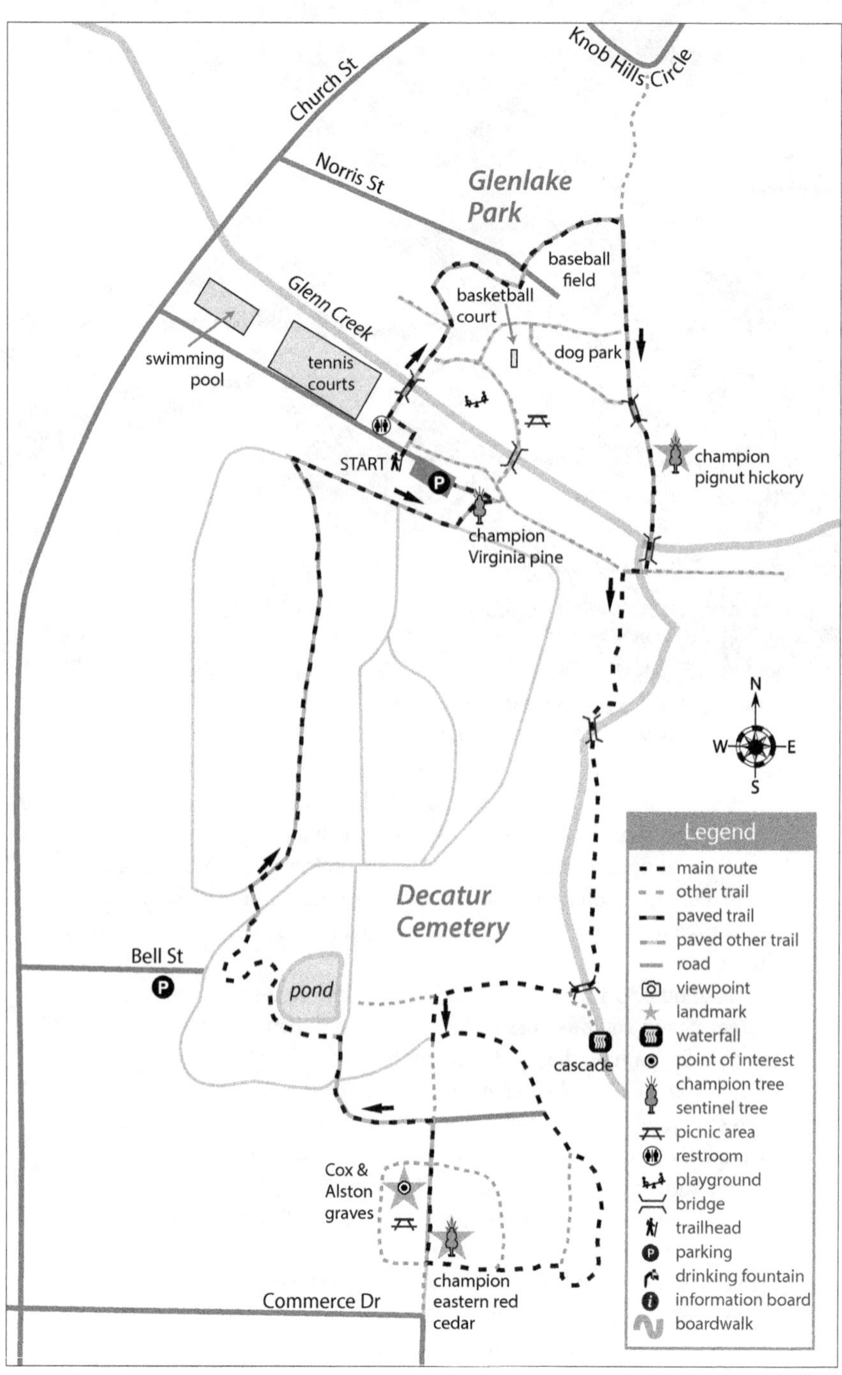
Church St
Knob Hills Circle
Norris St
Glenlake Park
baseball field
basketball court
Glenn Creek
swimming pool
tennis courts
dog park
START
champion pignut hickory
champion Virginia pine
N
W
E
S
Legend
main route
other trail
paved trail
paved other trail
road
viewpoint
landmark
waterfall
point of interest
champion tree
sentinel tree
picnic area
restroom
playground
bridge
trailhead
parking
drinking fountain
information board
boardwalk
Decatur Cemetery
Bell St
pond
cascade
Cox & Alston graves
champion eastern red cedar
Commerce Dr

follow this path to a small gravel road at the base of a set of stairs. Turn left onto this road and walk 0.1 mile into the historic section of Decatur Cemetery. Take a left at the first fork in the road, then another left when the road splits again at the Section 6 sign. Look around for old gravestones that have been weathered by years and overgrown with trees. The path curves to the right past a stand of large bamboo and then circles back up the hill.

After the path turns up the hill, turn left onto a small set of steps across from another Section 6 sign and walk past grave markers to reach another small road. Turn left, passing several hand-carved gravestones of Revolutionary War veterans at the corner on your right. It's worth spending some time in this part of the cemetery, as the old graves are particularly interesting; also, the champion eastern red cedar is in this section.

Continue walking on the gravel path to reach an intersection with a larger paved path that leads right to a gazebo. Turn right and look for the graves of Robert Alston and Edward Cox, just past the gazebo. At a T-intersection at the top of a flight of stone stairs, turn left and walk downhill to a small traffic circle.

Cross the traffic circle and walk on the grass (there is no path) past a swinging bench and around the left bank of the pond to find stairs on the opposite side. Continue up the stairs and follow the paved path to a veterans memorial on the right and a nice view of the cemetery. At the memorial, continue right toward the cemetery office. Before reaching the office, make a left on the first road, then an immediate right.

Walk 0.2 mile through a newer section of the cemetery past mature water oaks and grassy fields with graves, then turn right at a T-intersection at a Section 13 sign. In less than 0.1 mile, past a road on the right, reach a Walk There! Decatur sign near a grove of Virginia pines that includes one of the largest of this species in the city. Turn left on the pedestrian walkway and pass through a gate to reenter Glenlake Park at the far end of the parking lot where you began your hike.

Stay on the beaten path to help protect the environment in this old-growth research preserve.

Hahn Woods & Lullwater Preserve

Beautiful Lullwater Preserve sits in the center of the Emory University campus. The Hahn Woods route into Lullwater Preserve adds adventure to what is usually an easy stroll. Along the trail are city champion trees, two historic dams, and a suspension bridge. This greenspace is a research preserve set aside by Emory University for preservation and study. It is one of the last old-growth forests in metro Atlanta. Stewards of the preserve are working hard to heal and restore overused areas. Be sure to stay *on* the beaten path to avoid disturbing rare and fragile plants and animal habitat. These trails are reserved for Emory faculty, staff, and students only.

HOW TO GET THERE

Driving Distance from Downtown Atlanta: 7 miles
Address: 866 Houston Mill Road, Atlanta, GA 30329
Nearest Interstate: I-85
Neighborhood: Druid Hills / Emory
Public Transit: MARTA 6 or 816 bus + 0.4-mile walk
Parking: Circular gravel parking area; Emory parking hang tag required

HIKE DISTANCE

3-mile figure-8 loop

DIFFICULTY

Overall: Easy to moderate
Navigation: Map of Hahn Woods posted at parking area; no other blazes or trail signs
Terrain: Mostly hard-packed dirt trails with short sections of pavement, gravel, and mulch; trails connecting Hahn Woods and Lullwater Preserve can be overgrown and muddy in summer; the last leg includes a suspension bridge and an 18-inch sewer pipe used to cross a small creek
Elevation Change: Minimal elevation change—very level

SAFETY

Usage ★★★★★
Visibility ★★★★☆
Upkeep ★★★★☆
Parking ★★★★☆

HOURS	Daytime use only; closes at dusk
DOGS	Leashed dogs allowed
FACILITIES	• No toilets • Trash cans and some benches
FEES & PERMITS	Visitation restricted to Emory University faculty, staff, and students
LAND MANAGER	Emory University

Landmarks

HOUSTON MILL DAM

This dam dates from the 1860s and powered a grist mill until the early 1900s, when it was converted into DeKalb County's first hydroelectric plant. After a rain, water often cascades over the edge of the dam in a beautiful waterfall.

CITY CHAMPION LOBLOLLY PINE

- 131" circumference, 117' tall, 48' crown spread
- Loblolly pine trees are one of the most common species in Atlanta, but specimens this large are rare. This is one of only four known loblollies in the city with a circumference of over 10 feet. It towers almost 120 feet tall.

LULLWATER DAM

This dam was built across South Fork Peachtree Creek to fill Lullwater Lake and was later used to generate hydroelectric power (using machinery that was housed in the tower across the creek) for the Candler family's home and stables.

Hike Route

With your back to Houston Mill Road, start your hike on Upper Trail, to the left of the information board. This 0.1-mile trail curves back to the other side of the parking circle, then turns right and descends the hill. Take the left fork when the trail splits, then turn right to parallel South Fork Peachtree Creek. Pass an overlook platform on your left and stay left at a junction just past the overlook. Hike 0.1 mile along the creek, crossing a footbridge and climbing two small sets of stairs to reach the bottom of a longer staircase that leads up to the parking

You can explore the ruins of a historic hydroelectric dam at Lullwater Preserve.

area. Continue straight on a broken and uneven concrete path, then walk under the Houston Mill Road bridge to reach the historic Houston Mill Dam, built in 1863.

Continue straight along the path that parallels the creek for 0.35 mile before reaching the city champion loblolly pine on the right of the trail. The trail continues another 0.2 mile before passing under the suspension bridge and then reaching the paved path at Lullwater Dam, across from a historic tower. Go straight onto the pavement and walk 0.25 mile along the lakeshore, passing a southern magnolia on the left that children love to climb.

At the first junction, go straight onto the gravel path and continue to circle the lake. In 0.3 mile stay straight at a junction with a trail on your right and then keep an eye out for steps on your left in less than 100 yards. Hike down the stairs onto the floodplain and follow this mulched trail for 0.3 mile until you return to the junction with the paved path near the waterfall.

The route that follows can be fairly overgrown in the summer months and also includes balancing across an 18-inch sewer pipe to

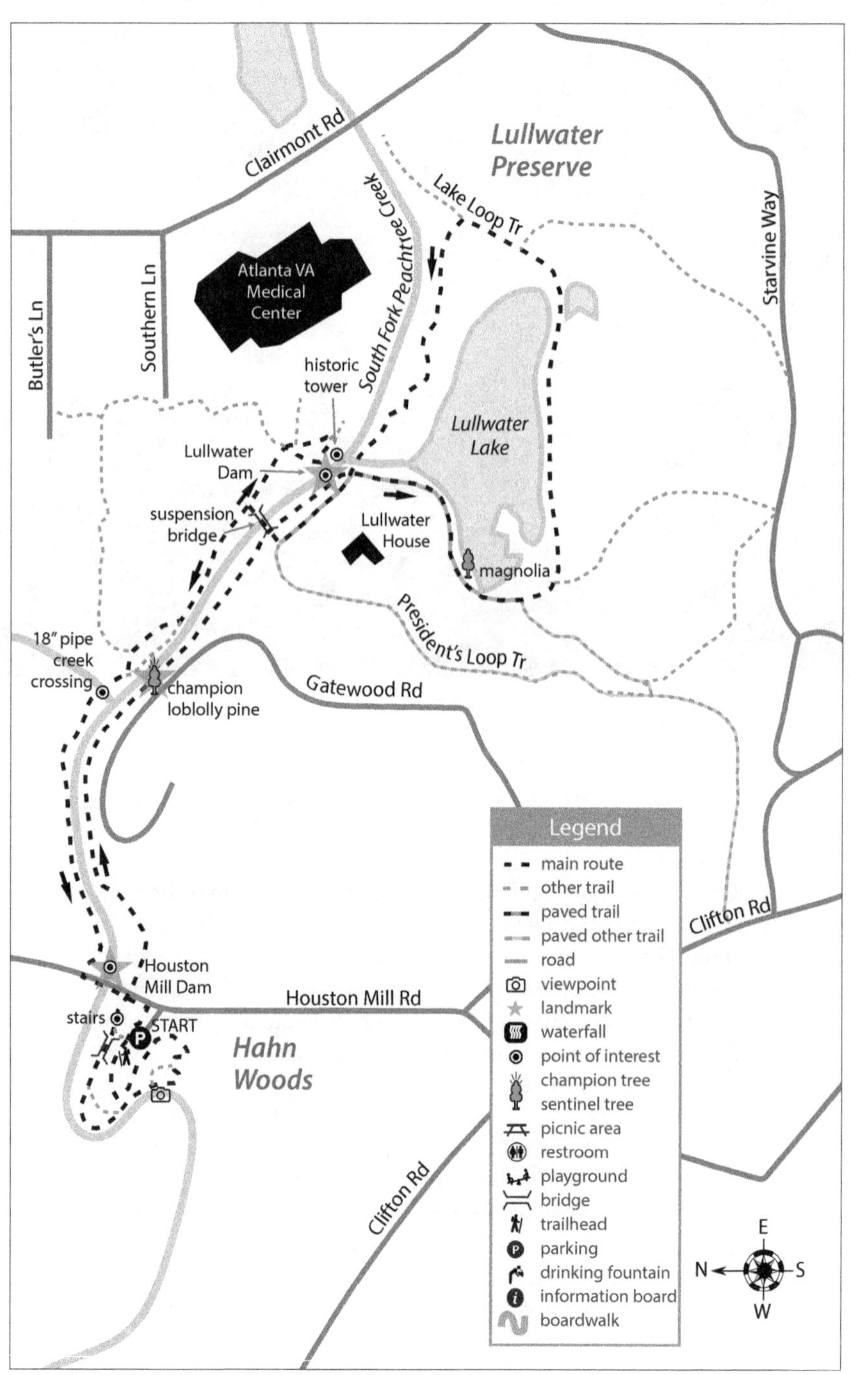
Clairmont Rd
Lullwater Preserve
Lake Loop Tr
South Fork Peachtree Creek
Starvine Way
Butler's Ln
Southern Ln
Atlanta VA Medical Center
historic tower
Lullwater Lake
Lullwater Dam
suspension bridge
Lullwater House
magnolia
President's Loop Tr
18" pipe creek crossing
champion loblolly pine
Gatewood Rd
Legend
main route
other trail
paved trail
paved other trail
road
viewpoint
landmark
waterfall
point of interest
champion tree
sentinel tree
picnic area
restroom
playground
bridge
trailhead
parking
drinking fountain
information board
boardwalk
Clifton Rd
Houston Mill Dam
Houston Mill Rd
stairs
START
Hahn Woods
Clifton Rd
E
N
S
W

cross the creek. If you want to avoid this, you can retrace your steps along the near side of the creek to return to Hahn Woods.

For the more adventurous route back, continue straight on the pavement and hike up the hill. Above you to your left is the Emory University president's residence—the historic Candler mansion. In 0.1 mile turn right onto the suspension bridge and cross the creek. Turn right on the far side of the bridge and hike 100 yards to a four-way junction near a police call button. Turn right and hike downhill to the historic but graffiti-covered tower. Continue straight past the tower, then turn left at the first junction to circle back to the police button. Go straight and return to the suspension bridge.

At the bridge, stay straight and walk 0.2 mile to a trail that leads left and down to the floodplain. Stay right on the high trail, then go left at the next trail and hike downhill.

In 100 yards cross a small creek on an 18-inch sewer pipe, which can be slippery even in dry weather. Walk another 0.25 mile, pass the old Houston Mill, then reach Houston Mill Road. Carefully cross the road (there is no crosswalk) and turn left, crossing the bridge and turning right into the Hahn Woods parking area to finish your hike.

Several giant trees, like this American beech, make Kittredge Park an urban oasis.

Kittredge Park

In the past decade, Kittredge Park has received a great deal of care and maintenance from dedicated volunteers and has become a hiking destination. A network of trails are blazed with signs installed, benches built, and invasive plants cleared. This park is home to many old trees, with one particularly impressive tulip tree on the ridge. Despite its proximity to the interstate highway, Kittredge's topography blocks out much of the traffic sound, making it a delightful and unexpected urban oasis.

HOW TO GET THERE	**Driving Distance from Downtown Atlanta:** 8 miles **Address:** 1520 Kittredge Park Road NE, Atlanta, GA 30329 **Nearest Interstate:** I-85 **Neighborhood:** Merry Hills / North Decatur **Public Transit:** MARTA 8 bus + 0.2-mile walk or MARTA 30 bus + 0.5-mile walk **Parking:** Paved parking lot near swimming pool; ADA parking down paved road near information board
HIKE DISTANCE	1.5-mile loop
DIFFICULTY	**Overall:** Easy to moderate **Navigation:** No maps posted, but wooden trail signs throughout the park mark the main trail loop **Terrain:** Hard-packed dirt or gravel trails with several wooden bridges and one paved section **Elevation Change:** Rolling hills with one steep ascent and descent
SAFETY	**Usage** ★★★★☆ **Visibility** ★★★☆☆ **Upkeep** ★★★★☆ **Parking** ★★★☆☆
HOURS	7:00 am to sunset
DOGS	Leashed dogs allowed

FACILITIES	• Toilet near playground near Holly Lane entrance to the park • Seasonally open swimming pool, picnic tables, benches, and playground
FEES & PERMITS	None
LAND MANAGER	DeKalb County Recreation, Parks & Cultural Affairs

Landmarks

CASCADE

We can find beauty even in this small urban creek. The water rushes between fissures in large boulders, making soothing sounds and a beautiful view. You can visit this cascade once toward the beginning of this hike and again near the end.

Loop Trail signs make the hiking at Kittredge Park easy and fun.

COUNCIL CIRCLE

When you arrive at the top of the hill, where a home once stood, you'll find a circular stone seating area surrounding a tree. At one time this was a fire circle for Scouting events. Today, it's a peculiar planter.

SENTINEL TULIP TREE

Besides being the largest tree (by far) on this ridge, this tree's bent shape and huge girth make it unmistakable and awe-inspiring. This tulip tree (commonly known as tulip poplar) is over 11 feet in circumference and was once used by Tree Climbers International as a climbing tree.

Hike Route

Park near the swimming pool and begin by walking downhill on the paved road past the barrier. In 0.1 mile pass a Loop Trail sign on your right that leads across the old baseball field, then look for a second path on your right. Take this trail to visit a small observation platform that provides a view of a small cascade in the creek. Return to the paved road and cross it to begin hiking Loop Trail up the hill on a dirt path.

Pass two benches and a picnic table before reaching a sentinel American beech with a bench beneath it. Follow the trail to the right and hike 0.1 mile to another junction. Follow the Loop Trail sign to the left and hike downhill, passing a bench before arriving at a wide gravel trail. Turn left and hike uphill, again following a Loop Trail sign.

This gravel trail leads to a playground and restroom at the top of the hill. But before reaching those landmarks, turn right onto a single-track dirt path that is marked with a Loop Trail sign. Hike downhill on Loop Trail to QueensBridge. Cross this bridge, turn right, and hike another 0.1 mile to reach another bridge, Nantahalla Crossing. Cross the bridge and then turn right at a Loop Trail sign.

At the next Loop Trail sign, hike left and up the rock stairs, pass a bench and two old beech trees, then continue uphill for 0.15 mile to reach a wide gravel path. This junction can be confusing. First, take a left on the wide gravel path to hike uphill about 50 yards to visit the Council Circle. Then return downhill to this same junction. This time, turn left onto a more narrow hiking trail and take an immediate right fork to begin descending the ridge on a switchback. At the second bench, look for the giant bent sentinel tulip tree. Follow the main trail

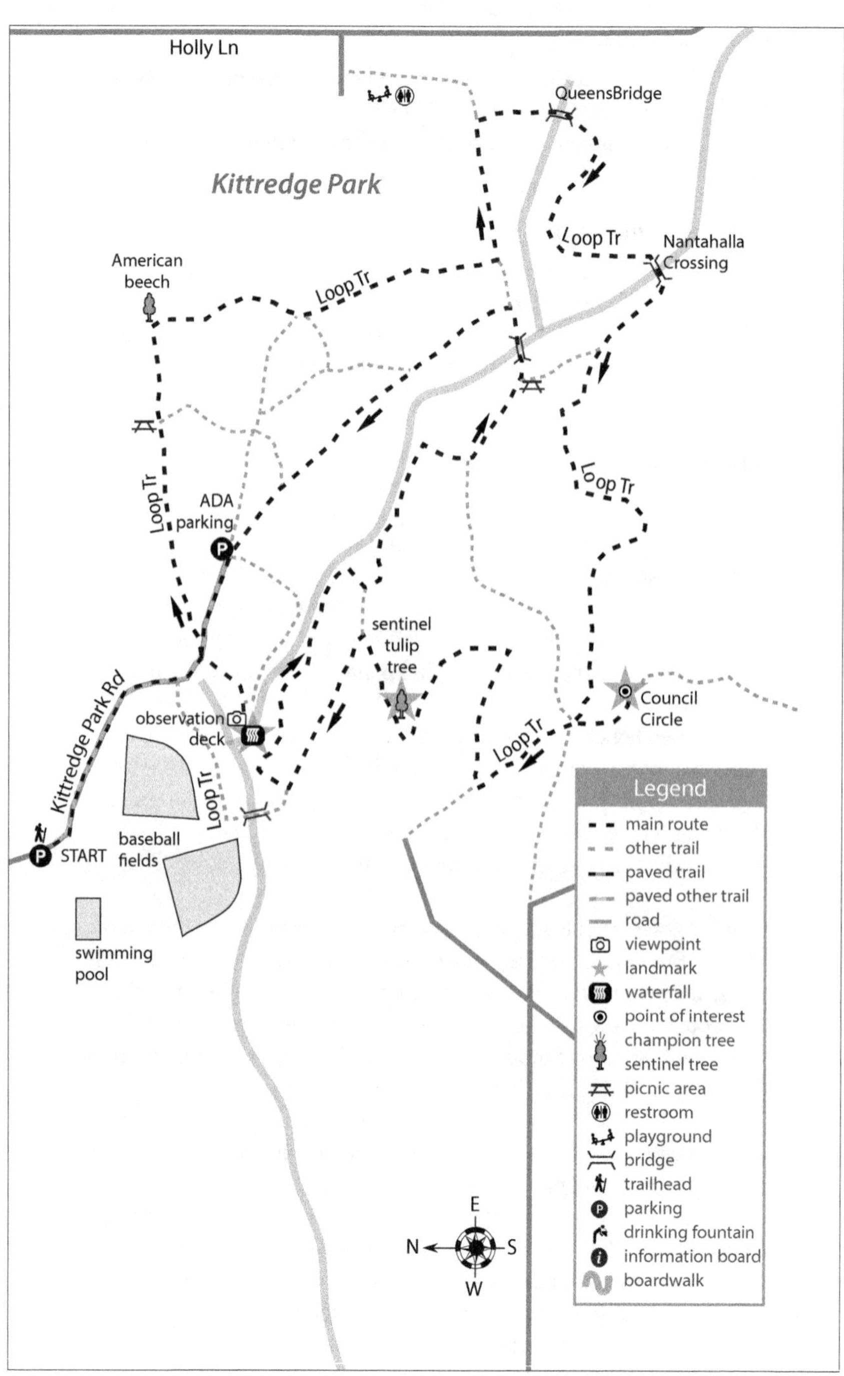
Holly Ln
QueensBridge
Kittredge Park
Loop Tr
Nantahalla Crossing
American beech
Loop Tr
Loop Tr
ADA parking
Loop Tr
sentinel tulip tree
Council Circle
Kittredge Park Rd
observation deck
Loop Tr
Loop Tr
START
baseball fields
swimming pool
Legend
main route
other trail
paved trail
paved other trail
road
viewpoint
landmark
waterfall
point of interest
champion tree
sentinel tree
picnic area
restroom
playground
bridge
trailhead
parking
drinking fountain
information board
boardwalk
E
N
S
W

as it curves past the tulip tree and then reaches another confusing junction. Make a hard left and continue hiking downhill. At the bottom of the hill you'll come to a large bridge over the creek. You can cross the bridge and the field beyond it to return to the parking area. But if you want more adventure, the following route has more in store for you.

Before the bridge, turn right on a small trail and hike parallel to the creek, past the cascade and a large flat rock that is perfect for sitting on. In 100 yards the trail makes a steep uphill turn to the right where you might have to use hands and feet to ascend. At the junction above, turn left and continue to parallel the creek until the trail curves right and slightly uphill to meet the wide gravel trail.

Turn left and hike downhill on the gravel trail. Pass a picnic area on the right, where you'll also find a Loop Trail sign. This time, do not follow it. Instead, go left and cross the bridge. Turn left at the first junction past the bridge and follow this wide trail through a meadow and past the ADA parking, and hike another 0.1 mile on the pavement to return to the parking area and finish your hike.

Legacy Park is no longer a farm, but it feels like a rural haven within the city.

Legacy Park

The United Methodist Children's Home has been a Decatur landmark for over 150 years. The property was home to orphaned children and a farm that boasted 100 dairy cows, 25 hogs, and 1,000 chickens. Recently, the City of Decatur purchased the 77-acre property and is transforming it into an amazing public space. The long-term vision includes nature trails, a sports complex, nonprofit offices, and affordable apartments. The park is swiftly changing, but the meadows, forests, wetlands, and ponds will continue to be a beautiful haven for nature. Come discover what you might find at this brand new nature park!

HOW TO GET THERE

Driving Distance from Downtown Atlanta: 7 miles
Address: 552 South Columbia Drive, Decatur, GA 30030
Nearest Interstate: I-20
Neighborhood: Winnona Park / Decatur
Public Transit: MARTA 114 bus + 0.25-mile walk
Parking: Turn into the park at its south entrance, near Katie Kerr Drive; once in the park, turn right, then left to reach several paved parking areas near the playground

HIKE DISTANCE

2.2-mile loop

DIFFICULTY

Overall: Easy to moderate
Navigation: No trail markers or signs
Terrain: Wide mowed trails through meadows, wide jogging trails through forests, and narrow single-track dirt trails that can be muddy
Elevation Change: Mostly flat with a few minor hills

SAFETY

Usage ★★★★☆
Visibility ★★★★☆
Upkeep ★★★☆☆
Parking ★★★★★

HOURS

7:00 am until 30 minutes after sunset

DOGS	Leashed dogs allowed
FACILITIES	• No toilets • Playground, picnic tables, sports fields, outdoor classroom
FEES & PERMITS	None
LAND MANAGER	City of Decatur in partnership with Legacy Decatur

Landmarks

HISTORIC TRACTOR

This tractor is left over from the days when residents of the United Methodist Children's Home planted fruit trees, cared for dairy cows, and farmed food crops such as potatoes, melons, okra, squash, cabbage, and corn.

BEAVER WETLANDS

Though the Postal Pond dam was constructed by the Children's Home, the wetlands below the pond are constructed by beavers, a keystone species that creates important habitat for many other animals.

SPRING-FED POND

The water in this small pond is incredibly clear. You'll often find tadpoles and frogs here. Even though the water is very inviting on a hot day, please stay out of the pond.

Hike Route

From the playground, look for an opening in the wooden fence to start your hike. Pass through the opening and follow the mowed path to the right past a white pine. Stay right at a possibly confusing junction where several mowed paths join, then keep to the main path, past two small trails to the right. In 0.1 mile the main trail splits again—stay right.

In 0.2 mile stay right on the main trail and hike another 0.15 mile past a cutoff trail that leads into the woods on the right. Stay on the mowed path through the meadow and pass the historic tractor in 0.1 mile. This is a great place for a photo.

The mowed trail continues along the edge of the forest for 0.1 mile, joining with a parallel mowed trail, then passing the old dairy barn on the left. Just after the barn but before reaching the edge of the lake, follow the trail right, into the woods. This trail curves through the forest and then passes through an area that once was a ropes course. Look for a decaying wooden wall, balance platform, and other remnants of the ropes course. At a four-way junction, stay straight. Then in 100 yards join a small trail to the wetland to the right. The trail can be very muddy, so stay on the main trail and hike uphill. In 50 yards turn right on another wide trail.

Pass an octagonal platform on your right, then pass another small trail on the right. The next trail on the right leads to a viewpoint of the wetland, which is worth a visit. It's only 100 yards down and back.

After visiting the wetland, continue on the main trail to reach the

Frogs abound in Legacy Park's small spring-fed pond.

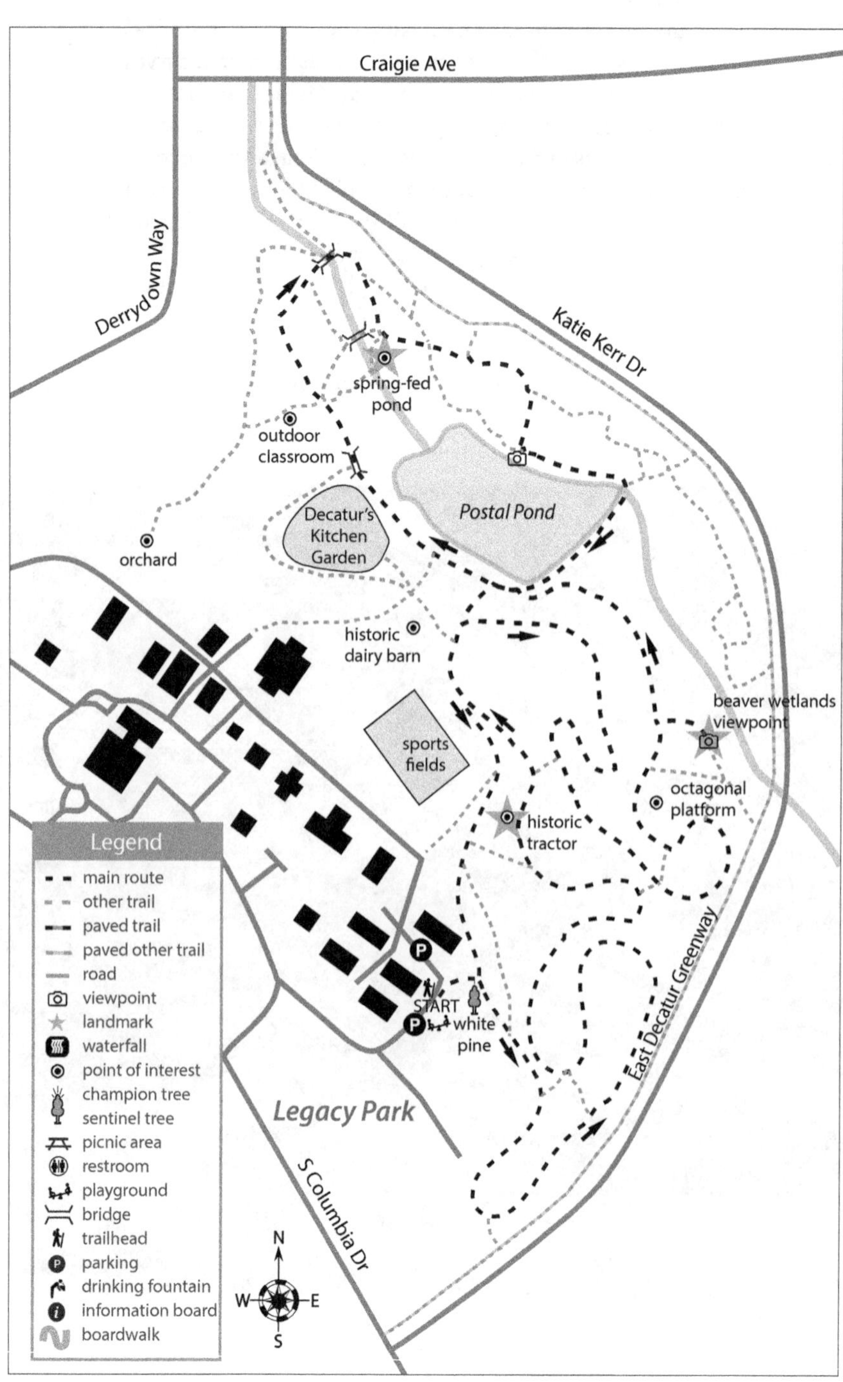
Craigie Ave
Derrydown Way
Katie Kerr Dr
spring-fed pond
outdoor classroom
orchard
Decatur's Kitchen Garden
Postal Pond
historic dairy barn
sports fields
beaver wetlands viewpoint
octagonal platform
historic tractor
START
white pine
East Decatur Greenway
Legacy Park
S Columbia Dr
Legend
main route
other trail
paved trail
paved other trail
road
viewpoint
landmark
waterfall
point of interest
champion tree
sentinel tree
picnic area
restroom
playground
bridge
trailhead
parking
drinking fountain
information board
boardwalk
N
W
E
S

edge of the Postal Pond in 0.1 mile. Stay straight through a grassy trail on the pond's edge.

Pass the historic dairy barn uphill on your left and then pass Decatur's Kitchen Garden, an immigrant-run farm, before arriving at a junction at a small boardwalk in 0.1 mile. Go right across the boardwalk and reach another junction in 50 yards at an old wire fence and gate. To the left is an outdoor classroom and seating area. Stay straight, parallel to the fence. Follow this trail 100 yards to cross a small wooden bridge over the creek near Katie Kerr Drive, then turn right and hike gradually downhill toward a spring-fed pond surrounded by a hexagonal concrete border. This is a good place to rest on a bench and nearby picnic table.

Stay straight on the trail that led you to the spring-fed pond. The trail gently slopes uphill to an opening in another fence. Pass through the opening and hike 100 yards to reach a junction. Turn right to hike down to the pond's edge, then left to follow the water's edge for 0.1 mile to a beaver dam and pond outflow.

Find a route across the beaver dam and then walk the 0.1-mile trail along Postal Pond's human-made dam. At the end of the dam, turn left and hike uphill toward the stone dairy barn. At a junction near the barn, stay left and hike uphill into the field, then stay right to pass the track-and-field area. At the top of the hill, stay straight on the mowed trail through the meadow toward a basketball court and the playground to end your hike.

The elevated boardwalk is one of the most beautiful places in this park.

Mason Mill Park

BURNT FORK TRAILS

Mason Mill Park has contained an extensive wetland for decades, but this important ecological area along the banks of Burnt Fork Creek is now accessible via the beautiful South Peachtree Creek Trail. This boardwalk is welcoming to both walkers and cyclists and leads from the DeKalb Tennis Center to North Druid Hills Road through floodplain, upland forest, and beaver-created wetlands. Mason Mill Park is a favorite of birders, but the boardwalk is also a great place to look for beavers, river otters, and turtles in the water below you. In addition, the hiking trails you can access from the midpoint of the boardwalk lead past two of Atlanta's champion trees.

HOW TO GET THERE

Driving Distance from Downtown Atlanta: 9 miles
Address: 1420 McConnell Drive, Decatur, GA 30033
Nearest Interstate: I-85
Neighborhood: Williamsburg / North Decatur
Public Transit: MARTA 19 bus + 0.4-mile walk
Parking: Large parking area near trailhead and DeKalb Tennis Center

HIKE DISTANCE

2-mile multiple-loop hike

DIFFICULTY

Overall: Easy to moderate
Navigation: Trail map and information board at start; maps posted at each trailhead; color-coded blazes and trail marker posts
Terrain: Paved trail, elevated boardwalk, and hard-packed dirt trails that can be muddy after a rain
Elevation Change: Mostly flat with one major elevation change on the boardwalk, plus a few other minor ascents and descents

SAFETY

Usage ★★★★★
Visibility ★★★★☆
Upkeep ★★★★★
Parking ★★★★★

HOURS

7:00 am to sunset

DOGS	Leashed dogs allowed; an off-leash dog park is accessible from this hike by hiking Dog Park Trail from the boardwalk and crossing Burnt Fork Creek on stepping-stones to reach a parking area, pavilion, and dog park at North Jamestown Road
FACILITIES	• Toilets near playground and at DeKalb Tennis Center • Playground, picnic tables, pavilions, water fountain, information boards, tennis courts, community garden
FEES & PERMITS	None
LAND MANAGER	DeKalb County Recreation, Parks & Cultural Affairs

Landmarks

BEAVER WETLANDS

Beavers are North America's largest rodents, and several generations have engineered the Mason Mill wetlands, building a series of five tiered dams that hold rainwater and create a perfect habitat for birds, reptiles, amphibians, and other mammals.

CITY CHAMPION RIVER BIRCH

- 134" circumference, 73' tall, 80' crown spread
- This is the largest river birch inside the I-285 perimeter and is over 11 feet in circumference. Look for the signature peeling and curling bark on the tree's upper branches.

CITY CHAMPION RED MAPLE

- 123" circumference, 88' tall, 108' crown spread
- Red maples love moist soil, so it's no surprise that the largest of this species in Atlanta is growing right on the banks of Burnt Fork Creek. This maple is over 10 feet around and 90 feet tall and just begging for a hug!

Hike Route

Start your hike on the paved, multiuse South Peachtree Creek Trail near the tennis courts. Go left, just past the information board with maps, and enter a boardwalk with tall wooden railings near a bench within 100 feet.

In 0.1 mile reach an overhead South Peachtree Creek sign at the top of stairs near a seating area. Turn right and hike the ramp downhill. At another seating area, the trail curves sharply left, passes the base of the stairs, then curves right. The boardwalk leaves the heavily forested hillside and winds through the Burnt Fork floodplain for 0.2 mile before reentering an upland forest and ascending a slight rise to reach a junction with a boardwalk exit and large seating area. This hike continues straight on the boardwalk from here but then returns.

Hike straight ahead on the elevated boardwalk to enter the beaver-created wetlands, which are full of animal life. Look for birds, turtles, snakes, frogs, and even river otters here. Hike 0.25 mile through the wetlands to a scenic viewpoint at a large open area of the wetlands. On a sunny day, it's fun to count turtles here. Continue hiking the boardwalk for another 100 yards to a bridge over Burnt Fork Creek. You can walk another 0.25 mile to North Druid Hills, but this hike turns around at the bridge.

Wildlife abounds in the Mason Mill wetlands, including this common snapping turtle.

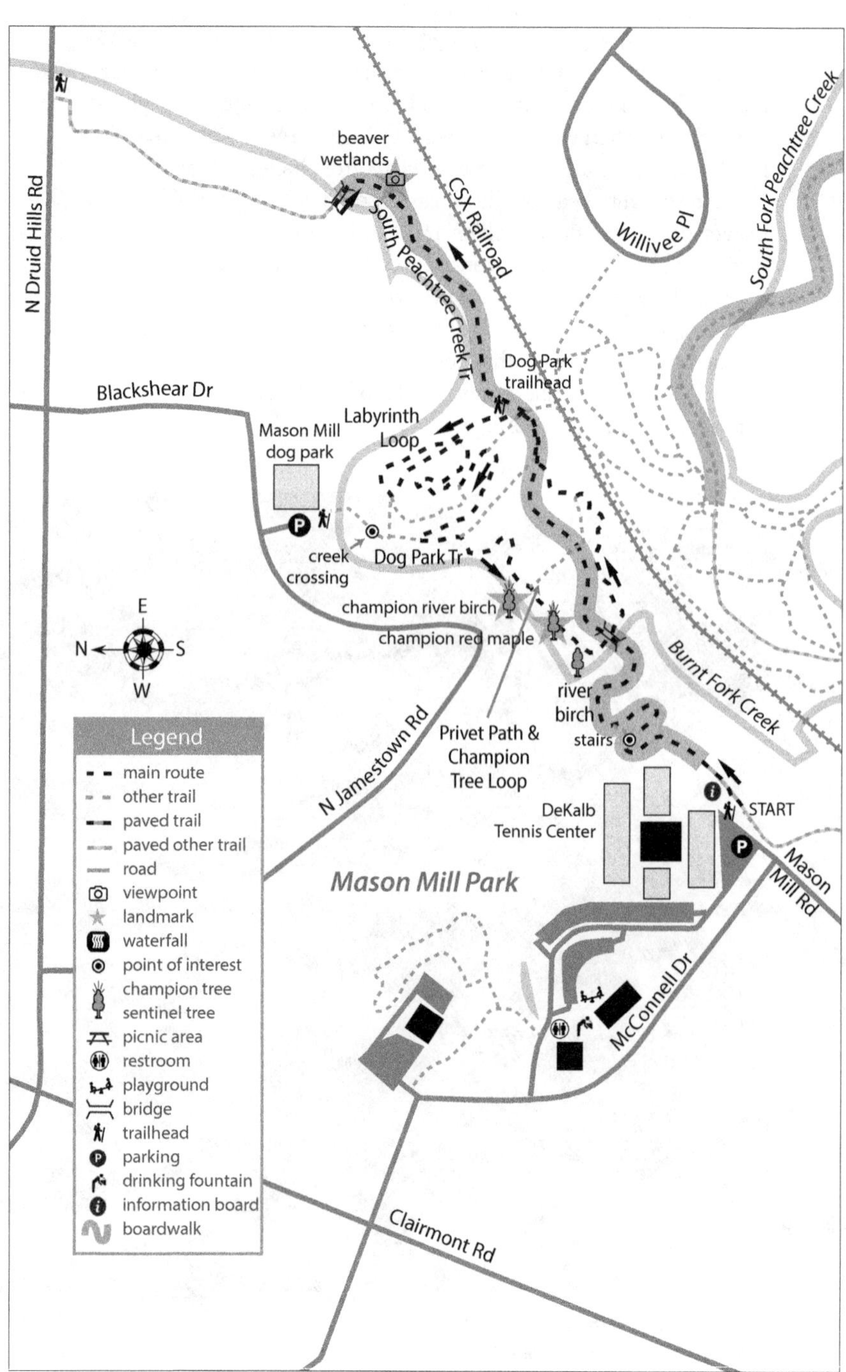
beaver
wetlands
CSX Railroad
Willivee Pl
South Fork Peachtree Creek
N Druid Hills Rd
South Peachtree Creek Tr
Dog Park
trailhead
Blackshear Dr
Labyrinth
Loop
Mason Mill
dog park
creek
crossing
Dog Park Tr
champion river birch
champion red maple
E
N
S
W
river
birch
stairs
Burnt Fork Creek
Privet Path &
Champion
Tree Loop
N Jamestown Rd
START
DeKalb
Tennis Center
Mason
Mill Rd
Mason Mill Park
McConnell Dr
Clairmont Rd
Legend
main route
other trail
paved trail
paved other trail
road
viewpoint
landmark
waterfall
point of interest
champion tree
sentinel tree
picnic area
restroom
playground
bridge
trailhead
parking
drinking fountain
information board
boardwalk

Follow the boardwalk back 0.3 mile to the seating area and boardwalk exit. The next part of this hike is on dirt trails. Turn right and descend three steps to leave the boardwalk and arrive at Dog Park trailhead. Turn right and hike the pink-blazed Labyrinth Loop 0.1 mile to arrive at a junction with a trail marker post labeled Loop, Spur, and Dog Park Trails. Go left and hike uphill to stay on the pink-blazed Labyrinth Loop for 0.1 mile. Just past a trail marker post with a pink arrow, turn sharply right and uphill to stay on Labyrinth Loop. In 0.1 mile reach a Loop/Spur trail marker post and turn left to stay on Labyrinth Loop. In 100 yards, at a Loop trail marker post, turn right on blue-blazed Dog Park Trail. Dog Park Trail reaches a junction with a wide sewer line access road in 0.1 mile. Turn left here and follow the white-blazed trail down the access road, then right into the forest, following trail marker posts with white arrows.

In 0.1 mile, at a Loop/Spur trail marker post, turn right on the orange-blazed Privet Path & Champion Tree Loop. You will immediately pass an information sign and the city champion river birch tree on the right and then in 50 yards the city champion red maple tree on the left, also with a corresponding information sign. After passing the champion trees, the trail curves left along Burnt Fork Creek near a large, leaning river birch tree and then passes underneath the boardwalk.

Follow orange blazes and trail marker posts for 0.1 mile to reach a junction with a Loop/Trailhead trail marker post. Turn right and follow this trail under the boardwalk, then to the right as it parallels the boardwalk, uphill to Dog Park trailhead and the boardwalk exit. Reenter the boardwalk and turn right. Hike 0.4 mile on the boardwalk back to the parking lot to end your hike.

The graffiti-covered ruins of the Old Decatur Waterworks are fun to explore.

Mason Mill Park

SOUTH FORK TRAILS

Nestled between Mason Mill, Medlock, and Melton Parks, the 100-acre forest along South Fork Peachtree Creek provides a very diverse hike, including an extended boardwalk, miles of paved and dirt trails, several creeks, a historic site, and peaceful forests. You'll pass mountain laurel, sourwood, and hop hornbeam trees, visit the confluence of Burnt Fork and South Fork Peachtree Creeks, and explore the Old Decatur Waterworks and its graffiti-covered buildings. This complicated route takes you past all the best sites, so use the map, refer to the directions, and have a great adventure.

HOW TO GET THERE	**Driving Distance from Downtown Atlanta:** 9 miles **Address:** 1420 McConnell Drive, Decatur, GA 30033 **Nearest Interstate:** I-85 **Neighborhood:** Williamsburg / North Decatur **Public Transit:** MARTA 19 bus + 0.4-mile walk **Parking:** Large parking area near trailhead and DeKalb Tennis Center
HIKE DISTANCE	3.3-mile multiple-loop hike
DIFFICULTY	**Overall:** Moderate **Navigation:** Trail map and information board at start; maps posted at each trailhead; color-coded blazes and trail marker posts **Terrain:** Paved multiuse trails and boardwalk, as well as hard-packed dirt trails and a creek crossing on stepping-stones **Elevation Change:** Rolling hills with short but steep ascents and descents
SAFETY	**Usage** ★★★★★ **Visibility** ★★★★☆ **Upkeep** ★★★★★ **Parking** ★★★★★
HOURS	7:00 am to sunset
DOGS	Leashed dogs allowed; an off-leash dog park is on North Jamestown Road

FACILITIES	• Toilets near playground and at DeKalb Tennis Center • Playground, picnic tables, pavilions, water fountain, information boards, tennis courts, community garden
FEES & PERMITS	None
LAND MANAGER	DeKalb County Recreation, Parks & Cultural Affairs

Landmarks

OLD DECATUR WATERWORKS

From 1907 until the mid-1940s, the City of Decatur got its water from Burnt Fork Creek and used the now-ruined buildings in this area to purify and treat it for drinking. Graffiti writers have been painting the buildings since the 1960s, and the art will be different every time you visit.

CITY CHAMPION BOX ELDER

- 99" circumference, 71' tall, 63' crown spread
- Box elder trees are in the maple family and are understory trees that prefer to grow near water. This one is the largest of its species inside the I-285 perimeter.

ABANDONED VOLKSWAGEN SQUAREBACK

This upside-down car wreck has been in these woods since at least the early 1980s. Abandoned by a local teenager and picked clean by scavengers, this car has sparked the curiosity of hikers for years.

Hike Route

Start your hike on the paved, multiuse South Peachtree Creek Trail near the intersection of McConnell Drive and Mason Mill Road. You've gone the wrong way if you enter a boardwalk within 50 yards. Hike steeply downhill on the paved trail, passing an information board with maps.

In 0.1 mile reach a paved circle and junction. Stay straight and hike uphill to the railroad bridge. After crossing the bridge over the tracks, pass a historic concrete water tower on your left, then switchback down the boardwalk. The path is paved again after the boardwalk ends. Pass an interpretive sign about Mason Mill history and then reach the Three Creeks trailhead. Turn right and follow purple blazes through the Old Decatur Waterworks ruins.

The creeks of Mason Mill Park are relaxing and peaceful.

Pass old granite stairs on the left, then loop around the graffiti-covered ruin of a rectangular water filtration tank, following the purple blazes painted on trees. This trail leads you to a creek crossing that can be impassable after a rain. Be very careful as you balance from boulder to boulder, crossing South Fork Peachtree Creek to enter Ira B. Melton Park. On the far side of the creek, hike up the stairs and go straight, still following the purple blazes of Three Creeks Trail.

In 0.1 mile reach a trail marker post for the white-blazed Native Plant Wetland Trail. Go right and hike this trail until it loops back to the main trail. Turn right and continue hiking Three Creeks Trail. Cross a seasonal creek on cobblestones; the trail then curves right. In 100 yards reach the Melton Park entrance at Desmond Drive. Continue on Three Creeks Trail to the right, passing a bench. Then pass the city champion box elder tree on the left.

In 0.1 mile cross a wooden bridge and then follow Three Creeks Trail as it curves to the right along the banks of South Fork Peachtree Creek. In 0.15 mile reach the creek crossing again. Turn left, cross the creek on the stones, and follow the purple-blazed Three Creeks Trail back to the paved South Peachtree Creek Trail.

Turn right on the paved trail, cross a stone bridge, and immediately turn right on a white-blazed trail. In 100 yards reach a junction with the blue-blazed Watershed Loop. Stay straight, following blue blazes past two giant American beech trees in a sandy area beside the creek. There are many unofficial trails in this area of the forest. Look around carefully and follow blue blazes to hike Watershed

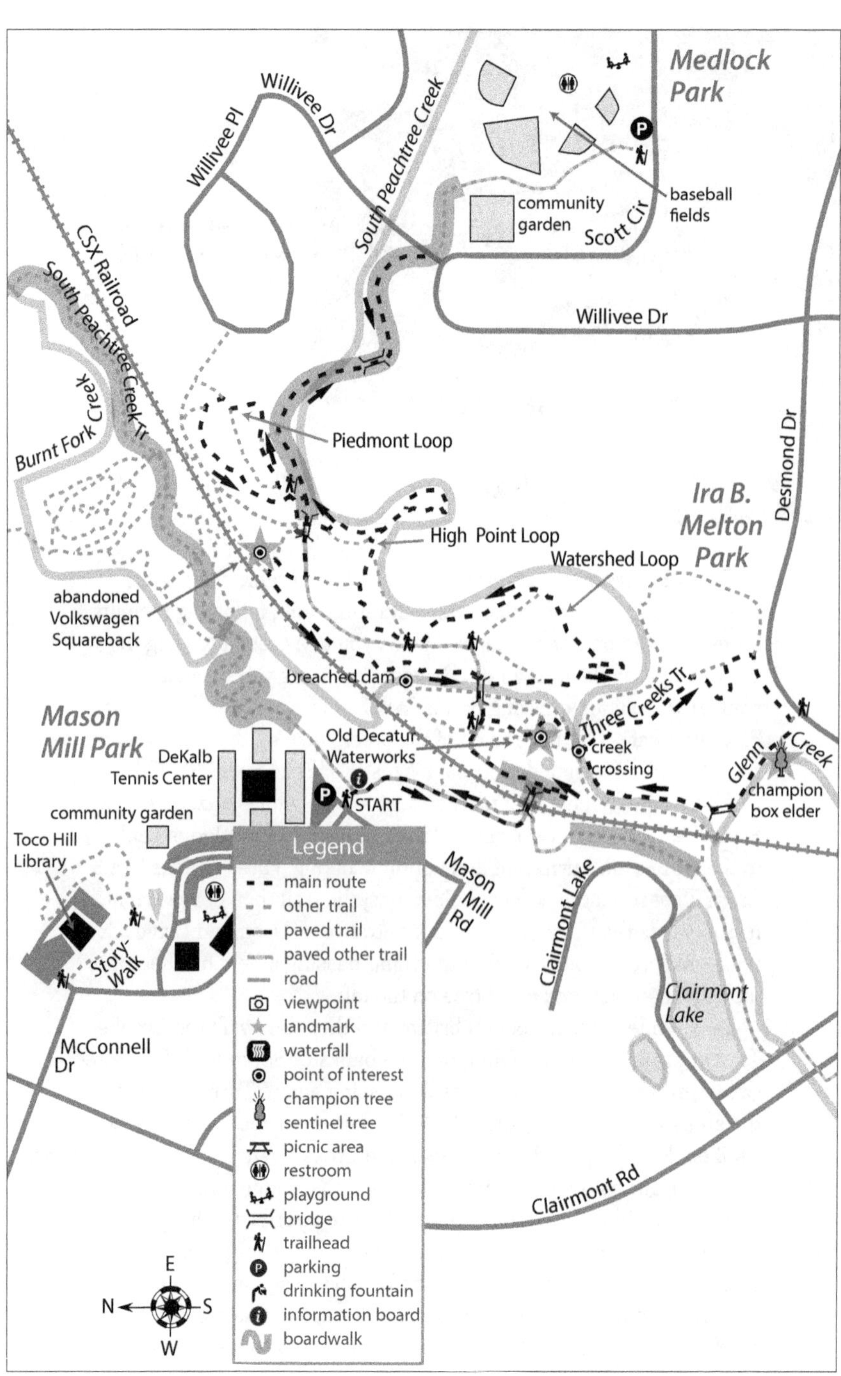

Medlock Park
baseball fields
community garden
Scott Cir
Willivee Pl
Willivee Dr
South Peachtree Creek
CSX Railroad
South Peachtree Creek Tr
Burnt Fork Creek
Willivee Dr
Piedmont Loop
High Point Loop
Watershed Loop
Ira B. Melton Park
Desmond Dr
abandoned Volkswagen Squareback
breached dam
Three Creeks Tr
Mason Mill Park
DeKalb Tennis Center
Old Decatur Waterworks
creek crossing
Glenn Creek
champion box elder
community garden
START
Toco Hill Library
Story-Walk
Mason Mill Rd
Clairmont Lake
Clairmont Lake
McConnell Dr
Clairmont Rd
Legend
main route
other trail
paved trail
paved other trail
road
viewpoint
landmark
waterfall
point of interest
champion tree
sentinel tree
picnic area
restroom
playground
bridge
trailhead
parking
drinking fountain
information board
boardwalk
E
N
S
W

Loop for 0.2 mile to reach a junction with a Loop/Spur trail marker post. Turn right and hike the white-blazed trail for 0.1 mile to reach the paved trail near the High Point trailhead.

Facing the High Point trailhead sign, hike uphill to the left, following red blazes. At a Loop trail marker post, take the right fork and hike downhill. Stay straight at a junction with a white-blazed trail on the right, then reach a junction with a wide trail that doubles as a sewer line access road. Turn right and hike steeply downhill to a saddle and then uphill again to reach a junction with a short, white-blazed loop. Hike the loop to the right, and when you get back to the loop junction, go right and hike downhill to the saddle again. This time, take a small unofficial trail to the right along South Fork Peachtree Creek. This trail winds through a grove of mountain laurel, American hornbeam, and hop hornbeam trees before meeting up with the red-blazed High Point Loop Trail in 100 yards. Turn right on this wide trail.

Hike under a bridge and immediately turn right on the white-blazed trail. Hike steeply uphill to the yellow-blazed Piedmont Loop Trail. Stay straight past a junction on the right and then past one on the left before reaching a junction with a Loop/Spur trail marker post. Go right and follow yellow blazes. In 0.1 mile go right at another Loop/Spur trail marker post and continue to follow yellow blazes to loop back to the South Peachtree Creek Trail boardwalk.

At this point, you can turn right and hike South Peachtree Creek Trail back to the parking lot. But because this boardwalk is one of the most beautiful parts of this park, this hike turns left and hikes the boardwalk 0.3 mile, parallel to South Fork Peachtree Creek, to reach Willivee Drive. You can continue across the road to a parking lot in Medlock Park, but this hike turns around at Willivee Drive. Hike back 0.3 mile to where the boardwalk ends and the trail is paved again. In 50 yards, just after passing a PATH Foundation sign, turn right on High Point Loop Trail at a Loop trail marker post. Hike downhill to a Loop/Spur trail marker post and turn left on the white-blazed trail, which passes above a wrecked Volkswagen Squareback car and then turns left on a steep, eroded path. This trail crests the hill and parallels the railroad tracks.

In 0.1 mile pass a historic water pipe marked with the year 1932 near a view of a historic railroad trestle that dates to the 1890s. Continue following white blazes for 0.1 mile past a breached dam to reach the paved South Peachtree Creek Trail again. Turn right and hike the paved multiuse trail 0.4 mile back to the parking lot.

Go ahead, hug a tree!

Mercer University Nature Trail

It's unusual to find an undulating hike route with old-growth trees on a small college campus, so this trail is a pleasant surprise. Used by many joggers, college students, and neighbors, the Mercer University Nature Trail is unique among intown hikes because it keeps to the ridges and away from creeks and floodplains. The forest is mostly pine and young hardwoods, but the trail also passes an old homesite with some interesting historical remains and a grove of large oak trees.

HOW TO GET THERE

Driving Distance from Downtown Atlanta: 14 miles

Address: 3000 University Circle, Atlanta, GA 30341

Nearest Interstate: I-85

Neighborhood: Embry Hills / DeKalb

Public Transit: MARTA 126 bus + 0.2-mile walk

Parking: Large parking lot and trailhead are on University Circle near the intersection with Flowers Road South; trailhead is across University Circle from the far south end of the parking lot

HIKE DISTANCE

1-mile loop

DIFFICULTY

Overall: Easy

Navigation: No blazes or maps; wooden posts mark each ¼ mile of trail

Terrain: Hard-packed dirt trails with significant erosion in places

Elevation Change: Rolling hills and several short, steep ascents and descents

SAFETY

Usage ★★★☆☆

Visibility ★★★☆☆

Upkeep ★★★☆☆

Parking ★★★★★

HOURS

Dawn to dusk

DOGS

Leashed dogs allowed

FACILITIES	• No toilets • No facilities open to the public
FEES & PERMITS	None
LAND MANAGER	Mercer University

Landmarks

OLD HOMESITE

- City champion American holly: 62" circumference, 64' tall, 40' crown spread
- To the right of the trail, just before the junction, is the site of what used to be someone's home. If you leave the trail and explore, you'll find foundations and other remnants of human habitation. But the trees are an even better sign—a city champion American holly, large eastern red cedars, and black walnut trees were likely planted by the family as yard trees.

SENTINEL OAKS

Likely remnants of the old homesite, these giant white oaks and a slightly smaller post oak stood sentinel and provided shade over the family's home when the surrounding area was farmland. Look for white oak leaves with narrow, rounded lobes and dark green post oak leaves with lobes that are roughly in the shape of a cross.

SENTINEL TULIP TREE

Tulip trees (commonly known as tulip poplars) thrive in the Piedmont region of Georgia, and this gorgeous tree is a prime example of how large they can get. This tree is over 15 feet in circumference and more than 125 feet tall. Though this one is probably only 150 years old, some tulip trees have been known to live for 500 years.

Hike Route

Enter the Nature Trail loop across University Circle from the parking lot and cross a small wooden bridge over a drainage ditch to reach a junction. Start your hike on the right fork. The trail winds uphill, fairly steeply at times, for 0.25 mile before leveling out and reaching an old homesite, several massive oak trees, and a trail junction.

On your right, just before the junction, are the remains of the homestead. If you explore the area, you'll find signs of the buildings,

Ancient trees tower over the surrounding forest.

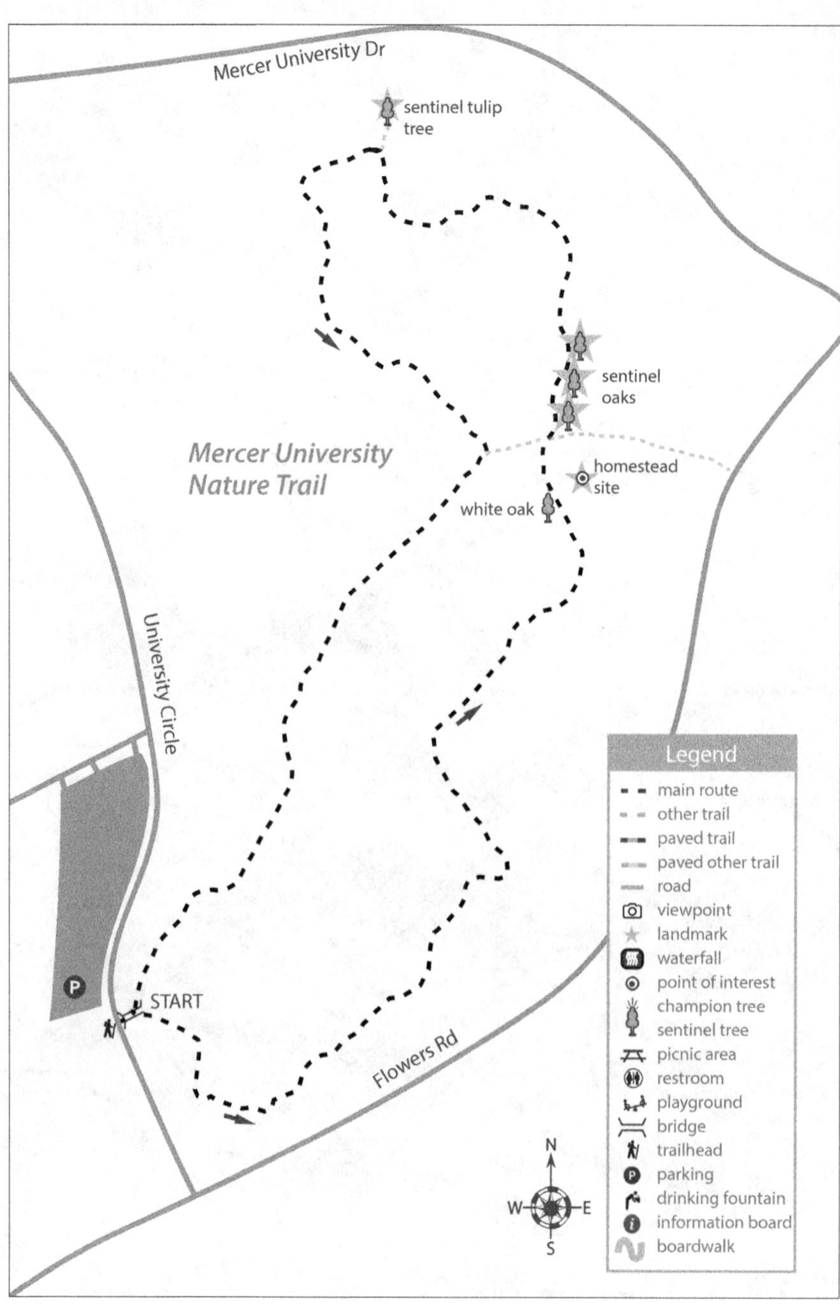

Mercer University Dr
sentinel tulip tree
sentinel oaks
Mercer University Nature Trail
homestead site
white oak
University Circle
START
Flowers Rd
Legend
main route
other trail
paved trail
paved other trail
road
viewpoint
landmark
waterfall
point of interest
champion tree
sentinel tree
picnic area
restroom
playground
bridge
trailhead
parking
drinking fountain
information board
boardwalk
N
W
E
S

roads, and plants built and planted by the family who lived here. To the right at the junction, a narrow, unmaintained trail leads to Flowers Road South, near DeKalb Fire Station 19. To the left, a trail leads to the other half of the loop.

Stay straight at the junction and pass two large white oaks on the right. The third tree on the right is a post oak, recognizable by its cross-shaped leaves and less flaky bark.

In 0.2 mile, about 100 yards after passing the half-mile marker, the trail reaches a low point. To your right is the sentinel tulip tree, by far the largest tree in this forest. Walking 50 yards downhill off the trail to visit the tulip tree is definitely worthwhile, but watch out for briars, poison ivy, and delicate trillium flowers growing on the forest floor.

Back on the trail, the route ascends and then curves left. In 0.2 mile pass the cutoff trail that leads back to the homesite and continue straight another 0.3 mile, mostly downhill, to finish your hike at the University Circle trailhead.

Take a moment to view South Fork Peachtree Creek from Morningside Nature Preserve's suspension bridge.

Morningside Nature Preserve

Formerly the Wildwood Urban Forest, Morningside Nature Preserve has become one of the premier destinations for intown hiking. Once just a neighborhood greenspace known only by locals, the preserve now contains a long staircase through the forest canopy, a suspension bridge over South Fork Peachtree Creek, and a two-mile network of trails through floodplain forests and Piedmont hills. Trillium, pawpaw, and many wildflowers flourish in the shade of old-growth trees in this peaceful nature preserve.

HOW TO GET THERE

Driving Distance from Downtown Atlanta: 6 miles
Address: 2020 Lenox Road NE, Atlanta, GA 30324
Nearest Interstate: I-85
Neighborhood: Morningside
Public Transit: MARTA 6 or 27 bus + 0.4-mile walk
Parking: Gravel parking area

HIKE DISTANCE

2-mile lollipop loop

DIFFICULTY

Overall: Easy to moderate
Navigation: Trails are wide and well-traveled, but there are no posted maps and only two trail markers
Terrain: Hard-packed dirt trails with a boardwalk, extended stairs, and a suspension bridge
Elevation Change: Mostly flat but with several steep ascents and descents

SAFETY

Usage ★★★★☆
Visibility ★★★☆☆
Upkeep ★★★★☆
Parking ★★★★★

HOURS

6:00 am to 11:00 pm

DOGS

Leashed dogs allowed

FACILITIES

- No toilets
- Bicycle rack, water fountain

FEES & PERMITS	None
LAND MANAGER	City of Atlanta Parks & Recreation

Landmarks

SUSPENSION BRIDGE AND SANDBAR

Built in 2010, this suspension bridge allows hikers to view South Fork Peachtree Creek from above and to safely cross, even in flood conditions. Below the bridge is a large sandy sandbar that draws families who want to connect with their local creek. Be aware that you'll probably see off-leash dogs here.

OLD-GROWTH TREES

The ridge above the creek's floodplain is home to many old-growth hardwood trees. A particularly scenic spot is found just after the main trail ascends from the floodplain. Here the trail passes two ancient white oaks, an American beech, and a giant southern red oak. A nearby, relatively young water oak was dated to 1930, so these larger trees are likely more than 200 years old.

"PENCIL TOWER" VIEWPOINT

Despite the power lines above your head, it's fun to glimpse a skyscraper in the middle of a nature preserve. Nicknamed the Pencil Tower, the Bank of America Plaza is Atlanta's tallest building and also the tallest in the southeastern United States. It is over 1,000 feet tall and has 55 stories of office space.

Hike Route

From the parking area, begin your hike at the information board. Looking up the hill, you'll see a power line clearing. To the left of this clearing, follow the trail into the woods, crossing a wooden footbridge and ascending the hill, passing two side trails on your right. When you come to a gate and small trail marker with a red arrow, bear right and continue up the hill until the trail curves right through a clearing under the power lines. You can see a Georgia Power substation below you, but right next to the trail you might see wildflowers and blackberries.

Upon reentering the forest, you'll come to a wooden staircase leading down the hill. Check out the forest canopy as you descend the stairs to the South Fork Peachtree Creek floodplain. At the base of the stairs, continue along a 100-yard boardwalk. After the boardwalk, bear left and hike 0.25 mile through a floodplain forest and power line clearing to reach a large suspension bridge spanning South Fork Peachtree Creek. Below the bridge is a large sandbar that is worth exploring. This is a great place to take your shoes off and dip your toes in the water, if you are so inclined.

Cross the bridge to reach a four-way trail junction. Turn right to follow the path parallel to the creek. Cross a bridge in 0.1 mile, then pass a trail junction leading uphill on the left and several trails that lead to the creekbank on the right. Continue straight on the main trail, and you'll notice a change in terrain as the trail curves away from the creek and uphill. As you leave the floodplain there are larger boulders and trees. In 0.1 mile the trail passes several particularly large

Wildflowers flourish in one of the largest nature preserves inside the perimeter.

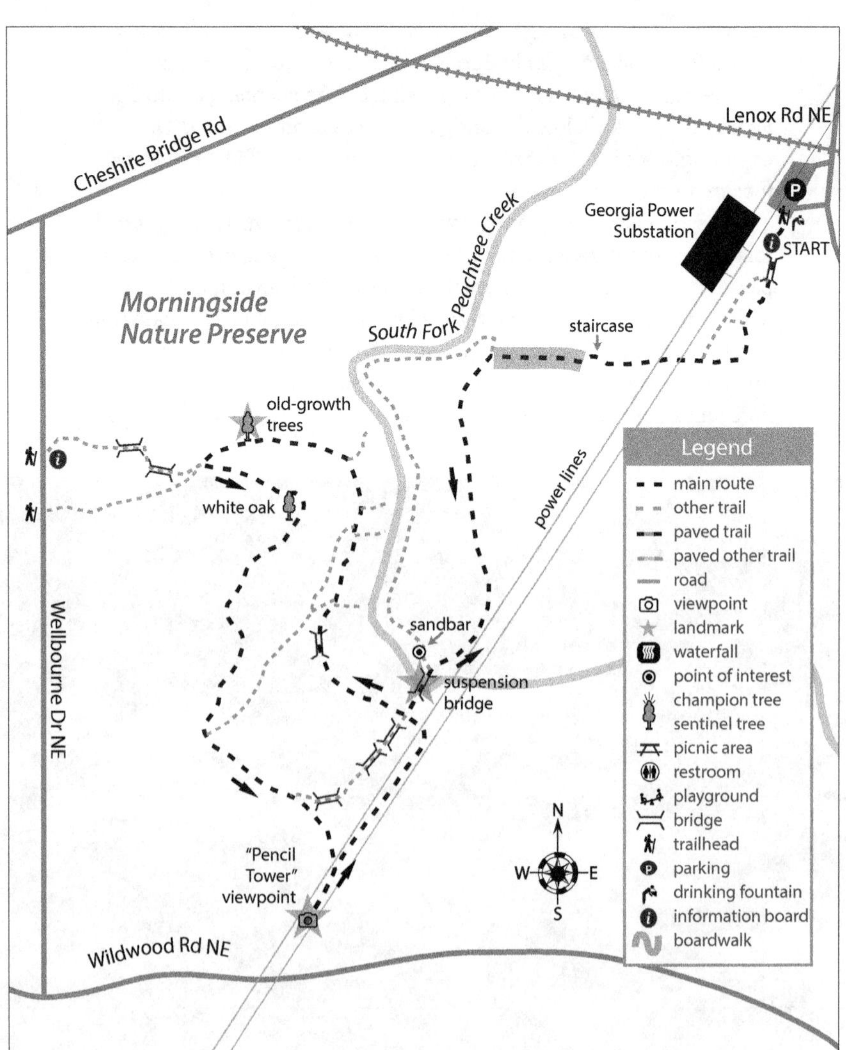

Cheshire Bridge Rd
Lenox Rd NE
Georgia Power Substation
START
Morningside Nature Preserve
South Fork Peachtree Creek
staircase
old-growth trees
white oak
power lines
sandbar
suspension bridge
"Pencil Tower" viewpoint
Wellbourne Dr NE
Wildwood Rd NE
N
W
E
S
Legend
main route
other trail
paved trail
paved other trail
road
viewpoint
landmark
waterfall
point of interest
champion tree
sentinel tree
picnic area
restroom
playground
bridge
trailhead
parking
drinking fountain
information board
boardwalk

old-growth trees—an American beech, two white oaks, and a southern red oak. In 100 yards reach a junction. Both trails on the right lead to Wellbourne Drive. Make a hard left and begin climbing the ridge. Immediately you'll notice Piedmont terrain and flora—a reminder that Atlanta is in the foothills of the Appalachians. Trillium and other wildflowers can be found here.

After heading uphill for 0.1 mile, the trail curves right past a particularly large white oak, 15 feet off the trail on the right. Look at the other trees around you—this is an especially beautiful area. Continue along the ridge for 0.2 mile until you reach a junction with a trail on the left, just before a footbridge over a small creek. Cross the bridge and look to your right. In the spring, Japanese azaleas light up the woods with their bright colors. We're used to seeing these ornamental shrubs in lawns, but it's a special treat to come across such stunning color in the deep green of the forest.

The trail ascends slowly to reach a junction with a trail on the left that descends the ridge to the suspension bridge. Instead, continue up the ridge to the right until the forest ends and the trail meets a gravel access road beneath the power lines. Turn right and hike uphill to the top of the ridge, where you'll be treated (on a clear day) to a view of the "Pencil Tower"—the Bank of America Plaza, the tallest building in Atlanta and the 23rd tallest in the United States.

Turn around to descend the hill. The most direct route is straight down the steep and rocky access road. A shady and less steep route is to backtrack into the woods on the trail you hiked to get here, then make the first right turn to descend the hill on a trail that crosses three small wooden bridges. Both routes lead back to the suspension bridge. Cross the bridge and then look for an informal trail to the left along the banks of South Fork Peachtree Creek. This route leads back to the boardwalk and stairs you hiked at the beginning, but vegetation overgrowth and creek flooding make this a questionable route in some seasons. Take the adventure if you'd like, or hike back on the same route as before—0.25 mile to the boardwalk, then up the staircase, across the power line clearing, and 0.1 mile down the wooded hill to reach the parking area and conclusion of your hike.

This section of Peavine Creek is rocky and lush and seems like a mountain stream.

Peavine Trail

Tucked between a university, grocery store, and television studio, Peavine Creek is an important tributary that flows from Decatur all the way to South Fork Peachtree Creek in Druid Hills. This trail gives hikers access to a particularly beautiful section of the creek and the mature forest on the ridge above. Peavine Trail inspires us to imagine what the Atlanta area must have looked like before modern development. And it is fitting that such a natural relic has its trailhead on the historic route of Old Briarcliff Road.

HOW TO GET THERE	**Driving Distance from Downtown Atlanta:** 6 miles **Address:** 808 Old Briarcliff Road NE, Atlanta, GA 30306 **Neighborhood:** Druid Hills **Nearest Interstate:** I-85 **Public Transit:** MARTA 6 or 816 bus + 0.3-mile walk **Parking:** Small gravel pulloff on the edge of Old Briarcliff Road; see map for alternative street parking on Emory Road
HIKE DISTANCE	1.5-mile figure-8 loop
DIFFICULTY	**Overall:** Easy to moderate **Navigation:** Trail information sign and map at trailhead; no other trail markers **Terrain:** Hard-packed gravel and dirt trails **Elevation Change:** Mostly flat with a few steep hills on the second half of the hike
SAFETY	**Usage** ★★☆☆☆ **Visibility** ★★★☆☆ **Upkeep** ★★★☆☆ **Parking** ★★☆☆☆
HOURS	Dawn to dusk
DOGS	Leashed dogs allowed
FACILITIES	• No toilets • Trailhead signs and one bench

FEES & PERMITS	None
LAND MANAGER	Emory University in partnership with South Fork Conservancy

Landmarks

RAIN GARDEN

The South Fork Conservancy is working to rehab the tributaries of South Fork Peachtree Creek by joining stormwater management, public use, and landscape architecture. This rocky rain garden slows stormwater flow, provides a hiking surface, and is planted with native plants.

AMERICAN CHESTNUT

In the early 1900s, American chestnut trees were everywhere on the East Coast, but an imported fungal blight wiped out almost all mature chestnut trees. Scientists are beginning to reestablish the species by planting blight-resistant hybrids of American and Chinese chestnut such as this specimen along Peavine Trail.

SENTINEL WATER OAK

Sometimes a particularly large tree like this water oak at the end of Peavine Trail can give us a clue about previous uses of this land. In this case, the oak tree was a yard tree planted by homeowners to shade their property. Now it's a unique giant in this otherwise young forest.

Hike Route

Start your hike at the South Fork Conservancy's Peavine Trail sign on the side of Old Briarcliff Road. Emory's Peavine Trail is about 50 yards north of this trailhead and crosses over Peavine Creek. This hike stays on the near side of the creek.

Your hike begins on a wide gravel trail. Stay straight for 0.2 mile to reach a rain garden and bench. Walk straight, crossing stones that are part of the rain garden, to reach a small planting of immature American chestnut trees on the right. Stay straight on the wide trail.

Peavine Creek, which runs parallel to the trail for the next 0.2 mile, might remind you of rocky-bottomed mountain streams with its boulders and small riffles and cascades. Stay straight at a junction on the right, then past a trail on the left that leads down to the creek. The next trail on the right leads to a trailhead on Emory Road. If in doubt, stay straight on the widest trail and hike 0.1 mile to a bridge followed immediately by a junction. To the right are stairs leading to another Emory Road trailhead. Go left and follow the trail as it curves back around to the bridge, past a giant water oak tree that used to shade the home that once stood on this spot.

Cross the bridge and backtrack on the main trail past a side trail on the left. At the next trail on the left, turn left and hike steeply uphill onto the ridge above Peavine Creek. The trail levels out and then climbs again to the edge of a chain-link fence below WAGA-TV's transmission tower before descending again.

Turn right at the next junction, then hike until you reach an old service road. Hike downhill to your right until you find a hiking trail

Botanists are trying to bring back the American chestnut from the brink of extinction.

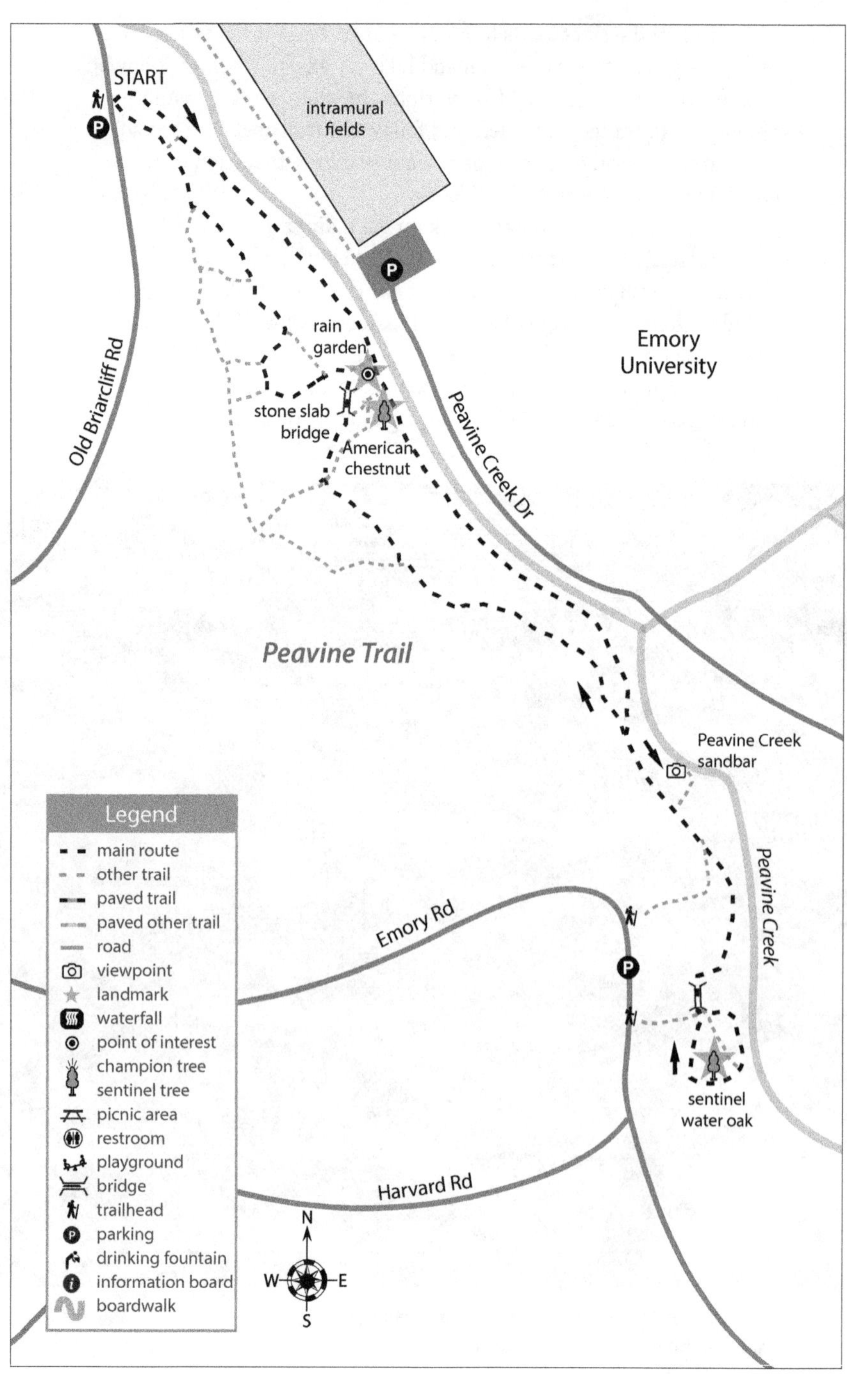
START
intramural fields
rain garden
stone slab bridge
American chestnut
Emory University
Old Briarcliff Rd
Peavine Creek Dr
Peavine Trail
Peavine Creek sandbar
Peavine Creek
Emory Rd
Harvard Rd
sentinel water oak
Legend
main route
other trail
paved trail
paved other trail
road
viewpoint
landmark
waterfall
point of interest
champion tree
sentinel tree
picnic area
restroom
playground
bridge
trailhead
parking
drinking fountain
information board
boardwalk
N
W
E
S

on the left that leads down to the creek and a stone-slab bridge. Cross the stone bridge, then go left and up the hill, not right toward the bench and main trail. At the first junction, take the less steep trail to the left and then pass a giant root ball from a fallen tree on your left.

This final section of trail has many side trails. The general rule of thumb here is to keep the downhill slope on your right until the trail descends to the floodplain near where you parked. Stay right at two junctions on the left, then at a T-junction, turn left. Finally, turn right at the last two junctions. The trail descends and parallels the main trail back to the trailhead and parking.

This park's trail system will make you feel like you're in an Appalachian Mountain hollow.

W.D. Thomson Park

Unlike many other forested parks in the Decatur area, W.D. Thomson Park is not situated in the bottomlands of South Fork Peachtree Creek. Instead, the park provides an excellent hike through an area of Piedmont forest through which several small, clear streams flow. The forest is mature, and the terrain, with its rocky soil and rolling hills, will remind you of the Appalachian Mountains. Within the forest of beech, tulip tree, oak, and hickory, you can even find one of the largest basswood trees in the whole state.

HOW TO GET THERE

Driving Distance from Downtown Atlanta: 8 miles
Address: 1001 Mason Woods Drive NE, Atlanta, GA 30329
Nearest Interstate: I-85
Neighborhood: Thomson Park / North Decatur
Public Transit: MARTA 19 bus + 0.5-mile walk
Parking: Turn off Mason Woods Drive into the park entrance, then turn right and drive downhill to the paved parking area near a picnic pavilion

HIKE DISTANCE

1.25-mile figure-8 loop

DIFFICULTY

Overall: Easy to moderate
Navigation: Trail maps posted in several places; each junction has color-coded trail markers
Terrain: Hard-packed dirt trails with lots of rocks and roots; bridges at most crossings, but there are two rock-hopping creek crossings on this route
Elevation Change: Rolling hills, but no major ascents or descents

SAFETY

Usage ★★★★☆
Visibility ★★★☆☆
Upkeep ★★★★☆
Parking ★★★★☆

HOURS

7:00 am to sunset

DOGS

Leashed dogs allowed

FACILITIES	• No toilets • Playground, basketball goal, tennis courts, picnic pavilion
FEES & PERMITS	None
LAND MANAGER	DeKalb County Recreation, Parks & Cultural Affairs

Landmarks

WATERFALL

Look upstream from the first creek crossing on the blue Eastside Trail. This rocky creek looks like a mountain stream in north Georgia. Upstream about 50 yards is a human-made dam through which the water trickles in a pleasing cascade.

SECRET VALLEY

The Secret Valley Trail is one of the most secluded areas of W.D. Thomson Park and can make you feel like you've left the city. Use your senses here to take a brief "forest bath"—touch tree bark, listen to the sounds of the forest, breathe in the scents of soil and water.

CITY CHAMPION BASSWOOD

- 94" circumference, 128' tall, 50' crown spread
- Basswood trees are often overlooked in Piedmont forests because they usually grow smaller than oak, hickory, sweetgum, and tulip trees, but this amazing basswood is over 7 feet in circumference and 130 feet tall. It's one of the largest basswoods in the entire state.

Hike Route

This park's network of trails can be hiked in many different ways. For the most simple and straightforward loop, start near the tennis courts and walk the paved trail to the basketball goal, then hike the blue-blazed Eastside Trail to the green-blazed Westside Trail.

The route described below is more adventurous and complicated, but it leads you past more of the park's highlights. Start your hike in the lower parking lot near the pavilion and playground. With your back to the playground and pavilion, look for a blue trail marker post at the right corner of the field. Cross the field on the right side, watching for soggy ground, which can easily soak your shoes. Near a native habitat restoration sign, cross the creek on rocks. Look upstream for a waterfall created by a small dam, then turn left on the far side of the creek.

In 100 yards reach a junction with the red-blazed Creekside Trail and blue-blazed Eastside Trail. Turn right, cross a small wooden footbridge, then go straight at the next junction to continue uphill on the blue Eastside Trail.

At a junction with the orange-blazed Secret Valley Trail, turn left and hike 0.1 mile to a junction with the white-blazed Central Ridge Trail. Turn left here. Then in 100 yards turn right at another junction onto the red-blazed Creekside Trail, cross a bridge, and stay right. Just before a junction where the red Creekside Trail splits from the green Westside Trail, pass the city champion basswood on the right. Then turn right onto the red Creekside Trail and follow this trail along the edge of the creek for 0.1 mile to reach a junction with the yellow-blazed High Point Trail. Turn right on the yellow High Point Trail and cross the bridge, then stay left on the white Central Ridge Trail, following the lip of a ravine on your left.

After 0.1 mile of uphill hiking, turn left onto the blue Eastside Trail, hike steeply down a rugged trail, then head back uphill to the

W.D. Thomson Park's state champion basswood tree is over 130 feet tall.

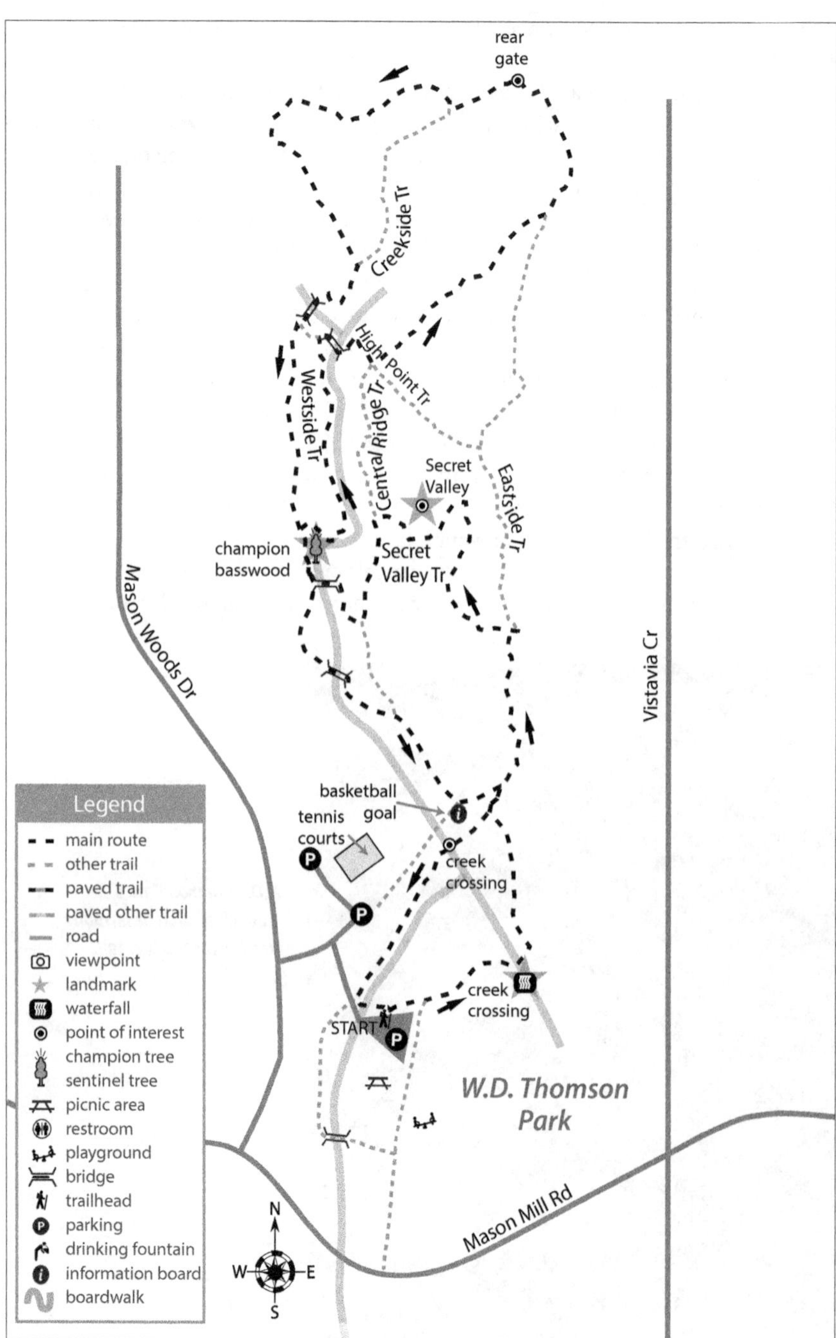
rear gate
Creekside Tr
High Point Tr
Westside Tr
Central Ridge Tr
Secret Valley
Eastside Tr
champion basswood
Secret Valley Tr
Mason Woods Dr
Vistavia Cr
basketball goal
tennis courts
creek crossing
creek crossing
START
W.D. Thomson Park
Mason Mill Rd
N
W
E
S
Legend
main route
other trail
paved trail
paved other trail
road
viewpoint
landmark
waterfall
point of interest
champion tree
sentinel tree
picnic area
restroom
playground
bridge
trailhead
parking
drinking fountain
information board
boardwalk

park's northeast gate and a junction with the green Westside Trail and red Creekside Trail. Go left and uphill, then take the green Westside Trail to the right. After 0.15 mile of steep ascents and descents, the green Westside Trail meets back up with the red Creekside Trail.

At the junction where the red and green trails rejoin, continue right and downhill, then cross a bridge over the creek at the bottom of the hill. Go straight after the bridge and stay on the green Westside Trail for the next several junctions. Pass the champion basswood again in 0.1 mile and stay right when the red Creekside Trail splits off to the left. At a junction with the white, red, and green trails, go right to the paved area with the basketball goal.

Cross the pavement to the left past the information board and go left into the woods on the red and blue trail. At the first junction, turn right and head downhill. Cross a small wooden footbridge and turn right onto the red Creekside Trail, continuing to hike downhill to a steep creek crossing on rocks. If this crossing is too difficult, backtrack to the blue Eastside Trail and follow it right, back to the parking area. Otherwise, cross the creek and follow the red trail to the parking lot, where you'll end your hike.

A cascade between boulders in Herbert Taylor Park's Rock Creek.

Zonolite Park & Herbert Taylor Park

Take a short, straightforward hike in either or both of these beautiful nature parks, or make an adventure out of it and connect the two loops, following a new trail along the banks of South Fork Peachtree Creek. Both Zonolite and Herbert Taylor Parks have dedicated volunteers who maintain and improve the trails, and the South Fork Conservancy is creating connectivity along the creek corridor. Parks that used to require a car to commute between are now connected by sidewalks and trails.

HOW TO GET THERE

Driving Distance from Downtown Atlanta: 7 miles

Address: Zonolite Park (Start): 1164 Zonolite Place NE, Atlanta, GA 30306; Herbert Taylor Park: 1385 Beech Valley Road NE, Atlanta, GA 30306

Nearest Interstate: I-85

Neighborhood: Morningside

Public Transit: MARTA 816 bus + 0.3-mile walk

Parking: Small gravel parking area at Zonolite Park; street parking at Herbert Taylor Park

HIKE DISTANCE

2.75-mile figure-8 loop

DIFFICULTY

Overall: Moderate

Navigation: Trailhead signs and maps; some trail markers in Herbert Taylor Park

Terrain: Hard-packed gravel trails, wide mulched trails, and some narrow dirt trails that can be very overgrown in the summer; route includes stairs, a rock-hop creek crossing, and a creek crossing on a wide, armored sewer pipe

Elevation Change: Mostly flat with a few minor hills

SAFETY

Usage ★★★★☆
Visibility ★★★★☆
Upkeep ★★★☆☆
Parking ★★★★☆

HOURS

7:00 am to sunset

DOGS

Leashed dogs allowed

FACILITIES	• No toilets • Community garden, pavilion with picnic tables, benches, information boards
FEES & PERMITS	None
LAND MANAGER	DeKalb County Recreation, Parks & Cultural Affairs (Zonolite Park), City of Atlanta Parks & Recreation (Herbert Taylor Park), in partnership with South Fork Conservancy

Landmarks

SENTINEL FIVE-TRUNKED MAPLE

Maple trees grow well near creeks, and Zonolite Park is a perfect habitat. This large maple tree on the right of the trail is unique because of how many trunks are growing from its base.

HERBERT TAYLOR CHAMPION TREES

Herbert Taylor Park has 14 city champion trees (one of the three largest of their species inside the I-285 perimeter). See how many you can find! At least seven are labeled with stone markers. See the full list of champion trees on page 399.

ROCK CREEK CASCADE

This beautiful section of Rock Creek includes large boulders and a small cascade. The water quality of the creek is monitored and protected by neighbors who formed the Rock Creek Watershed Alliance in 1998.

Hike Route

This route connects the 0.75-mile loop trail in Zonolite Park with the one-mile loop trail in Herbert Taylor Park. The connector trail between Johnson Road and Herbert Taylor Park can be confusing and very overgrown in the summer, so consider visiting these parks separately or using the alternative sidewalk connection.

Start your hike at the Zonolite parking lot and walk past the bollards to a circular junction with an information sign. Go straight, toward the Nickel Bottom Community Garden and an open field. Cross the field on the mulched trail, then cross a wooden bridge and arrive at a T-junction. Go left and walk 50 yards to a bench. Hike left on a riverstone-lined path that leads to stairs down to South Fork Peachtree Creek. Turn right and walk along the creek either on the

Repurposed curbstones make up the surface of part of the connector trail between Zonolite Park and Herbert Taylor Park.

gravel bar or on the higher sandbar to another set of stairs that leads back up to the main trail.

At the top of the stairs, turn left on the dirt trail (not the gravel trail you can see from where you are standing). Hike on this dirt trail, parallel to the creek, until you reach a junction with the crushed gravel trail. Along the way, you'll pass another set of stairs leading down to the creek and a five-trunked maple tree. At the gravel trail, turn right and then immediately left onto a boardwalk. The boardwalk passes a large sycamore tree on the left. Stay left at a junction just beyond the boardwalk, take a right just before the parking lot, then turn left at the next junction. In 0.1 mile reach the gravel path again.

Turn left and hike the gravel path across two wooden bridges, then turn left. This trail loops you through a woodland area, past a bridge leading to businesses on the left, to reach the first bridge you crossed in this park. Turn left and then cross the bridge and field to reach the circular junction near the Zonolite parking lot.

This time, turn right to begin the connector trail leading to Herbert Taylor Park. This trail has a series of stepping-stones made from repurposed City of Atlanta curbstones. In 0.1 mile cross Dalon Road and look for the trail on the far side of the road, to the left of a sign. Hike another 0.1 mile to reach an Emory bus parking lot. Cross this lot on the green painted path to arrive at Johnson Road. Turn right and use the sidewalk to cross the Johnson Road bridge over South Fork Peachtree Creek, then cross Johnson Road at the crosswalk. The trail connector to Herbert Taylor Park begins here.

In the summer, this trail can be almost impassable, so it is recommended that you follow the 0.3-mile detour on sidewalks to the main

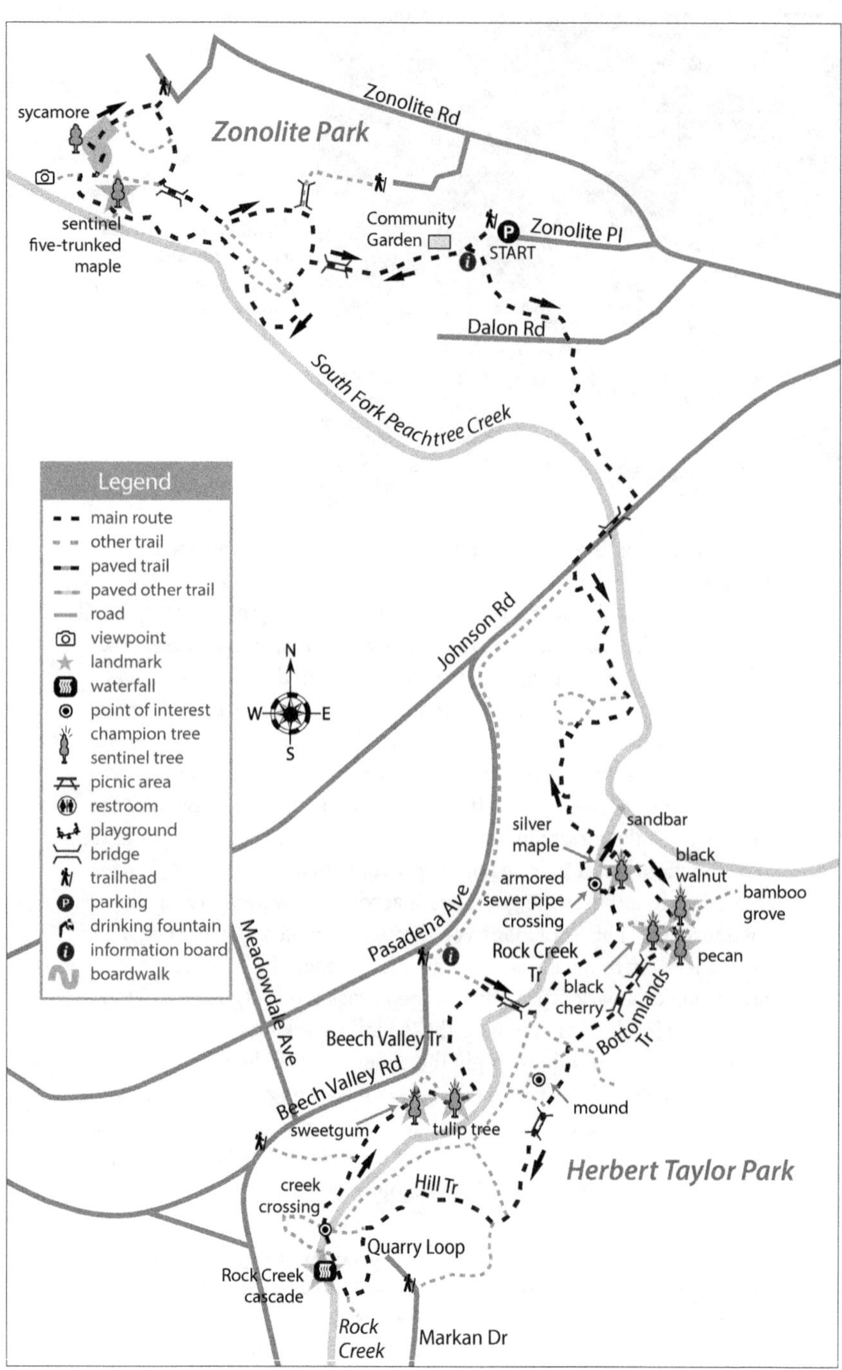

Zonolite Rd
Zonolite Park
sycamore
sentinel five-trunked maple
Community Garden
Zonolite Pl
START
Dalon Rd
South Fork Peachtree Creek
Legend
main route
other trail
paved trail
paved other trail
road
viewpoint
landmark
waterfall
point of interest
champion tree
sentinel tree
picnic area
restroom
playground
bridge
trailhead
parking
drinking fountain
information board
boardwalk
N
W
E
S
Johnson Rd
silver maple
sandbar
black walnut
bamboo grove
armored sewer pipe crossing
pecan
Rock Creek Tr
black cherry
Bottomlands Tr
Pasadena Ave
Meadowdale Ave
Beech Valley Tr
Beech Valley Rd
mound
sweetgum
tulip tree
Herbert Taylor Park
creek crossing
Hill Tr
Quarry Loop
Rock Creek cascade
Rock Creek
Markan Dr

park entrance (straight on Johnson Road, left on Pasadena Avenue, then left on Beech Valley Road). If you take the sidewalk, refer to the map to get your bearings once you are in Herbert Taylor Park.

Use the following instructions if you choose to take the connector trail to Herbert Taylor Park. Enter the forest near the crosswalk and hike downhill toward the creek. There are several trail options here, but stay generally parallel to the creek, and in 0.2 mile you will reach a steep gully behind some homes. After a steep down and up, descend wooden stairs on the left in 100 yards, then cross an armored sewer pipe across Rock Creek on the left.

Head up some rock steps to reach the junction with Rock Creek Trail. Turn left, passing two city champion silver maple trees almost immediately. In 25 yards a trail to the left leads to a sandy area on South Fork Peachtree Creek. Stay right. Pass a bench, then stay left along the banks of South Fork Peachtree Creek. As the trail curves right, away from the creek, a series of small informal trails lead left into a bamboo grove and the eventual location of a connection to DeKalb County's Briarcliff Bridge Park.

Back at the main trail, pass a champion black walnut tree on the left and a junction with North Spur Trail on the right. Look for the champion black cherry tree on the left and champion pecan on the right and continue straight, across two wooden bridges to reach another trail junction. Stay straight on Bottomlands Trail, cross another bridge, and pass Mound Trail on the right to reach the junction with Hill Trail and South Spur Trail in 0.1 mile.

Go straight, up the hill, and right to follow Hill Trail to Quarry Loop. In 0.1 mile stay left to hike Quarry Loop, which follows a narrow ridge above the quarry, then head down to the banks of Rock Creek. Turn right along the creek past a beautiful cascade between large boulders. Pass a bench on your right, then reach a junction and rock-hop creek crossing.

Cross the creek and stay straight on a wide gravel trail that ascends slowly. Look for the champion sweetgum tree on the hill below you. In 0.1 mile go right to stay in the woods on Beech Valley Trail. Pass a champion tulip tree on the right and hike another 0.1 mile to the main park entrance at Beech Valley Road.

Turn right, cross a large wooden bridge, then turn left on Rock Creek Trail. In 0.15 mile reach the junction on the left with the trail across the armored sewer pipe that leads back to Zonolite Park. Retrace your steps along the banks of South Fork Peachtree Creek to Johnson Road, then across the road and to the right to reach the Emory bus parking lot. Reenter the woods at the back of the parking lot and follow the connector trail back to the Zonolite parking lot to finish your hike.

ON THE PERIMETER–
EASTSIDE

Wildflowers and wildlife abound at Friendship Forest.

Friendship Forest Wildlife Sanctuary

The City of Clarkston knew it had a gem on its hands when it spent almost $2 million to turn the 19-acre Friendship Forest into the city's flagship nature park. This small greenspace packs a ton of interesting features into a small package. Paved trails and boardwalks, a viewing platform above South Fork Peachtree Creek, and additional hiking trails make this park an excellent adventure for just about anyone. The crown jewel is the wetland, which is beautiful for any nature lover and a paradise for birders.

HOW TO GET THERE

Driving Distance from Downtown Atlanta: 13 miles

Address: 4380 East Ponce de Leon Avenue, Clarkston, GA 30021

Nearest Interstate: I-285

Neighborhood: Clarkston

Public Transit: MARTA 120 bus + 100-yard walk

Parking: Paved parking area with restrooms and water fountain

HIKE DISTANCE

1.2-mile lollipop loop

DIFFICULTY

Overall: Easy

Navigation: Paved trail is easy to navigate, but there are no blazes or other trail markers

Terrain: Paved trails and boardwalks lead to the wetland; the remainder of this hike is on gravel and hard-packed dirt trails, which can be muddy

Elevation Change: Mostly flat, with a long, slow descent and ascent to and from the parking area

SAFETY

Usage ★★★★☆

Visibility ★★★★★

Upkeep ★★★★☆

Parking ★★★★★

HOURS

Dawn to dusk

DOGS

Leashed dogs allowed

FACILITIES	• Toilets and water fountains at parking area and at wetland pavilion • Picnic tables, bike rack, dog waste station, StoryWalk®, and lighting along the main trails
FEES & PERMITS	None
LAND MANAGER	City of Clarkston Parks & Recreation

Landmarks

WETLANDS

Wetlands are one of the most important ecological features in Atlanta because they provide habitat for such a wide variety of creatures. These areas also hold stormwater, helping remediate the flooding that is common along urban creeks. But wetlands are usually not easy to visit, because they are wet! Friendship Forest's trails and boardwalks are a great place to acquaint yourself with a wetland.

SENTINEL WATER OAK

As the name suggests, water oaks love to grow near creeks. This specimen is particularly picturesque, with a long, thick limb reaching out over the trail. Water oaks have small, barely lobed leaves and are one of the last oaks to lose their leaves in the autumn.

SOUTH FORK PEACHTREE CREEK VIEWPOINT

This creek is one of the most important waterways of DeKalb County, flowing from Tucker all the way to its confluence with North Fork Peachtree Creek near Lindbergh. This creek provides habitat for river otters, mink, spiny softshell turtles, fish, and many species of birds. What will you see at Friendship Forest today?

Hike Route

Start your hike on the paved, lighted path beyond the bollard and hike downhill, passing a series of StoryWalk® signs, in which librarians place pages of books for park visitors to read along the way.

In 0.15 mile, at the bottom of the hill, the trail splits. Take the right fork to the boardwalk, turn left, and cross the wetlands on the boardwalk to arrive back at the paved path. Turn right and hike along the edge of the wetland past an unusual rock garden on your left. The trail curves to the right to reach a pavilion with restrooms and a water fountain in 0.1 mile. Pass the pavilion and go right onto a boardwalk wetland viewpoint. This is a great place to observe wetland plants and look for and listen to birds. Retrace your steps along the boardwalk and turn right on the paved path. Walk 0.15 mile to a trailhead at Clark Street. Turn around at the bollard and hike back downhill the way you came.

When the grade flattens out, turn off the paved path at the first dirt trail you see on the left. Turn left in less than 100 yards at a green-painted, aboveground sewer access point. A sentinel water oak now stands in front of you, with a long branch snaking out over the trail. Follow this trail along the banks of South Fork Peachtree Creek until you reach the next aboveground sewer access point in 0.1 mile.

The Friendship Forest wetland is great for photography, birding, or just an afternoon stroll.

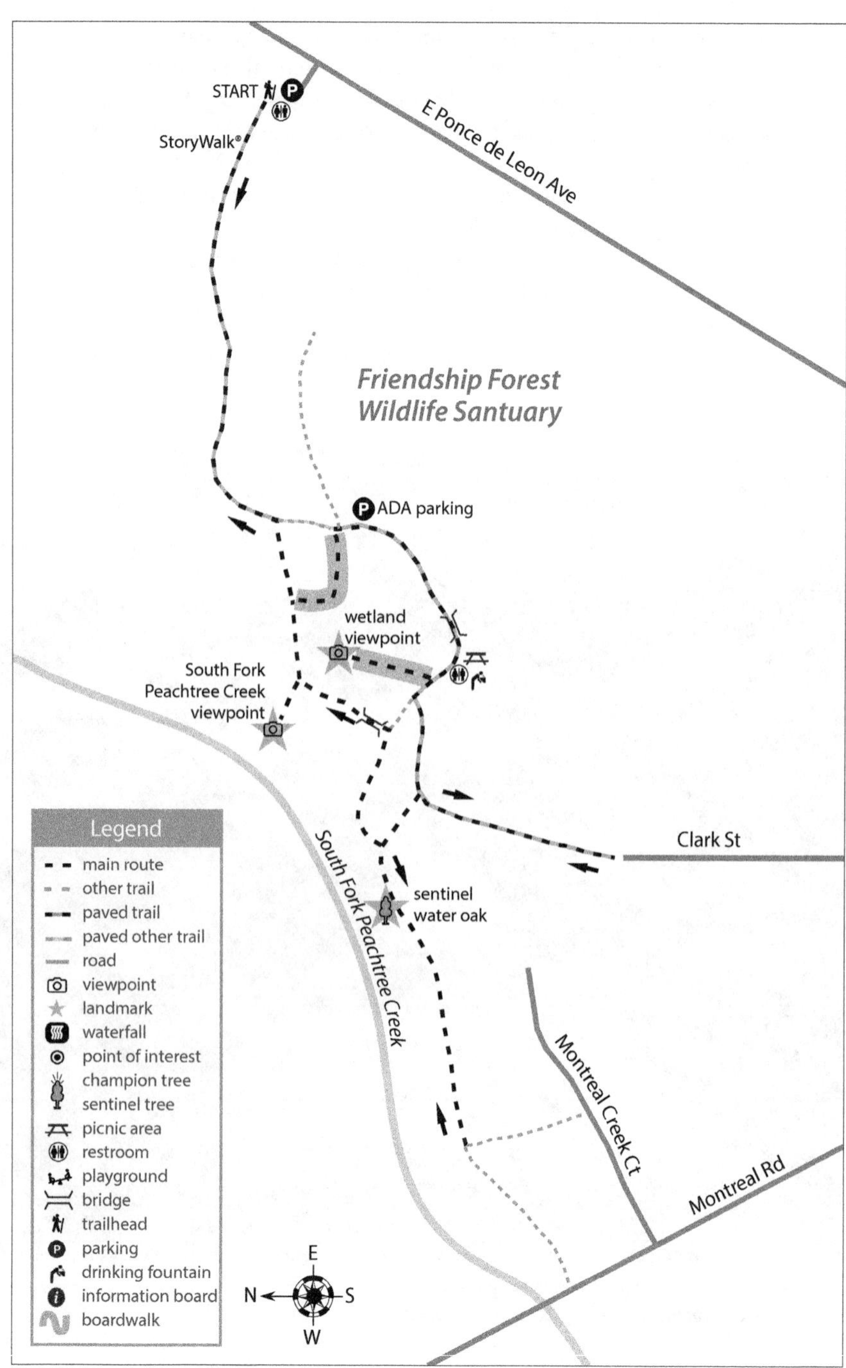

START
StoryWalk®
E Ponce de Leon Ave
Friendship Forest
Wildlife Santuary
ADA parking
wetland
viewpoint
South Fork
Peachtree Creek
viewpoint
Clark St
South Fork Peachtree Creek
sentinel
water oak
Montreal Creek Ct
Montreal Rd
Legend
main route
other trail
paved trail
paved other trail
road
viewpoint
landmark
waterfall
point of interest
champion tree
sentinel tree
picnic area
restroom
playground
bridge
trailhead
parking
drinking fountain
information board
boardwalk
E
N
S
W

Ahead of you is Montreal Road, but from here, this sewer access road becomes too muddy and overgrown to continue. Turn around and retrace your steps to the previous sewer access point.

Pass under the water oak again and stay left past the green sewer access point. Hike another 0.1 mile and then turn left at a junction with a bridge on the left, just before reaching the pavilion and wetland viewpoint. Cross the bridge to the left and then cross another one before arriving at the South Fork Peachtree Creek viewpoint deck on your left. Listen for birds such as belted kingfisher and eastern phoebe here, then hike the wide gravel trail along the edge of the wetland to reach the paved path.

Turn left to follow the paved trail back uphill to the parking lot to complete your hike.

The Serenity Garden and lake are two of the best spots within Hairston Park.

Hairston Park

DeKalb County has an amazing number of greenspaces, many of which are just being discovered by hikers. Hairston Park is an example of how a park known for its playground, playing fields, and picnic areas is becoming a destination for those who seek connection with nature. The double loop around the park's two lakes is beautiful and peaceful, as is the new Serenity Garden Trail. On these trails you can walk your dog, listen to and look at birds, sit and meditate, or even work out at the many fitness stations in the park.

HOW TO GET THERE

Driving Distance from Downtown Atlanta: 13 miles

Address: 911 South Hairston Road, Stone Mountain, GA 30088

Nearest Interstate: I-285

Neighborhood: South Hairston / DeKalb

Public Transit: MARTA 119 bus stops at park entrance

Parking: Paved parking lot near the park entrance

HIKE DISTANCE

1.25-mile double loop

DIFFICULTY

Overall: Easy

Navigation: Trail marker posts at start and end of Serenity Garden Trail; no other trail markers, but trail is easy to follow

Terrain: Paved, crushed slate, and hard-packed dirt trails; trail around the smaller lake is narrow, can be overgrown, and includes one difficult embankment to navigate

Elevation Change: Minimal elevation change—very level

SAFETY

Usage ★★★★☆

Visibility ★★★☆☆

Upkeep ★★★☆☆

Parking ★★★★☆

HOURS

7:00 am to sunset

DOGS

Leashed dogs allowed

FACILITIES	• No toilets • Playground, fitness stations, pavilion, picnic tables, benches, and the Serenity Garden
FEES & PERMITS	None
LAND MANAGER	DeKalb County Recreation, Parks & Cultural Affairs

Landmarks

GREEN ASH GROVE

Green ash trees are dying throughout the country because of an introduced beetle called the emerald ash borer. Because of this blight, Hairston Park's healthy grove of ash trees is a beauty to behold. Green ash prefers to grow near water and is related to maples. Its wood is prized for its strength.

LAKES

The two gorgeous lakes at Hairston Park are truly the gems of this greenspace. Beavers are active here at night. River otters have been seen at all hours. In the spring and fall, dozens of species of migrating birds call the lakes and surrounding forest their temporary home.

SERENITY GARDEN

This short trail was envisioned by the Friends of Hairston Park to entice park users into the forest, provide a calm, meditative space, and teach information about native trees and plants. It's a great place to sit quietly or have a picnic.

Hike Route

Facing the park with your back to the parking area, begin your hike at the bollards on your left. Walk straight on the paved path with the forest on your left. Pass several fitness stations and a grove of green ash trees on the right. Exit the paved path just before a park rules sign and cross the concrete bridge to reach the edge of the lake.

Hike straight across the dam, then turn left at the far end to circle a beautiful smaller lake. Listen for belted kingfishers and other birds. This trail can be overgrown, so watch for poison ivy in the summer. Halfway through this loop there is a steep embankment that can be difficult to cross. Turn back or skip this loop if your mobility requires it.

When the small lake loop reaches the dam, turn left and cross the dam again. This time, when you reach the far side of the dam, make a slight left to cross a small creek on rocks and then go right to circle the larger lake. Go past a trail on your left that leads to Hardwood Court. Hike along the edge of the lake for 0.2 mile. Keep your eye out for turtles sunning themselves on logs and great blue herons hunting fish and frogs. At the end of the lake, turn right. The sewer-line trail on the left leads to Elam Road near the East Central DeKalb Community & Senior Center.

Swinging benches offer great views and a place to relax on the lakeshore.

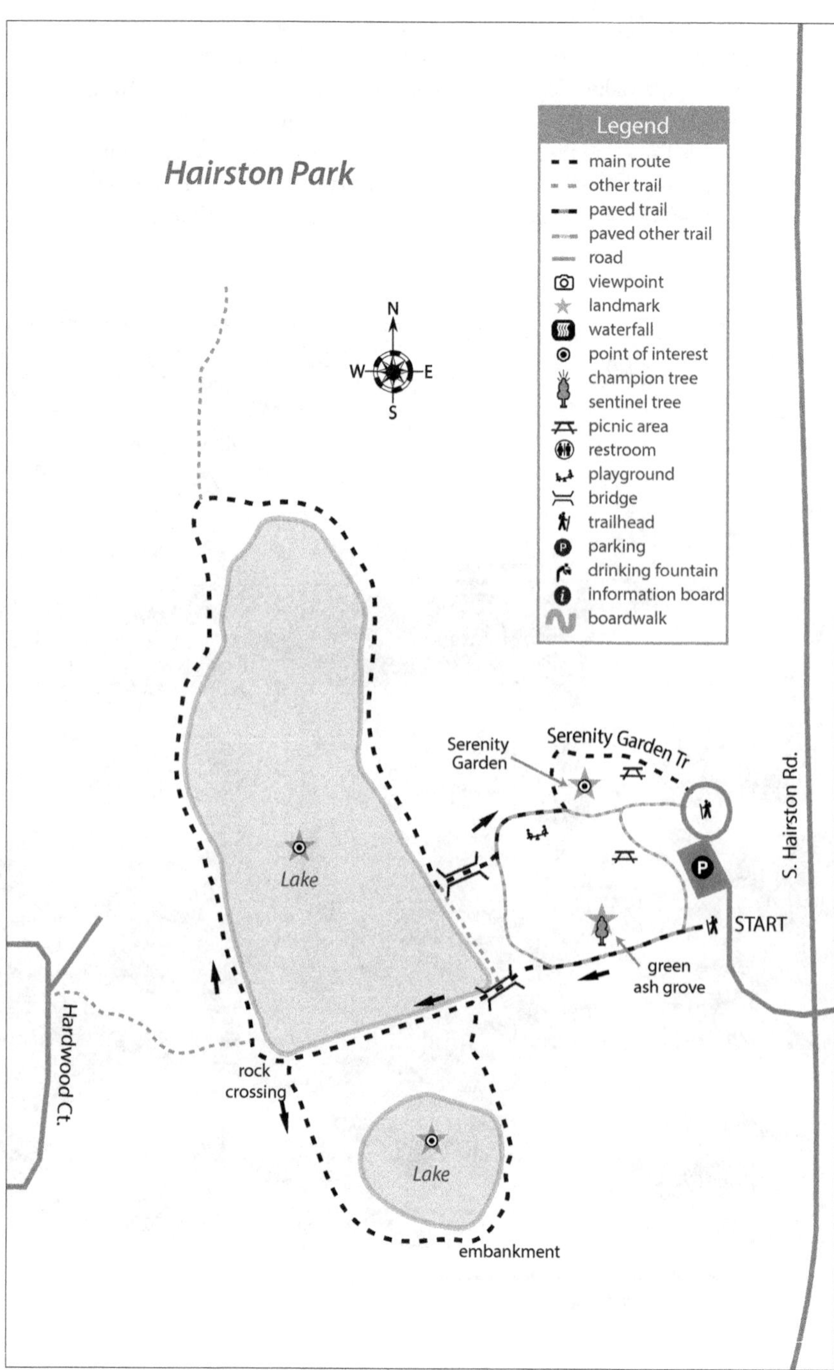
Hairston Park
Legend
main route
other trail
paved trail
paved other trail
road
viewpoint
landmark
waterfall
point of interest
champion tree
sentinel tree
picnic area
restroom
playground
bridge
trailhead
parking
drinking fountain
information board
boardwalk
N
W
E
S
Serenity Garden
Serenity Garden Tr
S. Hairston Rd.
START
green ash grove
Lake
Hardwood Ct.
rock crossing
Lake
embankment

Listen to the beautiful bubbling sounds of the creek on your left for the next 0.2 mile before reaching a grassy area with swinging benches that locals call their "lakefront seating." Cross a wooden bridge on your left and walk up the hill to the paved path near the playground. Turn left and walk about 100 feet to the Serenity Garden Trail. Enter the Serenity Garden on the left and walk the trail, generally to the right, through native plantings, past inspirational signs, and through a small picnic area. The Serenity Garden Trail ends near the parking lot, where your hike also ends.

Henderson Park's 30-foot waterfall is a unique attraction in this Tucker park.

Henderson Park

Many people know Henderson Park for its soccer fields, but its trail system is extensive and beautiful. This route will take you through coves of spring wildflowers, along the banks of scenic Lake Erin, and past wetlands, streams, and waterfalls. Though this route is only 2.5 miles long, you can hike over 8 miles at Henderson Park if you explore every trail. Even if you just came to watch a soccer game or visit the playground, when you venture into the forest, the hiking trails and impressively large hardwood trees will surely entice you to return to Henderson Park.

HOW TO GET THERE

Driving Distance from Downtown Atlanta: 16 miles

Address: 2723 Henderson Road, Tucker, GA 30084

Nearest Interstate: I-285

Neighborhood: Tucker

Public Transit: MARTA 124 bus + 0.9-mile walk

Parking: Paved parking in the Henderson Park Community Garden parking lot; overflow parking near the soccer fields on Henderson Road.

HIKE DISTANCE

2.4-mile loop

DIFFICULTY

Overall: Moderate

Navigation: Trail maps at several trailheads and trail markers at many junctions, but because there are so many unofficial, unmarked trails in this park, navigation can be difficult

Terrain: Hard-packed dirt trails, mostly wide and well-maintained; several creek crossings with and without bridges; a few short sections of paved trails or sidewalks

Elevation Change: Rolling hills, but no major ascents or descents

SAFETY

Usage ★★★☆☆

Visibility ★★★☆☆

Upkeep ★★★★☆

Parking ★★★★★

HOURS	Dawn to dusk
DOGS	Leashed dogs allowed; the dog park is located on Henderson Park Road, off Livsey Road
FACILITIES	• Toilets at trailhead • Community garden, two playgrounds, picnic areas, information boards, soccer fields, observation decks
FEES & PERMITS	None
LAND MANAGER	City of Tucker Parks & Recreation

Landmarks

NATIVE PLANT & WILDLIFE WALK

The paved trail loop near the trailhead is cared for by a dedicated group of DeKalb Master Gardeners and the Friends of Henderson Park. Along the route you'll find many native trees, shrubs, and wildflowers. See how many species you can identify!

LAKE ERIN

This lake is one of the most beautiful amenities at Henderson Park. Fed by multiple streams, the lake is home to waterfowl, turtles, and herons. The best viewpoints are from the east and west observation decks, the wetland boardwalk, and the dam.

HENDERSON WATERFALL

You might not expect to see a 30-foot cascading waterfall in an urban neighborhood, but here it is! Just after a rainstorm is the best time to see the waterfall in its full glory.

Hike Route

From the parking lot, begin your hike on the asphalt path next to the restrooms and hike toward a small gazebo. As you pass the gazebo on your left, the path enters the woods and switchbacks down the hill. This paved trail is part of Henderson Park's Native Plant & Wildlife Walk. After 0.2 mile, at the bottom of the switchbacks, look for a trail marker and stone steps on your right and walk down onto a dirt trail that leads farther down the hill. Turn right at the first junction you arrive at. This is Blue Trail, and it will lead you straight to a viewpoint on the edge of Lake Erin. There are many unofficial trails that lead

You can view scenic Lake Erin from multiple observation points within the park.

left and right off this main path, but if you generally stay straight, you will reach the lake. At the observation deck overlooking the lake, turn right and cross a wooden bridge. Stay straight to parallel the lake's edge past a trail junction on your right.

At the next junction, a steep dirt trail leads to the right, and wooden stairs lead left. After a rain, you may need to turn left and take the stairs to a boardwalk through a beautiful wetland. However, this skips Henderson Park's iconic waterfall, so we recommend going right and downhill on the dirt trail to reach the waterfall. Cross the creek below the two-tiered waterfall and continue on the far side of the creek. The trail leads to another creek crossing and then follows that creek downstream to a junction with the wetland trail. Turn right to continue your hike.

In 0.1 mile cross a bridge, then immediately go right over another bridge to follow Red Trail alongside a small creek. In 0.1 mile stay straight past a junction with a bridge on the left, then walk another 0.1 mile to a creek crossing with a small waterfall. After crossing the water, the trail begins to loop back toward Lake Erin. On this stretch

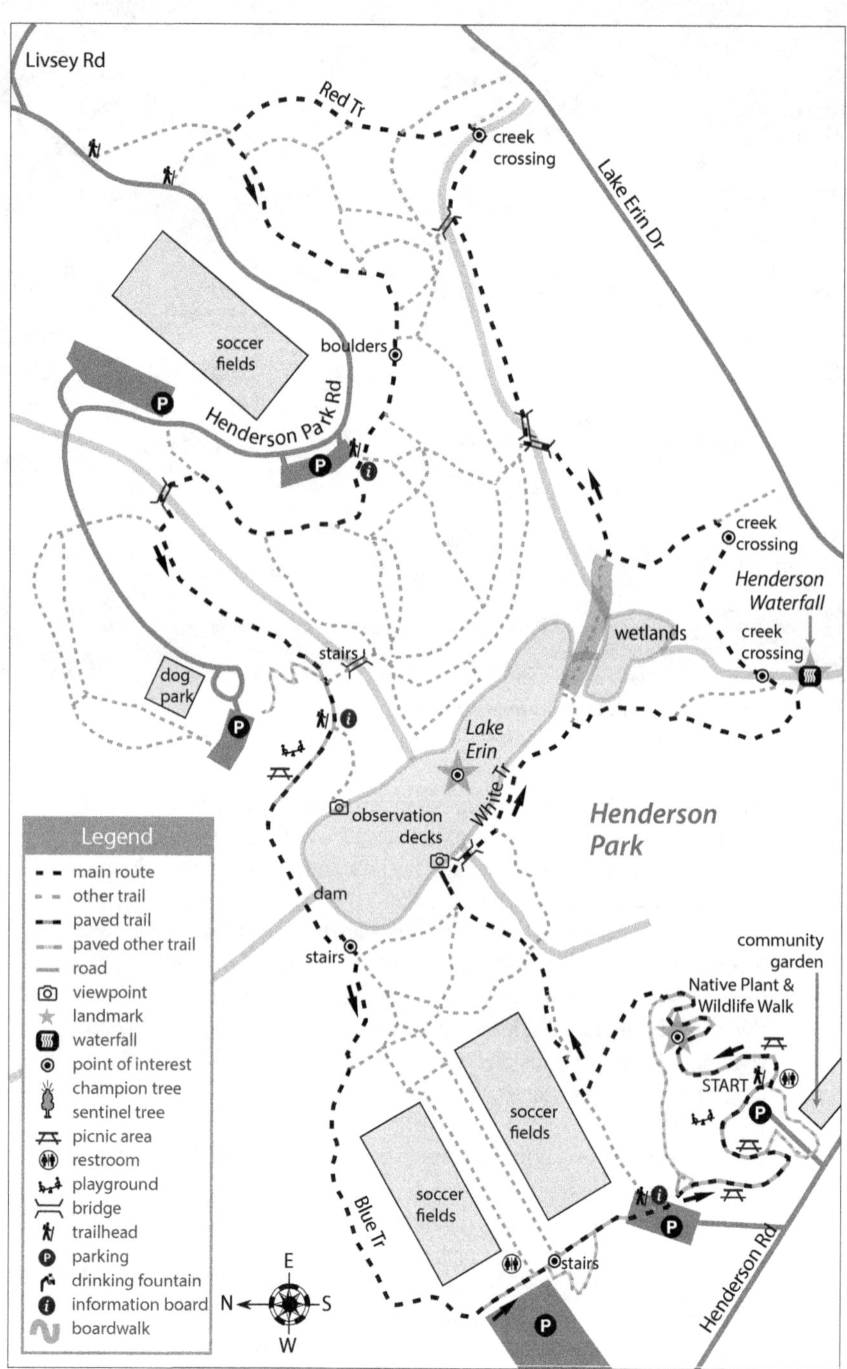
Livsey Rd
Red Tr
creek crossing
Lake Erin Dr
soccer fields
boulders
Henderson Park Rd
creek crossing
Henderson Waterfall
wetlands
creek crossing
stairs
dog park
Lake Erin
White Tr
observation decks
Henderson Park
dam
stairs
community garden
Native Plant & Wildlife Walk
START
soccer fields
soccer fields
Blue Tr
stairs
Henderson Rd
Legend
main route
other trail
paved trail
paved other trail
road
viewpoint
landmark
waterfall
point of interest
champion tree
sentinel tree
picnic area
restroom
playground
bridge
trailhead
parking
drinking fountain
information board
boardwalk
E
N
S
W

of trail, there are many unofficial trails that lead out of the park to the right or downhill to the left. Generally stay right on the most well-traveled path, and you will follow Red Trail along the perimeter of the park. Pass two junctions before reaching a trail junction on the right; it leads to the park's entrance on Henderson Park Road. Stay left on Red Trail and pass multiple junctions on the left that lead downhill into the park's interior. After passing an area of large boulders on your right, hike uphill to the right at the next junction to reach an information board and trailhead near the soccer fields. Pass the information board and hike back into the woods to continue on Red Trail. Stay straight past a few more side trails to reach a small wooden bridge.

Cross the bridge, then stay left at the next junction. The trail descends along a creek to reach a junction and paved path near a set of wooden stairs and a boardwalk that crosses the creek. Facing the paved path, go left on the pavement to reach the trailhead and information board near the playground and pavilion. Leave the paved path (which leads downhill to the left to a wooden observation deck near Lake Erin) and walk across the road toward the playground. Follow the sidewalk next to the playground and pavilion to reach White Trail, which leads left across the grassy dam on the edge of Lake Erin.

At the far side of the dam, walk up a set of stairs. At the top of the stairs, turn right on Blue Trail, then right again at the next junction. This trail circles the park's western soccer fields and in 0.25 mile emerges from the woods near a utility building and parking lot. Walk the sidewalk between the parking lot and soccer fields, then down a long flight of concrete stairs (an accessible ramp is available to the right). Parallel the lower soccer field, and when you reach the lower parking lot, look across it for a trailhead and information board. Cross the parking lot to this board and enter the woods on the paved path to the right. At the first junction, go right. The paved trail will curve through the woods past several picnic gazebos and the playground to reach the parking area, where your hike ends.

Volunteer-made bridges help hikers navigate Johns Homestead Park.

Johns Homestead Park

This 50-acre park is one of the up-and-coming natural gems of the metro area. Forests, lakes, wetlands, and an important historic site make Johns Homestead Park a great destination for just about anyone. However, implementation of the master plan is still in the early stages. The trail system is still a work in progress, and most bridges, built by dedicated volunteers, are homemade. With over two miles of hiking trails, each time you come to this park, you'll find something new!

HOW TO GET THERE	**Driving Distance from Downtown Atlanta:** 14 miles **Address:** 3117 Lawrenceville Highway, Tucker, GA 30084 **Nearest Interstate:** I-285 **Neighborhood:** Tucker **Public Transit:** MARTA 75 or 125 bus + 100-yard walk **Parking:** Small paved parking lot on the south side of Lawrenceville Highway
HIKE DISTANCE	1.5-mile loop
DIFFICULTY	**Overall:** Easy to moderate **Navigation:** Map at trailhead, at least one wooden trail sign, but no other trail markers **Terrain:** Hard-packed dirt trails that can be muddy; several homemade, single-track bridges that require good balance **Elevation Change:** Minimal elevation change—very level
SAFETY	**Usage** ★★★☆☆ **Visibility** ★★★☆☆ **Upkeep** ★★★☆☆ **Parking** ★★★★☆
HOURS	7:00 am to sunset
DOGS	Leashed dogs allowed
FACILITIES	• No toilets • Information boards, picnic pavilion

FEES & PERMITS	None
LAND MANAGER	City of Tucker Parks & Recreation

Landmarks

JOHNS HOMESTEAD

Take a look at the information board and see which structures you can learn about, including one of the oldest homes in DeKalb County. Notice the pecan and walnut trees, which were planted because of the food they provide.

BEAVER WETLANDS

Beavers are the largest rodent in North America and until recently have been a mammal that humans love to hate. But today, naturalists remind us that beavers are a "keystone species." They create wetlands like these, which provide unique and important habitat for amphibians, reptiles, birds, mammals, and fish.

TWIN LAKES

These picturesque lakes were also part of the Johns family property. Today they provide temporary homes for migrating birds, as well as habitat for many fish, reptiles, and mammals. Both lakes will soon be drained so dams can be repaired and rebuilt.

Hike Route

From the parking lot, don't enter the woods right away. Instead, face Lawrenceville Highway and walk left (west) on the sidewalk to visit the historic Johns house, for which this park is named. When you reach the retaining wall, walk onto the grass above the wall to reach the historic homestead. The main building was built by Mr. John Johns between 1829 and 1832 and is one of the oldest structures still standing in DeKalb County. You can read about the property's history on an information board here.

Next, enter the woods behind the house on Marsh Trail. In less than 100 yards there is a small unofficial trail that leads a few steps to the left where a horse-drawn hay baler is rusting in the woods. Watch out for poison ivy if you explore this side trail. Stay straight on Marsh Trail for 0.15 mile to reach benches and a short boardwalk. Stay right (do not cross the boardwalk) to reach a single-track bridge and a small side trail that leads to a wetland viewpoint. Cross the

A beaver-created wetland increases the biodiversity at this park.

small bridge and hike on a mulched path between townhomes and the beaver-created wetland.

Over the next 0.15 mile pass two side trails on the right that lead into the neighborhood and then walk straight between a set of metal poles that used to be a small barn. Cross another single-track bridge and hike another 0.1 mile to reach the first dam of the Twin Lakes section of this park. Look for old farming terraces on this section of trail.

At the dam go right, staying on higher elevation on a wide path covered with pine straw. In 0.1 mile reach a grassy area on the lakeshore with a pavilion and picnic tables. A trail to the right leads to a park entrance at Stapp Drive. Stay straight through the field toward the dam at the end of the lake and then curve left to cross the dam.

At the far side of the dam, the trail curves left again to circle the lake. On your right is a creek with very steep banks. Look at the root systems of the large trees on the right that have been exposed by erosion.

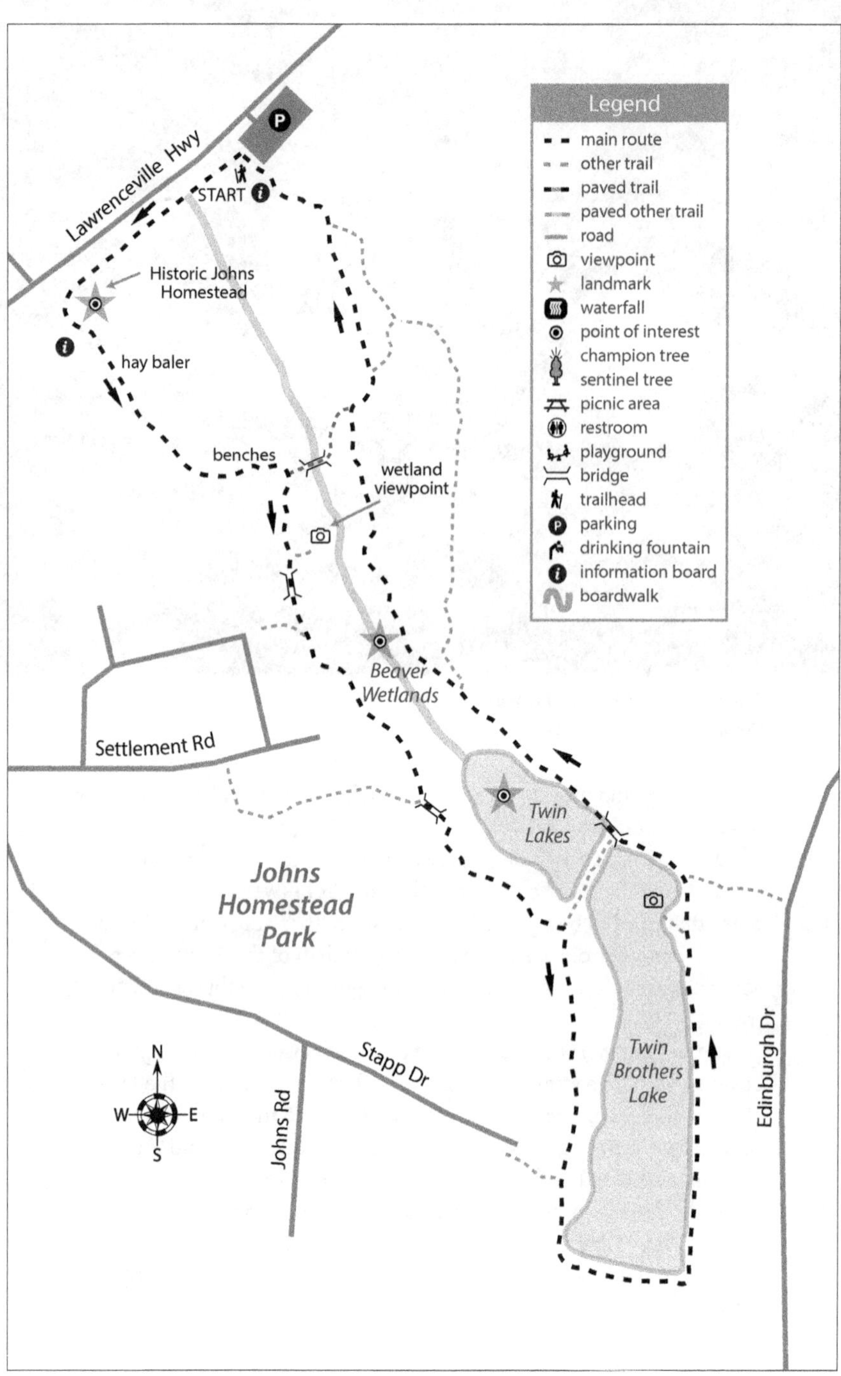
Legend
main route
other trail
paved trail
paved other trail
road
viewpoint
landmark
waterfall
point of interest
champion tree
sentinel tree
picnic area
restroom
playground
bridge
trailhead
parking
drinking fountain
information board
boardwalk
Lawrenceville Hwy
START
Historic Johns Homestead
hay baler
benches
wetland viewpoint
Beaver Wetlands
Settlement Rd
Twin Lakes
Johns Homestead Park
Twin Brothers Lake
Stapp Dr
Johns Rd
Edinburgh Dr
N
W
E
S

In 0.2 mile pass another grassy area with a bat house and sandy area on the edge of the lake. Stay straight through a narrow area of land between the lake and a wetland, passing stone steps and another small bridge that leads to another park entrance on Edinburgh Drive. Just past this side trail you'll reach the first dam again. A very sketchy bridge leads across the creek to the right. If you're feeling adventurous, follow this route across the lopsided bridge. If it doesn't look safe to you, cross the dam to the left and then turn right and use the map to backtrack to the boardwalk.

Across the sketchy bridge, the trail turns left and parallels the lake and wetlands. Stay left at a junction in 0.1 mile and then walk another 0.15 mile to reach the main trail near the boardwalk. This route goes right, but now is a good time to detour to visit the boardwalk and observe the wetlands from its viewing area, if you are curious. After a stop on the boardwalk, turn around and follow the main trail 0.15 mile, staying left at each junction you pass, to end your hike back at the parking lot.

A small dam across Snapfinger Creek creates a picturesque waterfall.

Pine Lake

Pine Lake is the smallest city in DeKalb County, but it is packed with amenities for nature lovers: an idyllic lake, beautiful wetlands, a swimming beach, and over a mile and a half of trails. When you visit this town of fewer than 700 residents, you'll learn how the lake helps manage flooding and the wetlands filter creek water before it enters the lake. In the summertime, you might wear your swimsuit and bring a towel to take a dip in the lake after your hike.

HOW TO GET THERE	**Driving Distance from Downtown Atlanta:** 12 miles **Address:** 4580 Lakeshore Drive, Pine Lake, GA 30083 **Nearest Interstate:** I-285 **Neighborhood:** Pine Lake **Public Transit:** MARTA 117 bus + 0.3-mile walk **Parking:** Angled parking spaces to the left of the clubhouse on Lakeshore Drive
HIKE DISTANCE	1.5-mile loop
DIFFICULTY	**Overall:** Easy **Navigation:** Information signs are posted along both wetland trails, but there are no other trail markers **Terrain:** Paved paths, wide gravel trails, hard-packed dirt trails, and shorts walks on quiet roads **Elevation Change:** Minimal elevation change—very level
SAFETY	**Usage** ★★★★☆ **Visibility** ★★★★☆ **Upkeep** ★★★★☆ **Parking** ★★★★★
HOURS	Dawn to dusk
DOGS	Leashed dogs allowed
FACILITIES	• No public toilets, though a portable toilet is available at the beach in the summer • Picnic tables, playground, swimming beach, and information signs

FEES & PERMITS	None
LAND MANAGER	City of Pine Lake

Landmarks

PINE LAKE BEACH

This small sandy beach is an amazing amenity for such a small town. In the summer it's one of the best places to cool off or let your kids play in the sand. The beach is open to anyone, so wear your swimsuit and bring a towel if you are hiking Pine Lake in the summer.

A sunny morning at Pine Lake can make you forget you're in a city.

WESTERN WETLANDS

In the early 2000s, the City of Pine Lake built these wetlands to help clean the water of Snapfinger Creek and to control flooding. In the process, the city's biodiversity has taken a huge leap. Reptiles, amphibians, mammals, and birds flock to this area. What creatures might you see?

EASTERN WETLANDS FLUME

The water diverted from Snapfinger Creek is cleaned by the constructed wetlands and then flows through the piped flume (water channel) into the lake. You can see the flume to your left along this section of trail.

Hike Route

From the parking area on Lakeshore Drive, start your hike facing the clubhouse and walk along Lakeshore Drive past the beach and playground. (Alternatively, if the bridges are open on the swimming berm that circles the clubhouse and beach area, you can walk that trail to get to the swinging bench near the playground.) In 0.1 mile you'll reach a junction near the playground and a swinging bench. The swimming berm trail is to the right. Stay straight along Lakeshore Drive as it curves along the edge of the lake.

In 100 yards cross the road to the left to enter the Western Wetlands loop. If you cross the road bridge over Snapfinger Creek, you've gone too far. Stay straight between bollards and hike past an information sign on the trail between the creek and wetlands. In 0.15 mile the trail curves left. Continue to stay left past a side trail on the right. This next section of trail circles the wetlands, leading through a cool, dark forest before arriving back at the bollards and Lakeshore Drive in 0.15 mile.

Turn left and cross the road, then turn right onto the paved path that runs along the lake's dam. Snapfinger Creek will be on your left, and the lake will be on your right. Walk 0.3 mile across the dam, with beautiful views of the lake, to reach Spruce Drive near a swinging bench and information sign.

Turn left on the road, cross a road bridge over Snapfinger Creek, then turn right onto the Eastern Wetlands Trail. This trail leads 0.3 mile through one of Georgia's first constructed wetlands past several information signs and a picturesque old well. At the end of the trail there is a dam that helps divert water from the creek into the lake. Turn around and retrace your steps to Spruce Drive. (Alternatively,

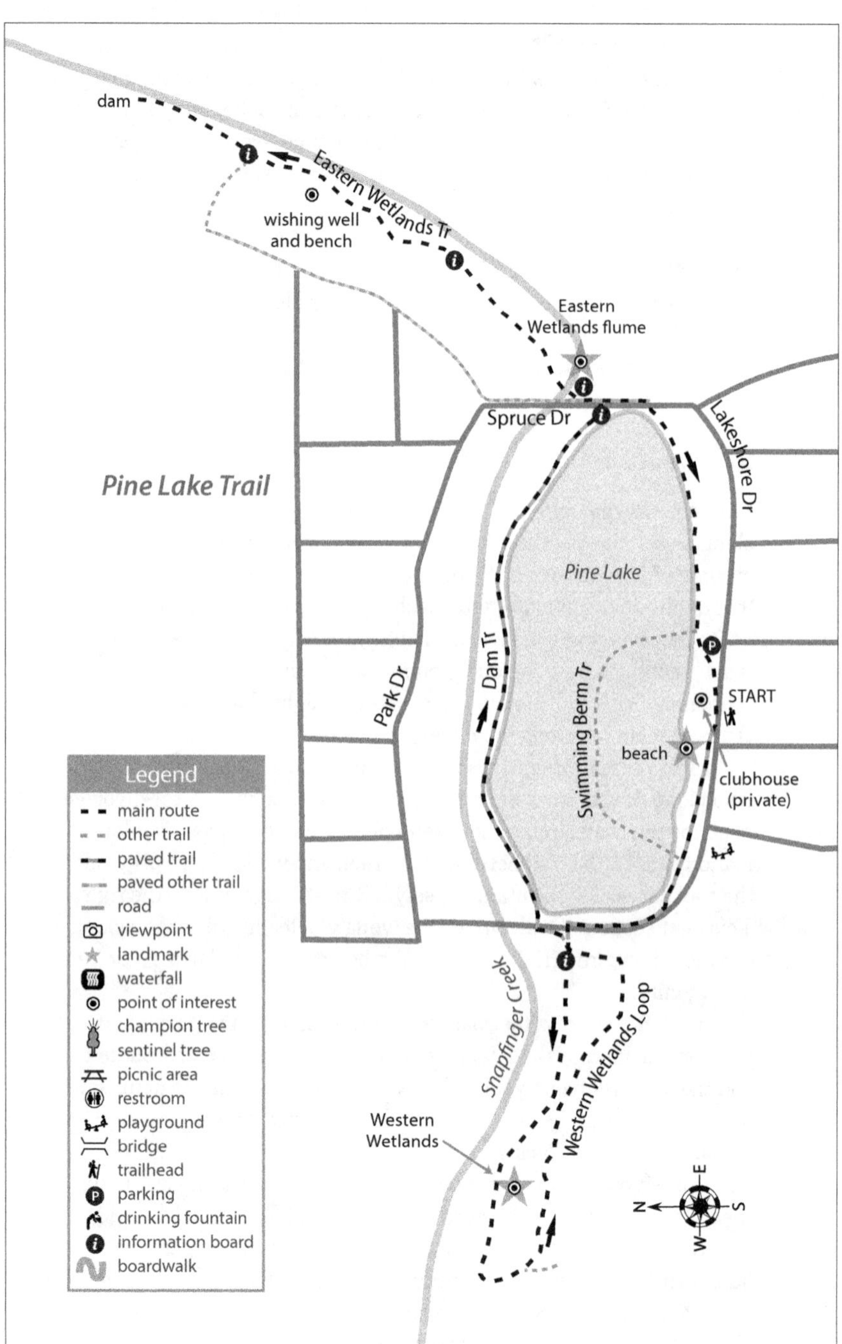
dam
Eastern Wetlands Tr
wishing well
and bench
Eastern
Wetlands flume
Spruce Dr
Lakeshore Dr
Pine Lake Trail
Pine Lake
Dam Tr
Swimming Berm Tr
Park Dr
START
beach
clubhouse
(private)
Legend
main route
other trail
paved trail
paved other trail
road
viewpoint
landmark
waterfall
point of interest
champion tree
sentinel tree
picnic area
restroom
playground
bridge
trailhead
parking
drinking fountain
information board
boardwalk
Snapfinger Creek
Western Wetlands Loop
Western
Wetlands
N
E
S
W

you can use a small trail near an information sign and bench to walk between houses to access Spruce Drive and return to the lake along the road.)

Back at the start of the Eastern Wetlands Trail at Spruce Drive, turn left on the road and cross the creek. Just before reaching Willow Road, turn right onto a trail at the lake's edge. From here it is 0.1 mile to return to the clubhouse and parking area and finish your hike.

BELTLINE CONNECTIONS–EASTSIDE

Freedom Park is a hike and an art exhibit in one.

Freedom Park Trail

Freedom Park is a 200-acre greenspace with trails that hold vast amounts of history and act as a connector for many of Atlanta's oldest intown neighborhoods. Legend says that General Sherman watched Atlanta burn in 1864 from Freedom Park. Today, visitors to the park can take in stunning views of the Atlanta skyline and public art along the paved multiuse trail. The park pays homage to the legacy of Atlanta's civil rights legends Martin Luther King Jr. and John Lewis and is also home to the Jimmy Carter Presidential Library and Museum.

HOW TO GET THERE

Driving Distance from Downtown Atlanta: 3 miles

Address: 453 John Lewis Freedom Parkway NE, Atlanta, GA 30307

Neighborhood: Inman Park / Candler Park

Nearest Interstate: I-75/I-85

Public Transit: MARTA 816 bus stops at the Carter Center

Parking: Monday through Friday: free parking at the Carter Center; Saturday and Sunday: street parking; recommend parking on North Highland Avenue or Austin Avenue

HIKE DISTANCE

3.5-mile out-and-back loop

DIFFICULTY

Overall: Easy to moderate

Navigation: Infrequent stone markers along the paved trail

Terrain: Paved multiuse path

Elevation Change: Mostly flat with a few minor hills

SAFETY

Usage ★★★★★

Visibility ★★★★★

Upkeep ★★★★★

Parking ★★★☆☆

HOURS

6:00 am to 11:00 pm

DOGS

Leashed dogs allowed

FACILITIES

- Toilets inside the Carter Presidential Library
- Water fountains, trash cans, and playground

FEES & PERMITS	None
LAND MANAGER	City of Atlanta Parks & Recreation

Landmarks

SENTINEL AMERICAN ELM

This eye-catching elm splits halfway up its trunk, creating an almost heart-shaped canopy of branches. Look for it at the left of the trail across from a large oak.

CHAMPION WATER OAK

The size of this oak suggests that it's a very old tree, possibly predating some of Atlanta's oldest intown neighborhoods.

THE BRIDGE ART INSTALLATION

Atlanta is brimming with civil rights history and was home to notable leaders of the movement, including John Lewis and Martin Luther King Jr. This art installation, located at the corner of John Lewis Freedom Parkway, was dedicated to the late congressman in 2005.

Hike Route

Begin your hike at the Jimmy Carter Presidential Library and Museum and the Carter Center. If you have time, take a few extra minutes to walk through the Carter Center gardens before or after your hike.

(If you are starting your hike from street parking on North Highland or Austin Avenue, refer to the map to make your way to Freedom Park Trail on the south end of the Carter Library, along John Lewis Freedom Parkway.)

From the Carter Library parking lot, with your back toward the circle of flags and main entrance of the Carter Library, begin your hike by exiting the main entrance gate at the far eastern side of the property into the circular road median. Take the sidewalk to the right and carefully cross the street. Stay right, carefully crossing the street again onto the main multiuse path. Be very careful crossing the streets, as there is no signage for cars to slow down or stop.

Once on Freedom Park Trail, turn right and explore the history and legacy of President Carter by reading the signage along the right side of the trail. In 0.25 mile, before reaching a fork in the path that leads downhill to the Eastside Beltline, take a looped section of path

The grassy fields of Freedom Park have several impressively sized trees that provide shade.

on the left to turn around and circle back the way you came. (If you continue straight and under the bridge, in one mile you will reach the Martin Luther King Jr. National Historical Park and the Dr. Eugene Thomas and Elmo James Overlook Intersection, one of the most iconic skyline views in the city. It may be worth the journey, especially if you are hiking close to sunset.) Continue back along Freedom Park Trail until you reach a crosswalk at North Highland Avenue. Enjoy the art installations on the side of the trail. Carefully cross the street and continue straight on the trail until you arrive at Moreland Avenue. Carefully cross this large road to enter Freedom Park.

Turn left, then stay to the right at the junction, following Freedom Park Trail into the park. In 100 yards you'll approach a beautiful water oak on the right side of the trail directly across from a perfectly split sentinel elm tree. Continue on the trail for another 0.4 mile, taking in the natural beauty and art installations along the trail. The creation of Freedom Park was the result of a fight to save this intown neighborhood from a proposed highway project in the early 1990s.

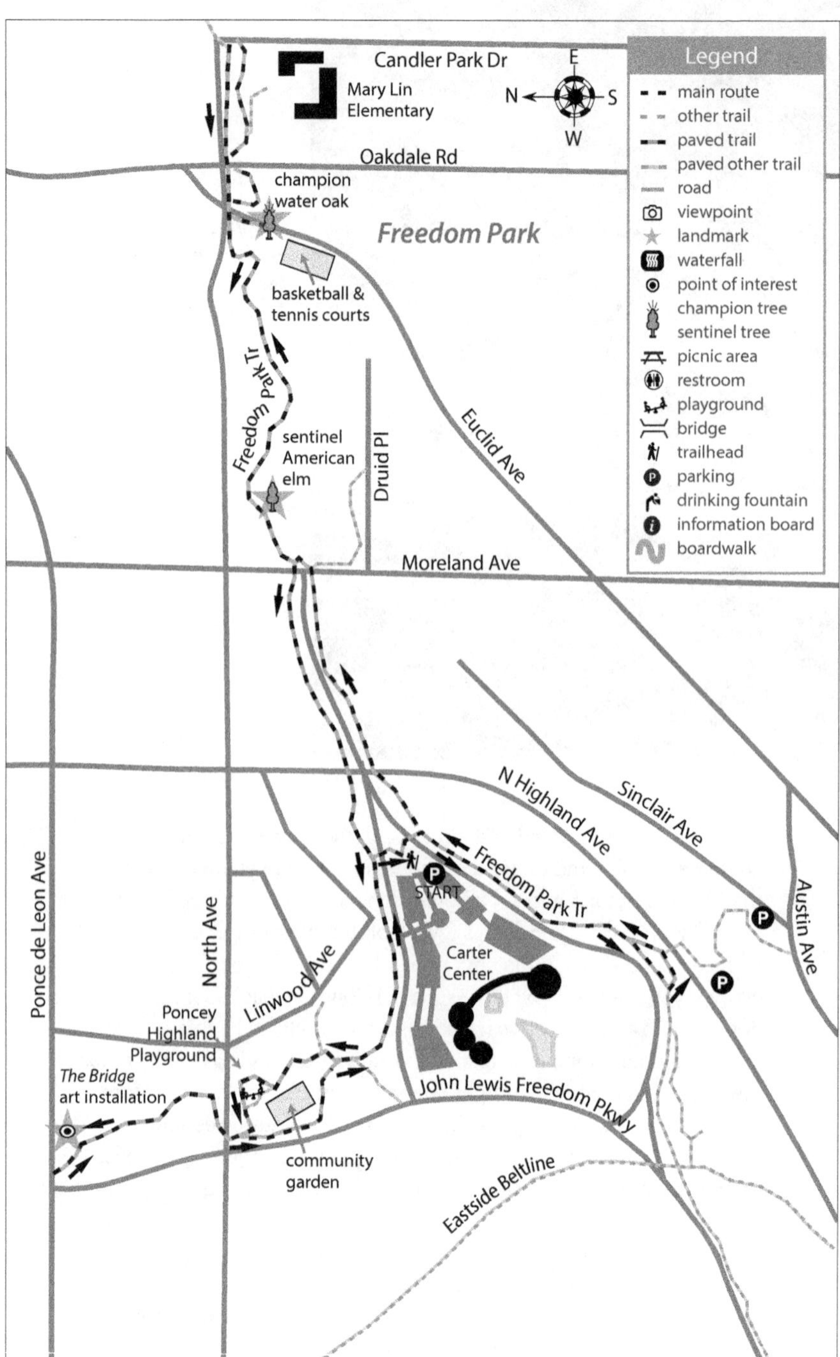

Legend
main route
other trail
paved trail
paved other trail
road
viewpoint
landmark
waterfall
point of interest
champion tree
sentinel tree
picnic area
restroom
playground
bridge
trailhead
parking
drinking fountain
information board
boardwalk
Candler Park Dr
Mary Lin
Elementary
N
S
E
W
Oakdale Rd
champion
water oak
Freedom Park
basketball &
tennis courts
Freedom Park Tr
Druid Pl
Euclid Ave
sentinel
American
elm
Moreland Ave
N Highland Ave
Sinclair Ave
Freedom Park Tr
START
Carter
Center
Austin Ave
Ponce de Leon Ave
North Ave
Linwood Ave
Poncey
Highland
Playground
The Bridge
art installation
community
garden
John Lewis Freedom Pkwy
Eastside Beltline

Keep an eye out for photographs along the trail depicting the transformation of the park from 1992 to the present day.

At Euclid Avenue, turn right before crossing the street and walk toward the tennis and basketball courts. Just before reaching them, you'll find a formidably sized city champion water oak at the edge of the road. After appreciating the tree, return to the path and carefully cross Euclid Avenue to the right.

Stay to the right as the trail winds uphill to another art installation. In a few feet carefully cross Oakdale Road, again staying to the right at the fork. The trail will bring you past a chimney swift tower that provides a home for these migratory birds. Stay left on the main path downhill to Candler Park Drive. Take a sharp left to walk the sidewalk along North Avenue to where it intersects with Oakdale Road. Carefully cross the street and continue on Freedom Park Trail, the section that you previously traveled.

In 0.5 mile, when you reach the Moreland Avenue intersection, take the first crossing to the opposite (north) side of Freedom Park Trail from which you previously hiked. Continue on the trail for 0.6 mile across North Highland Avenue and past the Carter Center before veering to the right. At the fork, stay straight, then take the first right and an immediate left to follow the trail downhill past a community garden and the Poncey Highland Playground. Take the wide trail around the playground to the left, arriving at North Avenue.

Carefully cross the street and continue to follow the path downhill and to the left. In 0.2 mile you will reach the 1961 Freedom Riders Route, which leads to *The Bridge*, a found-object art installation created by Thornton Dial to honor the legacy of John Lewis and the historic events at the Edmund Pettus Bridge in Selma, Alabama. Just past here the trail ends at Ponce de Leon Avenue. Turn around and return the way you came.

After carefully crossing North Avenue, stay straight on the path and all following junctions. In 0.4 mile take the stairs on the right to very carefully cross John Lewis Freedom Parkway onto the circle median at the eastern end of the Carter Center, where you began. Carefully reenter the Carter Center parking lot, where you'll end your hike.

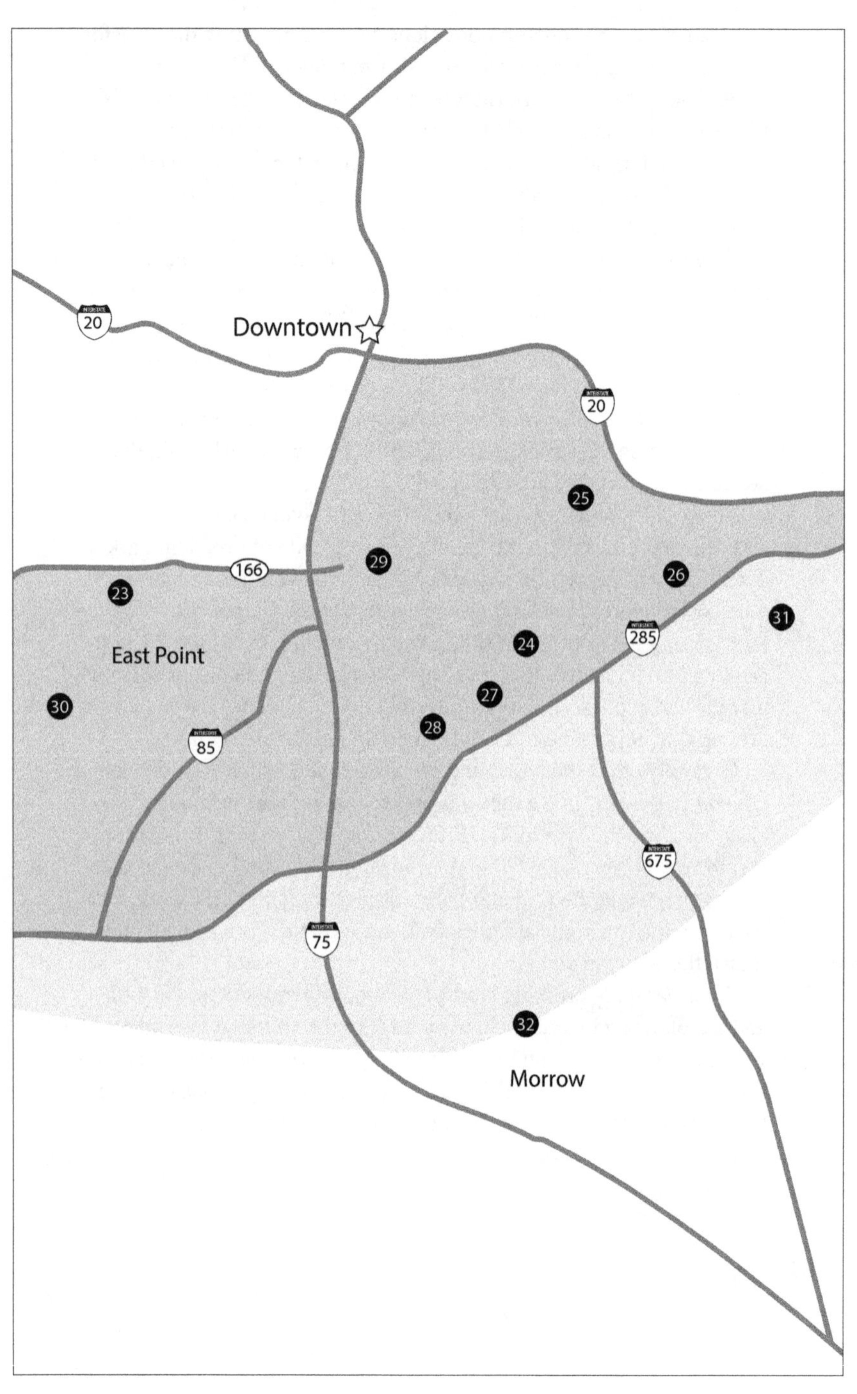

20
Downtown
20
25
166
29
26
23
31
East Point
285
24
27
30
28
85
675
75
32
Morrow

SOUTHSIDE

23. Connally Nature Park
24. Constitution Lakes Park
25. Glen Emerald Park
26. Gresham Park & South River Trail
27. Lake Charlotte Nature Preserve
28. Southside Park
29. Southtowne Trail & South Bend Park
30. Sykes Park
31. Michelle Obama Trail
32. Reynolds Nature Preserve

A tree with two trunks!
This tulip tree stands tall.

Connally Nature Park

Formerly a large plantation, Connally Nature Park is a hidden gem in East Point. It is an unassuming park from the street, but its forest holds a state cochampion white oak, and during late spring you may catch sight of rare pink lady's slippers. Wild blackberries and a small transitional field for birding make this an engaging hike south of the city. Recent forest restoration by Trees Atlanta will only continue to showcase the value of this forest.

HOW TO GET THERE

Driving Distance from Downtown Atlanta: 8 miles
Address: 2257 Mulberry Court, East Point, GA 30344
Nearest Interstate: I-85
Neighborhood: Semmes Park / East Point
Public Transit: MARTA 93 bus + 0.2-mile walk
Parking: Parking on paved circular drive off Mulberry Street near the corner of Connally Drive

HIKE DISTANCE

1.3-mile loop

DIFFICULTY

Overall: Easy
Navigation: Trails are not marked, and no trail map is posted, but trails are wide and easy to navigate
Terrain: Hard-packed dirt trails, one section of gravel service road
Elevation Change: Rolling hills, but no major ascents or descents

SAFETY

Usage ★★★☆☆
Visibility ★★★★☆
Upkeep ★★★★☆
Parking ★★★☆☆

HOURS

7:00 am to 10:00 pm

DOGS

Leashed dogs allowed

FACILITIES

- No toilets
- Dog waste station, benches and outdoor seating

FEES & PERMITS	None
LAND MANAGER	City of East Point Parks & Recreation

Landmarks

SENTINEL DOUBLE-TRUNKED TULIP TREE

Just past a bridge over a tributary of South Utoy Creek stands a towering double-trunked tulip tree. Trees may develop multiple trunks when regrowing from a cut stump.

STATE COCHAMPION WHITE OAK

- 199" circumference, 168' tall, 120' crown spread
- Given the nickname Hank Aaron, this massive oak is a state cochampion white oak. Because the tree belongs to a group of other sizable mature oaks in the forest, we assume Hank and its family were planted around the same time.

PINK LADY'S SLIPPERS

Catch sight of the park's pink lady's slippers, a rare wildflower, in late April to early May.

Hike Route

At the end of the U-shaped parking lot, look downhill to the right to find the start of the trail. Pass a mature mimosa tree and look for the beautiful pink blossoms in the summer. Begin your hike at the wooden bridge and Land and Water Conservation sign. Turn right onto the bridge and follow the winding trail uphill. In 0.1 mile stay to the left past a second parking lot off Mulberry Street. You will come to a footbridge in 100 yards. Cross it and immediately look to the left for an amazing three-trunked sourwood tree just off the trail. Continue hiking along the ridge with the East Point facilities fence to your right. In 0.15 mile stay to the right at the split and continue uphill on the trail.

You will pass a bench at the top of the hill in 0.1 mile. Follow the trail as it veers to the left onto a gravel access road. (This section of the hike follows the service road below power lines, but if you prefer, you can turn around and follow the trail back downhill. If you do so, turn right at the first junction to arrive at a wooden bridge, where you can continue to use this guide as a reference.) If you choose to

The state cochampion white oak nicknamed Hank Aaron is an impressive sight.

continue on the access road, you will come to a gate in 100 yards, next to the City of East Point Buildings and Grounds facility. Immediately turn left and continue down the gravel access road under the power lines. In the summer, be on the lookout for wild blackberries on either side of the path for a quick trail snack.

Follow the access road downhill with the forest on your left. The access road ends in 0.15 mile, where there is a nice transitional meadow to stop for birding at the bottom of the hill before heading back into the forest.

Turn left into the forest and almost immediately cross a bridge over a tributary of South Utoy Creek. As you cross, you will see a sentinel double-trunked tulip tree on your right. Cross a second bridge in 100 yards that will bring you to a junction near an interpretive sign describing Trees Atlanta's forest restoration work. Stay to the right and follow the trail uphill; the trail is lined with wooden

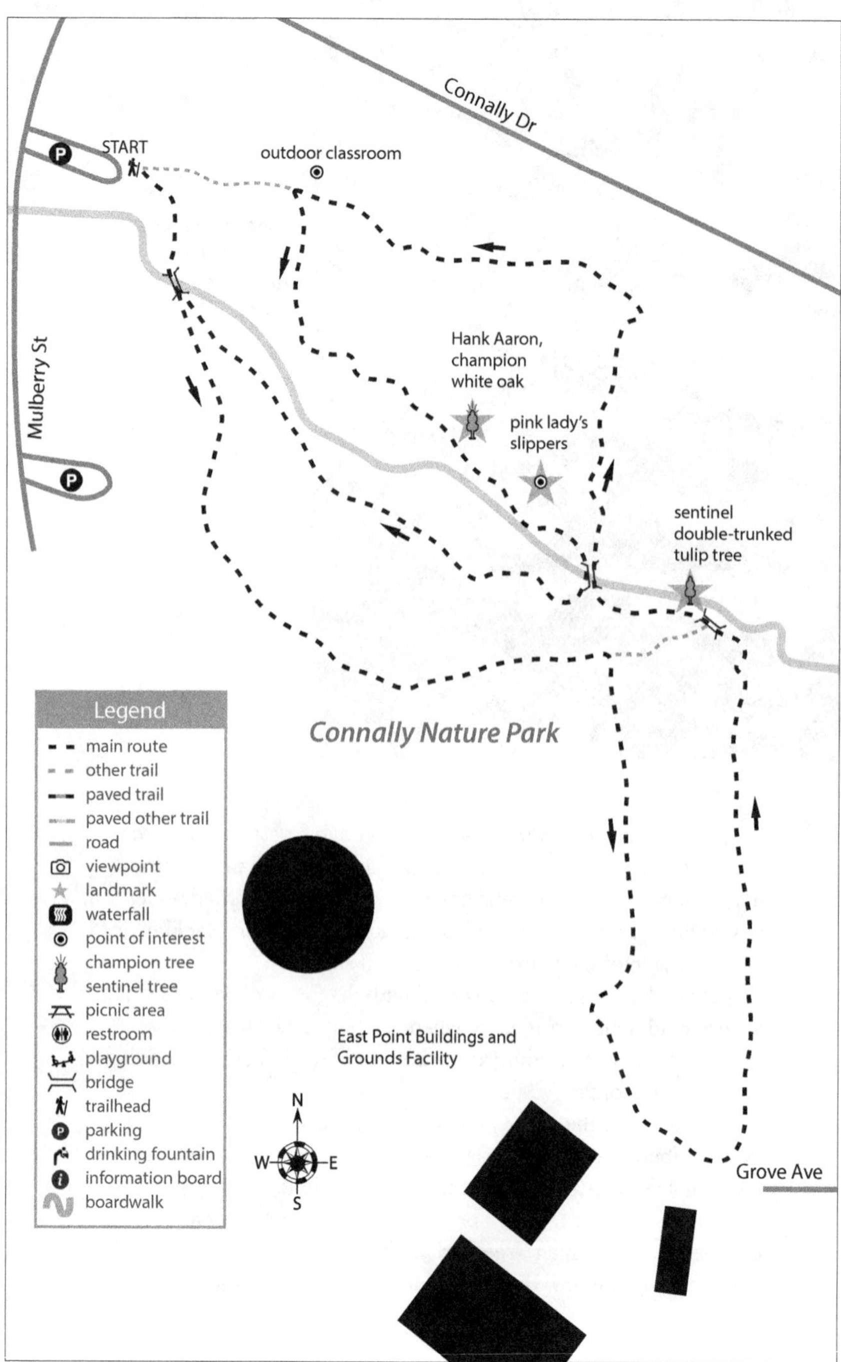
Connally Dr
START
outdoor classroom
Mulberry St
Hank Aaron,
champion
white oak
pink lady's
slippers
sentinel
double-trunked
tulip tree
Legend
main route
other trail
paved trail
paved other trail
road
viewpoint
landmark
waterfall
point of interest
champion tree
sentinel tree
picnic area
restroom
playground
bridge
trailhead
parking
drinking fountain
information board
boardwalk
Connally Nature Park
East Point Buildings and
Grounds Facility
N
W
E
S
Grove Ave

posts on either side. In this part of the forest, you will encounter a number of stunning old-growth oaks.

Continue for 0.15 mile to an outdoor classroom and stay to the left, following the trail downhill and staying to the left at any subsequent junctions. In 0.1 mile on your left you will pass the state cochampion white oak, benevolently nicknamed Hank Aaron. Hank is at least 168 feet tall, with a circumference of 200 inches. Just past the amazingly large tree is an area where pink lady's slippers are known to grow. Keep an eye out for these rare wildflowers in late April and early May. Watch your step and stay on the trail even if the flowers aren't in bloom.

Continue along the trail for another 0.1 mile back to the start of this loop. Stay right to hike the trail along the edge of the creek. Follow this less well maintained trail as it runs parallel to the creek. In 0.2 mile the trail will lead you back to the bridge and sign where you started. Hike uphill back to the meadow and parking lot to end your hike.

Enjoy the views of the lake from the boardwalk.

Constitution Lakes Park

Made famous by the unusual Doll's Head Trail, Constitution Lakes Park is a unique and thriving greenspace in an area that used to be a brick mine and factory. Whether you enjoy art, history, birds, turtles, or amphibians, there's something for everyone in this hidden gem in south DeKalb's industrial area. Though visitors are encouraged to enjoy the found-object art installations along the Doll's Head Trail, bringing in outside materials to add to the exhibit is discouraged.

HOW TO GET THERE

Driving Distance from Downtown Atlanta: 6 miles

Address: 1305 South River Industrial Boulevard SE, Atlanta, GA 30315

Neighborhood: Constitution / south DeKalb

Nearest Interstate: I-285

Public Transit: MARTA 49 bus + 0.5-mile walk

Parking: Gravel parking lot at the end of a gravel driveway

HIKE DISTANCE

2-mile loop

DIFFICULTY

Overall: Easy to moderate

Navigation: Handmade signs on wooden posts and found materials; some may be hard to spot

Terrain: Sections of paved path, hard-packed dirt trail, and boardwalks; dirt sections of this path can be very muddy, so proper shoes are encouraged

Elevation Change: Minimal elevation change—very level

SAFETY

Usage ★★★★★

Visibility ★★★☆☆

Upkeep ★★★☆☆

Parking ★★☆☆☆

HOURS

7:00 am to sunset

DOGS

Leashed dogs allowed

FACILITIES

- Portable toilet
- Trash cans, benches

FEES & PERMITS	None
LAND MANAGER	DeKalb County Recreation, Parks & Cultural Affairs

Landmarks

SENTINEL WILLOW OAK SNAG

Growing out of a brick mound left over from the brick factory's kiln floor, this now-dead oak was once the biggest documented willow oak inside I-285. The *Speed Racer* folk art tacked to the truck now keeps watch over the forest.

SENTINEL WILLOW OAK

This park is mostly young forest, but there are still notable larger trees like this willow oak growing at the water's edge. Willow oaks can be identified by their long, skinny leaves.

"SWEETWATER GOAK"

Just off the trail, a sweetgum and water oak tree grew in such close proximity that they appear to be intertwined.

Hike Route

Start your hike on the paved path leading into the forest on the left side of the parking lot. Pass through the bollards and stay on the paved path, as the side trails on the left will lead you back to the parking lot. Continue on the paved path for 0.5 mile until you reach the boardwalk. Even if you find the boardwalk under construction, it's worth it to make your way out onto the octagon platform for a view of Soapstone Ridge, a major geological formation just across the South River. The ridge is named for the soapstone that Native Americans used to make bowls. Civil War ruins and Native American artifacts have been found on the ridge.

The platform is also a great spot for birding, and you may catch sight of a variety of native wading birds. Night herons have been spotted in this park, so keep an eye out!

Backtrack off the platform and follow the sign pointing to the dirt trail through the forest, an alternative path if the boardwalk is impassable. In 0.1 mile turn left at a sign for a frog pond. The sign is a few feet off the main trail and can be easy to miss. Depending on the time of year, you may see bountiful frog eggs, just hatched tadpoles,

Bring binoculars to look for wading birds that inhabit the lake.

and/or several native frog species in the pond. When finished, return to the trail the way you came.

Take a left and continue on the trail, crossing foot bridges labeled Mansfield and Audubon. When the trail intersects a wider path, stay straight, following signs toward Doll's Head Trail. In 0.2 mile you will reach the start of Doll's Head loop. Stay to the right, and in 100 feet, immediately on your left, is a willow oak snag (standing dead tree). Once the largest documented willow oak inside the perimeter, this tree grew out of a pile of bricks left over from the brickwork factory's kiln floor. Take the small loop to get a closer view of the tree and look at the various writings on the remaining bricks. Turn right at the end of the loop and backtrack to the start of the Doll's Head Trail.

Start the trail by turning right, then staying to the right at any junctions. Enjoy the found-object art for which this trail is known. The art is the work of volunteers and Joel Slaton, whose creative use of recycled materials gives this trail its unusual character. They're also responsible for the handwritten wayfinding signs found throughout the

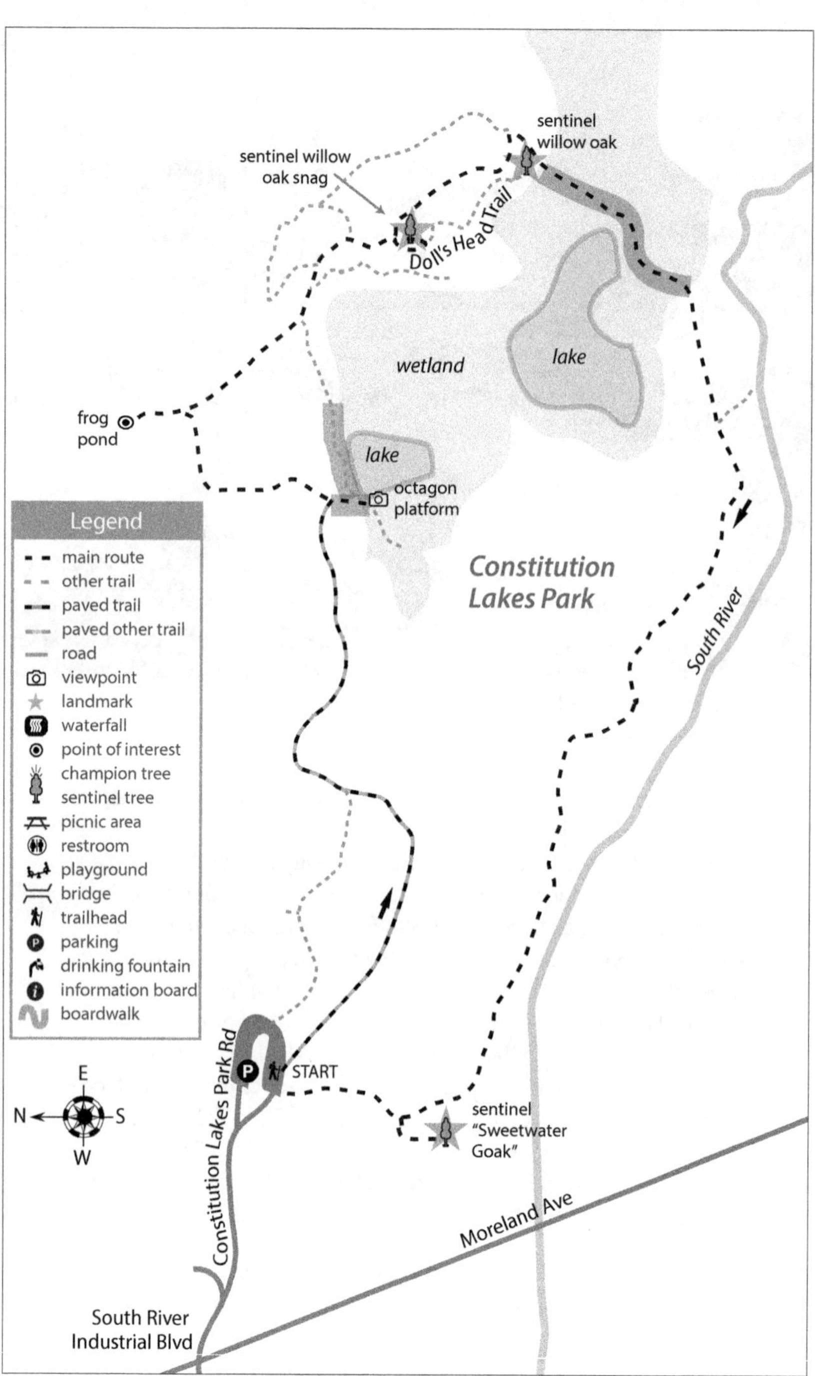
sentinel willow oak
sentinel willow oak snag
Doll's Head Trail
wetland
lake
frog pond
lake
octagon platform
Constitution Lakes Park
South River
Legend
main route
other trail
paved trail
paved other trail
road
viewpoint
landmark
waterfall
point of interest
champion tree
sentinel tree
picnic area
restroom
playground
bridge
trailhead
parking
drinking fountain
information board
boardwalk
E
N
S
W
Constitution Lakes Park Rd
START
sentinel "Sweetwater Goak"
Moreland Ave
South River Industrial Blvd

park. The Doll's Head Trail and Constitution Lakes Park are great examples of how community care and investment can turn a former industrialized wasteland into a hiking trail with pizzazz.

Enjoy the art and musings along the trail for another 0.2 mile until the trail comes to an intersection. Take a left and immediately go to the right, heading toward the boardwalk. Just before you reach the boardwalk, on your right, across from a bench, is a beautiful sentinel willow oak growing by the water's edge. Willow oaks like wet areas and are easily identified by their long, skinny leaves.

From here, you can continue on Doll's Head loop and retrace your steps back to the parking lot. Or follow this route across the boardwalk for some of the prettiest views in the park. Be aware that this next section of trail can be more adventurous and muddy and is prone to overgrowth and downed trees.

Continue onto the boardwalk across the wetland. Take your time, and you may be rewarded with sights of turtles (or snakes!) swimming and sunbathing and wading birds hunting. The view from the boardwalk is worth taking in.

Continue on the boardwalk to where it ends at the compact dirt path. Immediately on the left is a spur that leads to a viewing area of the South River. Follow the main path for another 0.7 mile, crossing several more boardwalks and a long footbridge. At the end of the long footbridge, in 100 yards take the spur trail on the left to the "Sweetwater Goak." This aptly named pair of mature trees—a sweetgum and a water oak—grew so close to each other that they appear to be intertwined. After visiting these trees, continue on the main trail until it ends at the parking lot.

Explore historic remnants in the rock garden.

Glen Emerald Park

Located in the Gresham Park neighborhood, Glen Emerald Park has been newly renovated and has a variety of options for spending the afternoon outdoors. This family-friendly hike circles beautiful Glen Emerald Lake, which is fed by a tributary of Intrenchment Creek. Don't miss the spectacularly intriguing Glen Emerald Rock Garden—a crumbling but impressive feature built in the 1930s as part of a nature retreat for wealthy Atlantans. Hidden within the rock garden is a soapstone bowl quarry stone that was worked by humans over 3,000 years ago.

HOW TO GET THERE

Driving Distance from Downtown Atlanta: 6 miles
Address: 1479 Bouldercrest Road, Atlanta, GA 30316
Nearest Interstate: I-20
Neighborhood: Gresham Park / South DeKalb
Public Transit: MARTA 32 bus stops at park entrance
Parking: Paved parking lot at park entrance

HIKE DISTANCE

1.2-mile figure-8 loop

DIFFICULTY

Overall: Easy
Navigation: No maps or blazes, but most trails are wide and easy to follow
Terrain: Wide compact dirt and gravel trails, plus paved sidewalks; the route within the rock garden has stairs and uneven surfaces
Elevation Change: Mostly flat with a few minor hills

SAFETY

Usage ★★★☆☆
Visibility ★★★★★
Upkeep ★★★★☆
Parking ★★★★★

HOURS

7:00 am to sunset

DOGS

Leashed dogs allowed

FACILITIES

- No toilets
- Water fountain, playground, basketball court, tennis court, picnic pavilions, benches

FEES & PERMITS None

LAND MANAGER DeKalb County Recreation, Parks & Cultural Affairs

Landmarks

SENTINEL SOUTHERN RED OAK

This large tree is a relic of the time before this lake was built on what was formerly a farm. Likely over 100 years old, it dwarfs most of the other trees in this park.

GLEN EMERALD ROCK GARDEN

In the 1930s, when the owners of this land weren't able to make enough money farming it, they envisioned a nature retreat and hired landscape architect William Monroe to build a unique rock garden in this spot. Look around at the unique features built from local granite, gneiss, and soapstone.

SOAPSTONE BOWL QUARRY STONE

See if you can find the form of a bowl that humans started carving on a soapstone boulder over 3,000 years ago. The quarry stone is on the right as you ascend the last set of steps to Foxhall Lane and looks kind of like a mushroom.

Hike Route

From the parking lot, begin your hike by following the sidewalk between the tennis court and playground. Turn right at a picnic pavilion in the woods and then continue downhill to the start of the lake loop. Directly in front of you, to the right of stairs leading down to the lake, is a sentinel southern red oak.

Turn left onto the compact crushed gravel trail passing a trail on the left that leads back to the parking lot. Stay straight and follow the gravel path as it curves behind a residential area before opening up to a view of the lake. Even from the trail, you may be able to see turtles and fish swimming below.

At a small ruined pump house where the trail curves right, the side trail to the Glen Emerald Rock Garden begins across the drainage ditch. The easiest way to access this trail is to hike on the main trail to the dam. Turn onto the grass at a bench and trash can, then hike back the way you came along the fenceline, parallel to the gravel trail and drainage ditch. The rock garden trail turns right across from the pump house. Hike uphill to the first rock garden pond and make your way uphill, generally staying right, to reach a rock patio with tables made from millstones and a tall fireplace. From the patio, cross the stone bridge, then hike up the rock stairs to the Foxhall Lane trailhead. Look for a soapstone boulder on the right as you walk up the last set of stairs. This quarry stone was moved here in the 1930s when the rock garden was built. The human carvings on this stone are at least 3,000 years old. With your back to Foxhall Lane, hike right and downhill through the rock garden to reach the lowest pond, then backtrack to the lake trail.

This hike circles the sparkling waters of Glen Emerald Lake.

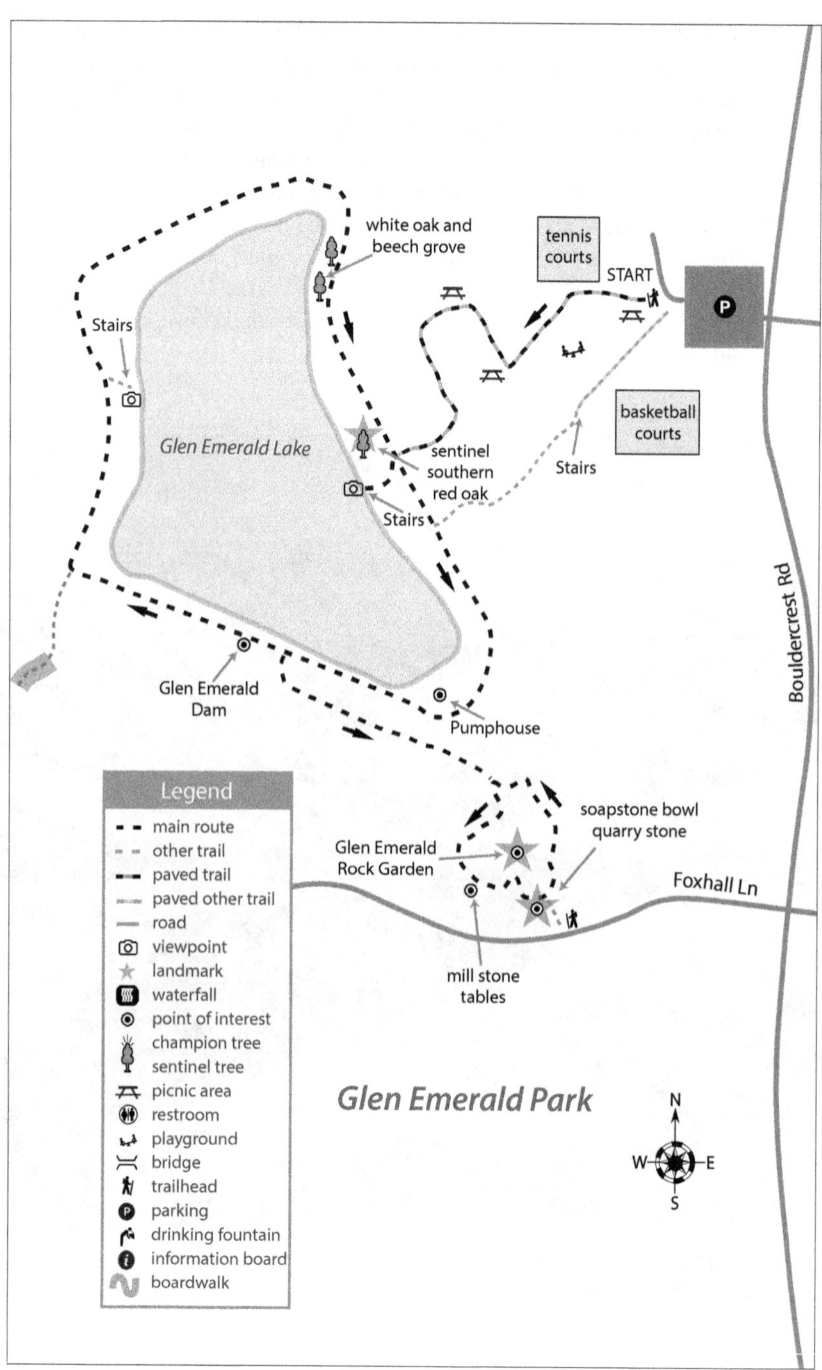
white oak and beech grove
tennis courts
START
Stairs
Glen Emerald Lake
sentinel southern red oak
Stairs
basketball courts
Stairs
Bouldercrest Rd
Glen Emerald Dam
Pumphouse
Legend
main route
other trail
paved trail
paved other trail
road
viewpoint
landmark
waterfall
point of interest
champion tree
sentinel tree
picnic area
restroom
playground
bridge
trailhead
parking
drinking fountain
information board
boardwalk
soapstone bowl quarry stone
Glen Emerald Rock Garden
Foxhall Ln
mill stone tables
Glen Emerald Park
N
W
E
S

Back at the bench and trash can, turn left and cross the Glen Emerald Dam on a rubberized mulch surface and continue on the trail as it curves to the right around the lake. (A boardwalk below you on the left will eventually create a connection to the neighborhood on Lakeview East Drive.)

As you hike, you'll come to stairs leading down to closer views of the lake. In 0.1 mile reach a swampy area of the lake, which is a good place to view wading birds. Continue for 0.15 mile to where the trail rounds the final corner of the lake. Here a small grove of bamboo grows on the left side of the trail. In 50 feet on the right pass a grove of white oak and beech trees. Finish the lake loop at the sentinel southern red oak where you began the loop and take the paved path left, back to the parking area to end your hike.

The South River Trail winds through peaceful south DeKalb neighborhoods.

Gresham Park & South River Trail

A welcome escape into nature is located in the Gresham Park neighborhood of south DeKalb County. The South River Trail has a special magic that's unexpected in its urban setting. The trail is a sensory delight with a diversity of colorful native plants, peaceful calls of birds and frogs, and tasty trailside blackberries. Whether you are hiking, biking, or jogging, you will be delighted by this trail. Soon this trail will also be a gateway to the trails of nearby but currently closed Intrenchment Creek Park.

HOW TO GET THERE

Driving Distance from Downtown Atlanta: 8 miles
Address: 3113 Gresham Road SE, Atlanta, GA 30316
Neighborhood: Gresham Park / south DeKalb
Nearest Interstate: I-285
Public Transit: MARTA 34 bus + 0.3-mile walk
Parking: Paved parking lot at Gresham Park Recreation Center

HIKE DISTANCE

3-mile out-and-back

DIFFICULTY

Overall: Easy to moderate
Navigation: PATH signage along route
Terrain: Paved multiuse path
Elevation Change: Mostly flat with a few minor hills

SAFETY

Usage ★★★★☆
Visibility ★★★★☆
Upkeep ★★★★☆
Parking ★★★★★

HOURS

7:00 am to sunset

DOGS

Leashed dogs allowed

FACILITIES

- Toilets in recreation center (check online for hours) and across Gresham Road near picnic pavilion and playing fields
- Recreation center, playground, water fountain, basketball court, football field, bike rack, pavilion, pool

FEES & PERMITS	None
LAND MANAGER	DeKalb County Recreation, Parks & Cultural Affairs

Landmarks

SENTINEL WATER OAK

This staggering big water oak is one of the largest trees in this forest.

MEADOW

The trail unexpectedly opens up into a meadow that stretches in both directions and is near a wetland. Though the clearing is for a gas pipeline, in the evenings you'll likely see grazing deer and hear frogs. Bring your binoculars for a birding session during the daytime.

SENTINEL PECAN

Sometimes the best way to identify a tree is to find its seeds on the ground. In this case, you'll likely find pecan nuts or shells under this large pecan tree. You'll find over a dozen pecan trees in this area, a sign that this land was recently farmed.

Hike Route

Facing the recreation center, find the trail at the far right of the parking lot between the two cement blockades. Enter the paved trail and walk past a football field and basketball court on the left, then curve to the right over a bridge. Hike past an outdoor fitness area and an open field.

Continue on the wide paved path for half a mile as it runs parallel to the street before the trail curves left and enters a boardwalk over Sugar Creek, a major tributary to the South River, which is listed as one of America's most endangered rivers from sewage and runoff pollution. Just before reaching the end of the boardwalk, look to the left to find an enormous sentinel water oak about 50 feet off the trail on the bank of the creek.

From here the trail parallels the creek for a while. Hike 0.2 mile past the boardwalk, then just before reaching the Mile 11 marker, you'll pass a large tree that stands alone on the side of the trail. This sentinel pecan tree is part of a grove of pecan trees that likely were planted when this was farmland. Look on the pavement for the remains of pecan shells, which can help you identify the tree. Hike 0.1 mile farther before reaching a junction to a neighborhood on the left.

Take in the view of Sugar Creek from the boardwalk.

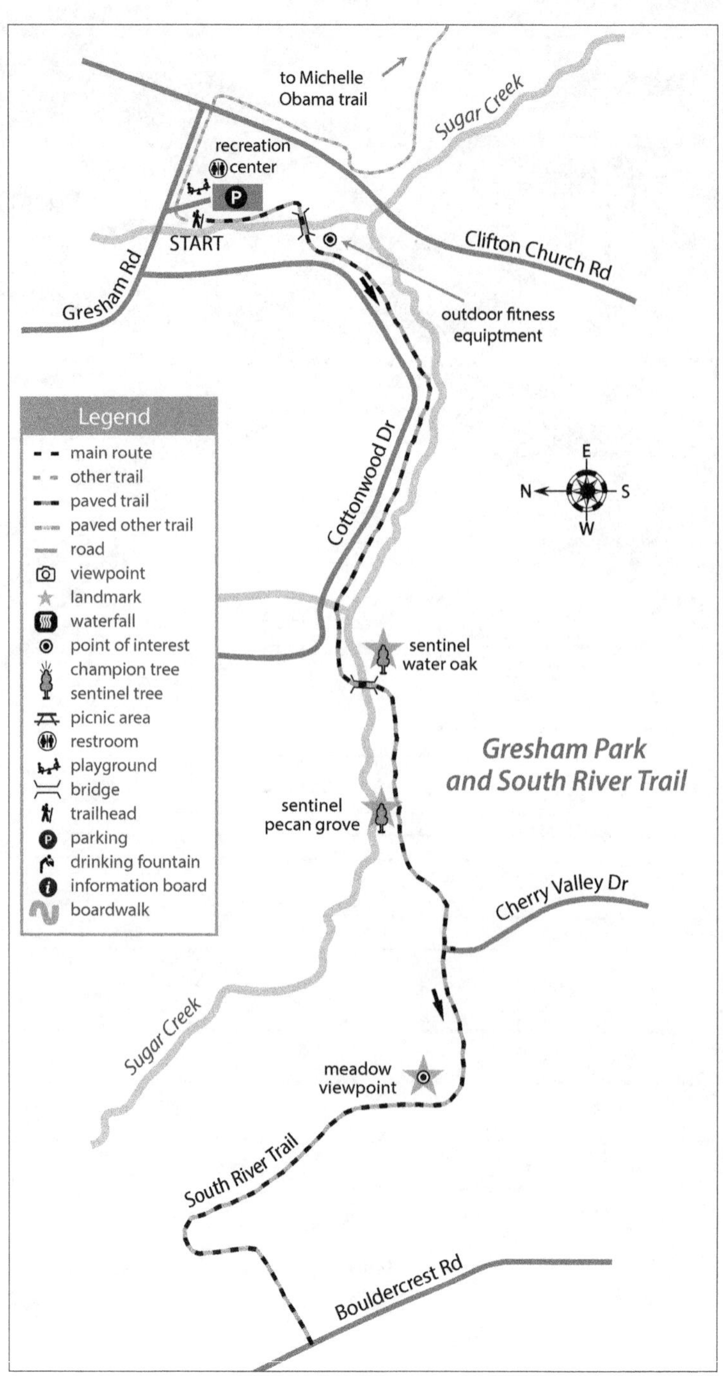
to Michelle Obama trail
Sugar Creek
recreation center
START
Gresham Rd
Clifton Church Rd
outdoor fitness equiptment
Legend
main route
other trail
paved trail
paved other trail
road
viewpoint
landmark
waterfall
point of interest
champion tree
sentinel tree
picnic area
restroom
playground
bridge
trailhead
parking
drinking fountain
information board
boardwalk
Cottonwood Dr
E
N
S
W
sentinel water oak
Gresham Park and South River Trail
sentinel pecan grove
Cherry Valley Dr
Sugar Creek
meadow viewpoint
South River Trail
Bouldercrest Rd

Continue straight and in 0.2 mile come to an open meadow and wetland in a gas pipeline clearing. Go slow here. This is a good spot for bird-watching or listening to frog calls in the spring and summer. The trail continues past two benches on the hill to the left. As you continue hiking, you'll likely see wild blackberries growing on either side of the trail in the summer.

Leave the clearing and hike along the forested path as it twists through the South River Forest, a place that holds cultural significance to the Muscogee Nation. In 0.3 mile the trail ascends, passes a bench and trash can, then reaches a tunnel and barricade. Beyond this barricade, the trail runs adjacent to an area involved in a controversial Police Training Facility development proposed by the City of Atlanta. Though not part of the proposed development, Intrenchment Creek Park was closed to the public in 2023 to the disappointment of many. When the park reopens, the South River Trail will provide access to miles of hiking trails in Intrenchment Creek Park.

Turn around here and retrace your steps back to the parking lot to end your hike. If you want more miles, the South River Trail continues along Gresham Road and then into the forest across Clifton Church Road to connect with the Michelle Obama Trail (page 199) in about 3 miles.

Stunning old-growth trees like this beech can be seen throughout the preserve.

Lake Charlotte Nature Preserve

Lake Charlotte Nature Preserve is an up-and-coming park with lots of character. The area was once threatened by pollution from the now-closed Live Oak Landfill, but several advocates successfully fought to preserve the 216-acre woodland. Though the lake itself has been drained, several still-intact structures from the 1920s remain on the property. As you traverse this mature forest (one of the largest remaining in Atlanta), you'll be greeted by ferns, mature shagbark hickories, and towering beech trees. Though restoration efforts and trail expansions are currently under way, the preserve is still somewhat of a secret.

HOW TO GET THERE

Driving Distance from Downtown Atlanta: 7 miles
Address: 2802 Forrest Park Road SE, Atlanta, GA 30354
Neighborhood: South River Gardens / southeast Atlanta
Nearest Interstate: I-285
Public Transit: MARTA 55 bus + 1-mile walk
Parking: Limited street parking along Forrest Park Road

HIKE DISTANCE

2-mile figure-8 loop

DIFFICULTY

Overall: Easy to moderate
Navigation: Red spray-painted arrows on trees that can be easy to overlook
Terrain: Hard-packed dirt and gravel trails
Elevation Change: Mostly flat with a few short, steep ascents and descents

SAFETY

Usage ★★☆☆☆
Visibility ★★★☆☆
Upkeep ★★★★☆
Parking ★☆☆☆☆

HOURS

6:00 am to 11:00 pm

DOGS

Leashed dogs allowed

FACILITIES

None

FEES & PERMITS None

LAND MANAGER City of Atlanta Parks & Recreation

Landmarks

SENTINEL AMERICAN BEECH TREE

About 0.1 mile into the hike, a stunning beech stands on the left side of the trail. Unmarked by carvings, it's a reminder that mature forests still exist in Atlanta.

LAKE CHARLOTTE VIEWPOINT

This viewpoint is a great place to stop and consider the history of the preserve. This spot was once part of the dam that held in the water of the lake. From here you can view the basin of the old lake, see the now-closed landfill, and appreciate the preservation of this woodland.

BRICK CHIMNEY

An impressive brick chimney stands tall, a reminder of the houses that used to sit on the property in the 1920s.

Hike Route

Start your hike at the green Lake Charlotte Nature Preserve sign along Forrest Park Drive, walking through the bollards and into the woods to the start of your hike. This trail is still being developed by the City of Atlanta, but soon an information sign will be directly on your left as you enter. Enjoy the lush clusters of ferns on the right as you make your way farther down the trail.

Continue on the trail as it curves left, then on your left, in 100 feet, is a stunning American beech tree. It's rare to see such an old, large beech without carvings on the trunk, a benefit of this trail being relatively new and secret.

About 0.4 mile after passing a junction on the right, you will come to a fork and a Dead End sign. Take the trail to the left and continue. As you hike, you'll pass remnants of an old brick structure on your left, possibly the

What historic remains might you find on this hike?

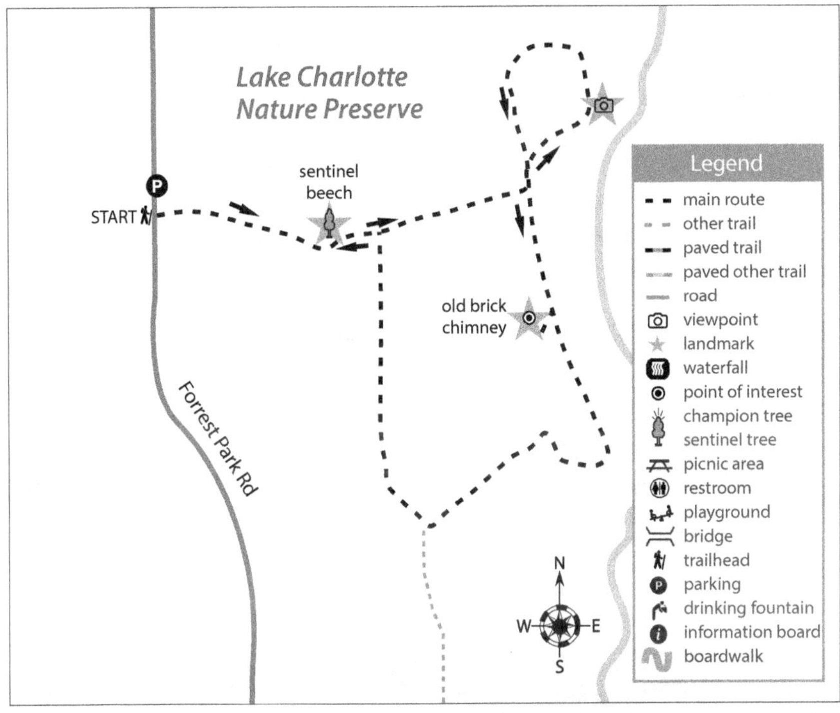

water pump for the former lake. In 100 yards you'll reach a ridge that extends out over the old lake. It's a great spot to watch planes arriving and departing from Hartsfield-Jackson Atlanta International Airport, and if you're lucky, you might spot a deer or two down below. You can also see the top of the old landfill just over the tree line. After taking in the view, continue on the trail as it veers to the left.

There are some large boulders on this section of the trail, and the XPO Logistics truck yard will be on your right. After 100 yards, take the trail to the left past a fallen oak tree. Continue on this path until it intersects with the larger main trail. A large two-trunked oak tree marks the joining of the trails. Turn right onto the trail and continue straight, past the Dead End sign.

In 0.25 mile follow a trail spur on the right to an old brick chimney. Return to the main trail and hike to the right as it winds uphill, passing more remnants of old buildings. This section of trail can be overgrown in the summer.

Continue hiking the trail up an incline for another 0.4 mile before reaching an intersection. Take the trail to the right, leading you uphill. Hike for 0.35 mile as the path inclines and then descends, connecting back to the wide trail you hiked at first. Take a left and follow this wide trail back to the entrance of the preserve to end your hike.

Watch for wildlife crossing the trails, such as this eastern box turtle.

Southside Park

Southside Park is a well-used mountain bike destination in the South River Gardens neighborhood. The park's trails twist and wind behind sports fields and through a young forest with lots of character. Though encircled by roads, the highway, and power lines, this park is a gem that provides a perfect afternoon getaway into nature. On nice weekends, you'll likely encounter bikers on the trail, so be mindful to hike the *opposite* direction bikers are directed on the trailhead sign. This hike route is based on Sunday directions.

HOW TO GET THERE

Driving Distance from Downtown Atlanta: 9 miles
Address: 3460 Jonesboro Road SE, Atlanta, GA 30354
Neighborhood: South River Gardens / southeast Atlanta
Nearest Interstate: I-285
Public Transit: MARTA 55 bus + 1-mile walk
Parking: Large paved parking lot; trailhead is on the far left side of the parking lot

HIKE DISTANCE

4-mile loop

DIFFICULTY

Overall: Easy to moderate
Navigation: Occasional but infrequent blazes and maps along route
Terrain: Hard-packed dirt and gravel trails
Elevation Change: Rolling hills, but no major ascents or descents

SAFETY

Usage ★★★★☆
Visibility ★★★★★
Upkeep ★★★☆☆
Parking ★★★★★

HOURS

6:00 am to 11:00 pm

DOGS

Leashed dogs allowed

FACILITIES

- No toilets
- Benches, trash cans, baseball fields, outdoor soccer field, bike rack

FEES & PERMITS	None
LAND MANAGER	City of Atlanta Parks & Recreation

Landmarks

SENTINEL WATER OAK

Located on a spur trail that leads to the park's entrance road, this water oak stands out among the other trees on the route with its wide crown and large size.

SENTINEL TULIP TREE

This forest is filled with tulip trees (commonly known as tulip poplars), but this one at the edge of the baseball field is one of the largest.

THREE-TRUNKED TULIP TREE

Just off the right side of the green trail, this tulip tree seems like any other. But upon closer view, you'll notice that it has three trunks stemming from its base.

Hike Route

The trails at Southside Park were built for mountain bikes. Hikers are welcome, but please be aware and courteous to bicyclists. Be sure to hike the *opposite* direction bikers are directed on the trailhead sign. These instructions are based on Sunday directions: Bikers counterclockwise (right), and hikers walk clockwise (left). Pay special attention while hiking uphill, because bikes may be coming downhill toward you at fast speeds. Always keep your eyes open and listen while hiking on trails shared with mountain bikers.

Facing the baseball fields, begin your hike at the far left end of the parking lot and enter the woods by the trail marker. At the map post, take note of the direction for hikers. This route is based on Sunday directions.

Start on the green-blazed Evergreen Trail by turning left at the map post. Pass under an arching maple in 0.25 mile. At the next junction with a spur trail on the left, walk 100 feet to visit a sentinel water oak. Return to the main trail and continue. Stay right at the next junction. Hike for another 0.35 mile as the trail takes a slight incline past large white oaks and magnolia trees. In 0.2 mile you'll come to an area of the forest with a more open understory.

Found-object art marks a trail junction at Southside Park.

Continue for 0.5 mile to reach the end of the green Evergreen Trail and a junction with the blue-blazed North Connector Trail. End your hike here or turn left onto the blue North Connector Trail to continue. Take North Connector Trail for 0.35 mile to come to a sentinel tulip tree on your right, just before coming to a ridge behind the baseball field fence. Hike behind the baseball field for 0.1 mile to reach a junction with South Access Trail on the right.

Turn left and cross a small culvert and bridge to reach a junction with the blue-blazed Oak and Hickory Trails. Stay right and hike on the blue trail for 50 yards to a directional post and map. Remember to follow the appropriate hiking direction, which is opposite of that for bikers, depending on the day of the week. These are Sunday hiking directions, so turn left here on the blue-blazed Oak Trail.

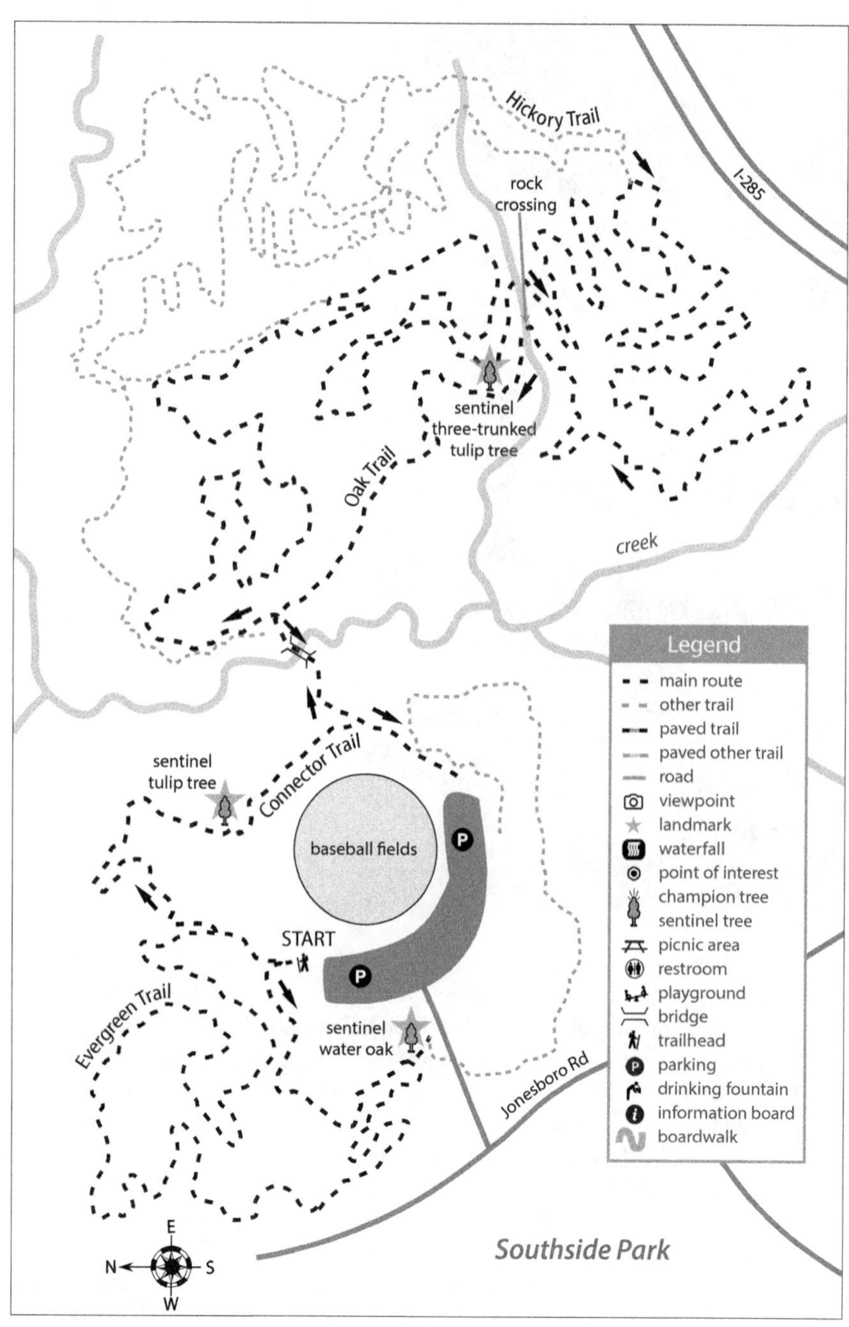
Hickory Trail
I-285
rock
crossing
sentinel
three-trunked
tulip tree
Oak Trail
creek
Legend
main route
other trail
paved trail
paved other trail
road
viewpoint
landmark
waterfall
point of interest
champion tree
sentinel tree
picnic area
restroom
playground
bridge
trailhead
parking
drinking fountain
information board
boardwalk
sentinel
tulip tree
Connector Trail
baseball fields
START
Evergreen Trail
sentinel
water oak
Jonesboro Rd
Southside Park
E
N
S
W

The trail switchbacks through the woods for 0.6 mile where it begins to parallel the open power line clearing. Hike for 0.15 mile through the field before the trail switchbacks down into the floodplain. At the next junction in 0.4 mile, keep to the left and cross rocks at the bottom of the floodplain. After hiking at a slight incline for 0.5 mile, you will see the highway from the trail.

Reach a junction with Hickory Trail in 0.1 mile and stay to the right on the blue Oak Trail. The trail begins to curve away from the highway and back down into the floodplain and through a grove of bamboo. In 0.8 mile, the trail curves around a wetland. At the next junction in 0.2 mile, stay to the left and immediately pass the sentinel three-trunked tulip tree on your right.

In 0.2 mile the trail begins to run parallel to the creek. Hike for 100 yards to reach the junction where you began the blue Oak Trail. Stay left, cross the bridge and culvert, and continue straight onto South Access Trail. Continue straight on the gravel South Access Trail until it exits the forest at the far southeast corner of the park. Walk past the sports fields to the parking lot to end your hike. Otherwise, turn right at the North Connector Trail junction and hike for 0.35 mile back to the Evergreen trailhead. Turn left out of the forest at the map board and end your hike.

Get up-close views of the South River along this trail.

Southtowne Trail & South Bend Park

This multiuse trail connects South Bend Park and the Swann Nature Preserve. The South Bend section of the trail is lined with playgrounds and giant bug sculptures for kids, making it a great trail for a family outing. During the hike you'll have the chance to get up close to the South River, one of only two urban-origin rivers in Georgia. While the first half of the hike is flat or downhill, take note that on the return you will be going mostly uphill.

HOW TO GET THERE

Driving Distance from Downtown Atlanta: 4 miles
Address: 2002 Lakewood Avenue SE, Atlanta, GA 30315
Nearest Interstate: I-75/I-85
Neighborhood: Lakewood Heights
Public Transit: MARTA 42 bus + 0.1-mile walk
Parking: Large paved parking lot

HIKE DISTANCE

3-mile out-and-back

DIFFICULTY

Overall: Easy to moderate
Navigation: Trail marked by black posts with signage attached
Terrain: Paved multiuse path
Elevation Change: Flat in some sections; several steep ascents and descents

SAFETY

Usage ★★☆☆☆
(note: park facilities are heavily used, but the trail itself is less traveled)
Visibility ★★★☆☆
Upkeep ★★★★☆
Parking ★★★★☆

HOURS

6:00 am to 11:00 pm

DOGS

Leashed dogs allowed

FACILITIES

- No toilets
- Playgrounds, picnic pavilions, water fountains, baseball field, tennis court, basketball court, outdoor soccer field

FEES & PERMITS	None
LAND MANAGER	City of Atlanta Parks & Recreation

Landmarks

ANCHORED SAIL ART INSTALLATION

Created in 2009 by artist Phil Proctor, this towering metal art installation stands at the entrance to the park.

SENTINEL TWO-TRUNKED MAPLE

A beautiful two-trunked maple tree stands over the southeast corner of the baseball field.

DRAGONFLY PLAY STRUCTURE

For the kids or kids at heart, this fun and imaginative play structure includes interpretive signage about dragonflies, which are important in water ecosystems.

Hike Route

Enter South Bend Park from Lakewood Avenue and park near the entrance at the top of the hill by the playground and large picnic pavilion. The trail begins at the very top of the hill near Lakewood Avenue on the playground side of the parking area. You'll find the interesting *Anchored Sail* art installation near the picnic pavilion across the parking lot from the playground.

Follow the trail as it begins downhill, passing a row of three beautiful southern magnolias on your right, directly across from the playground. Continuing down the hill, you may hear the sound of flowing water. In about 100 yards you can follow an unofficial side trail down to a rock outcropping to view the creek up close. Continue on the paved path, passing a picnic pavilion on your right in 0.1 mile before coming to a children's outdoor theater and playground. Soon after, you will reach a boardwalk. Enter the boardwalk and stay to the right, passing an old well in 0.1 mile on your right. You will soon come to a baseball field and third playground. Take note of the beautiful two-trunked maple that drapes over the southeast corner of the baseball field.

In 100 yards a kid's tunnel and ant playscape will be on the right side of the trail. Soon after, you'll reach a giant rideable dragonfly sculpture below a beautiful mature oak. In a few yards the trail

Several unique play structures line the South Bend Park section of the hike.

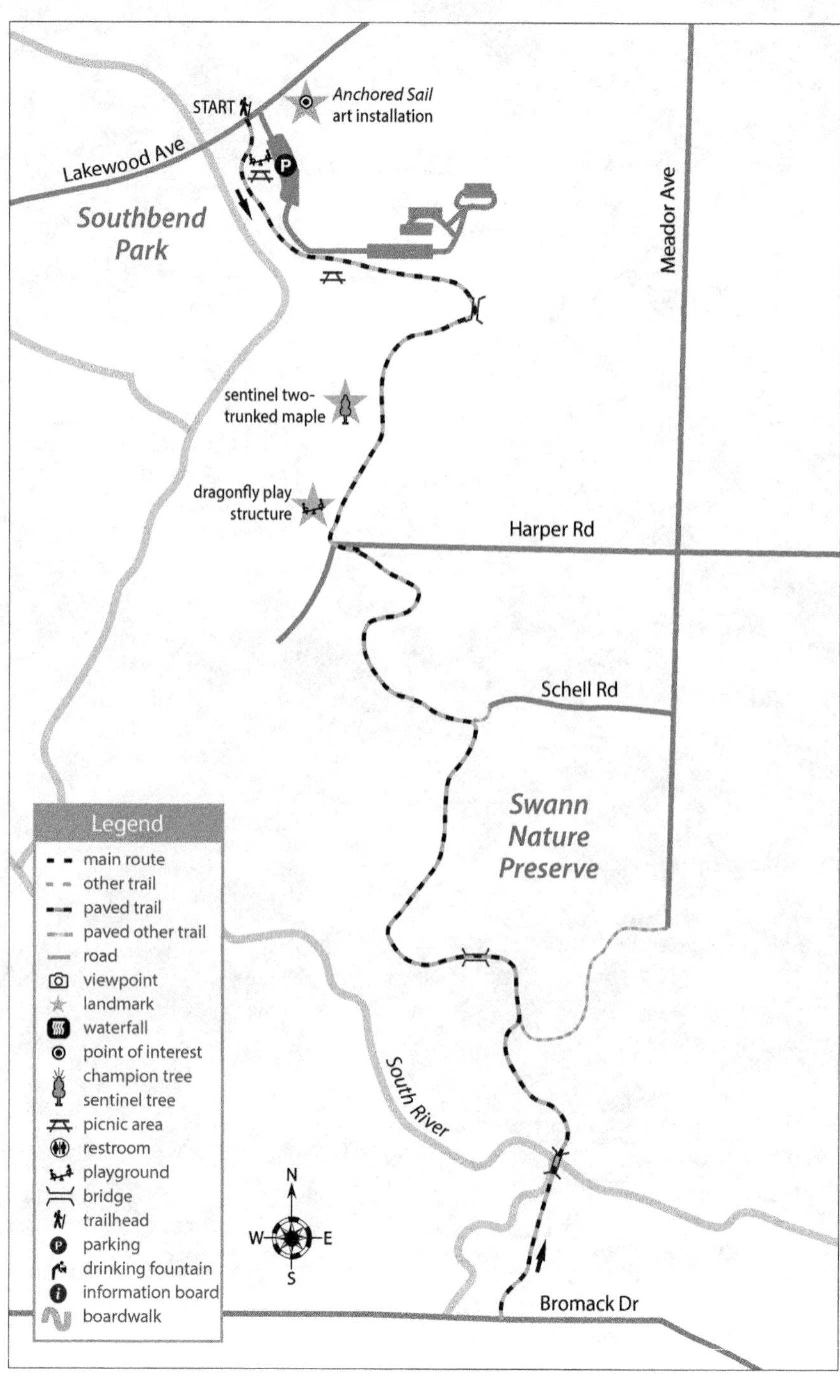

START
Anchored Sail
art installation
Lakewood Ave
Southbend
Park
Meador Ave
sentinel two-
trunked maple
dragonfly play
structure
Harper Rd
Schell Rd
Swann
Nature
Preserve
South River
Bromack Dr
N
W
E
S
Legend
main route
other trail
paved trail
paved other trail
road
viewpoint
landmark
waterfall
point of interest
champion tree
sentinel tree
picnic area
restroom
playground
bridge
trailhead
parking
drinking fountain
information board
boardwalk

crosses Harper Road. Look to the left to find the continuation of the trail. At this point, the trail enters the Swann Nature Preserve. Remember to occasionally look up for a chance to catch sight of hawks and woodpeckers. There are a number of stunning mature beech trees on this section of the trail as well. You will come to one on your left in about 0.15 mile from the road crossing. Stay right at the next intersection to continue the trail as it winds downhill to a boardwalk in 0.3 mile. You will soon come to another junction with a trail on the left. Continue to the right and downhill. In 0.2 mile you'll reach a boardwalk that crosses the South River. At the end of the boardwalk, the trail continues for another 0.3 mile, where it ends at Bromack Drive. From here, turn around and follow the trail back uphill, staying to the left at each junction, including at the road crossing. End your hike back at the top of the hill at South Bend Park where you parked.

A series of footbridges over seasonal creeks add to the beauty of this trail.

Sykes Park

When you arrive at Sykes Park you may feel like you're the first person to ever visit for hiking. This secluded park in East Point has long been a spot for basketball, tennis, playgrounds, and parties, but Sykes Park has recently become a hiking, biking, and trail-running destination thanks to the hard work of the Atlanta mountain biking community. The rolling hills, well-manicured trails, boulders, creeks, and towering trees provide a cool forest hike. Invite along a human or canine friend for this adventure. Bring your bike or scooter and try out the pump track, or stick around after your hike for basketball, tennis, or a picnic.

HOW TO GET THERE

Driving Distance from Downtown Atlanta: 9 miles
Address: 3224 Dodson Drive Connector, East Point, GA 30344
Neighborhood: East Point
Nearest Interstate: I-85
Public Transit: MARTA bus 84 + 0.3-mile walk
Parking: Paved parking lot near tennis and basketball courts

HIKE DISTANCE

1.5-mile loop

DIFFICULTY

Overall: Easy to moderate
Navigation: Trails marked at some junctions; information sign at trailhead
Terrain: Trails built for mountain bikes: hard-packed dirt trails with berms and rock features
Elevation Change: Rolling hills with many short, steep ascents and descents

SAFETY

Usage ★☆☆☆☆
Visibility ★★☆☆☆
Upkeep ★★★☆☆
Parking ★★★☆☆

HOURS

7:00 am to 8:30 pm

DOGS

Leashed dogs allowed

FACILITIES	• Toilets • Tennis courts, basketball courts, playground, multiple pavilions and picnic tables, water fountain, pump track, and mountain bike trails
FEES & PERMITS	None
LAND MANAGER	City of East Point Parks & Recreation in partnership with MTB Atlanta

Landmarks

BOULDER FIELD

Sykes Park is on the eastern edge of a geological formation that includes nearby Boat Rock Preserve and Cascade Springs Nature Preserve (page 213). The boulders in this area are made of Ben Hill granite and likely formed 250 million years ago.

PUMP TRACK

Though this landmark is visible from the trail, you'll have to use the pavement to access it. A pump track is a circular path of rolling rises and banked turns that is designed so you can generate momentum on your bike or scooter by "pumping" your body weight instead of pedaling or pushing with your feet. Bring your helmet and bike or scooter and give it a try!

MOONTOWER WATER TOWER

Though not its official name, "Moontower" certainly is fitting, isn't it? This orb of white rising from the forest provides drinking water for the city of East Point. It is also a reminder that Sykes Park is one of the highest points in the city.

Hike Route

The trails at Sykes Park were built for mountain bikes. Hikers are welcome, but please be aware and courteous to bicyclists. Be sure to hike the *opposite* direction bikers are directed on the trailhead sign. These instructions are based on Saturday directions: Bikers ride clockwise (left), and hikers walk counterclockwise (right). Pay special attention while hiking uphill because bikes may be coming downhill toward you at fast speeds. Always keep your eyes open and listen while hiking on trails shared with mountain bikers.

Start your hike near the green pavilion at the trail information sign beside the black gates. Though not always marked with signs, the trails in this park are named Blue Trail (which circles the exterior of the park) and Green Trail (on the interior). Follow Blue Trail to the right as it skirts the edge of the parking lot and then winds downhill through a field of interesting boulders.

In 0.3 mile cross the pavement and reenter the woods, still on Blue Trail. You might be able to see the concrete pump track to the left as you descend. At the bottom of the hill, the winding trail parallels a tributary of North Fork Camp Creek and then passes a small trail on the left that allows access to the asphalt drive and other trails.

Sykes Park is a young forest with a wide diversity of trees: tulip poplar, loblolly pine, beech, hickory, and oak.

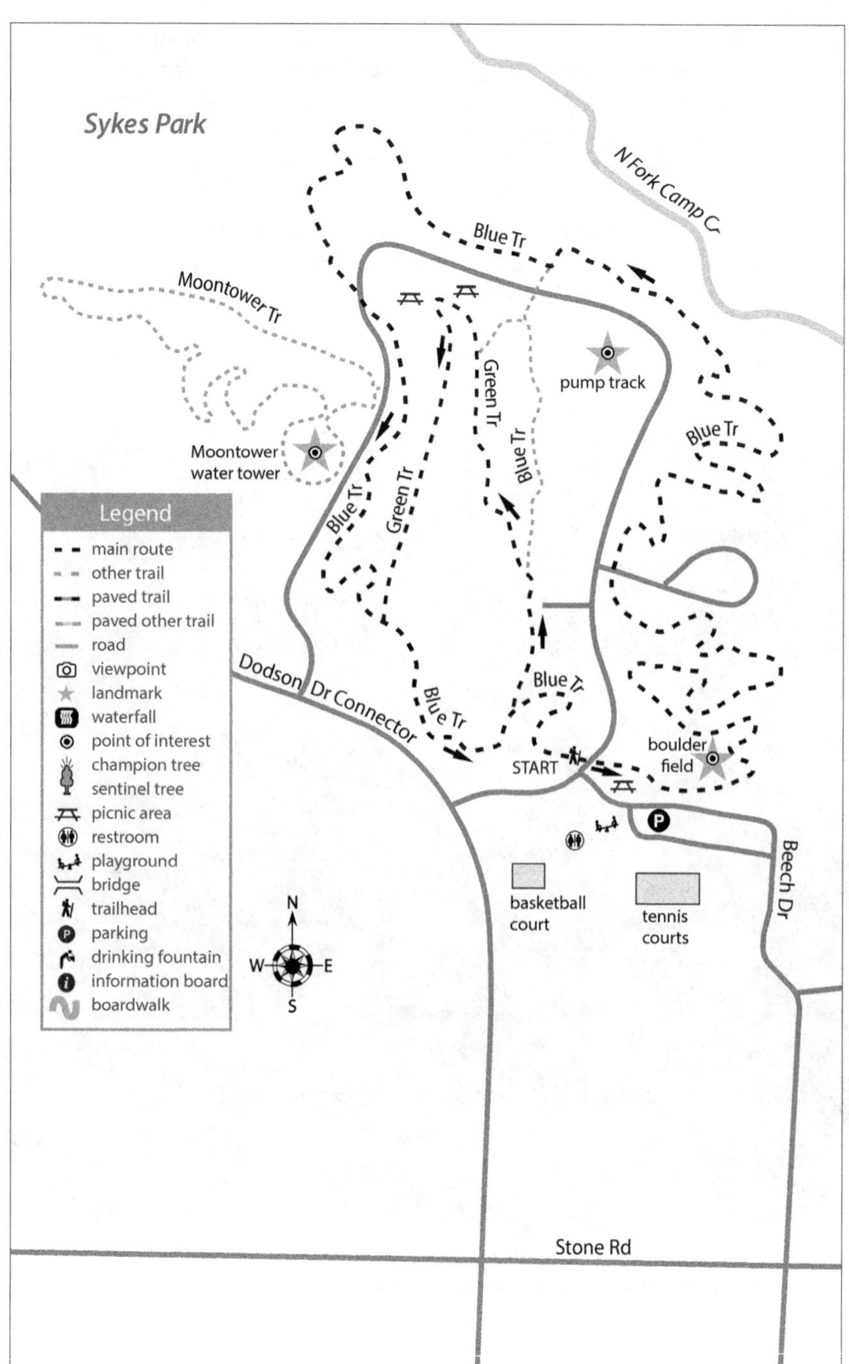
Sykes Park
N Fork Camp C
Blue Tr
Moontower Tr
Green Tr
Blue Tr
pump track
Moontower
water tower
Blue Tr
Green Tr
Blue Tr
Blue Tr
Legend
main route
other trail
paved trail
paved other trail
road
viewpoint
landmark
waterfall
point of interest
champion tree
sentinel tree
picnic area
restroom
playground
bridge
trailhead
parking
drinking fountain
information board
boardwalk
Dodson Dr Connector
Blue Tr
Blue Tr
START
boulder
field
Beech Dr
basketball
court
tennis
courts
N
W
E
S
Stone Rd

Continue straight on the near side of the pavement, passing a pink pavilion in 0.1 mile. In another 100 yards reach the paved drive again. To the right, just up the hill, is the 0.5-mile Moontower Loop, which is for bikers only. Cross the pavement and reenter the woods just above a teal pavilion and continue on Blue Trail.

Hike uphill for 0.2 mile, looking up for a unique view of the East Point Moontower water tower on the right. At a Blue Trail marker, continue straight. In 0.1 mile cross a bridge and walk toward another Blue Trail marker. This time, turn left and hike downhill on Green Trail near an outdoor fitness area. Cross the pavement, pass a nature trail sign, and stay left to follow Green Trail.

Cross two wooden bridges and stay on Green Trail for 0.25 mile before making a sharp left U-turn just below the teal pavilion. Stay on Green Trail as it winds uphill to reach Blue Trail in another 0.1 mile. Turn left and hike 0.1 mile to the bridge you crossed before. Cross the bridge and hike toward the Blue Trail marker as you did before, but this time go right to stay on Blue Trail.

In 0.1 mile the hike ends at the pavement and green pavilion where you began.

ON THE PERIMETER— SOUTHSIDE

Long boardwalks stretch over wetlands.

Michelle Obama Trail

Inspired by the former First Lady's "Let's Move" initiative to reduce chilhood obesity, the Michelle Obama Trail is a paved multiuse path at Georgia State University's Perimeter College and will someday help connect the Beltline to Arabia Mountain. This route covers just a few of the trail's five linear miles and leads you past several river and wetland views. It's a great trail to see native wildlife, including deer, birds, and butterflies. And because the trail is paved and has few hills, it is popular among bikers and walkers with strollers.

HOW TO GET THERE

Driving Distance from Downtown Atlanta: 10 miles
Address: 2901 Clifton Springs Road, Decatur, GA 30034
Neighborhood: Panthersville / south DeKalb
Nearest Interstate: I-20
Parking: Large paved parking lot; may be crowded when classes are in session
Public Transit: MARTA 34 or 15 bus + 0.3-mile walk

HIKE DISTANCE

4-mile out-and-back; optional longer hike of up to 10 miles

DIFFICULTY

Overall: Moderate to strenuous based on length
Navigation: PATH Foundation markers on black metal posts and on boardwalks
Terrain: Paved multiuse path and boardwalk
Elevation Change: Mostly flat

SAFETY

Usage ★★★★☆
Visibility ★★★★☆
Upkeep ★★★★★
Parking ★★★★★

HOURS

7:00 am to sunset

DOGS

Leashed dogs allowed

FACILITIES

- No toilets
- Benches

FEES & PERMITS	None
LAND MANAGER	DeKalb County Recreation, Parks & Cultural Affairs

Landmarks

WETLAND

This wetland at the end of a long boardwalk is a prime spot along the route to listen to frog calls and look for and listen to wading birds. Wetlands are important but sensitive ecosystems that provide habitat for a large variety of amphibians, reptiles, mammals, and birds.

SENTINEL TULIP TREE

This massive tulip tree (commonly known as tulip poplar) has three trunks. Tulip tree leaves are distinguishable by their tulip shape, which some people say looks like a cat's face.

FERNS OF THE WORLD GARDEN

Nationally renowned for its collection of ferns, this nearby garden is the personal collection of George Sanko, a botany professor who began planting ferns here in 1990. Walking through the fern garden conjures images of a prehistoric time.

Hike Route

Begin your hike in the southwest corner of the parking lot, with the university buildings on your left. There is a boardwalk and commemorative Michelle Obama plaque here. Take the first left on the boardwalk to descend onto the paved trail. In partnership with DeKalb County Libraries, park officials sometimes post poems along the path. Stop and read a few during your hike.

While the Michelle Obama Trail has existed since 2018, this section of the trail is the most recent addition, completed in 2021. Continue on the trail, keeping an eye out for wildlife. You can sometimes spot families of deer grazing on either side of the trail.

In 0.35 mile pass under Panthersville Road, with views of the South River on your right. In 100 feet you will come to a long (0.2 mile) boardwalk over a wetland. Despite tires and other trash that you can see in the water, if you're lucky you may still catch sight of wading birds. At the end of the boardwalk pass a food distribution warehouse on the left. The paved trail then passes a large, less polluted wetland off the trail on the left. Depending on the time of day, you might hear a cacophony of frog calls.

The native plants along the trail provide nectar for pollinators.

Continue on the trail with the South River on your right. In any season, this is truly a sensory hike. For instance, in the spring, the trail offers sweet wild blackberries and delightful scents from the honeysuckles and jasmine. In the late summer, wildflowers, butterflies, and birdsong abound.

In another half mile, cross a second boardwalk, and soon after you will come to a third boardwalk. After crossing the third boardwalk, in 0.1 mile reach the magnificent three-trunked tulip tree (say that five times fast) on the left side of the trail across from a "Curving Trail" sign at mile marker 5.41. A tree may develop multiple trunks for various reasons: as regrowth after being cut, from two seeds sprouting closely together, or as just an uncommon but natural development of the tree.

Continue on the path, passing under Warriors Path road. In 0.2 mile from the underpass you will come to a bridge that crosses over Shoal Creek. And 0.25 mile after the bridge the trail ends at Waldrop Road. Turn around and retrace your steps to the trailhead.

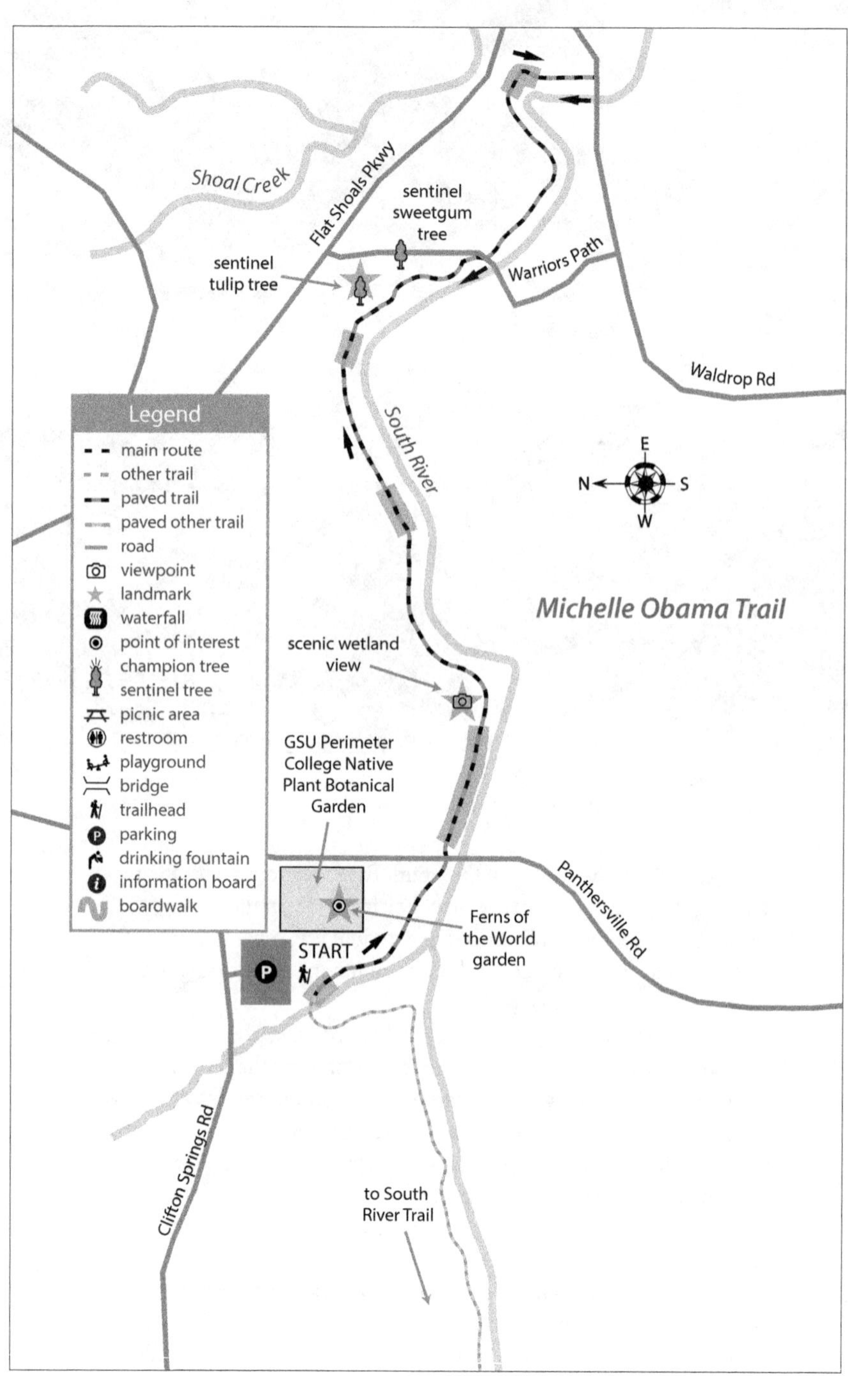
Shoal Creek
Flat Shoals Pkwy
sentinel sweetgum tree
sentinel tulip tree
Warriors Path
Waldrop Rd
Legend
main route
other trail
paved trail
paved other trail
road
viewpoint
landmark
waterfall
point of interest
champion tree
sentinel tree
picnic area
restroom
playground
bridge
trailhead
parking
drinking fountain
information board
boardwalk
South River
E
N
S
W
Michelle Obama Trail
scenic wetland view
GSU Perimeter College Native Plant Botanical Garden
Panthersville Rd
Ferns of the World garden
START
Clifton Springs Rd
to South River Trail

There are two ways you can extend your hike, if you want more walking and adventure. First, the Michelle Obama Trail continues about 3 miles to Gresham Park Recreation Center on Bouldercrest Road where it joins the South River Trail. Take a left at the boardwalk near the trailhead and continue over Doolittle Creek to hike this other section of the Michelle Obama Trail. It is a six-mile round trip hike to Gresham Park and back.

The second option is to visit the nearby Ferns of the World garden, which boasts one of the largest collections of fern species in the United States. The fern garden is directly adjacent to the Georgia State University Perimeter College Native Plant Botanical Garden, and both are free and open to the public. You can walk there on the sidewalk or drive to the opposite side of campus where the garden is located: 3355 Panthersville Road, Decatur, GA 30034.

Built in the late 1800s, the barn on this property is still standing.

Reynolds Nature Preserve

Formerly owned by Judge William Reynolds, Reynolds Nature Preserve was donated to Clayton County in 1967 and contains miles of trails that curve through stands of old-growth forests along the edges of human-made ponds and natural creeks. Well-maintained and loved by locals, this preserve is a hidden gem where you can walk for miles without seeing other hikers. Or you can stay near the entrance and visit the butterfly garden, native azaleas, and nature center. Either way, the preserve offers an excellent outing for families and individuals.

HOW TO GET THERE

Driving Distance from Downtown Atlanta: 14 miles
Address: 5665 Reynolds Road, Morrow, GA 30260
Neighborhood: Morrow
Nearest Interstate: I-75
Public Transit: MARTA 193 bus + 0.6-mile walk or MARTA 55 or 195 bus + 1-mile walk
Parking: Small gravel parking lot

HIKE DISTANCE

2-mile loop

DIFFICULTY

Overall: Easy to moderate
Navigation: Map posted at trailhead and posts with trail names along trails
Terrain: Hard-packed dirt trail
Elevation Change: Rolling hills, but no major ascents or descents

SAFETY

Usage ★★★★☆
Visibility ★★★★☆
Upkeep ★★★★☆
Parking ★★★☆☆

HOURS

8:00 am to dusk; nature center open 9:00 am to 5:00 pm Monday through Friday

DOGS

Leashed dogs allowed

FACILITIES	• Toilets • Water fountain, nature center, picnic tables, outdoor classroom
FEES & PERMITS	None
LAND MANAGER	Clayton County Parks & Recreation

Landmarks

SENTINEL WHITE OAK

Look for this impressively large white oak immediately after you turn onto the Crooked Creek Trail. The oak and tulip trees in this grove are fast growing but are still the oldest specimens in the park.

SENTINEL TULIP TREE

Along the Crooked Creek Trail, this tulip tree (commonly known as tulip poplar) is memorable both for its size and for the young maple growing out of its root system.

BIG POND OVERLOOK

Built by Judge Reynolds when he owned this property, this pond is a great spot for a variety of wildlife viewing. Just remember: no fishing.

Hike Route

Begin your hike at the map board next to the parking lot and walk straight on the paved path toward the nature center. Turn left in front of the building. Just past a gazebo on your right go left at the sign for Crooked Creek and Brookside Trails.

Continue on Brookside Trail, passing two junctions with smaller trails on the right. In 0.2 mile at a small footbridge, stay left, continuing on Brookside Trail. Continue straight for another 0.1 mile past a closed parking lot on your left, until you reach the Big Pond pier on your right. This is a great place to view turtles, ducks, geese, and other wildlife—but as the sign says, no fishing and no swimming! (Not that Big Pond is that enticing for swimmers.)

Continue on Brookside Trail until you reach a large metal gate on your left. Turn right at the gate onto Back Mountain Trail, which crosses the dam. After the dam the trail climbs uphill for 0.1 mile until you reach the junction with High Springs Trail.

Turn right. High Springs Trail winds along the slope above the ponds. Depending on the season, you'll see a variety of interesting

Boardwalk Trail crosses over a lush bed of ferns.

fungi along the path. The trail climbs uphill again past another junction on the right. Stay straight. In another 0.1 mile make a hard left turn onto Hickory Stump Trail (there is no sign at this junction) and hike uphill. After 0.2 mile you'll reach a junction (again no signage, but marked with a yellow birdhouse) with Back Mountain Trail. Turn right and hike another 0.2 mile. This area of the preserve brings you closest to the surrounding neighborhood on Phillips Drive. At a chain-link gate, Back Mountain Trail turns right and becomes Crooked Creek Trail. Immediately after this sign, turn right onto Burstin' Heart Trail.

Walk up the ridge on Burstin' Heart Trail, then downhill past a junction with Oak Ridge Trail on your left. Just after this junction you'll see large tulip trees and oaks on the left that make up Poplar Park (a section of older-growth forest along Crooked Creek). One-tenth of a mile beyond Oak Ridge Trail, turn left onto Crooked Creek Trail. You'll immediately pass the sentinel white oak on your left. This

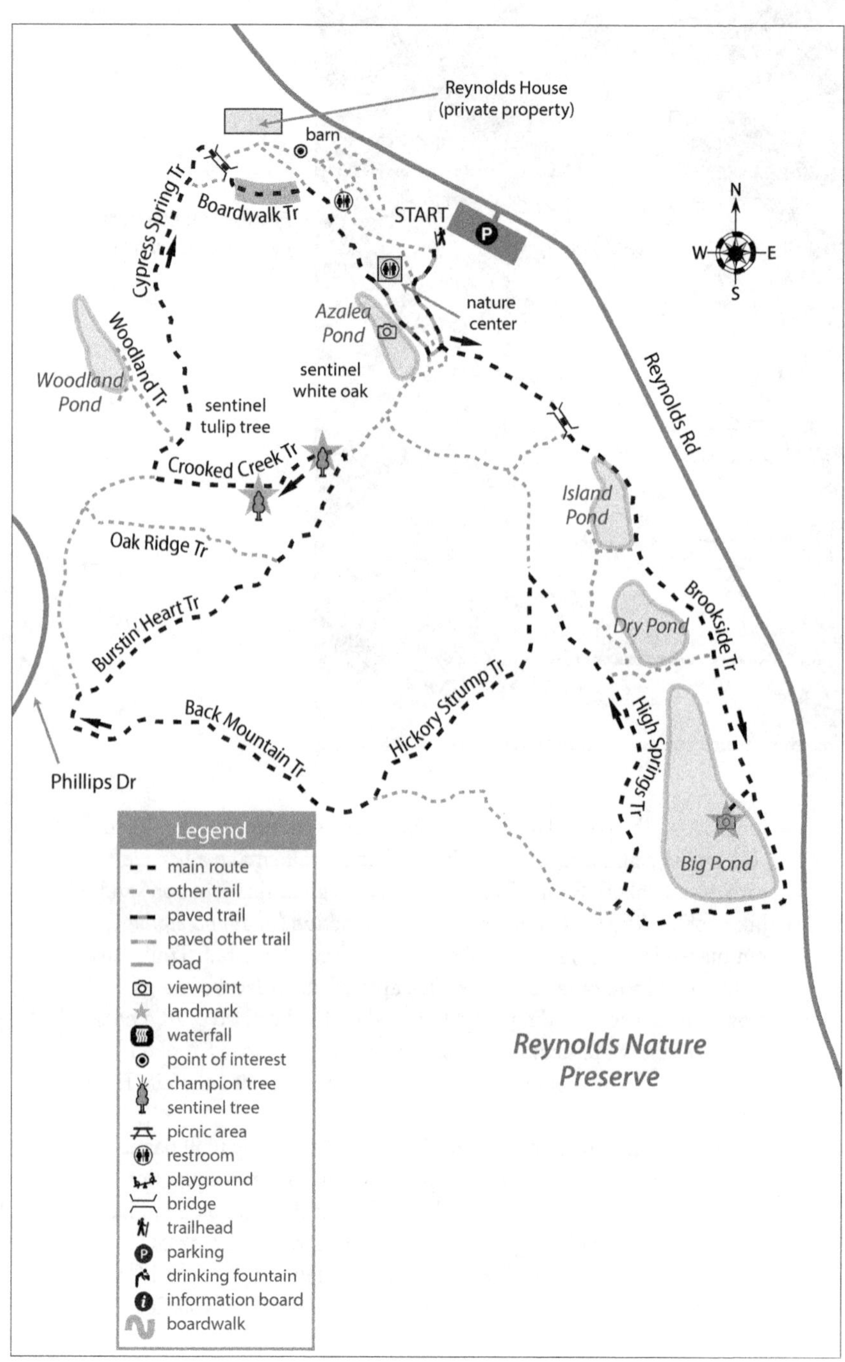

Reynolds House
(private property)
barn
Cypress Spring Tr
Boardwalk Tr
START
P
N
W
E
S
Azalea
Pond
nature
center
Woodland Tr
Woodland
Pond
sentinel
white oak
sentinel
tulip tree
Reynolds Rd
Crooked Creek Tr
Island
Pond
Oak Ridge Tr
Burstin' Heart Tr
Dry Pond
Brookside Tr
Back Mountain Tr
Hickory Strump Tr
High Springs Tr
Phillips Dr
Big Pond
Legend
main route
other trail
paved trail
paved other trail
road
viewpoint
landmark
waterfall
point of interest
champion tree
sentinel tree
picnic area
restroom
playground
bridge
trailhead
parking
drinking fountain
information board
boardwalk
Reynolds Nature
Preserve

section of trail also has opportunities to view native mountain laurels, which bloom in the late spring.

Continue on Crooked Creek Trail and pass a small stone wall. After passing through a patch of rhododendrons, you'll come to the sentinel tulip tree on your left. The tree has a young red maple tree growing out of its massive root system. In another 100 yards leave Poplar Park and turn right onto Cypress Spring Trail.

There's no sign here, but the trail is obvious. Cross a small footbridge, pass the junction with Woodland Pond Trail, cross another small footbridge, then hike uphill through a forest of oak trees. After 0.1 mile and a bench, the trail descends to meet Boardwalk Trail in 0.1 mile. At the bottom of the hill, pass a small cutoff trail on the right and walk 25 yards farther as the trail curves to the right to reach the official junction and sign for Boardwalk Trail.

Turn right onto Boardwalk Trail and cross a bridge between a boxed spring on the right and an enormous fallen tulip tree on the left. Then hike along the boardwalk until you come to an outdoor classroom, old barn, and pollinator garden. Depending on the season, the pollinator garden provides a burst of colors from both flowers and visiting butterflies. Turn right after the outdoor classroom and head back into the woods. (To reach restrooms and a picnic area, go up the small hill to the gravel path and turn right.)

The path through the woods on the right leads you 0.1 mile to the rear of the nature center and two viewing platforms above a small pond on the right. After passing the nature center, turn left across from the second viewing platform and walk up the stairs and to the left, circling back to the front of the building on the brick path. The paved path in front of the nature center leads back to the parking area to end your hike.

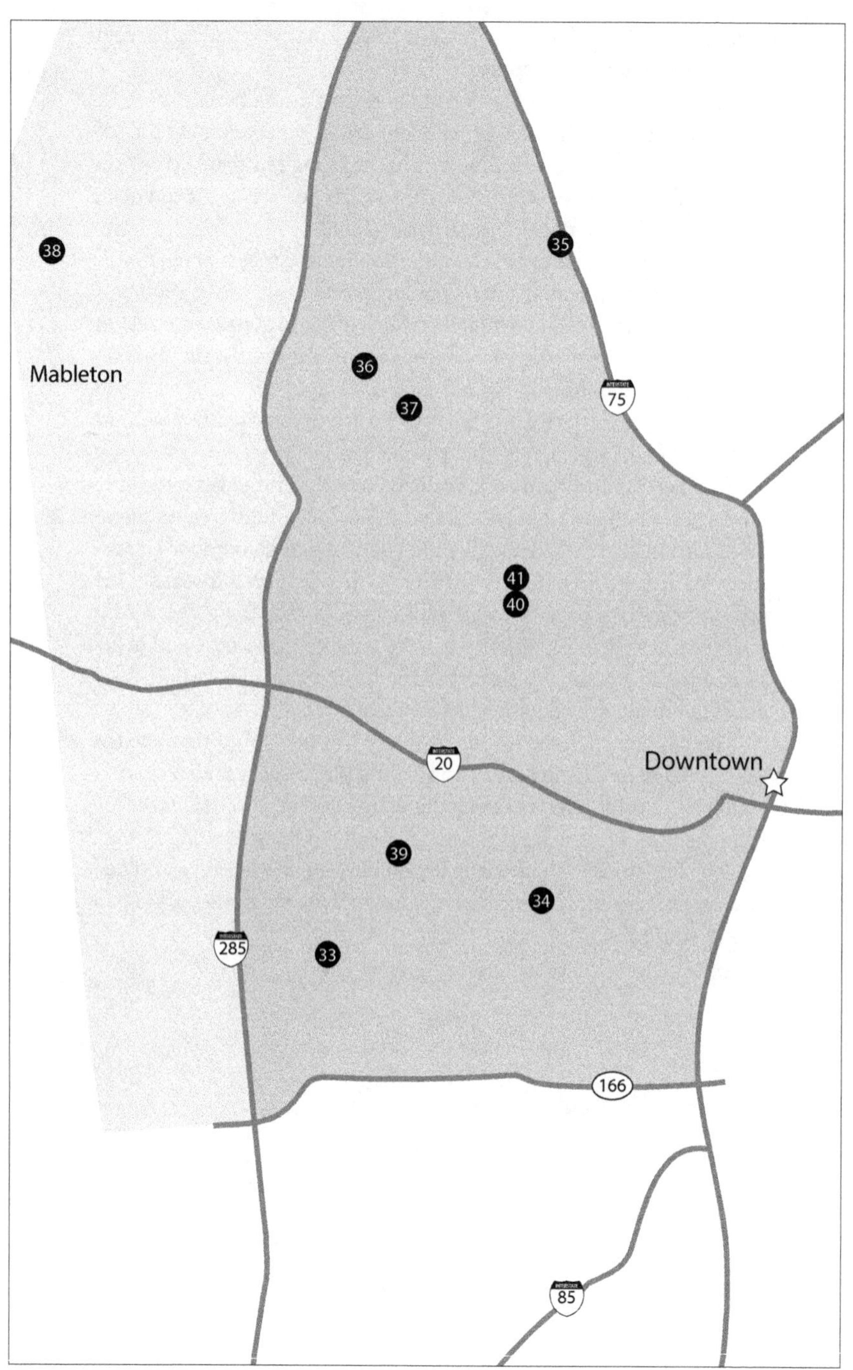

38
Mableton
35
36
37
75
41
40
20
Downtown
39
34
285
33
166
85

WESTSIDE

33 Cascade Springs Nature Preserve

34 Outdoor Activity Center

35 Paul Koshewa Trail

36 Riverwalk Atlanta & Whittier Mill Park

37 Spink Collins Park

38 Heritage Park

39 Lionel Hampton Park & Beecher Hills Park

40 Proctor Creek Greenway

41 Westside Park

Turkeyfoot Falls is one of Atlanta's most beautiful hidden secrets.

Cascade Springs Nature Preserve

Cascade Springs Nature Preserve has become one of the go-to hiking destinations for intown Atlantans. The 135-acre park has something for everyone—champion trees, interesting geology, historic ruins, creekside trails, rolling hills, and even a waterfall. The beauty of the land has been drawing visitors for over a century, and you can still find the remains of a spa and nature retreat, a spring house (where the water from "Cascade Spring" was bottled and sold in the early 1900s), and farming terraces.

HOW TO GET THERE	**Driving Distance from Downtown Atlanta:** 7 miles **Address:** 2852 Cascade Road SW, Atlanta, GA 30311 **Neighborhood:** Audubon Forest / southwest Atlanta **Nearest Interstate:** I-285 **Public Transit:** MARTA 71 bus stops near the entrance **Parking:** Large gravel parking area
HIKE DISTANCE	2-mile loop
DIFFICULTY	**Overall:** Easy to moderate **Navigation:** Trails marked by posts at most junctions and a map at the trailhead; this park contains many unofficial trails, so navigation can be difficult **Terrain:** Hard-packed dirt trails that can be overgrown in the summer, short sections of paved paths, and boardwalks **Elevation Change:** Rolling hills, but no major ascents or descents
SAFETY	**Usage** ★★★★☆ **Visibility** ★★★★☆ **Upkeep** ★★★☆☆ **Parking** ★★★★☆
HOURS	6:00 am to 11:00 pm
DOGS	Leashed dogs allowed

FACILITIES	• No toilets • Several picnic areas, water fountain, bicycle racks
FEES & PERMITS	None
LAND MANAGER	City of Atlanta Parks & Recreation

Landmarks

STATE CHAMPION SOURWOOD

- 74" circumference, 99' tall, 38' crown spread
- Normally, sourwoods are understory trees, but this one reaches all the way to the top of the canopy. At 99 feet tall, it is one of the tallest known sourwoods in the state. Find it on the hillside just behind the frog pond.

TURKEYFOOT FALLS

A waterfall inside the perimeter? Though it's small, Turkeyfoot Falls is certainly beautiful and is a great place to rest, contemplate, and take photographs. You might also see fruit on the rocks, left as an offering in this sacred place.

SENTINEL BEECH

This massive American beech with smooth gray bark is one of the most memorable trees in the forest. Its branches stretch high and wide. Some of the graffiti carved into its trunk is higher than we can even reach. How did it get there?

Hike Route

Start your hike on the boardwalk next to the water fountain and information board. Continue on the paved path when the boardwalk ends, passing the ruins to your left of a pump house from the old Cascade Inn, a nature resort from the 1920s.

Cross the bridge over Turkeyfoot Creek and inspect the spring house, which once provided crystal clear drinking water. Take the paved path on the right for 0.1 mile, where you'll come to a frog pond and the state champion sourwood tree. Loop back on the paved path to the spring house and continue straight, following yellow-capped posts parallel to the creek for 0.15 mile. At the end of a short boardwalk, just past a second ruined spring house, you can see a champion bigleaf magnolia across the creek on your left. Continue straight to the waterfall.

Even the stumps of fallen trees are massive and eye-catching at Cascade Springs.

At Turkeyfoot Falls hike uphill on the trail to a bench, then make a hard right to continue on Ridge Trail. This trail winds through rolling hills past an unofficial trail junction on the left and across three seasonal creeks to reach Spring Trail in 0.2 mile. You'll find a wooden sign and yellow-capped post at this junction. Go left to stay on Ridge Trail and hike uphill for a few more yards to reach another junction at an orange-capped post. Stay left on Ridge Trail and pass a large white oak tree on your left.

Hike 0.15 mile, staying right at several unmarked junctions, until you reach a junction at another orange-capped post. Turn left and hike 0.1 mile to a four-way junction. Straight ahead, you can choose to visit the sentinel beech tree and an interesting collection of large boulders. This hike turns right and follows the main trail for about 100 yards to reach a junction at an orange-capped post. Turn left and descend to the Utoy Creek floodplain. Stay right at the first junction and then left at the next to switchback down the hill and reach a flat gravel trail. Turn right and hike along Utoy Creek for 0.1 mile, then pass a junction on the right below a large hillside rock outcrop.

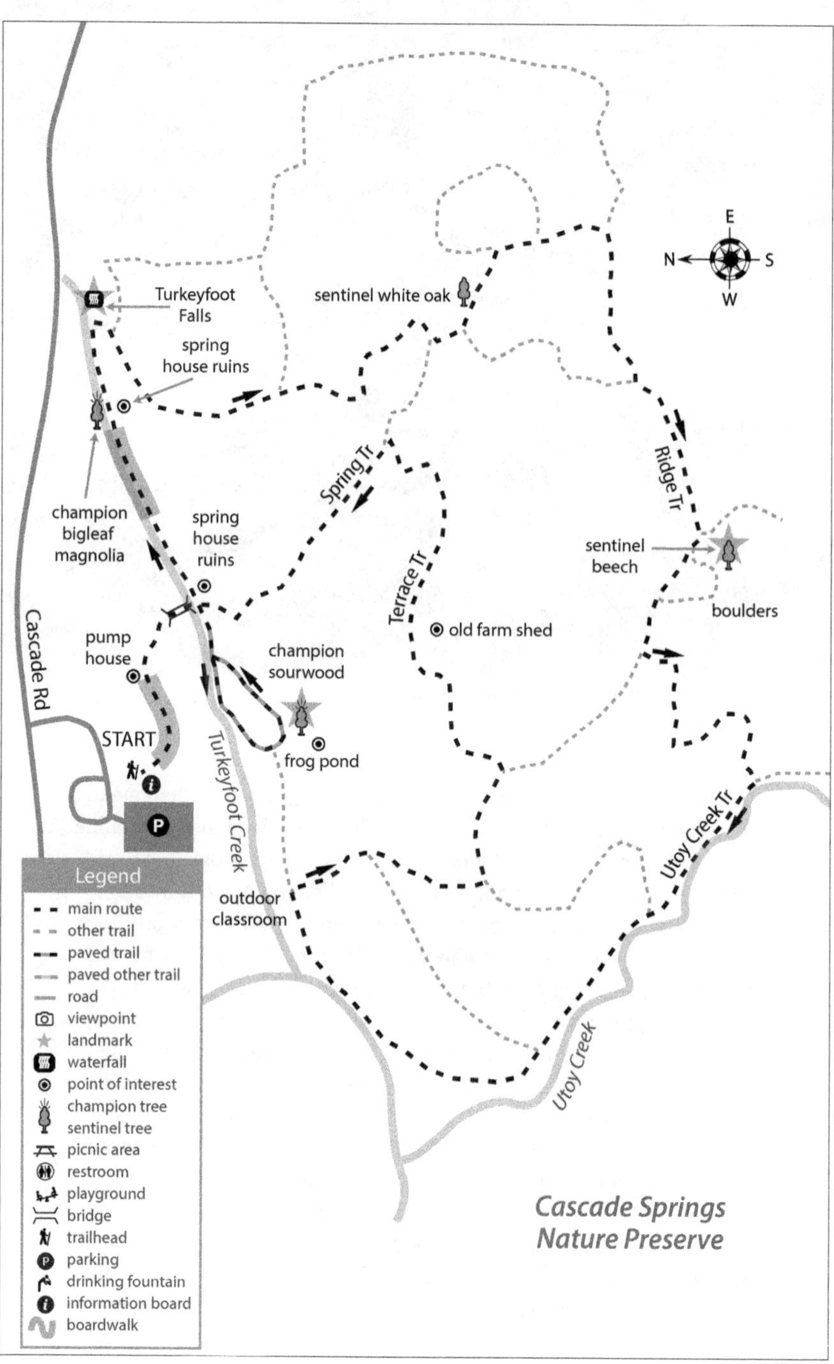
Turkeyfoot Falls
spring house ruins
sentinel white oak
E
N
S
W
champion bigleaf magnolia
spring house ruins
Spring Tr
Terrace Tr
Ridge Tr
sentinel beech
boulders
old farm shed
pump house
champion sourwood
Cascade Rd
START
frog pond
Turkeyfoot Creek
Utoy Creek Tr
outdoor classroom
Utoy Creek
Legend
main route
other trail
paved trail
paved other trail
road
viewpoint
landmark
waterfall
point of interest
champion tree
sentinel tree
picnic area
restroom
playground
bridge
trailhead
parking
drinking fountain
information board
boardwalk
Cascade Springs Nature Preserve

After another 0.1 mile, veer right at a black-capped post and continue another 0.2 mile to an outdoor classroom. Look for another black-capped post and turn right, up the hill.

Over the next 0.15 mile, stay straight past two wooden Utoy Creek signs before turning left onto Terrace Trail at an orange-capped post. Follow Terrace Trail for 0.2 mile, passing an old farm shed on your right, before arriving at a junction with Spring Trail. Turn left at a yellow-capped post and hike 0.15 mile to return to the spring house near Turkeyfoot Creek. Continue straight, cross the bridge, and walk the paved path back up the hill to the parking area to end your hike.

The towering Grandfather Beech is one of the oldest trees in the forest.

Outdoor Activity Center

The Outdoor Activity Center is a 26-acre urban nature preserve managed by the West Atlanta Watershed Alliance (WAWA), which supports a variety of environmental activities and educational programs. To access the hiking trails, you'll pass a community garden, composting station, and playground, all intended to engage community members of all ages in outdoor learning. Enjoy a peaceful hike through this old-growth forest with notable Atlanta history.

HOW TO GET THERE	**Driving Distance from Downtown Atlanta:** 4 miles **Address:** 1442 Richland Road SW, Atlanta, GA 30310 **Neighborhood:** Oakland City / West End **Nearest Interstate:** I-20 **Public Transit:** MARTA 71 bus + 0.4-mile walk or MARTA 68 bus + 0.5-mile walk **Parking:** Small gravel parking lot
HIKE DISTANCE	1-mile loop
DIFFICULTY	**Overall:** Easy to moderate **Navigation:** Colored wooden posts **Terrain:** Hard-packed dirt trail **Elevation Change:** Mostly level with one steep ascent and descent
SAFETY	**Usage** ★★☆☆☆ **Visibility** ★★★☆☆ **Upkeep** ★★★★☆ **Parking** ★★★★☆
HOURS	9:00 am to 4:00 pm, Monday through Saturday
DOGS	Leashed dogs allowed
FACILITIES	• Toilets • Nature center with water fountain, outdoor classroom, playground
FEES & PERMITS	None

LAND MANAGER	City of Atlanta Parks & Recreation and West Atlanta Watershed Alliance

Landmarks

CITY CHAMPION GRANDFATHER BEECH

- 136" circumference, 121' tall, 90' crown spread
- The centerpiece of this urban forest, Grandfather Beech, is labeled as a Civil War–era tree. The older graffiti on its trunk is stretched by the growth of the tree's bark, giving credence to the claim of the tree being more than 150 years old.

SENTINEL WINGED ELM

This tree stands in one of the lowest spots in the forest along a creek bed near a trail junction. Elms used to make up a larger percentage of the forest across the eastern United States but were decimated by the fungal Dutch elm disease.

HISTORIC NEGRO LEAGUE BASEBALL FIELD

The Atlanta Black Crackers was a Negro League baseball team that used this field on Bush Mountain to practice. For home games, the Black Crackers were only allowed to use Atlanta's Ponce de Leon Park when the white Atlanta Crackers team was not playing.

Hike Route

Start your hike in the parking lot at the right side of the nature center. Follow the trail to the right around the building past the compost demonstration area. At the back of the building, take the dirt trail to the back of the property past the outdoor classroom and play area and arrive at the gate at the right of the fence. This gate may be locked. Other gates along the fence may be open for you to enter; otherwise, you might need to ask someone in the building to unlock the gate for you.

After passing through the gate, take the trail for 0.1 mile, following the blue wooden posts to a junction with a bridge. Do not cross this bridge but stay straight, hiking until you reach a second bridge on your left and a neighborhood access trail on your right. Turn left, cross the bridge, and stay right on the trail. Follow the red wooden posts as the trail ascends a ridge.

In 0.1 mile pass a marker in the ground and a small platform. In 50 yards pass a substantial oak on your right as the trail comes to the

Escape the urban landscape with a walk through an old-growth forest.

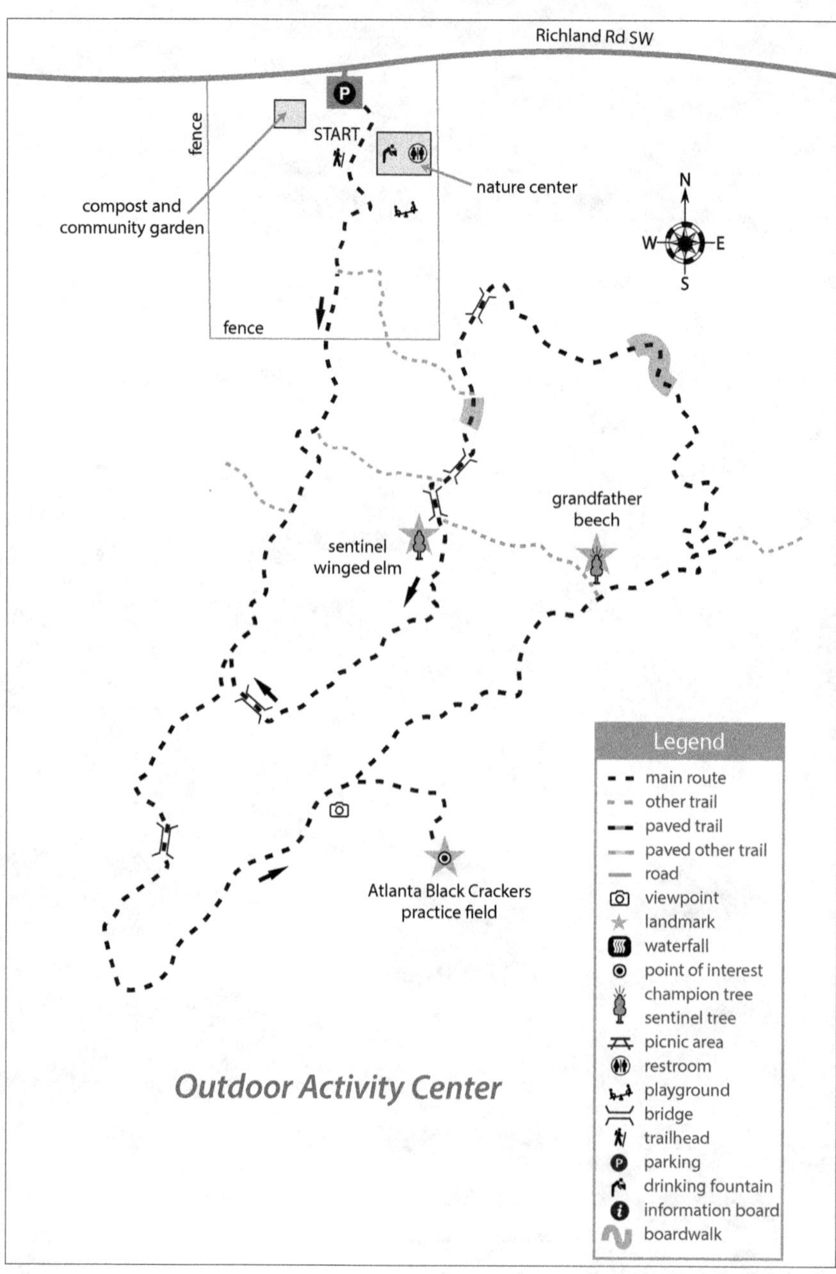
Richland Rd SW
fence
START
compost and
community garden
nature center
N
W
E
S
fence
grandfather
beech
sentinel
winged elm
Atlanta Black Crackers
practice field
Outdoor Activity Center
Legend
main route
other trail
paved trail
paved other trail
road
viewpoint
landmark
waterfall
point of interest
champion tree
sentinel tree
picnic area
restroom
playground
bridge
trailhead
parking
drinking fountain
information board
boardwalk

top of the ridge. In 100 yards reach an overlook with three benches. Just past this overlook, turn right on a small trail that leads 50 yards uphill to an open area that used to be the practice field for Atlanta's Negro League baseball team, the Atlanta Black Crackers. After visiting the field, return to the main trail and turn right to continue the loop.

In 0.1 mile reach a platform and benches surrounding the city champion Grandfather Beech. Go right at the tree and reach another junction. Stay left, following the yellow wooden posts. In 0.1 mile cross a small boardwalk across the bottom of the floodplain. In another 0.1 mile the trail curves to the left around a large white oak.

Continue on the trail, with the fence to your right, passing two gates on your right. Stay left at the junction, following the blue wooden post and crossing a boardwalk. Pass a granite signpost and cross two small bridges after the boardwalk ends. At the next junction, look to your right to see the sentinel winged elm. Then turn right and walk 0.1 mile to a junction with a bridge. Cross the bridge and turn right, returning to the fenceline in 0.1 mile. Go through the gate and follow this trail back to the parking lot to end your hike.

This peaceful nature trail is used regularly by the Westminster cross-country track team.

Paul Koshewa Trail

One of Atlanta's best hikes along Nancy Creek is on the campus of one of the city's exclusive private schools: The Westminster Schools. This cross-country course and nature trail is named after military hero and longtime track-and-field coach Colonel Paul Koshewa. Along the two-mile loop you'll see rock outcrops, peaceful running water, and quiet upland forests. Westminster allows its neighbors to use the trail, but because this trail is on private property, be sure to follow all rules posted on signs along the trail.

HOW TO GET THERE

Driving Distance from Downtown Atlanta: 10 miles

Address: 1424 West Paces Ferry Road NW, Atlanta, GA 30327

Nearest Interstate: I-75

Neighborhood: West Paces Ferry / Buckhead

Public Transit: MARTA 12 bus + 0.5-mile walk

Parking: The best trail parking is along the campus loop road (West Paces Ferry Road), just across from the Westminster facilities driveway; if the Westminster Schools gates are closed, you can find street parking near 3077 Clarendale Drive and get to the Koshewa Trail via an unofficial connector trail across from Sanders Memorial Baptist Church

HIKE DISTANCE

2-mile loop

DIFFICULTY

Overall: Moderate

Navigation: Trail is wide and easy to follow; no maps or trail markers, but mileage is posted at intervals

Terrain: Hard-packed gravel and dirt trails

Elevation Change: Rolling hills with several steep ascents and descents

SAFETY

Usage ★★★★☆

Visibility ★★★★☆

Upkeep ★★★★★

Parking ★★★★★

HOURS	Closed at dark
DOGS	Leashed dogs allowed
FACILITIES	• No toilets • No facilities open to public
FEES & PERMITS	None
LAND MANAGER	The Westminster Schools; this trail is on private property, and members of the public may use the trail at their own risk

Landmarks

NANCY CREEK ROCK LEDGE

This unusual rock outcrop overhangs the water of Nancy Creek. Erosion has created a gravity-defying visual effect. The rock is likely made up of gneiss, a metamorphic rock that is common in Atlanta.

SENTINEL SOUTHERN RED OAK

The trees along the Koshewa Trail are fairly young, but this large specimen is significantly older than the surrounding forest. You can recognize southern red oaks by the particularly skinny terminal lobes on their leaves.

CORSO ATLANTA VIEWPOINT

Near the end of this hike there is a break in the trees, and you get a view of the stunning buildings of Corso Atlanta, billed as Atlanta's most luxurious senior living community. This view reminds you that even after 2 miles of forested walking, you are still in Buckhead.

Hike Route

Start your hike where the Koshewa Trail crosses the physical plant driveway. With your back to the road, hike left on the trail. At the first junction in 100 yards, turn left and hike downhill to a junction at the edge of Nancy Creek. The Koshewa loop trail leads left, but first hike to the right on a small trail along the bank of the creek to reach an interesting rock ledge overhanging the creek. Then backtrack to the junction and continue on the trail under the bridge. The trail parallels the creek and skirts the edge of the Westminster sports

This is one of the most beautiful spots along Nancy Creek in the city.

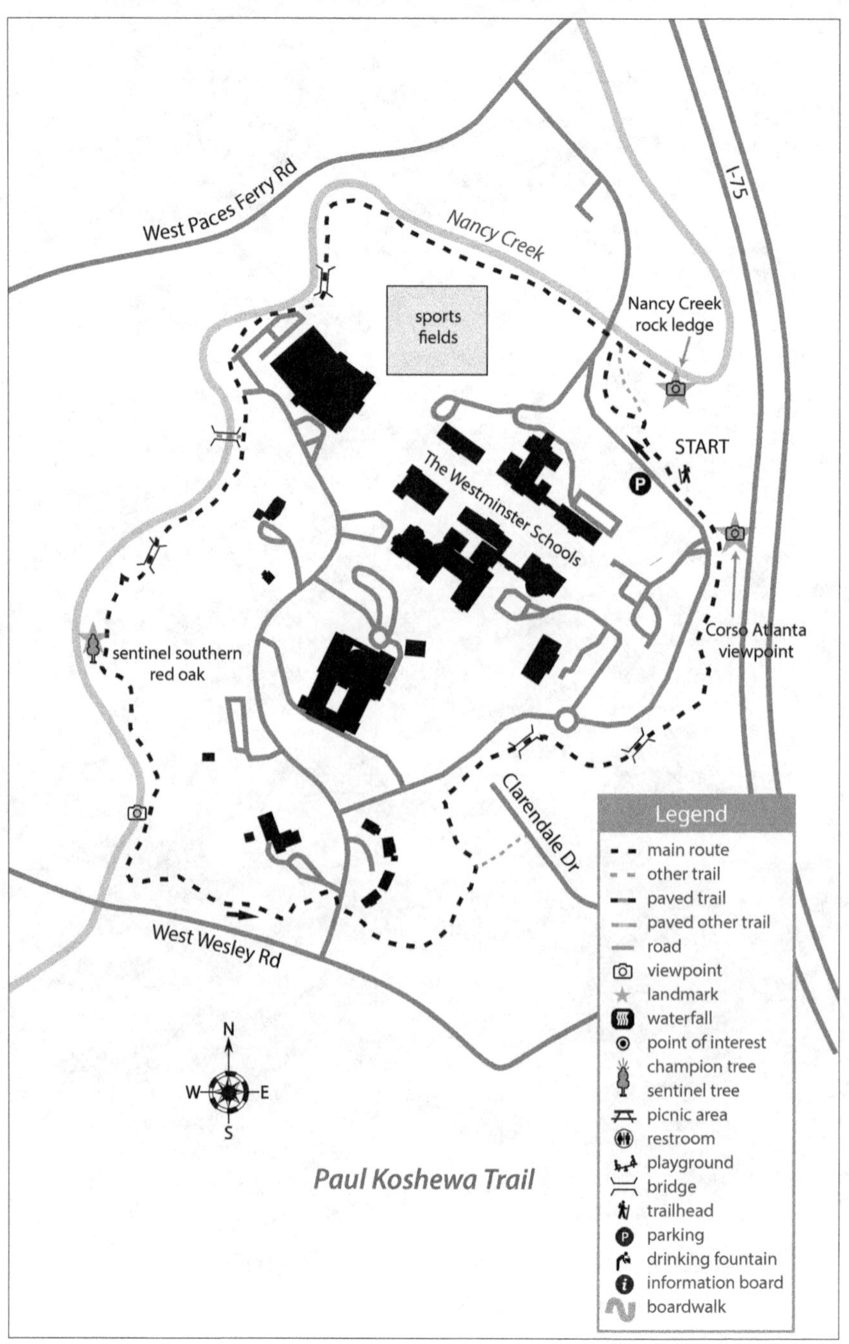
West Paces Ferry Rd
Nancy Creek
I-75
sports fields
Nancy Creek rock ledge
START
The Westminster Schools
Corso Atlanta viewpoint
sentinel southern red oak
Clarendale Dr
West Wesley Rd
N
W
E
S
Paul Koshewa Trail
Legend
main route
other trail
paved trail
paved other trail
road
viewpoint
landmark
waterfall
point of interest
champion tree
sentinel tree
picnic area
restroom
playground
bridge
trailhead
parking
drinking fountain
information board
boardwalk

complex for 0.25 mile, when the trail curves left and passes an emergency button.

Hike 0.1 mile to a bridge, then cross and turn right. The trail skirts the edge of a parking lot, dips down to the creek's edge, then skirts the parking lot again. After the parking lot, the trail curves right and passes under an elevated sewer pipe. To the right is a bridge over Nancy Creek that leads to Westminster's multiuse fields and ropes course. Stay straight for 0.2 mile to reach another emergency button. After passing the button, look on the right for a large sentinel southern red oak, just before the trail enters a clearing. This is one of the largest trees you'll pass on this hike.

After the clearing, stay right along the creek, passing an interesting rock outcrop. In 0.1 mile the trail curves left, away from the creek, and parallels West Wesley Road. Hike 0.2 mile to reach West Paces Ferry Road near Tull Hall. Cross the road at a crosswalk and hike back into the forest on a very steep uphill grade. Just after passing a 2.4-kilometer marker, look for a trail on your right. This side trail leads to Clarendale Drive in the adjacent neighborhood and is a good access point for the Koshewa Trail if Westminster's gates are closed.

Stay on the wide gravel trail as it curves downhill for 0.15 mile. After crossing a wooden bridge, hike steeply uphill 0.1 mile to a bench and a 2-kilometer marker. The trail descends to another bridge, then climbs again to the highest point on the trail, so close to I-75 you can hear the roar of the cars. From here, you have 0.2 mile left in your hike. Along the way, look to your right for a surprising view of the palatial buildings of Corso Atlanta. When you reach the physical plant driveway, your hike is complete.

Views of the Chattahoochee are a great reason to explore Riverwalk Atlanta.

Riverwalk Atlanta & Whittier Mill Park

This hike is more of an urban adventure than a walk in the park. The route includes an active railroad crossing, several utility clearings, and homemade bridges. This is the initial section of what will someday become Riverwalk Atlanta, a sweeping vision for human access and pedestrian connectivity along the Chattahoochee River corridor. Though the trails feel secluded and secret, a dedicated group of volunteers maintains the trails and removes invasive plants. Peaceful woods, giant champion trees, and river vistas will bring you back to this trail again and again. Each time you hike, look for progress being made by volunteers, and maybe you'll be inspired to pitch in.

HOW TO GET THERE

Driving Distance from Downtown Atlanta: 10 miles

Address: 2486 Paul Avenue NW, Atlanta, GA 30318

Nearest Interstate: I-285

Neighborhood: Riverside / Whittier Mill Village

Public Transit: MARTA 60 bus + 0.6-mile walk

Parking: Street parking just beyond the curve along Paul Avenue; the trail entrance is from a gravel lot and adjacent Georgia Power gravel road (there is an alternative entrance to these trails if you park at Whittier Mill Park on Wales Avenue)

HIKE DISTANCE

3-mile multiple figure-8 loop

DIFFICULTY

Overall: Moderate

Navigation: No maps or trail markers on this confusing network of trails

Terrain: Hard-packed dirt trails that can be muddy and overgrown, several wooden bridges, and a few gravel and grassy paths; this trail also includes an active railroad crossing

Elevation Change: Minimal elevation change—very level

SAFETY

Usage ★☆☆☆☆

Visibility ★☆☆☆☆

Upkeep ★★★☆☆

Parking ★☆☆☆☆

HOURS	Dawn to dusk
DOGS	Leashed dogs allowed
FACILITIES	None
FEES & PERMITS	This land is owned by Georgia Power
LAND MANAGER	These trails are on Georgia Power land and are adjacent to City of Atlanta's Lower Paul Park and Whittier Mill Park

Landmarks

CHATTAHOOCHEE VIEWPOINT

Access to Atlanta's famous river is transforming before our eyes. Since the late 1970s, when the federal government first started protecting the land on the banks of the river, Atlantans have been growing more and more interested in protecting the Chattahoochee. You might even see an adventurous soul kayaking in the current below you.

CITY CHAMPION SILVER MAPLE

- 176" circumference, 103' tall, 80' crown spread
- Wow, this is a big tree! Silver maples (*Acer saccharinum*) grow best in wet soil, so the Chattahoochee's floodplain is a perfect habitat for the largest silver maple in the whole city. This tree is almost 15 feet around and over 100 feet tall.

RIVER CANE AND PAWPAW GROVE

- City champion pawpaw: 23.5" circumference, 25' tall, 15' crown spread
- Before privet was introduced and took over many areas of the American South, river cane (a type of native bamboo) and pawpaw trees were among the most common plants growing up and down the Chattahoochee corridor. Here at Riverwalk Atlanta you'll pass between a stand of river cane and a grove of pawpaws that includes a city champion. Look up these native species and see if you can identify both.

Hike Route

Because these trails are not maintained by an official group, you'll need to pay attention to your surroundings and get your bearings based on two major landmarks: the Chattahoochee River and the railroad tracks. This route stays between the river and the tracks, so

Look for wildflowers and champion trees on this hike.

keep the river on your right for the first half, then the railroad tracks on your right for the second half. If you get turned around, find the railroad tracks and follow them back to your vehicle.

From the street parking on Paul Avenue, find a gravel access road with a gate and an empty gravel parking area near the curve on Paul Avenue. Walk through the gravel area toward the railroad tracks and skirt around a silt fence to reach an active railroad crossing on the gravel road. Carefully cross the tracks and then curve left on a mowed gravel track. In 100 yards reach a junction and turn right to hike along the edge of the Chattahoochee River with great views. Though no trail signs are posted, this trail has been named Levy Trail by volunteers.

In 100 yards reach another junction. Turn left onto the smaller trail and enter the woods, passing a city champion silver maple tree on the left. This forested trail meets back up with Levy Trail very soon. Turn left and pass a small trail on the right leading to a popular fishing spot and another viewpoint on the river. The rapids below you are created by a weir built to control river flow. Continue on Levy Trail, passing a stand of river cane—Atlanta's native bamboo species—on the right and a pawpaw grove on the left that includes a city champion pawpaw. In 0.1 mile stay straight on Levy Trail at a junction on the left and then straight at another junction immediately on the right.

In 100 yards Levy Trail jogs right and then left to cross a gas line clearing. Hike another 0.1 mile; the trail then curves left to reach a series of two bridges over O'Neal Creek. Cross the first bridge, then

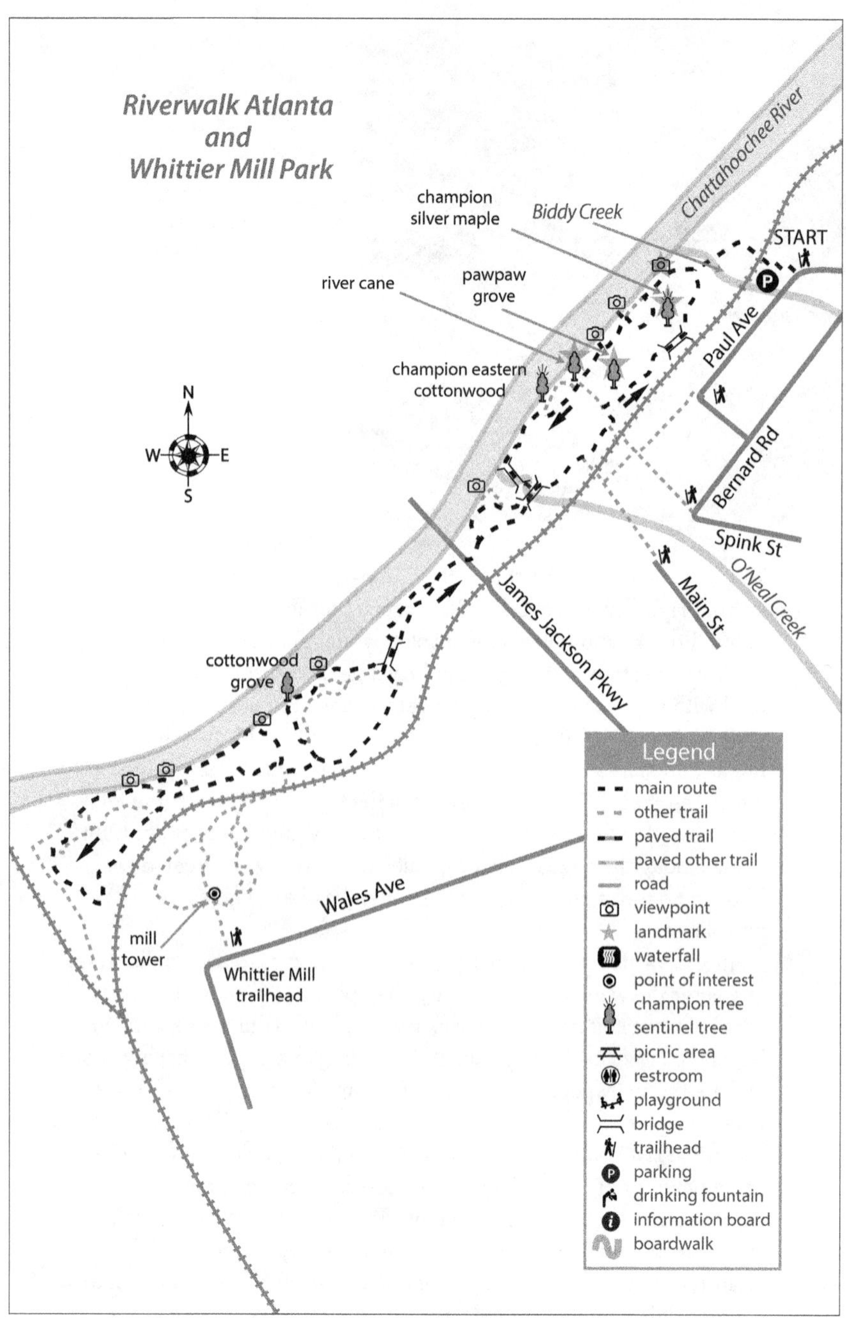
Riverwalk Atlanta
and
Whittier Mill Park
champion
silver maple
Biddy Creek
Chattahoochee River
START
river cane
pawpaw
grove
champion eastern
cottonwood
Paul Ave
Bernard Rd
Spink St
O'Neal Creek
Main St
James Jackson Pkwy
N
W
E
S
cottonwood
grove
Wales Ave
mill
tower
Whittier Mill
trailhead
Legend
main route
other trail
paved trail
paved other trail
road
viewpoint
landmark
waterfall
point of interest
champion tree
sentinel tree
picnic area
restroom
playground
bridge
trailhead
parking
drinking fountain
information board
boardwalk

turn to the right and cross the second and turn right again. In 100 yards pass two trails on the right that are often overgrown in the summer. In another 100 yards reach a junction next to a highway underpass. To the right is a trail under James Jackson Parkway that connects to an additional network of trails that are hikeable but less regularly maintained. You can stay left to circle back to your car, but this route continues to the right and under the James Jackson Parkway bridge.

Hike under the bridge and into the woods on the far side. In 100 yards turn right at a junction and hike 0.1 mile to the next junction, near a large water oak tree. Turn right and cross a makeshift wooden bridge. One hundred yards past the bridge, turn right and then immediately right again and hike downhill. This trail leads to a beautiful view of the Chattahoochee and then curves left to parallel the river. Stay right at the next junction and walk through a grove of giant cottonwood trees. Turn right at a junction in 0.1 mile. The next portion of the hike brings you back to the edge of the river. Walk parallel to the river and stay right at each junction until the trail enters a clearing and you can see a railroad bridge ahead of you.

Once in the clearing, look for trails on your left. You can take either one, but the second junction is the more direct trail. Turn left there and then stay right at each junction for 0.2 mile, when you'll reach a junction with a trail that crosses the railroad track on your right. The trail across the tracks leads to Whittier Mill Park. This route stays straight to parallel the tracks and return to Riverwalk Atlanta. Turn right at a junction in 100 yards. Hike another 0.15 mile, curve left, then turn right at the next junction, which leads downhill to the wooden bridge you crossed before. Turn right after crossing the bridge and right at one more junction to return to the James Jackson Parkway bridge.

On the far side of the bridge, enter the woods and turn right on the trails of Riverwalk Atlanta. In 0.1 mile arrive at the bridge over O'Neal Creek, cross, and turn right to follow the trail that parallels the railroad tracks. Volunteers have named this unmarked trail Trackside Trail. Stay on Trackside Trail as it crosses several gas line clearings. The trail then curves left to reach a junction in the woods. Go right to stay on Trackside Trail and hike 0.25 mile across a bridge to a junction in a clearing. Turn right and hike back to the railroad crossing and gravel lot to finish your hike.

Large, mostly intact ruins are fun to explore, and they allow us to ponder the history of the land.

Spink Collins Park

This park is a hidden gem in the Collins Park neighborhood in west Atlanta, and you'll not likely encounter many (if any) other hikers along this trail. Though less traveled, the 21-acre greenspace offers a breath of fresh air and seclusion in the woods. Hike past a creek, large boulders, mature trees, and stone ruins. While the park is still being developed, what it lacks in facilities it more than makes up for with an adventurous network of trails through the woods.

HOW TO GET THERE

Driving Distance from Downtown Atlanta: 11 miles
Address: 2101 Collins Drive NW, Atlanta, GA 30318
Neighborhood: Collins Park
Nearest Interstate: I-285
Public Transit: MARTA 60 bus + 0.2-mile walk
Parking: Limited street parking in a residential neighborhood

HIKE DISTANCE

1-mile loop

DIFFICULTY

Overall: Easy to moderate
Navigation: None
Terrain: Hard-packed dirt trail
Elevation Change: Rolling hills with a few short but steep ascents

SAFETY

Usage ★★☆☆☆
Visibility ★★★☆☆
Upkeep ★★★☆☆
Parking ★★★☆☆

HOURS

6:00 am to 11:00 pm

DOGS

Leashed dogs allowed

FACILITIES

- No toilets
- Playground, picnic tables, benches, trash cans, outdoor fitness equipment

FEES & PERMITS	None
LAND MANAGER	City of Atlanta Parks & Recreation

Landmarks

STONE RUINS

This mostly intact stone foundation and brick chimney are a pleasant surprise just off the trail. This was once a lodge built by one of the oldest Boy Scout troops in Atlanta.

LEANING SENTINEL TULIP TREE

Hard to miss, this large sentinel tulip tree (commonly known as tulip poplar) leans over the trail before you enter a grove of ferns at the bottom of the floodplain. There are several large tulip trees in this area, but this one leans charismatically over the trail.

SENTINEL BEECH

Though you'll pass several mature beech trees on this hike, this one stands out for obvious reasons. The huge hollow in the trunk evokes a spooky feeling. Trees can develop large cavities made by animals, storm damage, insects, or illness and decay. Healthy trees can usually heal and continue to live and grow normally.

Hike Route

Park on the street and enter the park. Turn left at the wooden information board and take the trail down to the playground. Just behind the playground take the small trail leading into the woods. This trail parallels a tributary of Whetstone Creek and passes outdoor fitness equipment. In the summer, the trail is lined with jewelweed, the natural remedy for poison ivy. In 0.15 mile pass a double-trunked sweetgum on the right.

Continue on the trail as it curves slightly to the left and over a small bridge. Hike past a forked tulip tree on the right as the trail curves right, away from the creek. The trail continues slightly uphill with the fence on the left. In 0.1 mile, just past another fitness station, take the small trail on the left. If you find yourself back at the entrance and picnic tables, you've gone too far.

The trail ascends past large boulders. Then hike downhill to a floodplain and curve to the right past the large leaning sentinel tulip tree immediately off the trail. The trail narrows as you walk along the

A spooky beech hollow grabs your attention on this hike.

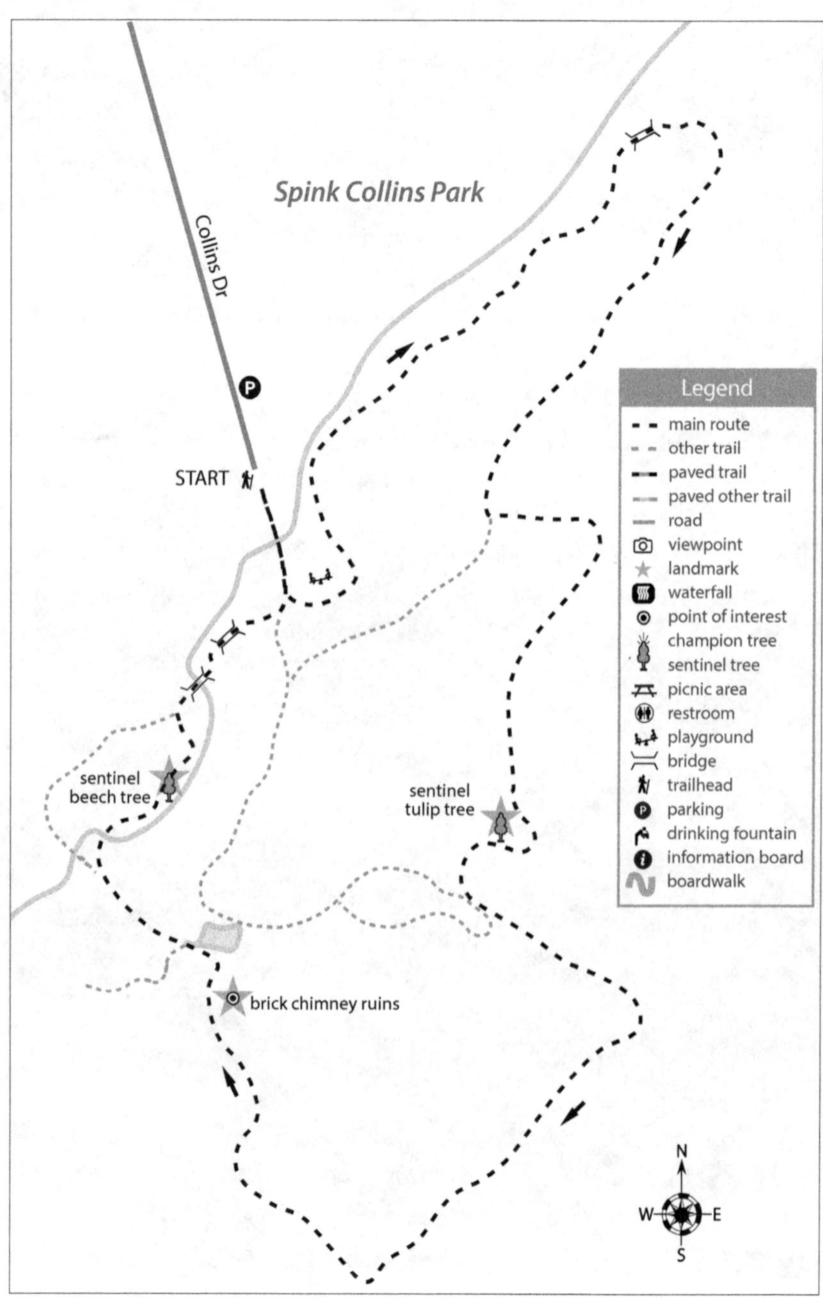
Spink Collins Park
Collins Dr
START
sentinel beech tree
sentinel tulip tree
brick chimney ruins
Legend
main route
other trail
paved trail
paved other trail
road
viewpoint
landmark
waterfall
point of interest
champion tree
sentinel tree
picnic area
restroom
playground
bridge
trailhead
parking
drinking fountain
information board
boardwalk
N
W
E
S

creek bank through a colony of ferns. Walk through a grove of several large old-growth tulip trees before coming to a junction.

Go left and hike uphill past overgrown picnic tables on the left. At the top of the hill, turn right and walk along an old road. In 100 feet, just before the trail reaches the power lines, turn right and head back into the forest. There is a fire hydrant here that is a good marker for the trail. Follow the trail as it winds downhill, providing a view of the meadow under the power lines before it curves back into the forest.

Soon you'll reach an old stone structure and brick chimney, the remains of an old Boy Scout lodge. After exploring the structure, continue on the trail to reach a four-way junction. Stay straight. In 50 feet, at another junction, stay to the right and come to a sentinel beech with a large hollow in the trunk. Continue on the trail, crossing a bridge and immediately turning right over another bridge to a picnic area and stone chimney. Follow the trail up the stairs to the playground and picnic tables. Turn left to leave the park and end your hike.

ON THE PERIMETER—WESTSIDE

The Civil War–era Concord Woolen Mill is an interesting historic relic to explore.

Heritage Park

Heritage Park is a great place to escape into the woods from the crowded pavement of the popular Silver Comet Trail. This hike passes the ruins of the historic Concord Woolen Mill on Nickajack Creek, destroyed by Union forces during the Civil War because it produced uniforms for the Confederate army. The far end of the trail brings you to a small waterfall, a covered bridge, and information about the Battle of Ruff's Mill.

HOW TO GET THERE

Driving Distance from Downtown Atlanta: 16 miles
Address: 60 Fontaine Road SW, Mableton, GA 30126
Neighborhood: Mableton
Nearest Interstate: I-285
Public Transit: CobbLinc 25 bus + 2.5-mile walk
Parking: Paved parking lot at the corner of Nickajack Road and Fontaine Road

HIKE DISTANCE

4-mile out-and-back

DIFFICULTY

Overall: Easy to moderate
Navigation: Infrequent posts and maps along the route
Terrain: Wide gravel and hard-packed dirt trails, plus a boardwalk
Elevation Change: Minimal elevation change

SAFETY

Usage ★★★★☆
Visibility ★★★★☆
Upkeep ★★★★★
Parking ★★★★★

HOURS

Sunrise to sunset

DOGS

Leashed dogs allowed

FACILITIES

- Toilets
- Water fountain, picnic tables

FEES & PERMITS	None
LAND MANAGER	Cobb County Parks & Recreation

Landmarks

SENTINEL BEECH

Just before beginning the hike, stop to look at this enormous American beech tree on the right. This tree's smooth gray bark is relatively unblemished by graffiti, a rare sight compared to many other trees of its species.

SENTINEL RED MAPLE AND BOX ELDER

These two trees grow almost as one at the end of the bridge over Nickajack Creek. At first glance, it appears that poison ivy is growing in the red maple tree, but closer inspection shows it is just shoots of the box elder, whose leaves resemble the poisonous plant.

CONCORD WOOLEN MILL RUINS

You can get up close and explore the ruins of the woolen mill, which is close to the trail. Historically, this mill had nearly four hundred spindles in operation.

Hike Route

Begin your hike at the far left end of the parking lot along Nickajack Road. Just before entering the trail, pass a sentinel beech tree on the right, directly behind a bench.

On this first section of the hike you will notice labeled native plants, courtesy of volunteers from the Georgia Native Plant Society. Follow the trail as it descends to the floodplain, then reaches a boardwalk in 0.1 mile. In the late summer and spring, you may catch glimpses of native butterflies pollinating flowers. Follow the boardwalk for 0.15 mile, cross a bridge over Nickajack Creek, then turn left. Immediately on the left next to the bridge is a sentinel red maple and box elder.

Follow this trail along the creek for 1.15 miles, passing a few good spots to view the creek and crossing two bridges. Turn left at a junction with a gravel access road on the right, then reach the mill ruins in less than 100 yards.

Take the trail to the right as it comes to a picnic table and passes between the two mill buildings propped up by steel girders. On the

Long boardwalks through the wetland provide views of native plants and pollinators.

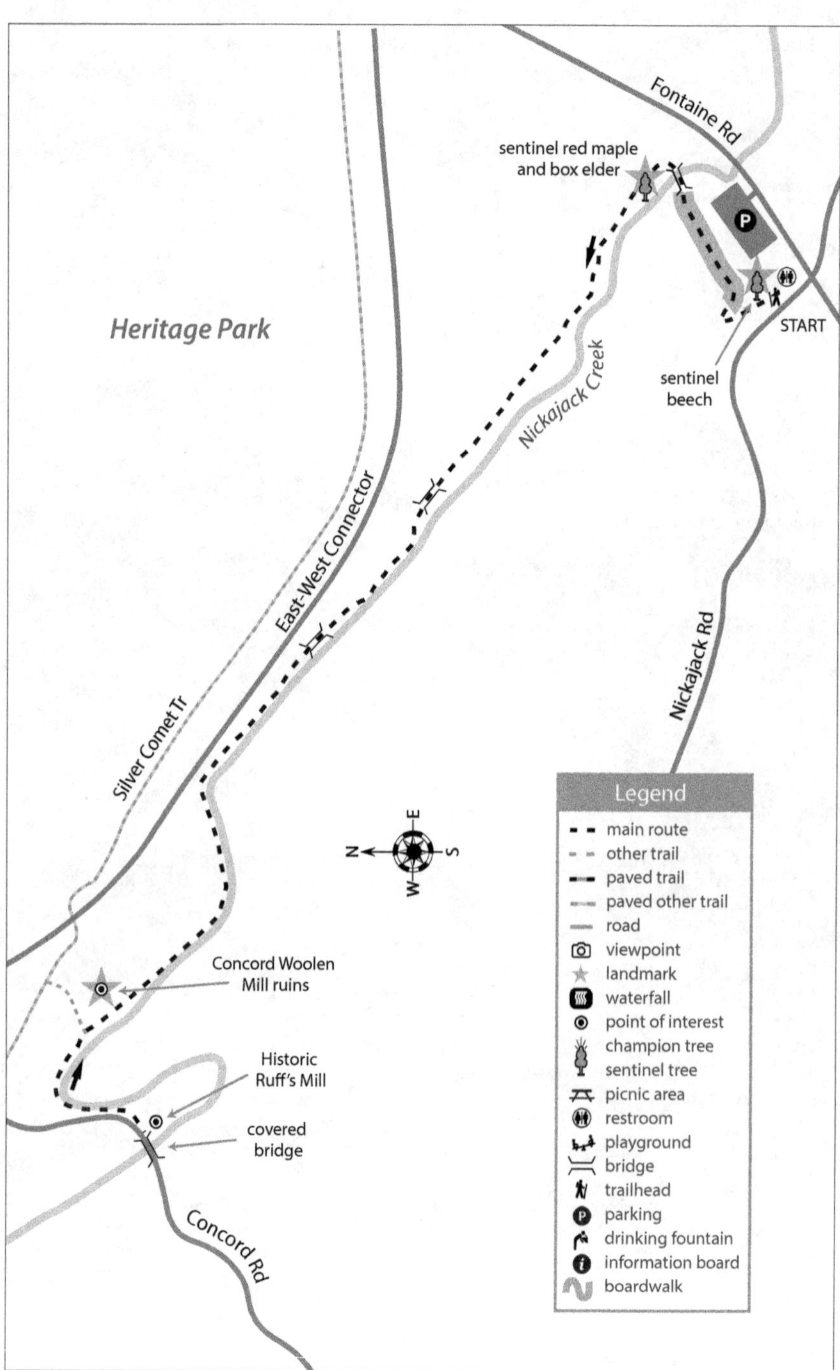
Fontaine Rd
sentinel red maple
and box elder
START
Heritage Park
sentinel
beech
Nickajack Creek
East-West Connector
Nickajack Rd
Silver Comet Tr
Legend
main route
other trail
paved trail
paved other trail
road
viewpoint
landmark
waterfall
point of interest
champion tree
sentinel tree
picnic area
restroom
playground
bridge
trailhead
parking
drinking fountain
information board
boardwalk
N
S
E
W
Concord Woolen
Mill ruins
Historic
Ruff's Mill
covered
bridge
Concord Rd

right are two small trails that connect to the Silver Comet Trail. Stay to the left, passing a map sign. Thirty yards from the end of the ruins is a large tulip tree on the left. Continue straight at a junction with an access road. In 100 feet, at a junction with a small trail on the right, continue straight, hiking across wooden planks. In 0.1 mile the trail ends at the Concord Road covered bridge and a historical marker about the Battle of Ruff's Mill. Below you is a small waterfall on Nickajack Creek.

Turn around here and retrace your steps to the mill ruins, then continue back to the Nickajack Creek bridge and the boardwalk, which leads to the parking area, where your hike ends.

BELTLINE CONNECTIONS–WESTSIDE

Hike through lush green
undergrowth in the summer.

Lionel Hampton Park & Beecher Hills Park

This hike takes you along a creek, through a Civil War–era Union army trench line, and past stunning mature trees. The paved, multiuse trail is also a connection to the Beltline's Westside Trail. Lionel Hampton was a jazz musician and the previous owner of this beautiful land. The 100-acre nature preserve spans two parks: one named for Hampton and one named after the local Beecher Hills neighborhood. Both parks are rich in history and natural beauty.

HOW TO GET THERE	**Driving Distance from Downtown Atlanta:** 6 miles **Address:** 2257 Bolling Brook Drive SW, Atlanta, GA 30311 (this is the address for Beecher Hills Elementary School, which is the closest address for the trailhead) **Neighborhood:** Beecher Hills **Nearest Interstate:** I-20 **Public Transit:** MARTA 68 bus + 0.5-mile walk **Parking:** Street parking on Bolling Brook Drive SW or parking at Beecher Hills Elementary School on the weekends
HIKE DISTANCE	3-mile figure-8 loop
DIFFICULTY	**Overall:** Moderate **Navigation:** PATH markers along paved route and metal posts with images along dirt trails **Terrain:** Paved multiuse path and compact dirt trails **Elevation Change:** Rolling hills, but no major ascents or descents
SAFETY	**Usage** ★★★★☆ **Visibility** ★★★☆☆ **Upkeep** ★★★★★ **Parking** ★★★☆☆
HOURS	6:00 am to 11:00 pm
DOGS	Leashed dogs allowed
FACILITIES	• No toilets • Trash cans, playground, water fountain

FEES & PERMITS	None
LAND MANAGER	City of Atlanta Parks & Recreation in partnership with West Atlanta Watershed Alliance

Landmarks

PAWPAW PATCH

Pawpaw is a native but lesser known Georgia fruit. Pawpaws are understory trees and grow clonally, so an entire pawpaw patch might be one organism. The trees produce a creamy, green fruit that ripens at the end of summer. This patch is between the paved path and Utoy Creek.

CITY CHAMPION BITTERNUT HICKORY

- 119" circumference, 116' tall, 50' crown spread
- Also called "swamp hickory" because it grows best in moist valleys, a bitternut hickory has hard, durable wood that is valued for lumber. This champion hickory is about 20 yards off the path.

SENTINEL TULIP TREE

From the path, the only obvious feature of this tulip tree (commonly known as tulip poplar) is its impressive size. But when you view it from behind, you'll see it has a massive cavern that stretches nearly the entire length of the trunk.

Hike Route

Enter the trailhead at the dead end of Bolling Brook Drive onto the paved multiuse Southwest Connector Trail. Follow the trail as it runs parallel to Utoy Creek. In 0.25 mile cross a small bridge and enter a small field with a beautiful winged elm on the right just off the path. Winged elms are identifiable by their broad wing-shaped branches. Cross a second bridge and at the junction go left, following the signs for Lionel Hampton Trail.

In 100 feet there is a large three-trunked sweetgum on the left, just off the bank of the creek. Right next to it is a patch of pawpaw trees. In the late summer, you can spot the mature green fruits on the branches. Pawpaw is a Georgia native, and its fruits fall to the ground when ripe and make a tasty (though messy) trail treat. Continue on the path as it ascends slightly before crossing under the power lines. In 100 feet at the next junction, go left off of Southwest Connector Trail and onto Lionel Hampton Trail.

Some trail junctions are marked with found objects.

In 100 feet at a four-way junction with the paved path and gravel trails, go right into the forest on the gravel trail. In 50 feet at a junction, take the trail on the right marked with a no dirt bikes sign and tree stumps decorated with found objects. Follow this narrow trail as it snakes uphill through the woods, transporting you to a dense forest. It is hard to believe that this forest is only a few miles from the highway.

In 0.25 mile go right at a junction. There's a small side trail immediately on the left in a few feet, but stay on the main path. Depending on the time of year and amount of rain, you may be lucky enough to see a variety of mushrooms sprouting on the ground as you continue your hike.

In 0.4 mile at the next junction with a signpost, go left and then left again at a junction with a display of old glass bottles on a rack to the right. Follow the trail downhill for 100 feet. Before you curve to the right, look straight ahead 20 yards off the path to see the city champion bitternut hickory. It's the largest tree in this immediate area.

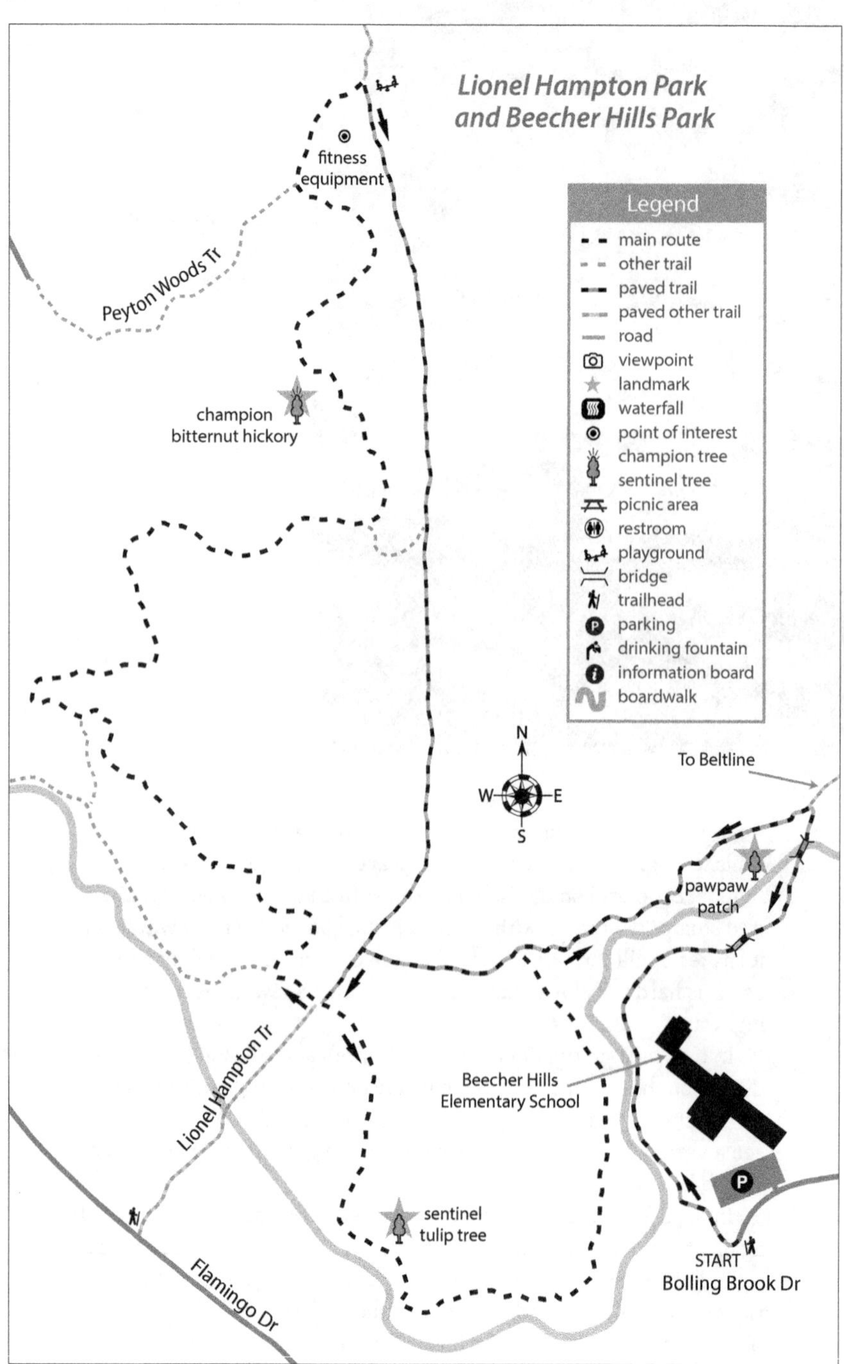

Lionel Hampton Park and Beecher Hills Park
Legend
main route
other trail
paved trail
paved other trail
road
viewpoint
landmark
waterfall
point of interest
champion tree
sentinel tree
picnic area
restroom
playground
bridge
trailhead
parking
drinking fountain
information board
boardwalk
fitness equipment
Peyton Woods Tr
champion bitternut hickory
N
W
E
S
To Beltline
pawpaw patch
Beecher Hills Elementary School
Lionel Hampton Tr
sentinel tulip tree
START
Bolling Brook Dr
Flamingo Dr

Turn right and continue for 0.3 mile to the next junction, then go right once more. The trail joins with the paved Lionel Hampton Trail at the playground in 50 yards.

Go right, passing the playground and outdoor fitness equipment. The trail descends, and as you hike along the path, look on your right, and you'll see a Union army trench line that dates from 1864, during the Civil War. About 0.3 mile from the playground, you'll find a blue marker labeling the site. When you reach the junction for Southwest Connector Trail, go straight for 100 feet to again reach the four-way gravel trail / paved trail junction. This time, go left onto the gravel path along Utoy Creek.

In 0.2 mile pass several beautiful mature beech trees on your right along the edge of the creek. Immediately to your left is a staggering sentinel tulip tree, so tall that it is hard to see its crown from the forest floor. Continue on the trail as it crosses under the power lines and back into the forest. Hike the trail through the floodplain for 0.2 mile before the trail reconnects with the paved Southwest Connector Trail. Go right, following the trail back the way you came, bearing right, to reach Bolling Brook Drive and end your hike.

The wide, shady trails make this an excellent path for all types of outdoor activities.

Proctor Creek Greenway

This scenic trail runs along Proctor Creek through the Grove Park neighborhood and will soon connect to the Westside Beltline Trail. Enjoy large trees, native edible plants such as elderberry, and long, shady stretches of trail. This hike is favored by bikers, joggers, and dog walkers for its mostly flat, wide paved path. This route follows the more shaded north section of the trail, but to add extra miles to your hike, you can also hike the south section of the greenway to the Bankhead MARTA Station. For a full afternoon of outdoor fun, bring a picnic and a blanket and enjoy views of the Atlanta skyline from Westside Park (page 265).

HOW TO GET THERE

Driving Distance from Downtown Atlanta: 7 miles

Address: 1660 Johnson Road NW, Atlanta, GA 30318

Neighborhood: Grove Park

Nearest Interstate: I-20

Public Transit: You can access the southern end of this trail directly from the MARTA Bankhead Station

Parking: Two large paved parking lots within Westside Park

HIKE DISTANCE

3-mile out-and-back

DIFFICULTY

Overall: Easy to moderate

Navigation: Trail markers along the path; maps posted inside Westside Park

Terrain: Paved multiuse trail

Elevation Change: Mostly flat; minimal elevation change

SAFETY

Usage ★★★★☆

Visibility ★★★★☆

Upkeep ★★★★★

Parking ★★★★★

HOURS

Dawn to dusk

DOGS

Leashed dogs allowed; dog park off Sanford Drive

FACILITIES	• Toilets in Westside Park • Benches and bike racks; water fountains, playgrounds, picnic areas, and maps in Westside Park
FEES & PERMITS	None
LAND MANAGER	City of Atlanta Parks & Recreation

Landmarks

SENTINEL WATER OAK

This massive water oak is growing at the base of a hill at the edge of the Boyd Elementary parking lot. With limited competition from other trees, it has been able to grow without restriction.

SENTINEL LOBLOLLY PINE

Incredibly large for this species, this pine is right on the side of the trail. Loblolly pines can be distinguished from other pine species by their 5- to 8-inch needles, which grow in bundles of three.

SENTINEL EASTERN COTTONWOOD

Cottonwood trees are fairly common in North America and can usually be found by water sources. In the summer they produce tiny, cotton-like seeds that are dispersed by the wind. This tree is growing right on the creekbank at almost a 45-degree angle.

Hike Route

Start your hike at the Westside Reservoir parking lot. Facing the *Birth of Atlanta* art installation, take the wide asphalt path to the right. In 0.2 mile this trail intersects with Proctor Creek Greenway at map D7. Turn right onto the paved multiuse path near a Proctor Creek Greenway sign.

Cross a bridge in 0.2 mile and follow the trail as it curves to the right. Along the greenway, you'll pass large patches of elderberry. In the summer you'll notice the dark berries lining the path. In 0.4 mile the path passes under power lines, bringing you to a grove of mature water oaks behind a residential neighborhood.

Continue straight. Just after mile marker 2.64, the trail curves right and then intersects with Johnson Road. Carefully cross to the other side and stop. Look to your right onto the school property: about 100 feet away, at the bottom of a hill, is a massive sentinel water oak.

A large water oak casts its shadow over the hillside.

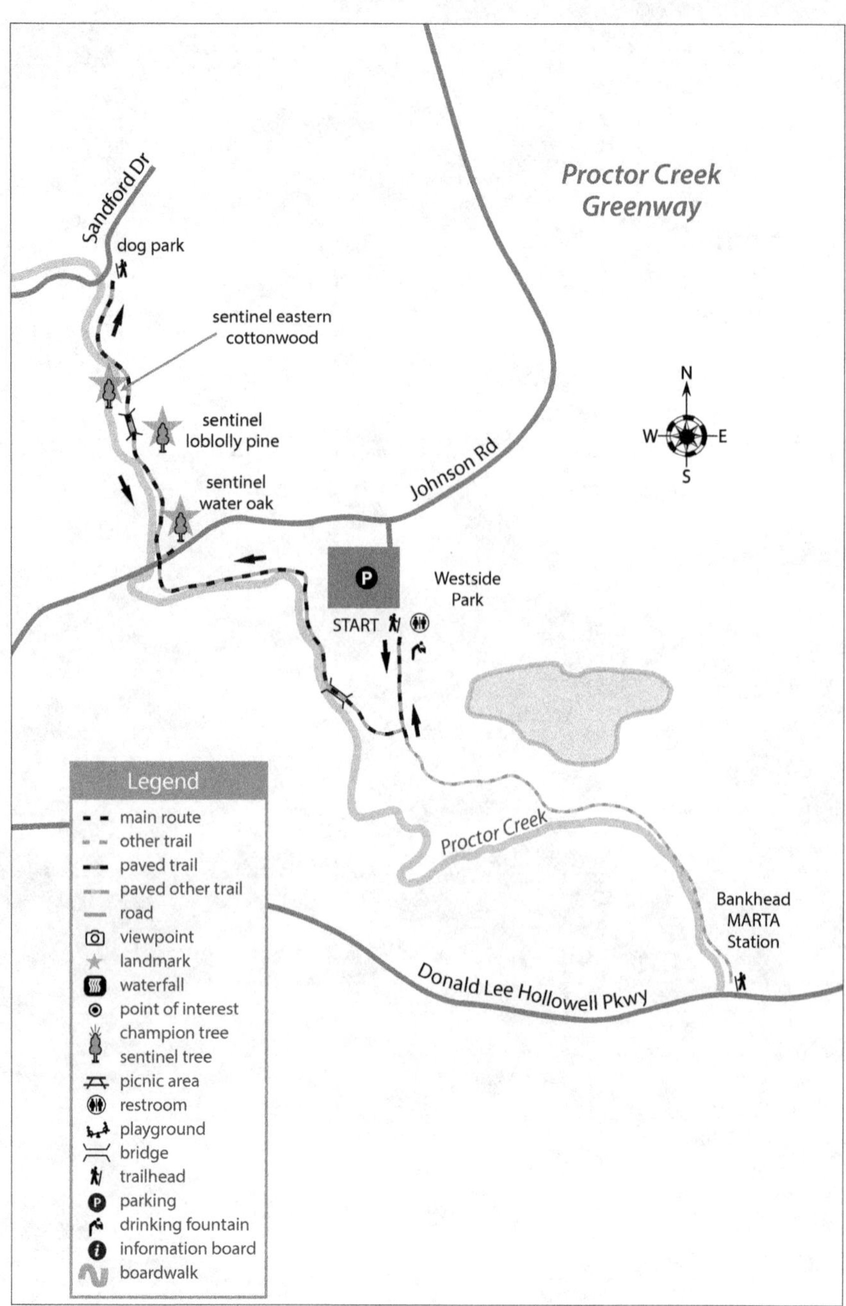
Proctor Creek
Greenway
Sandford Dr
dog park
sentinel eastern
cottonwood
sentinel
loblolly pine
sentinel
water oak
Johnson Rd
Westside
Park
START
N
W
E
S
Proctor Creek
Bankhead
MARTA
Station
Donald Lee Hollowell Pkwy
Legend
main route
other trail
paved trail
paved other trail
road
viewpoint
landmark
waterfall
point of interest
champion tree
sentinel tree
picnic area
restroom
playground
bridge
trailhead
parking
drinking fountain
information board
boardwalk

After marveling at the tree, continue your hike on the paved path, away from Johnson Road. In 0.2 mile, just before reaching a field and chain-link fence, pass a sentinel loblolly pine on your right. Reenter the forest and hike to the next bridge. As you cross, look for a sentinel eastern cottonwood tree leaning over the tributary creek on the left.

In another 0.1 mile the tree canopy opens up as the trail winds behind a housing development and residential area. In 0.3 mile the trail ends at Sandford Drive near a dog park and a mature mimosa tree at the edge of the streambank. The flowers and bark of mimosa trees are used in Chinese medicine as an herbal supplement for heart health. Turn around and return the way you came, about 1.5 mile, to reach the trail leading back into Westside Park. At this junction, you can turn left to return to your vehicle and end your hike.

To extend your hike, continue straight onto the southern section of the Proctor Creek Greenway, which stretches another 1.5 mile through power line clearings, across an elevated walkway, and past a unique rocky section of Proctor Creek. The trail terminates at the Bankhead MARTA Station, where it will someday connect with the Westside Beltline.

Take in the view of the Atlanta skyline and the quarry reservoir all at once.

Westside Park

Westside Park is one of Atlanta's newest and largest public parks. It features over two miles of paved, multiuse trails, open fields, and playgrounds. The park's trails connect to the historic Grove Park neighborhood and someday soon to the Westside Beltline. The centerpiece of the park is the 35.5-acre reservoir. The City of Atlanta purchased the land, previously a quarry site, from Bellwood Quarry in 2006. Westside Park is both a reminder of Atlanta's history and a beacon for its future.

HOW TO GET THERE

Driving Distance from Downtown Atlanta: 7 miles
Address: 1660 Johnson Road NW, Atlanta, GA 30318
Neighborhood: Grove Park
Nearest Interstate: I-20
Public Transit: MARTA Bankhead Station + 1.5-mile walk on the Proctor Creek Greenway
Parking: Two large paved parking lots

HIKE DISTANCE

2-mile loop

DIFFICULTY

Overall: Moderate
Navigation: Maps, color-coded posts, numbered circular markers on the ground along trails
Terrain: Paved multiuse path
Elevation Change: Rolling hills with a few short but steep ascents and descents

SAFETY

Usage ★★★★★
Visibility ★★★★★
Upkeep ★★★★★
Parking ★★★★★

HOURS

6:00 am to 11:00 pm

DOGS

Leashed dogs allowed

FACILITIES

- Toilets in multiple locations around the park

- Water fountains, playgrounds, picnic tables, pavilions, maps, benches, bike racks

FEES & PERMITS None

LAND MANAGER City of Atlanta Parks & Recreation

Landmarks

GATEWAY ARCH

You'll pass through this skeletal installation, which is not quite a tunnel, not quite a bridge, to enter the park. The work of Portman Architects, the Gateway Arch is made of over 60 tons of steel and is a unique way to enter a unique park.

GRAND OVERLOOK VIEW & RESERVOIR

Formerly the site of Bellwood Quarry, the current reservoir was filled with water in April 2020. From after the Civil War until the 1940s, the quarry was part of the Bellwood convict labor camp.

BIRTH OF ATLANTA SCULPTURE

Commissioned in 1996 for the Centennial Olympic Games, the artwork is an abstract representation of a phoenix, the unofficial symbol of Atlanta—a city that rose from the ashes after being burned during the Civil War.

Hike Route

Start at the *Birth of Atlanta* art installation, which can be seen from the parking lot by the bathrooms and pavilion. The installation features repurposed materials from the Olympics and from Underground Atlanta and welcomes visitors to the park.

This hike follows the purple route on the maps. Each map is labeled with a letter and number code. To begin from the D2 map, facing the *Birth of Atlanta* installation, take the wide, asphalt multiuse trail to the right. At map D5 in 100 feet, with your back to the map, take the concrete trail to the right that slopes uphill, parallel to the asphalt trail. Follow the path to the top of the hill, and at map D6 take the short loop trail on the right that leads to the grand overlook. From here you'll have a phenomenal view of the reservoir and Atlanta skyline. The reservoir holds up to 2.4 billion gallons of water and is 400 feet deep. For reference, all of the Mercedes-Benz Stadium could fit

The Birth of Atlanta ***installation marks the start of this hike.***

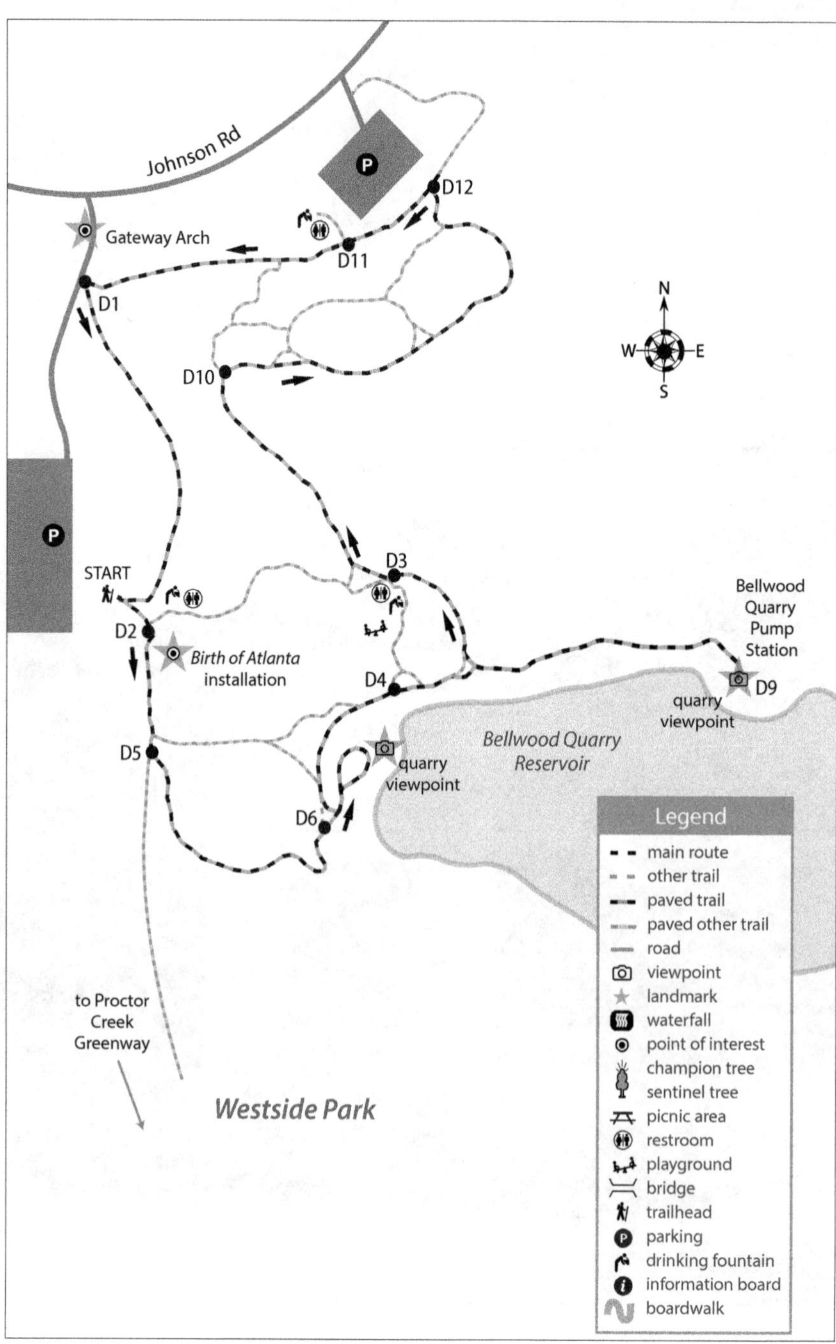

Johnson Rd
P
D12
Gateway Arch
D11
D1
N
W
E
S
D10
P
START
D3
Bellwood
Quarry
Pump
Station
D2
Birth of Atlanta
installation
D4
D9
quarry
viewpoint
Bellwood Quarry
Reservoir
D5
quarry
viewpoint
D6
Legend
main route
other trail
paved trail
paved other trail
road
viewpoint
landmark
waterfall
point of interest
champion tree
sentinel tree
picnic area
restroom
playground
bridge
trailhead
parking
drinking fountain
information board
boardwalk
to Proctor
Creek
Greenway
Westside Park

inside it. The reservoir is supplied by the Chattahoochee River via five miles of underground tunnels and could provide 30 days of emergency water reserves.

Return to the main trail at map D6 and continue to the right downhill, staying right at an immediate junction. As you hike, you'll notice several large rock boulders that likely came from the quarry. At the bottom of the hill continue straight past map D4, then past two more forks in the trail to hike North Rim Trail. This trail leads 0.1 mile along the edge of the reservoir past several viewpoints and a pond to reach the pump house and map D9. Enjoy the views of the reservoir, then turn around and hike back to the first junction you come to.

Turn right and hike about 50 feet to a restroom, playground, and picnic pavilion at map D3. With your back to the map, take a soft right on the trail that leads uphill in a steep incline.

Ascend steeply past two benches, then at the top of the hill stay right at map D10. Keep the open fields to your left and follow the green posts as the trail circles around the fields, passing numerous boulders. You can catch another view of the Atlanta skyline here.

In 100 yards, as the trail curves around the far field, take the first right to reach map D12 at the parking lot. Facing the map, take the trail behind you parallel to the parking lot toward the bathrooms. Just past the bathrooms, find map D11 and hike the trail on the right. When the trail forks near trail marker R08, take the fork that leads downhill to the right. At the bottom of the hill, at map D1, you'll get another view of the entrance gateway you drove through to enter the park. Architect Pierluca Maffey, who worked on the gateway, describes it as "an opportunity to pause and enjoy the moment." After taking a moment to view the gateway, go left at map D1 and follow the red posts along a wide asphalt path back to the *Birth of Atlanta* art installation and parking lot to end your hike.

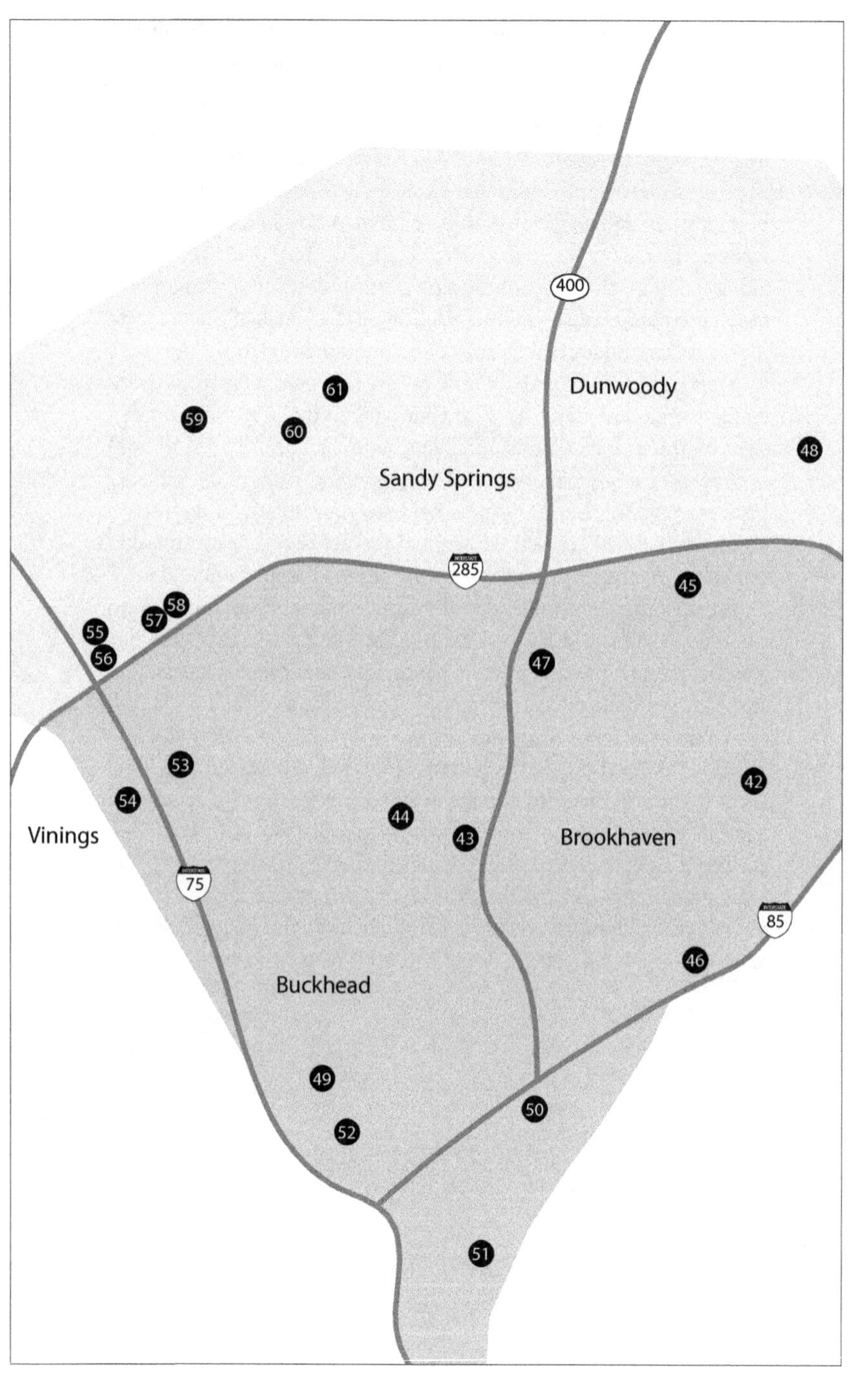
400
Dunwoody
61
59
60
48
Sandy Springs
285
45
58
57
55
56
47
53
42
54
44
43
Vinings
Brookhaven
75
85
46
Buckhead
49
50
52
51

NORTHSIDE

- 42 Ashford Forest Preserve
- 43 Blue Heron Nature Preserve
- 44 Chastain Memorial Park
- 45 Murphey Candler Park
- 46 Peachtree Creek Greenway
- 47 Ridgeview Park
- 48 Brook Run Park & Pernoshal Park
- 49 Atlanta Memorial Park
- 50 Confluence Trail & Cheshire Farm Trail
- 51 Piedmont Park & Eastside Beltline
- 52 Tanyard Creek Park & Northside Beltline
- 53 East Palisades
- 54 West Palisades
- 55 Bob Callan Trail
- 56 Rottenwood Creek Trail
- 57 Cochran Shoals
- 58 Powers Island
- 59 Sope Creek
- 60 Johnson Ferry South
- 61 Johnson Ferry North & Hyde Farm

Spring wildflowers such as trillium flourish at Ashford Forest Preserve.

Ashford Forest Preserve

This is one of north DeKalb's newer parks, but the land has a long and rich history—the homeland of the Muscogee (Creek) people, farmland, the site of Camp Gordon during World War I, and part of the runway protection zone for the Peachtree DeKalb Airport. Today, you'll find a mature, relatively undisturbed forest that includes springs, a small creek, native wildflowers, mature trees, and pleasant hiking trails. And if you want more miles, you can continue your hike at Georgian Hills Park, only 0.25 mile south on Clairmont Road from the preserve entrance.

HOW TO GET THERE	**Driving Distance from Downtown Atlanta:** 12 miles **Address:** 3890 Clairmont Road, Brookhaven, GA 30341 **Nearest Interstate:** I-85 **Neighborhood:** Brookhaven **Public Transit:** MARTA 19 bus + 0.1-mile walk **Parking:** Large fenced gravel parking area across the street from the Peachtree DeKalb Airport
HIKE DISTANCE	1.5-mile figure-8 loop
DIFFICULTY	**Overall:** Easy to moderate **Navigation:** No maps or regular trail markers; there are three wooden signs that point toward trailheads **Terrain:** Main trails are wide, but certain side trails are narrow and can be overgrown in summer; surface is hard-packed dirt or mulch and can be muddy after rain **Elevation Change:** Mostly flat with a few minor hills
SAFETY	**Usage** ★★★☆☆ **Visibility** ★★★☆☆ **Upkeep** ★★★☆☆ **Parking** ★★★★☆
HOURS	7:00 am to sunset
DOGS	Leashed dogs allowed; many locals do not follow this rule, so be prepared to meet off-leash dogs in this park

FACILITIES	• No toilets • Dog waste station, trash cans, benches
FEES & PERMITS	None
LAND MANAGER	City of Brookhaven Parks & Recreation

Landmarks

RAVINE

The ravine is the most undisturbed and biodiverse area in this park. Look for giant oak and tulip trees growing along a small stream. In the spring, keep your eye out for ephemeral flowers such as Solomon's seal, trillium, and bloodroot.

SENTINEL TWIN TULIP TREES

Tulip trees (commonly known as tulip poplars) are some of the tallest-growing trees in the metro Atlanta area. These two are growing on either side of the trail, almost serving as a welcome gate from the park's Skyland Drive entrance.

HISTORIC RUNWAY LIGHT

In 1917, when Camp Gordon was built where the Peachtree DeKalb Airport stands today, runway approach lights were installed in the farmland across Clairmont Road. You can still find one of these runway lights in the woods along the trails of Ashford Forest Preserve.

Hike Route

There are currently no signs leading onto trails from the gravel parking lot. Facing the forest, with your back to Clairmont Road, take the trail leading into the woods from the far right corner of the parking lot. Within 20 yards turn right on a single-track trail that dips down and through a small gully and then curves left. In 100 yards reach a Wildlife Habitat sign and wooden bench. Stay straight and hike 0.1 mile, passing two small trails that lead into the steep ravine on the left, to reach a junction with a wooden sign pointing right, toward the Park Lane trailhead. Turn left and hike downhill. As the trail levels off in the ravine, pass a giant tulip tree and a small cascade. Follow the trail across the creek and continue steeply up the far side of the ravine. Trillium and Solomon's seal thrive here alongside buckeye, bloodroot, and cranefly orchid.

Stay right at the next two junctions to take a small, narrow trail that winds through a section of younger forest for 0.1 mile before reaching a junction with the wide main trail. Look to the right to see twin tulip trees that stand sentinel on either side of the trail. Turn left and follow the main trail for 0.3 mile, passing several side trails on the left. Once the trail curves left and crests a small rise, start looking for a small trail leading downhill to the right. This short side trail leads you past a seasonal wetland and then curves back uphill to the main trail, near the trailhead and parking lot. Look to your left and you'll see a historic runway light still standing on a wooden pole on the left of the trail. You can end your hike here or continue the adventure on the park's interior trails.

This peaceful forest is across the street from the state's second busiest airport.

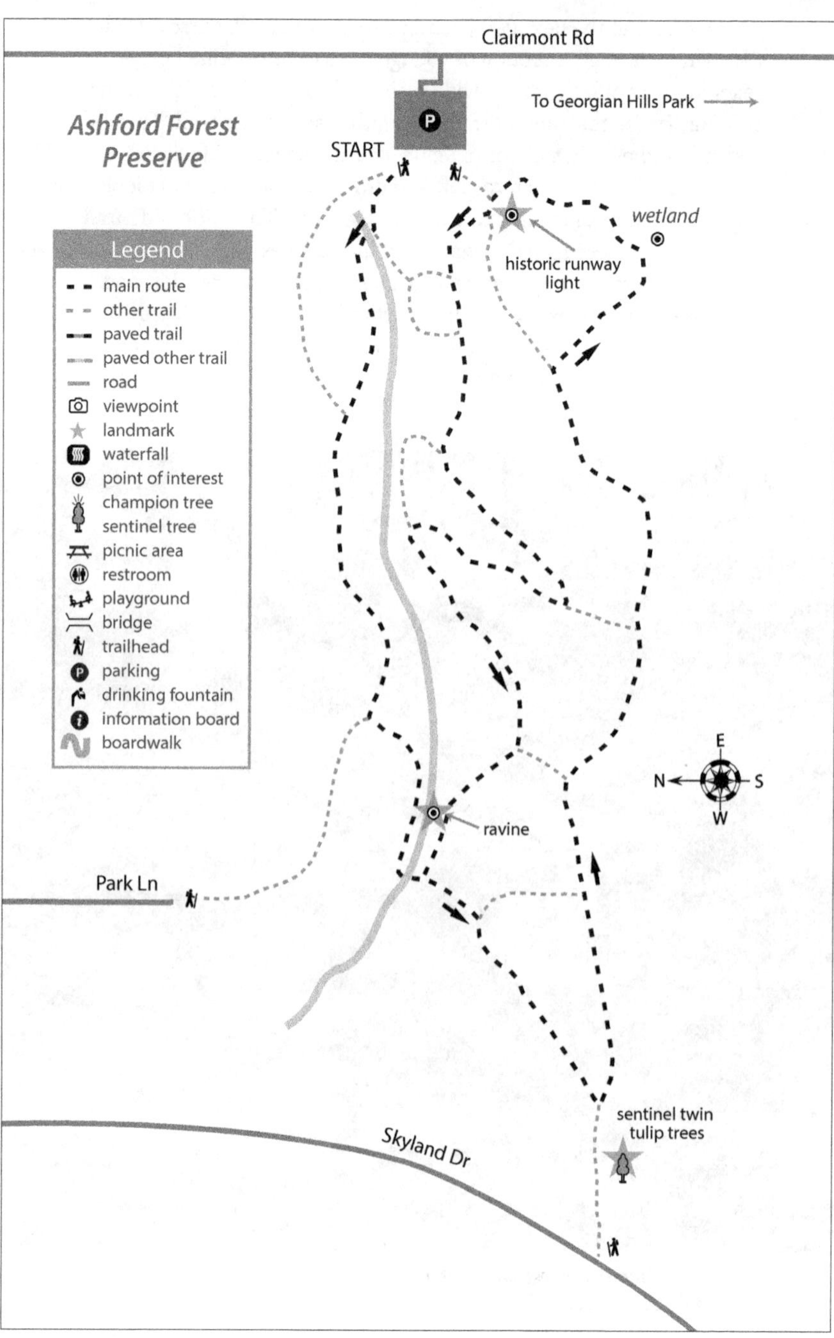
Clairmont Rd
To Georgian Hills Park
Ashford Forest Preserve
START
wetland
historic runway light
Legend
main route
other trail
paved trail
paved other trail
road
viewpoint
landmark
waterfall
point of interest
champion tree
sentinel tree
picnic area
restroom
playground
bridge
trailhead
parking
drinking fountain
information board
boardwalk
E
N
S
W
ravine
Park Ln
sentinel twin tulip trees
Skyland Dr

Turn left (away from the parking lot) and immediately hike right and downhill. At the bottom of the berm, go left and stay straight on a wide, flat trail, keeping the berm on your left. At a T-junction in 0.15 mile, turn right and hike downhill for 100 yards before taking a hard left and staying on the high ground for 0.1 mile, turning right at the next two T-junctions to reach the bottom of the ravine, where you've been before.

Cross the creek and hike out of the ravine. Turn right at the junction with the Park Lane sign and then follow the trail 0.2 mile to return to the parking lot and end your hike.

Unique stone stairs lead up to the old Eidson Mill dam and waterfall.

Blue Heron Nature Preserve

One of the city's most beautiful hidden forests is right on one of its busiest streets, Roswell Road. This nature preserve provides an immediate escape from the hustle and bustle of the city. Nancy Creek, one of the important tributaries of the Chattahoochee River, flows through the middle of the Blue Heron Nature Preserve and provides a good habitat for birds and other animals. Within the last decade, the preserve has expanded its trail system dramatically, adding boardwalks and bridges through the forests and wetlands off Mill Creek. Look for an old mill dam and waterfall, peaceful wetlands, and an amphibian research station.

HOW TO GET THERE

Driving Distance from Downtown Atlanta: 11 miles
Address: 4055 Roswell Road NE, Atlanta, GA 30342
Nearest Interstate: GA 400
Neighborhood: Buckhead
Public Transit: MARTA 5 bus stops at the preserve
Parking: Paved parking area near the Urban Ecology Center

HIKE DISTANCE

2-mile triple loop

DIFFICULTY

Overall: Easy
Navigation: Maps posted at trailheads; many trail junctions are marked with signs
Terrain: Hard-packed dirt trails and many wooden boardwalks and bridges; one rock staircase
Elevation Change: Mostly flat with a few minor hills

SAFETY

Usage ★★★★☆
Visibility ★★★★☆
Upkeep ★★★★★
Parking ★★★★★

HOURS

6:00 am to 11:00 pm

DOGS

Leashed dogs allowed

FACILITIES	• Portable toilet near the Field Research Center, but no other public toilets • Benches and picnic tables, community garden, USGS streamgaging station, interpretive signs
FEES & PERMITS	None
LAND MANAGER	City of Atlanta Parks & Recreation

Landmarks

NANCY CREEK

Along with Peachtree Creek, Nancy Creek is one of the primary watersheds on the northeast side of Atlanta. You can get down to the water in multiple places in the nature preserve: at the wooden viewpoint platform, from the road bridges, and at several sandbars that are accessible from this trail.

EIDSON MILL DAM

A mill owned by William Jefferson Eidson once stood near the site of the crumbling dam. The lower pond above the small dam near Lakemoore Drive was also part of the mill complex. Today, both dams slow the flow of stormwater and provide picturesque waterfalls.

BEAVER DAM ANALOGUES

After a rain, this creek can become a torrent, leading to erosion and habitat loss. To help nature solve this problem, the City of Atlanta has installed poles in the creek that act like dams to slow the water down. These "beaver dam analogues" help give beavers a starting point for transforming this eroded creek into an ecologically diverse wetland.

Hike Route

Start your hike across the parking lot from the Urban Ecology Center and walk through the arbor next to the map and information board. Turn right on the curving boardwalk and then stay straight on the crushed gravel Woodland Loop Trail when the boardwalk ends. In 0.15 mile cross a bridge and then reach a Nancy Creek viewpoint.

Continue straight to reach Rickenbacker Drive and go left on the road, cross the bridge over the creek, then make a left back onto Woodland Loop Trail. Hike through a stand of river birches with very flaky bark. In less than 100 yards, pass a United States Geological Survey streamgaging station, then come to a junction with a creek

Nancy Creek is a beautiful oasis right next to busy Roswell Road.

access trail on the left and then a boardwalk. Go right on the boardwalk for 100 yards, past a junction with a dirt trail on the left. The boardwalk ends at the Girl Scout pavilion. Walk through the pavilion to reach a T-junction near the community garden. Turn left, skirting a small gravel parking area, and then reenter the woods on Woodland Loop Trail. Pass beehives on the right, then reach a small bridge and junction. Hike up the stairs to the left and reach a sidewalk.

Turn left and cross the bridge over Nancy Creek. This short section of sidewalk trail on the edge of busy Roswell Road is the least peaceful part of this walk. Luckily, it's less than 0.1 mile before the trail dips back into the woods to the left and crosses the nature preserve driveway to meet Painted Turtle Trail. Go right and follow Painted Turtle Trail around the edge of the wetland for 0.15 mile until you reach a crosswalk at Lakemoore Drive. Cross the road near a small waterfall and enter the woods on flagstones near an information board to begin Eidson Mill Trail. Climb the rock stairs, then stay left on the crushed gravel path. (Extra steps on the right lead up to private homes.)

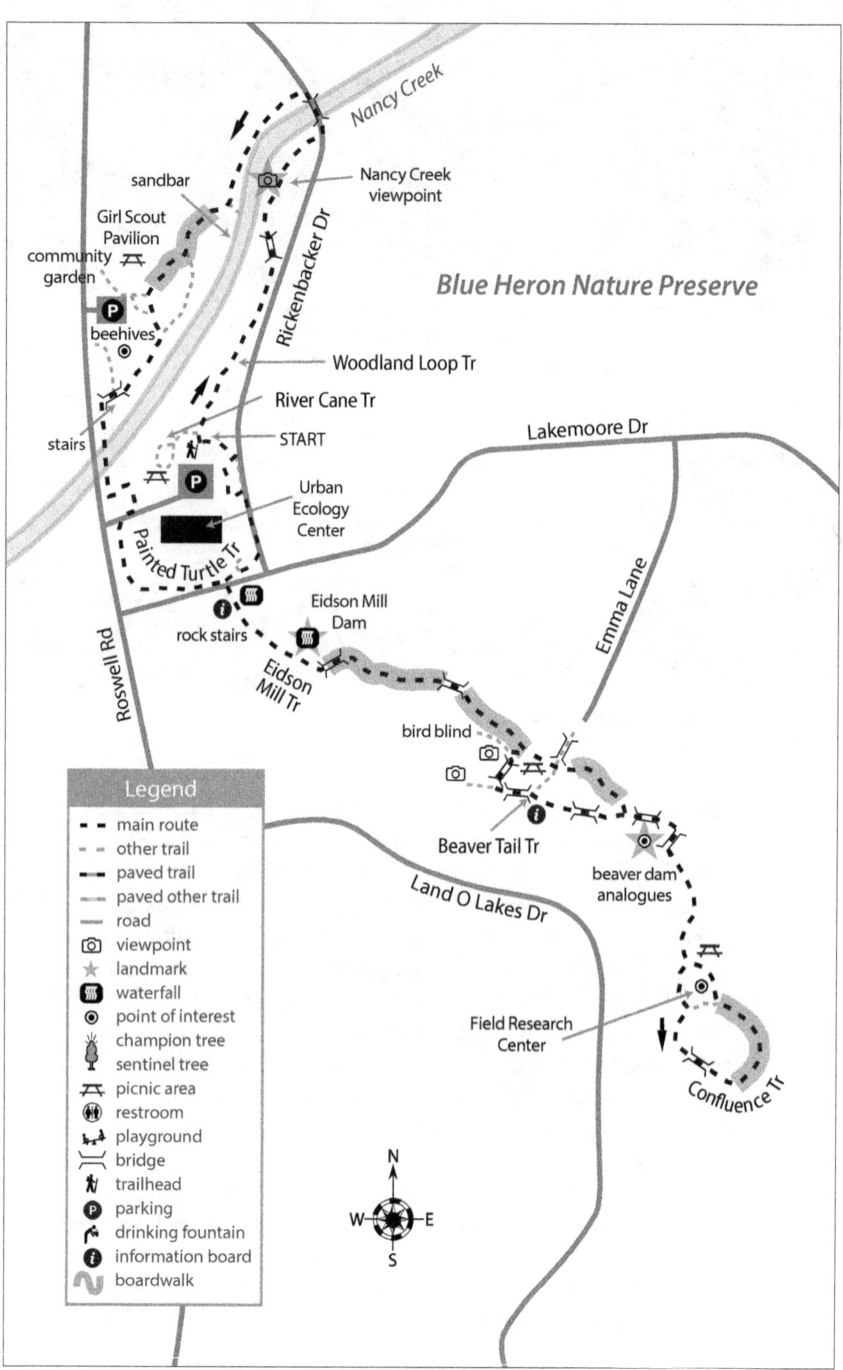

Nancy Creek
sandbar
Nancy Creek viewpoint
Girl Scout Pavilion
community garden
Blue Heron Nature Preserve
beehives
Rickenbacker Dr
Woodland Loop Tr
River Cane Tr
START
stairs
Lakemoore Dr
Urban Ecology Center
Painted Turtle Tr
Eidson Mill Dam
rock stairs
Eidson Mill Tr
Emma Lane
Roswell Rd
bird blind
Beaver Tail Tr
beaver dam analogues
Land O Lakes Dr
Field Research Center
Confluence Tr
Legend
main route
other trail
paved trail
paved other trail
road
viewpoint
landmark
waterfall
point of interest
champion tree
sentinel tree
picnic area
restroom
playground
bridge
trailhead
parking
drinking fountain
information board
boardwalk
N
W
E
S

In 100 yards reach the historic Eidson Mill dam and a beautiful waterfall. Cross a wooden bridge above the dam and hike 0.2 mile over two boardwalks to reach a three-way junction at a group of picnic tables. The trail to the immediate right leads to a bird blind. Take Beaver Tail Trail to the picnic tables and then right. Pass two wetland overlooks and then a small dirt trail on the right. Cross a boardwalk and pass an information sign as the trail parallels the creek.

At another Beaver Tail Trail junction, bear right and hike 0.1 mile to the Field Research Center, crossing a bridge over the creek on the way. From the bridge you can see human-built beaver dam analogues in the creek. Go around the Field Research Center building on the right, cross the small parking area, and continue on a bricked path to reach another set of picnic tables with a Woodland Field Education Center sign. Take the Confluence Trail past the tables, then cross a bridge and follow a boardwalk that will circle you back to the Field Research Center. At the base of a set of stairs on the left, stay right and pass amphibian research tanks to arrive back at the picnic tables and Mill Creek Trail junction. Go straight and hike Mill Creek Trail back to a junction with Beaver Tail Trail. Take the right fork. Cross a boardwalk, then pass the Emma Lane trailhead in 100 yards. Stay straight until you arrive at a junction with Eidson Mill Trail, where you'll bear right to hike back past the dam and down the rock stairs to Lakemoore Drive and Painted Turtle Trail.

Cross the road and turn right on Painted Turtle Trail. A trail on the left leads to Discovery Dock and a nice view of the wetlands. Painted Turtle Trail continues up to Rickenbacker Drive. In less than 100 yards a small trail leads left into the butterfly garden next to the Urban Ecology Center. Walk through the butterfly garden and then follow a small trail up stone steps to rejoin the main path. Hike left and downhill to return to the parking area and finish your hike.

Native flowers add beauty and color along the route.

Chastain Memorial Park

Nestled among Buckhead neighborhoods, Chastain Memorial Park is a 260-acre greenspace with a multitude of outdoor activities. At Atlanta's third largest park visitors can enjoy golf, tennis, soccer, and horseback riding or hike the paved multiuse path that encircles the park. Although you'll never forget you're in a city on this hike, you'll be treated to the sight of gorgeous, mature trees throughout the park.

HOW TO GET THERE

Driving Distance from Downtown Atlanta: 11 miles

Address: 140 Chastain Park Avenue NW, Atlanta, GA 30342

Nearest Interstate: GA 400

Neighborhood: Chastain Park / Buckhead

Public Transit: MARTA 5 bus + 0.8-mile walk

Parking: Ample street parking plus paved and gravel parking lots near sports fields and Chastain Park Gymnasium

HIKE DISTANCE

3.25-mile loop

DIFFICULTY

Overall: Easy to moderate

Navigation: Maps and wayfinding signs posted along route

Terrain: Paved path, sidewalk, and hard-packed dirt and gravel trail

Elevation Change: Rolling hills with a few steep ascents and descents and a few extended ascents and descents

SAFETY

Usage ★★★★★

Visibility ★★★★★

Upkeep ★★★★★

Parking ★★★★★

HOURS

6:00 am to 11:00 pm

DOGS

Leashed dogs allowed

FACILITIES

- Toilets
- Playgrounds, picnic areas, water fountains, information signs, sports fields, golf course, pool (check hours and fees ahead of time)

FEES & PERMITS	None
LAND MANAGER	City of Atlanta Parks & Recreation in partnership with Chastain Park Conservancy

Landmarks

AVENUE OF OAKS

Chastain Park Avenue is lined by rows of beautiful mature oak trees. White oaks, red oaks, water oaks, and willow oaks are tall and stately and provide a shady canopy for walking. One of the largest trees in this stretch is a willow oak near the last ballfield before Lake Forrest Drive. Female willow oaks produce an acorn that's a preferred snack for whitetail deer, squirrels, and songbirds.

CHAMPION GREEN ASH

- 135" circumference, 100' tall, 60' crown spread
- Sitting at the bank of the creek, this green ash is nearly 100 feet tall and the second largest in the city.

SENTINEL SAWTOOTH OAK

Aptly named for their jagged-edged leaves, sawtooth oaks were introduced to the United States in the 1800s. The size of this tree is impressive, as are the two subsequent sawtooth oaks you'll pass.

Hike Route

To start your hike, exit the parking lot with your back to the gymnasium and turn right onto the paved Chastain Park Trail, which parallels the road. As you walk along Chastain Park Avenue, you'll pass multiple beautiful mature oaks and maples on your right and across the street to your left. Among the largest is a willow oak in 0.2 mile on the right at the edge of a baseball field. In another 100 feet, at Lake Forrest Drive, turn right at a map sign, pass large boulders, and continue downhill on the trail.

In 0.2 mile, after passing the baseball fields and a gravel parking lot, the trail makes a short but steep descent as it curves down into the floodplain past a large white oak tree on the left. Cross a small bridge and continue with the golf course on your right.

Hike for another 0.25 mile before reaching three large water oaks growing on the right at the edge of the golf course. Immediately after that, look for a gate and bench on the left and a horse hitching post and pet waste bag dispenser on the right. This is a great place to hike

The hike offers several spots to rest and enjoy nature.

a dirt trail through the nearby forested area. Turn right onto the dirt trail and enter the forest. Reach a junction in 100 yards and go left to get to the edge of Nancy Creek. Turn left and follow the trail along the creek back to the paved path. On the right, just before the trail reconnects with the paved path, is a young pawpaw tree, distinguishable by its long, oblong-shaped leaves.

Once you are back on the paved path, before crossing a bridge, you'll see a gorgeous water oak next to a small paved path leading to some benches.

Cross the bridge over Nancy Creek and continue hiking for another 0.25 mile to come to another bridge. Before crossing, look on the left for a native habitat restoration sign and a dirt trail. Follow this trail to see the ongoing work to remove invasive species and restore this section of forest. You may see flags on the ground marking where native species have been protected or planted. In 50 feet, just before reaching a small footbridge, look right to find the city champion green ash on the opposite bank of the creek, with its roots exposed by erosion.

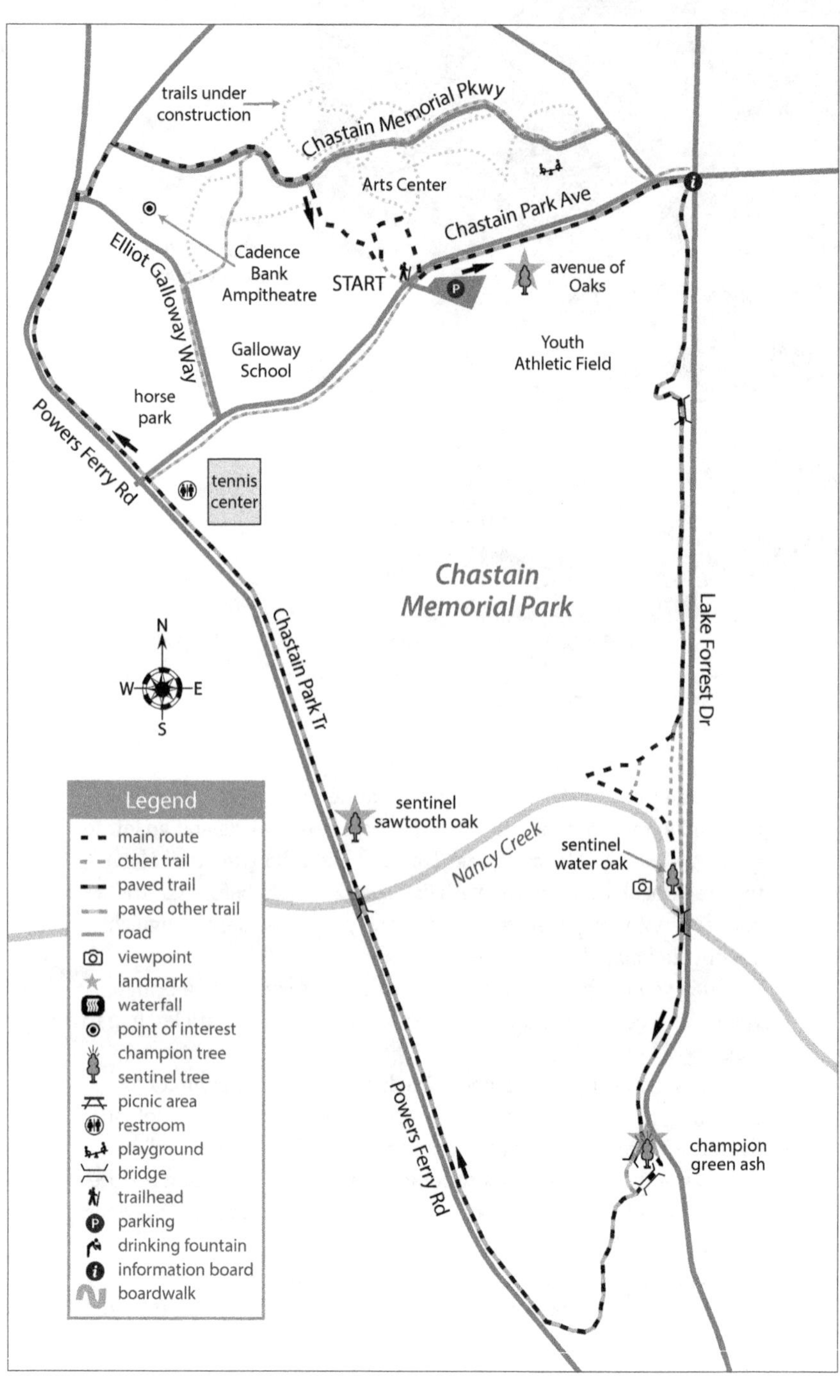
trails under construction
Chastain Memorial Pkwy
Arts Center
Chastain Park Ave
Cadence Bank Ampitheatre
START
avenue of Oaks
Elliot Galloway Way
Galloway School
Youth Athletic Field
horse park
Powers Ferry Rd
tennis center
Chastain Memorial Park
Chastain Park Tr
Lake Forrest Dr
N
W
E
S
sentinel sawtooth oak
Nancy Creek
sentinel water oak
champion green ash
Powers Ferry Rd
Legend
main route
other trail
paved trail
paved other trail
road
viewpoint
landmark
waterfall
point of interest
champion tree
sentinel tree
picnic area
restroom
playground
bridge
trailhead
parking
drinking fountain
information board
boardwalk

After crossing the bridge, climb the stairs to reconnect with the paved path. Turn left and hike uphill. In 0.25 mile the trail begins to curve to the right around the golf course and continues along Powers Ferry Road. Reach a sign about the Civil War cavalry at Nancy Creek in 0.4 mile before crossing a bridge. Just after the bridge, at another Civil War information sign, there is a massive sentinel sawtooth oak on the right, followed by two more of the same species.

Stay on the trail for 0.4 mile before coming to the intersection at Chastain Park Avenue and Powers Ferry Road. On the right are restrooms beside the tennis courts. If you're ready to end your hike, turn right and continue along the sidewalk until you reach the parking lot. Otherwise, carefully cross Chastain Park Avenue and continue straight on the path parallel to Powers Ferry Road.

The trail ascends a hill past the horse park on your right and a soccer field to the left. At the top of the hill, in 0.2 mile, take a right onto Elliot Galloway Way and an immediate left onto Stella Drive. The sidewalk ends here, so be very careful of traffic. Turn right at the first intersection onto Chastain Memorial Parkway (also called Alex Cooley Parkway), walking behind the Chastain Park Amphitheater.

Continue straight, passing a Chastain Park Trail junction on your right. You have entered the Northwoods area of Chastain Park. There are many unofficial dirt trails that wind through these woods, and the Chastain Park Conservancy and Park Pride are working to improve the trails and develop an official trail system. The proposed trail network is included on the map in this guidebook, but you can explore the trails in whatever order suits you.

To return to your vehicle on paved routes, continue along Chastain Memorial Parkway to Dudley Lane, where the trail curves right. Take another right on Chastain Park Avenue to return to the parking area.

To use dirt trails for the remainder of your hike, turn right into a gravel parking lot between a soccer field and picnic pavilion. At the far end of the parking lot, find the dirt trail and hike downhill to where it connects with a large gravel lot with stone chimneys and picnic tables. Continue right through the gravel lot to a gate at Chastain Park Avenue across from the parking area, where you'll end your hike.

Painted sewer access points at Murphey Candler Park will make you smile.

Murphey Candler Park

Watching the reflection of clouds on the lake's surface is just the beginning of a beautiful hike through Brookhaven's Murphey Candler Park. Once known primarily for its youth sports programs, the park was built in the 1950s and now includes a two-mile trail through hardwood forests and beaver-created wetlands and along the lakeshore. This trail also connects with the Nancy Creek Trail, which can add a 1.6-mile paved extension to your hike through nearby Blackburn Park.

HOW TO GET THERE

Driving Distance from Downtown Atlanta: 16 miles

Address: 1600 West Nancy Creek Drive NE, Brookhaven, GA 30319

Nearest Interstate: I-285

Neighborhood: Brookhaven

Public Transit: Dunwoody MARTA Station + 1.6-mile walk

Parking: Paved parking area at the corner of West Nancy Creek Drive and Candler Lake West; overflow parking across the dam on the southeast side of the lake

HIKE DISTANCE

2-mile figure-8 loop

DIFFICULTY

Overall: Easy

Navigation: Trails are well-maintained but have no marking system or maps

Terrain: Most trails are hard-packed dirt, with several sections of boardwalk and paved path

Elevation Change: Mostly flat with a few minor hills

SAFETY

Usage ★★★★★

Visibility ★★★★★

Upkeep ★★★★★

Parking ★★★★★

HOURS

Dusk to dawn

DOGS

Leashed dogs allowed

FACILITIES

- Toilets available near baseball fields across the street from the parking area

- Benches, picnic areas, playgrounds, swimming pool, sports fields

FEES & PERMITS	None
LAND MANAGER	City of Brookhaven Parks & Recreation in partnership with the Murphey Candler Park Conservancy

Landmarks

BOARDWALK WETLANDS VIEWPOINT

Stop in the middle of the Murphey Candler boardwalk to look for birds, signs of beavers, and wildflowers. You'll see fantastic views of the lake.

NORTH FORK NANCY CREEK TRASH TRAP

A short access road from the main trail allows you to view a strange contraption that makes a huge difference. This "trash trap" collects floating plastic garbage, keeping Nancy Creek clean here in Brookhaven and downstream through Sandy Springs and Buckhead.

THE THREE SISTERS

Growing at the edge of the floodplain right next to the trail are three mature sentinel trees, each of a different species. Look for the sweetgum's star-shaped leaves and spiky seed pods, the American beech's smooth gray bark, and the tulip tree's (commonly known as tulip poplar) leaves, shaped like a cat's face.

Hike Route

From the parking lot, walk toward the lake, then turn left onto the asphalt path along the lakeshore. Pass several picnic pavilions and a set of slides built into rock features before reaching a junction with the park's main boardwalk. Turn right and walk the length of the 0.1-mile boardwalk. You'll get to walk the boardwalk twice on this hike, but be sure to soak in the beauty of the wetlands, the creek, and the lake as you cross them.

At the end of the boardwalk, turn left, and you'll see two parallel trails. Hike the left fork and reach a gravel access road in 0.1 mile. This short gravel road leads left to a trash trap—a unique method that the City of Brookhaven uses to reduce plastic trash in Nancy Creek.

After visiting the trash trap, walk back to the trail and turn left toward a bench and information board, then downhill to a series of two wooden bridges. After these bridges, the trail becomes rooty and skirts beaver-created wetlands on your left. Hike for 0.25 mile, passing a side trail to Brawley Drive on your right before arriving at a boardwalk and bridge over North Fork Nancy Creek.

After crossing the bridge, use the trail on your right to bypass a section of wet trail and then ascend the hill past the "three sisters," triplet sentinel trees—a sweetgum, a tulip tree, and a beech. This next section of trail winds through a mature forest of hardwood trees and buckeye, mountain laurel, silverbell, and native azalea. There are also good views of the wetlands below you.

After crossing two bridges, you'll reach the boardwalk again. Turn left to cross, then turn right at the end of the boardwalk. This next

The lake at Murphey Candler Park provides many scenic viewpoints along this hike.

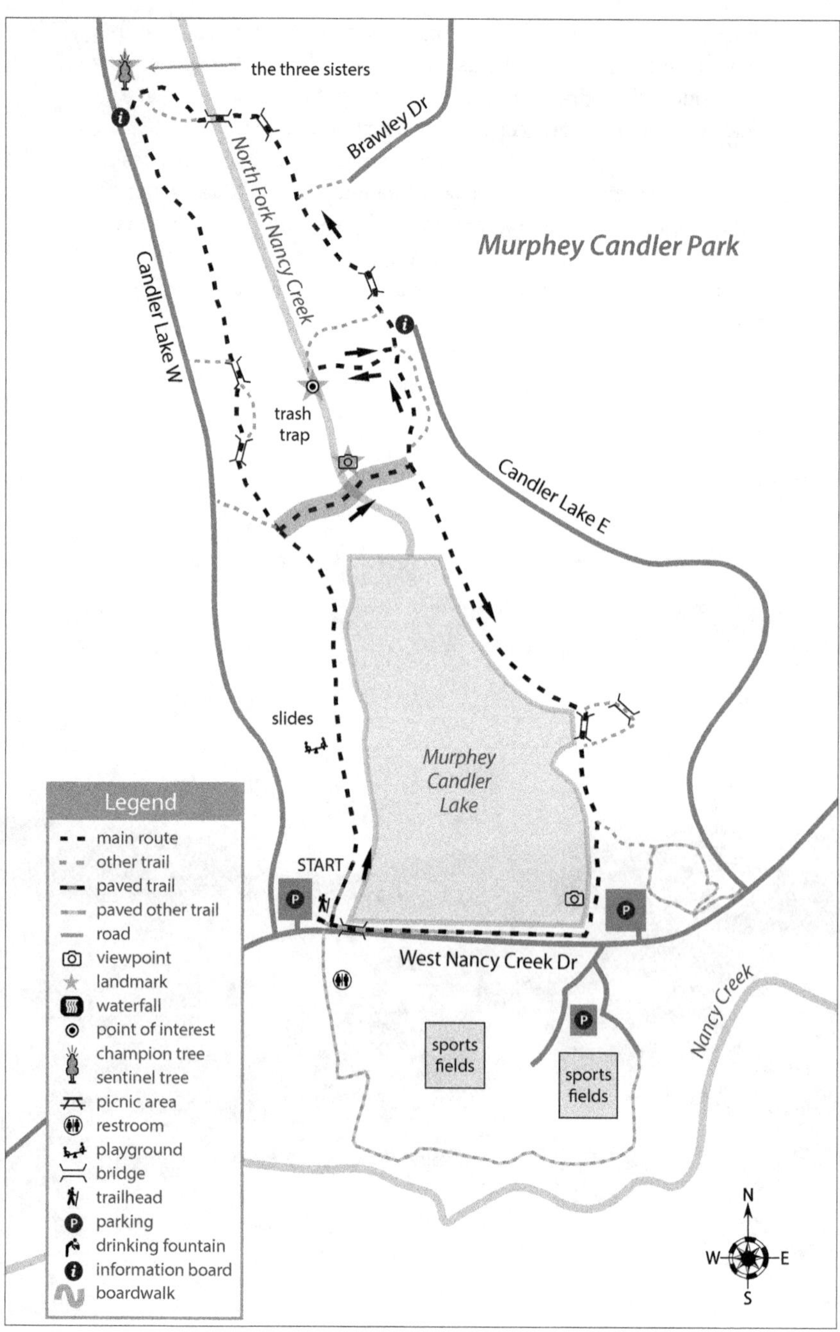

the three sisters
Brawley Dr
North Fork Nancy Creek
Murphey Candler Park
Candler Lake W
trash trap
Candler Lake E
slides
Murphey Candler Lake
START
West Nancy Creek Dr
Nancy Creek
sports fields
sports fields
Legend
main route
other trail
paved trail
paved other trail
road
viewpoint
landmark
waterfall
point of interest
champion tree
sentinel tree
picnic area
restroom
playground
bridge
trailhead
parking
drinking fountain
information board
boardwalk
N
W
E
S

section of trail has great lakeside views. The sewer access points have been painted to look like a mallard duck, a Canada goose, and a northern cardinal. Can you find all three? Hike 0.25 mile to a large steel bridge. Cross and hike the paved trail another 0.4 mile past several benches and pavilions to arrive at an observation deck and overflow parking area.

Turn to the right and cross the dam to return to the parking area and end your hike. Alternatively, you can cross West Nancy Creek Drive and walk a paved multiuse path behind the sports fields along the banks of Nancy Creek to return to the parking area.

Humans aren't the only creatures that enjoy hiking the Peachtree Creek Greenway.

Peachtree Creek Greenway

This "model mile" of a planned 15-mile trail along North Fork Peachtree Creek will help you fall in love with this waterway. Tucked between office parks, apartment buildings, and Atlanta's (in)famous Pink Pony adult entertainment club, the Peachtree Creek Greenway promises exercise, connection to nature, and family recreation. This paved path is truly multiuse, as you'll pass birders with binoculars, dog walkers, bicyclists, joggers, office and construction workers on their lunch breaks, and families out on an adventure. This well-maintained, well-lit, and creatively designed trail will get you excited for more greenway.

HOW TO GET THERE

Driving Distance from Downtown Atlanta: 11 miles

Address: 1793 Briarwood Road NE, Brookhaven, GA 30329

Neighborhood: Brookhaven

Nearest Interstate: I-85

Public Transit: MARTA 47 bus to trailhead or MARTA 39 bus + 0.3-mile walk

Parking: Paved parking area off Briarwood Road with overflow parking behind Brookhaven Public Safety building on weekends; parking also available at the North Druid Hills Road trailhead

HIKE DISTANCE

2.5-mile out-and-back

DIFFICULTY

Overall: Easy

Navigation: Regular trail mileage markers and signs

Terrain: Paved multiuse path is fully ADA accessible

Elevation Change: Mostly flat with a few minor hills

SAFETY

Usage ★★★☆☆

Visibility ★★★★★

Upkeep ★★★★★

Parking ★★★★★

HOURS

6:00 am to 11:00 pm

DOGS

Leashed dogs allowed

FACILITIES	• Toilets and water fountain in Public Safety building, • Many benches, a bike repair station, dog waste stations, slides, hammocks, swings, and picnic tables
FEES & PERMITS	None
LAND MANAGER	City of Brookhaven Parks & Recreation in partnership with Peachtree Creek Greenway, Inc.

Landmarks

SENTINEL SYCAMORE

This sycamore tree is a landmark because of its massive size, but it also stands as a reminder of the forests that used to line the banks of North Fork Peachtree Creek. Step off the pavement here and view the creek more closely.

SLIDES AND HAMMOCKS

The City of Brookhaven has installed some unique amenities along this trail. You can take a break from hiking to play on slides (and climb rocks) and then relax in a hammock or bench swing overlooking the creek.

NORTH FORK BRIDGE

Floodplains and high water levels during storms required this bridge to be very tall. You'll get great views of the creek from here, but the bridge really shines at dusk, when it is lit by beautiful LED lights.

Hike Route

Begin your hike near the Peachtree Creek Greenway sign next to the parking area. Eventually, the trail will continue under Briarwood Road to the left, but for now, hike to the right down an extended ramp and onto the floodplain alongside North Fork Peachtree Creek.

In 0.1 mile pass the Brookhaven Public Safety building on your right. Restrooms and water fountains are available here. About 100 yards farther pass a bench, a bike rack, and mileage marker 4.09. Though the current Peachtree Creek Greenway is only 1.25 miles, there are plans for over 15 miles of additional trail, extending from the Northside Beltline near Lindbergh MARTA Station to the Gwinnett County line. The mileage markers on this section of trail reflect the distance from the eventual beginning at the Beltline.

Hammocks along the trail are perfect for relaxing!

In 0.1 mile, just before hiking under high-tension power lines, pass a giant sentinel sycamore tree and a good viewpoint of the shoals of North Fork Peachtree Creek on your left.

The trail splits in 0.1 mile to allow you to play on two slides built into a rock feature beside the trail. After sliding on the slides (or not), you'll come to another trail split and unique feature in 0.1 mile—a group of hammocks and swinging benches overlooking the creek.

Continue the hike for 0.3 mile past two trail entrances from adjacent apartment complexes to reach the sizable bridge across North Fork Peachtree Creek. Keep your eyes out for birds such as great blue herons and belted kingfishers. Just past the bridge, you can access Corporate Square. In another 0.3 mile there is another entrance to the large Corporate Square complex.

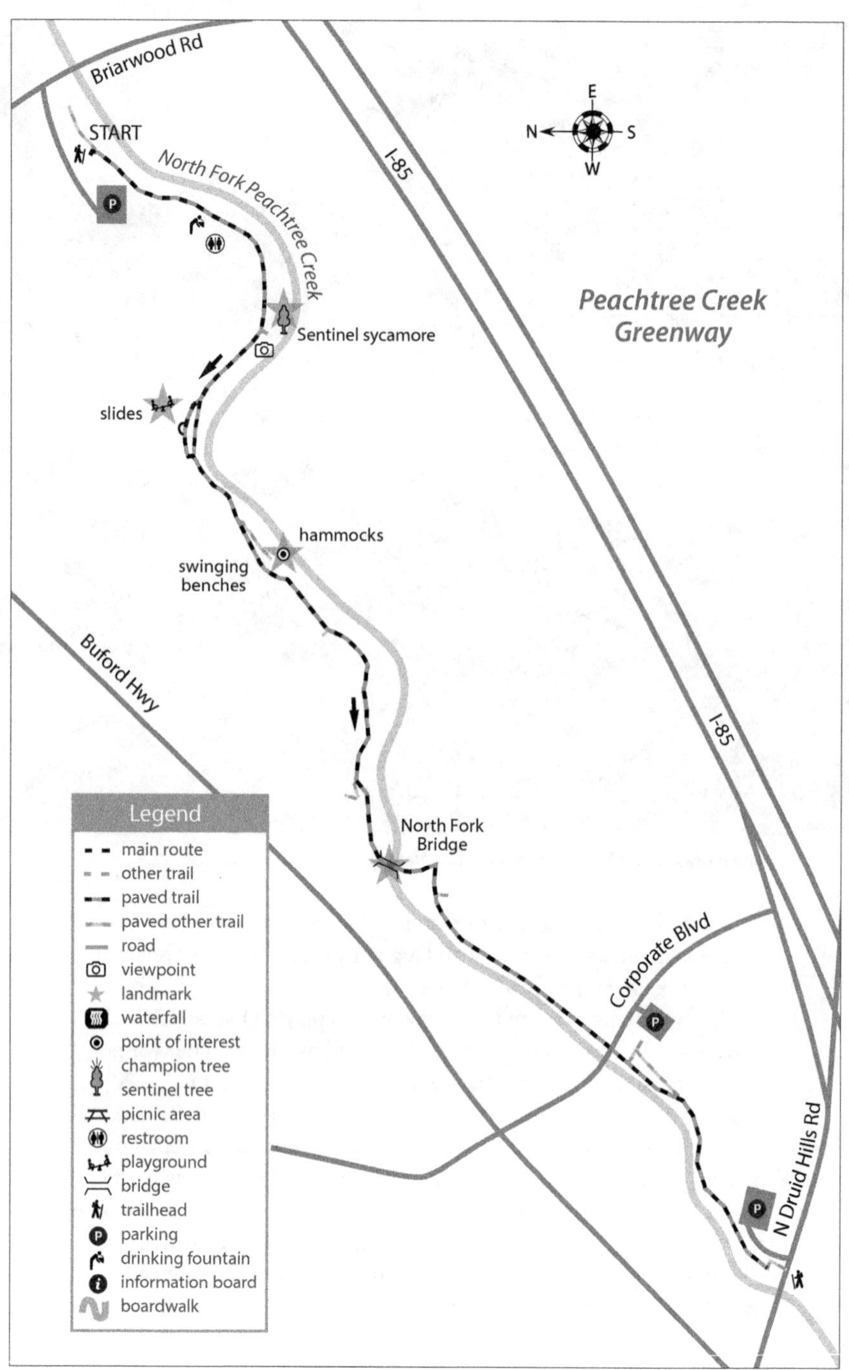

Briarwood Rd
START
North Fork Peachtree Creek
I-85
E
N
S
W
Peachtree Creek Greenway
Sentinel sycamore
slides
hammocks
swinging benches
Buford Hwy
I-85
North Fork Bridge
Corporate Blvd
N Druid Hills Rd
Legend
main route
other trail
paved trail
paved other trail
road
viewpoint
landmark
waterfall
point of interest
champion tree
sentinel tree
picnic area
restroom
playground
bridge
trailhead
parking
drinking fountain
information board
boardwalk

Continue straight on the paved trail for 0.2 mile. The trail is closest to the creek here and can be impassable during flooding. Sand deposited on the trail after a flood can be a hazard here as well. Look for mature floodplain trees along the banks of the creek, including cottonwood, black willow, green ash, and river birch.

The trail currently ends at North Druid Hills Road. Turn around and hike 1.25 miles back to your vehicle.

Trail markers installed by a local Scout troop welcome you to the trails of Ridgeview Park.

Ridgeview Park

This small community park near GA 400 has a hidden secret: over a mile of beautiful trails through a healthy, mature forest. Two small creeks join to form a tributary of Nancy Creek, and the trail traverses a steep ridge, winds through a unique woodland cove, and parallels the flowing water. This park is also a great place for picnicking, tennis, and a visit to the forest-themed playground.

HOW TO GET THERE	**Driving Distance from Downtown Atlanta:** 14 miles **Address:** 5200 South Trimble Road, Sandy Springs, GA 30342 **Neighborhood:** Sandy Springs **Nearest Interstate:** GA 400 **Public Transit:** MARTA Medical Center Station + 2-mile walk **Parking:** Paved parking area below tennis and pickleball courts
HIKE DISTANCE	1-mile figure-8 loop
DIFFICULTY	**Overall:** Moderate **Navigation:** No map, but trail direction posts mark many junctions **Terrain:** Mostly hard-packed dirt trails with lots of roots plus short sections of mulched trail, sidewalk, and grass **Elevation Change:** Several short but steep ascents and descents
SAFETY	**Usage** ★★★☆☆ **Visibility** ★★★☆☆ **Upkeep** ★★★☆☆ **Parking** ★★★☆☆
HOURS	7:00 am to dusk
DOGS	Leashed dogs allowed

FACILITIES	• No toilets • Water fountain, picnic area, pickleball and tennis courts, playground, and bike rack
FEES & PERMITS	None
LAND MANAGER	City of Sandy Springs Recreation & Parks

Landmarks

NINE-TRUNKED SWEETGUM GROVE

This grove of sweetgum trees almost looks like one organism. The nine trunks are at least eight separate trees. However, several are growing so close together that they can actually exchange and share nutrients in a process called inosculation.

Fungi are some of the many organisms that thrive in Ridgeview's woodland cove.

RIDGE VIEW

The large beech, tulip, oak, and hickory trees of Ridgeview Park are fun to view from the ridge above the creek. After hiking the steep trail up the ridge, stop and marvel at the various shapes and sizes of the trees in this section of forest.

WOODLAND COVE

Sometimes the steep walls of a ravine can protect an ecosystem from human development. This small woodland cove within Ridgeview Park is notable for exactly this reason. Look for large majestic trees and for smaller moments of beauty—fungi, moss, and running water.

Hike Route

From the parking area near the tennis and pickleball courts, walk down the sidewalk parallel to the playground. At the information board and bicycle rack, leave the sidewalk and continue straight, down the hill. There is no marked trail to follow here, but the entrance to this park's nature trail is directly in front of you at the bottom of the long hill. Walk downhill across mulch and grass with the picnic area on your left. Pass a mulched area that until recently housed a fitness station on your left and continue downhill. The grassy area narrows, then widens again and flattens out as you enter a wide field. It is here that you'll pass an interesting cluster of sweetgum trees with nine trunks.

Look for a trail marker across the clearing ahead of you and enter the woods to the left. Cross a bridge over a tributary of Nancy Creek and curve right. In 100 feet reach a junction and go left and immediately right. (The trail on the left ascends the hill to reach Green Pine Drive.)

Hike steeply uphill for almost 0.1 mile before the trail levels off on the ridge just below a house and provides scenic woodland views through the mature forest. At the next junction you reach, turn right and hike downhill. Just before reaching the creek, take the left fork at an unofficial junction. Then turn left and hike uphill along the creek, entering a woodland cove, where you'll find large beech, oak, and tulip trees as well as understory trees such as umbrella magnolia, hornbeam, and sourwood. In 0.1 mile reach a trail marker with a stop symbol. The trail curves left here and ascends the rolling terrain for 0.1 mile. When you reach a junction on the ridge, turn left and hike back downhill to the creek on the trail you hiked before.

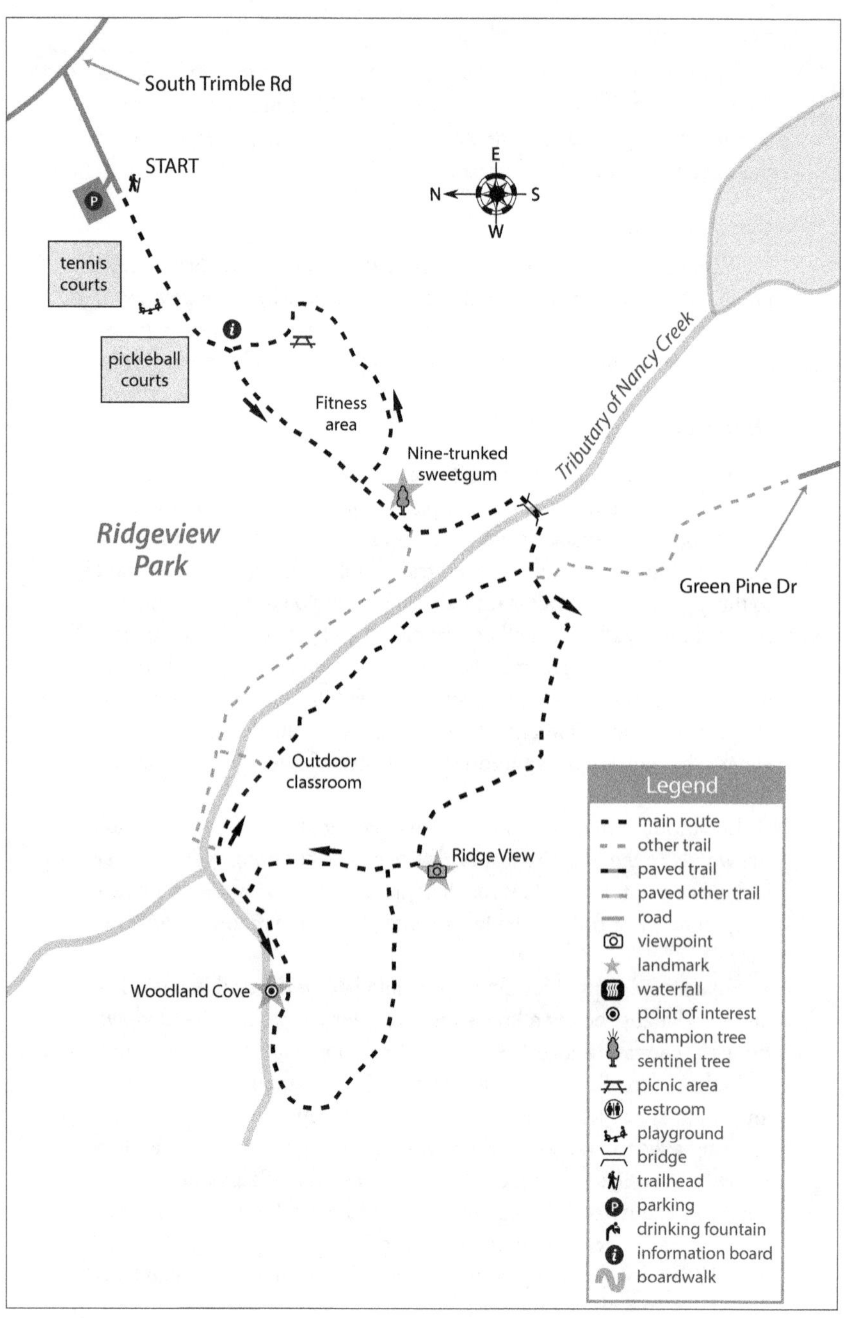
South Trimble Rd
START
E
N
S
W
tennis courts
pickleball courts
Fitness area
Nine-trunked sweetgum
Tributary of Nancy Creek
Ridgeview Park
Green Pine Dr
Outdoor classroom
Ridge View
Woodland Cove
Legend
main route
other trail
paved trail
paved other trail
road
viewpoint
landmark
waterfall
point of interest
champion tree
sentinel tree
picnic area
restroom
playground
bridge
trailhead
parking
drinking fountain
information board
boardwalk

This time, turn right at the creek and hike 0.1 mile to an outdoor classroom and several places where you can choose to cross the creek if you don't mind risking wet feet. (In fact, this is a great spot to get your feet wet, if creek exploration is your thing.) Stay on this side of the creek and continue straight on the main trail, passing the outdoor classroom on your right. Reach a trail junction in 0.1 mile. Go left, cross the bridge, then reenter the clearing near the nine-trunked sweetgum grove.

Walk past the sweetgums on your left, and this time turn right and skirt the slope below the old fitness area to reach the far side of the picnic area. This is not an official trail, but it's a nice shady walk through an area with beautiful moss growing on the ground. Cross the picnic area to reach the information board and turn right to hike uphill on the sidewalk to finish your hike.

ON THE PERIMETER—NORTHSIDE

White-tailed deer abound in this busy suburban park.

Brook Run Park & Pernoshal Park

Brook Run Park is Dunwoody's flagship park and offers just about any park experience you seek—from disc golf to a skate park to an amphitheater. Special community events are held here regularly. For a park with so many amenities, it's easy to overlook the fantastic hiking on the park's paved multiuse loop trail and 0.5-mile spur, which connects to Pernoshal Park. Peaceful forests, bubbling creeks, and a well-marked and well-maintained trail make Brook Run Park a great place for the whole family.

HOW TO GET THERE

Driving Distance from Downtown Atlanta: 19 miles

Address: 4770 North Peachtree Road, Dunwoody, GA 30338

Nearest Interstate: I-285

Neighborhood: Dunwoody

Public Transit: MARTA 103 and 132 buses stop at the park entrance

Parking: Several large paved parking areas; for easiest trailhead access, use the lot between the playground and the skate park

HIKE DISTANCE

2.8-mile loop

DIFFICULTY

Overall: Easy

Navigation: Mile markers every quarter mile along the main loop; information boards with park maps at each junction

Terrain: Wide paved multiuse path

Elevation Change: Mostly flat with a few minor hills

SAFETY

Usage ★★★★★

Visibility ★★★★★

Upkeep ★★★★★

Parking ★★★★★

HOURS

7:00 am to sunset

DOGS

Leashed dogs allowed; this trail has a large off-leash dog park near mile marker ½.

FACILITIES	• Restrooms and water fountains at several locations • Bicycle repair station, benches, picnic pavilions, skate park, playground, athletic fields, disc golf course, basketball courts, and a veterans memorial
FEES & PERMITS	None
LAND MANAGER	City of Dunwoody Parks & Recreation

Landmarks

RUINED BRIDGE

Half of a concrete bridge across a tributary of Nancy Creek is still standing, the remnant of an old road before this area became a park. Today the bridge is a landmark for urban explorers. You might even see people doing photo shoots.

A scenic pedestrian bridge connects Brook Run Park and Pernoshal Park.

SENTINEL LONGLEAF PINE

Longleaf pine forests used to stretch across much of Georgia and Alabama. Though most have been logged, today many parks plant these trees. Look for needles that are up to a foot long and much larger cones than those of the more common loblolly pines.

APIARY

Though many of us are afraid of stinging insects, we realize that bees are highly important to agriculture. This group of beehives (also known as an apiary) was placed here to entice these pollinators to visit the nearby community garden.

Hike Route

Start your hike at the trailhead between the skate park and the playground at mile marker 0, an information board, and a bicycle repair station. Hike to the left on the paved multiuse trail that parallels Peeler Road and then curves left in 0.1 mile. Pass a pavilion on the left and mile marker ¼ on the right. Cross the park road at a crosswalk and reenter the woods near Treetop Quest.

The next section of trail is crisscrossed by disc golf course side trails. You'll also pass the dog park on the left near mile marker ½. The disc golf trails and other unmarked dirt trails lead through the park's central forest. For more adventure you can explore these trails.

Continue on the paved path to mile marker ¾ and turn right onto a paved spur trail that leads to Pernoshal Park. Within the first 50 feet, you'll see a small dirt trail to the left. This unmaintained trail leads 0.3 mile through a nice area of woodlands to an unofficial trailhead at Chowning Way.

Continue straight on the paved path, and in another 100 feet a dirt trail on the right parallels the paved path on the banks of a tributary of Nancy Creek. The parallel paved and dirt trails lead you past the graffiti-covered ruins of a concrete bridge and then to a steel pedestrian bridge in 0.1 mile. Continue across the bridge, past an entrance to apartments, and over a boardwalk bridge. The trail narrows and cuts between a privacy fence and an apartment complex to reach Pernoshal Park in 0.15 mile.

Hike through Pernoshal Park, passing fitness stations and unique play structures on the right. Stay straight to loop around an open field. In the open field, a small stand of trees includes a sentinel longleaf pine. Once the trail loops around to the parking lot, walk left on a sidewalk between a pavilion and basketball court. Back at the multiuse path, turn right to hike back the way you came to Brook Run Park.

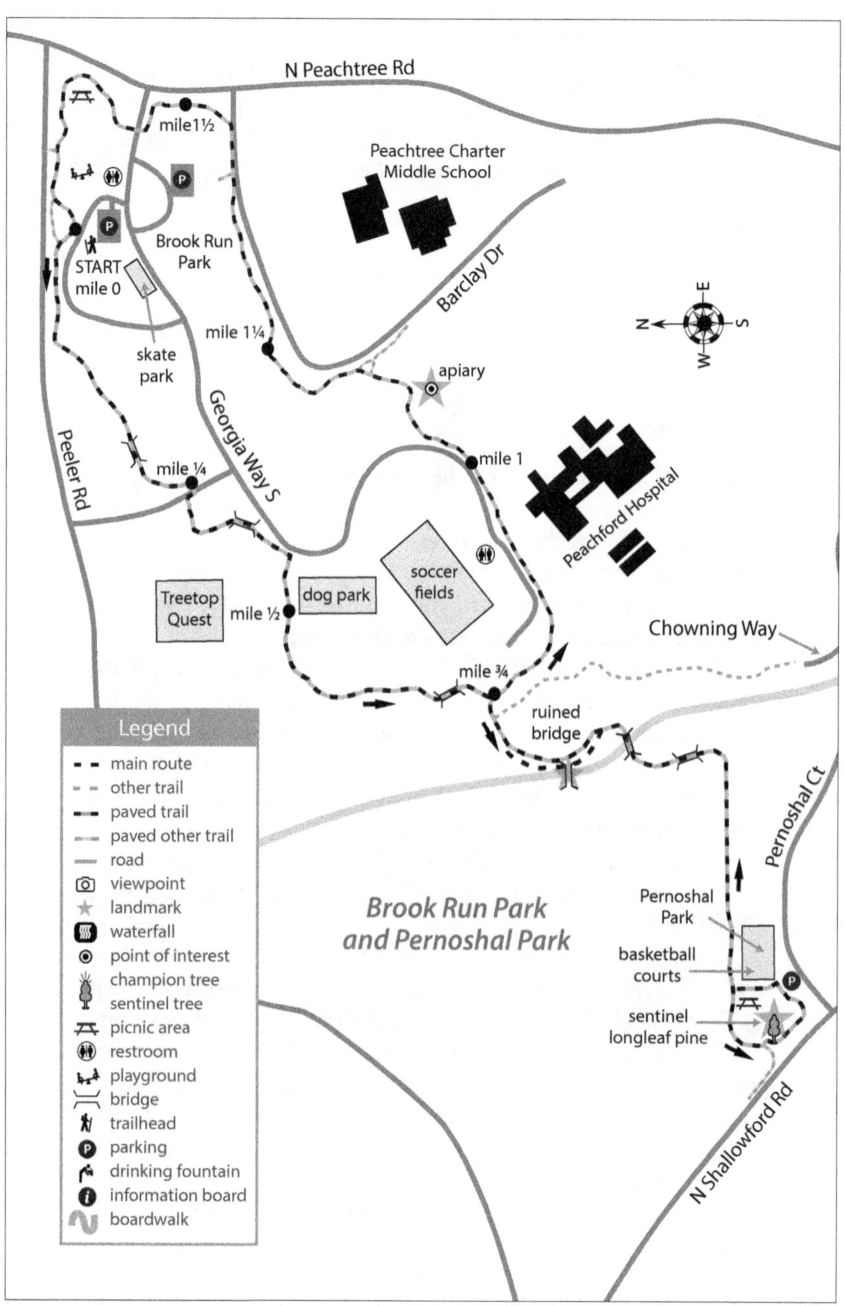
N Peachtree Rd
mile 1½
Peachtree Charter
Middle School
Brook Run
Park
START
mile 0
Barclay Dr
skate
park
mile 1¼
apiary
Georgia Way S
Peeler Rd
mile ¼
mile 1
Peachford Hospital
soccer
fields
Treetop
Quest
mile ½
dog park
Chowning Way
mile ¾
ruined
bridge
Pernoshal Ct
Legend
main route
other trail
paved trail
paved other trail
road
viewpoint
landmark
waterfall
point of interest
champion tree
sentinel tree
picnic area
restroom
playground
bridge
trailhead
parking
drinking fountain
information board
boardwalk
Brook Run Park
and Pernoshal Park
Pernoshal
Park
basketball
courts
sentinel
longleaf pine
N Shallowford Rd

In 0.5 mile arrive back at the main trail near mile marker ¾. Turn right and follow the paved trail as it curves around a parking lot. A mature hardwood forest is just past a fence to your right and is a much nicer view than the asphalt to your left. In 0.15 mile pass restrooms near the athletic fields on the left, then pass mile marker 1.

After crossing a park road, look for a sign about the Daffodil Project on your left and an apiary (beehives) behind a fence on the right. In 100 yards stay left at a circular trail junction. Then stay straight at the next trail junction, near a pavilion with restrooms and mile marker 1¼.

The trail parallels Barclay Drive for 0.2 mile and then turns left to reach mile marker 1½ near a bench. In 0.1 mile cross a park road and hike 0.2 mile farther around a grassy field past the playground to reach mile marker 0, where you'll end your hike.

BELTLINE CONNECTIONS–NORTHSIDE

This hike offers several opportunities to view Peachtree Creek.

Atlanta Memorial Park

Adjacent to the Bobby Jones Golf Course and Northside Beltline Trail, this park is home to some of the largest and most interesting trees in Atlanta. It was also the site of the Civil War Battle of Peachtree Creek. Because the trails here are close to many roads, you'll never forget you are in a city while you are on this hike, but you'll be awed by Atlanta's natural beauty just the same.

HOW TO GET THERE	**Driving Distance from Downtown Atlanta:** 6 miles **Address:** 650 Wesley Drive NW, Atlanta, GA 30305 **Nearest Interstate:** I-75 **Neighborhood:** Peachtree Battle / Buckhead **Public Transit:** MARTA 12 bus stops at the Howell Mill Road side of the park **Parking:** Ample street parking on Wesley Drive
HIKE DISTANCE	2-mile loop
DIFFICULTY	**Overall:** Easy to moderate **Navigation:** Occasional mile markers and maps along the trail **Terrain:** Hard-packed dirt trail, sidewalk **Elevation Change:** Mostly flat with one minor hill
SAFETY	**Usage** ★★★★☆ (park facilities and the adjacent Beltline trail are heavily used, but this hiking trail is less populated) **Visibility** ★★★★★ **Upkeep** ★★★★★ **Parking** ★★★★☆
HOURS	6:00 am to 11:00 pm
DOGS	Leashed dogs allowed
FACILITIES	• No toilets • Playground, picnic areas, benches

FEES & PERMITS None

LAND MANAGER City of Atlanta Parks & Recreation

Landmarks

CHAMPION GREEN ASH

- 123" circumference, 104' tall, 60' crown spread
- Green ash trees are valued for their speedy growth and strong, hardy wood. Recently, this species has become threatened by the emerald ash borer beetle, which is decimating populations of ash trees across the country.

CHAMPION OSAGE ORANGE

- 120" circumference, 90' tall, 71' crown spread
- Though not related to the orange—it's in the mulberry family—this species produces an orange-sized fruit that looks a little like a small green brain. The tree's dense wood withstands rot and has been used for centuries to build tool handles. This is the second largest Osage orange in Atlanta.

CHAMPION RIVER BIRCH

- 120" circumference, 74' tall, 75' crown spread
- This river birch is unusual because it stands very straight upright and is very large. Most river birches lean diagonally over streambanks. Find it along Woodward Way.

Hike Route

Park on the street on Wesley Drive. Take the sidewalk and walk east toward Northside Drive. Just before Northside Drive, at the Atlanta Memorial Park sign, turn sharply left into the park and take the first left onto a compact gravel path.

In about 100 feet on the left of the path you will reach the champion green ash tree. About 50 feet down from the champion ash, also marked with a small sign, is the champion Osage orange tree. Return to the path after visiting the trees and soon pass a nice picnic area on the left, close to the playground. A few feet after the picnic area you will come to a junction. You can take any trail, but if you stay to the far left, you will pass through a grove of bald cypress trees and a climbable box elder tree.

The city champion Osage orange tree is 10 feet in circumference and nearly 100 feet tall.

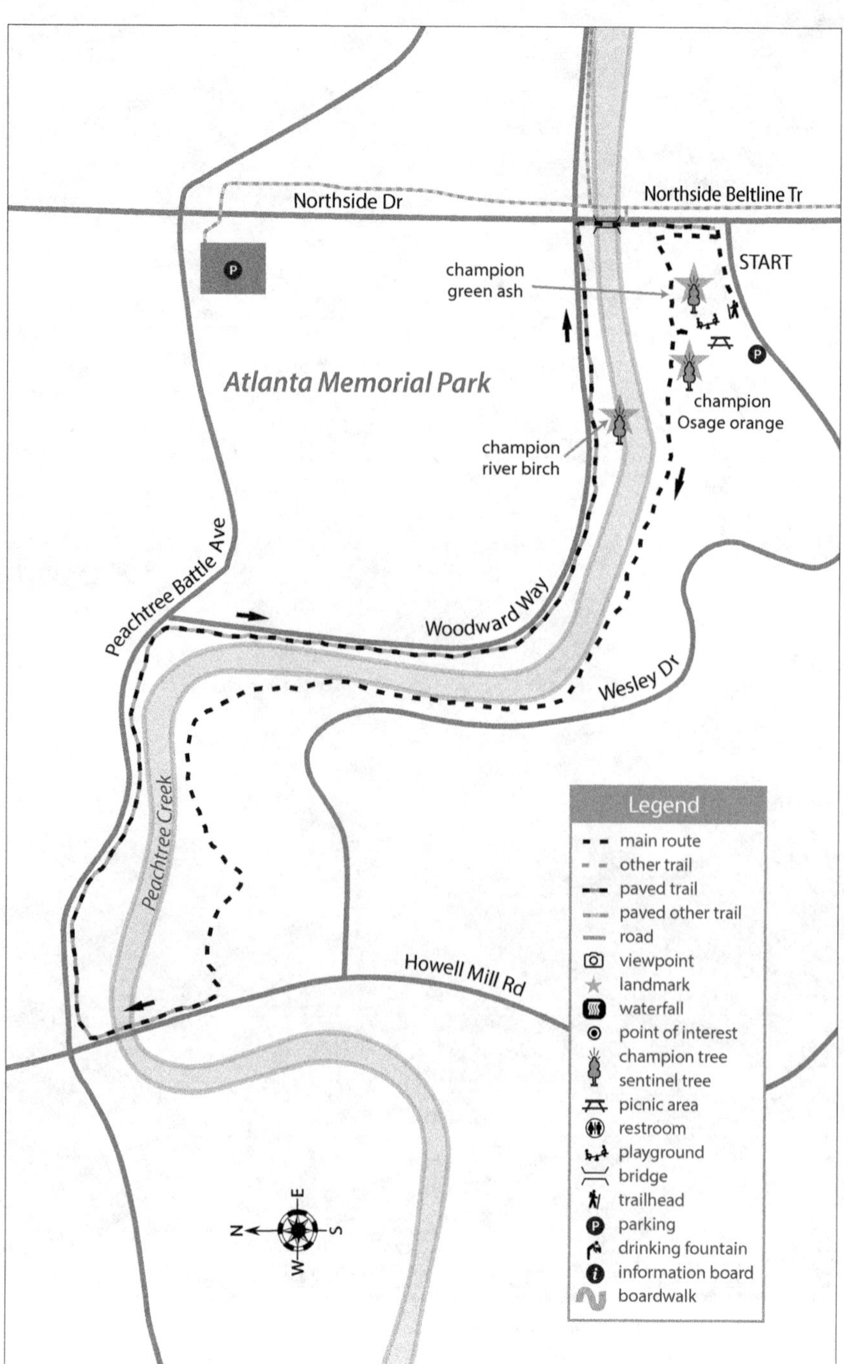
Northside Dr
Northside Beltline Tr
START
champion
green ash
Atlanta Memorial Park
champion
Osage orange
champion
river birch
Peachtree Battle Ave
Woodward Way
Wesley Dr
Peachtree Creek
Howell Mill Rd
Legend
main route
other trail
paved trail
paved other trail
road
viewpoint
landmark
waterfall
point of interest
champion tree
sentinel tree
picnic area
restroom
playground
bridge
trailhead
parking
drinking fountain
information board
boardwalk
N
E
S
W

Continue on the trail with Peachtree Creek on your right. In 0.15 mile the gravel trail becomes a compact dirt trail. After a small rock crossing, you'll pass a beautiful water oak on the right and then come to a junction. Stay to the left. In 0.15 mile at another junction go right over a small footbridge.

In 0.1 mile ascend the hill where the trail reaches the sidewalk at Howell Mill Road. Turn right and continue on the sidewalk past three historical markers about the Civil War battle that was fought here, as well as information about Howell's Mills, for which the road was named. Cross over Peachtree Creek to the corner of Howell Mill Road and Peachtree Battle Avenue (this is also the bus stop for this hike). Turn right and follow the Peachtree Battle sidewalk along Peachtree Creek.

In 0.3 mile reach the corner of Woodward Way and Peachtree Battle Avenue and a sign for Atlanta Memorial Park. Turn right and in 0.4 mile reach the champion river birch on the right. Reach Northside Drive in 0.1 mile after passing a large willow oak on the right. (Across Northside Drive and to the left is a 0.25-mile trail extension through Haynes Manor Park.) Turn right on the sidewalk to cross the Northside Drive bridge over Peachtree Creek and then turn right onto Wesley Drive to end your hike back where you started. For a longer hike, you can walk the paved multiuse trail at the corner of Wesley Drive and Northside Drive to cross underneath Northside Drive and connect with the two-mile Northside Beltline Trail around the Bobby Jones Golf Course.

A beautiful wooden sculpture of native wildlife welcomes you to the Confluence Bridge.

Confluence Trail & Cheshire Farm Trail

Get ready for an inspiring and unusual urban adventure on these trails. A natural marvel is situated almost directly underneath a feat of engineering: a confluence under an interchange. The place where North Fork and South Fork Peachtree Creek flow together is called their confluence, and you'll find it right next to a 15-lane highway interchange. The South Fork Conservancy has developed a trail system along the creeks that allows us to hike to the beautiful nature areas below these interstate bridges. Prepare for stretches of hiking under dark bridges, through remote areas between neighborhoods, and past human encampments. Invite along a human or canine friend, and you'll have a great adventure.

HOW TO GET THERE

Driving Distance from Downtown Atlanta: 8 miles

Address: 2177 Armand Road NE, Atlanta, GA 30324

Neighborhood: Lindbergh

Nearest Interstate: I-85

Public Transit: MARTA 6 bus + 0.4-mile walk, or walk 0.6 mile from the Lindbergh Transit Center to the trailhead at Adina Drive

Parking: Street parking in a small cul-de-sac near the entrance to Armand Park

HIKE DISTANCE

3.2-mile out-and-back

DIFFICULTY

Overall: Easy

Navigation: Trail maps and South Fork Conservancy signage, but no blazes; trails are obvious

Terrain: Hard-packed gravel, asphalt, and a short section of hard-packed dirt trails; some trails might be difficult for strollers

Elevation Change: Mostly flat with a few minor hills

SAFETY

Usage ★★☆☆☆

Visibility ★☆☆☆☆

Upkeep ★★★★☆

Parking ★★★★☆

HOURS	Dawn to dusk
DOGS	Leashed dogs allowed
FACILITIES	• No toilets • Playground, picnic tables, benches
FEES & PERMITS	None
LAND MANAGER	City of Atlanta Parks & Recreation in partnership with South Fork Conservancy

Landmarks

AMERICAN CHESTNUTS

One of the most important trees of the eastern United States was almost entirely wiped out by a fungal blight in the early 1900s. Scientists have been working to breed a strain of blight-resistant American chestnut. Several of these hybrid trees have been planted to the right of the trail on the embankment just below the interstate. See if you can find these young trees, marked with signs.

NATIVE ANIMAL SCULPTURES

Two wooden sculptures flank the trail near the Confluence Bridge, depicting many of the common animals found along Peachtree Creek: beaver, cottontail rabbit, great blue heron, red fox, white-tailed deer, raccoon, Canada goose, and red-tailed hawk.

CONFLUENCE BRIDGE

The crown jewel of this trail, the Confluence Bridge, has created safe pedestrian and bicycle access across the creek. This bridge will eventually connect the trails of South Fork Peachtree Creek with Buckhead's PATH400 trail, the Northside Beltline, and the Peachtree Creek Greenway.

Hike Route

Facing the playground, start your hike on the left side of Armand Park near the South Fork Conservancy trail sign and follow the crushed gravel path downhill and then to the right. On your right is a rain garden that helps filter stormwater from the street before it flows into South Fork Peachtree Creek. Enter the woods near a small South Fork Conservancy trail sign, then pass a picnic area with a view of the creek on your left.

These trails pass underneath interstate highway bridges multiple times.

In 100 yards pass a small trail on the left leading to a creekside kayak launch. Hike another 0.2 mile, and the trail makes its first pass under an interstate bridge. You'll hike under the bridge for 0.1 mile before emerging in a meadow-like trail above the creek. About 100 yards after leaving the interstate bridge, look on the embankment to your right, just before crossing a stormwater runoff channel, to find a small grove of hybrid American chestnut trees that have been planted as part of a project to bring back the once mighty American chestnut forests of the eastern United States.

Past the chestnuts, the trail passes between two wooden statues of native animals, and then you'll reach the Confluence Bridge. Before crossing the bridge, take the trail on the right to curve under the bridge to reach an overlook and steps that lead down to the confluence of South Fork and North Fork Peachtree Creeks. After viewing the creek, turn back and take the path on the right to loop back to the bridge entrance.

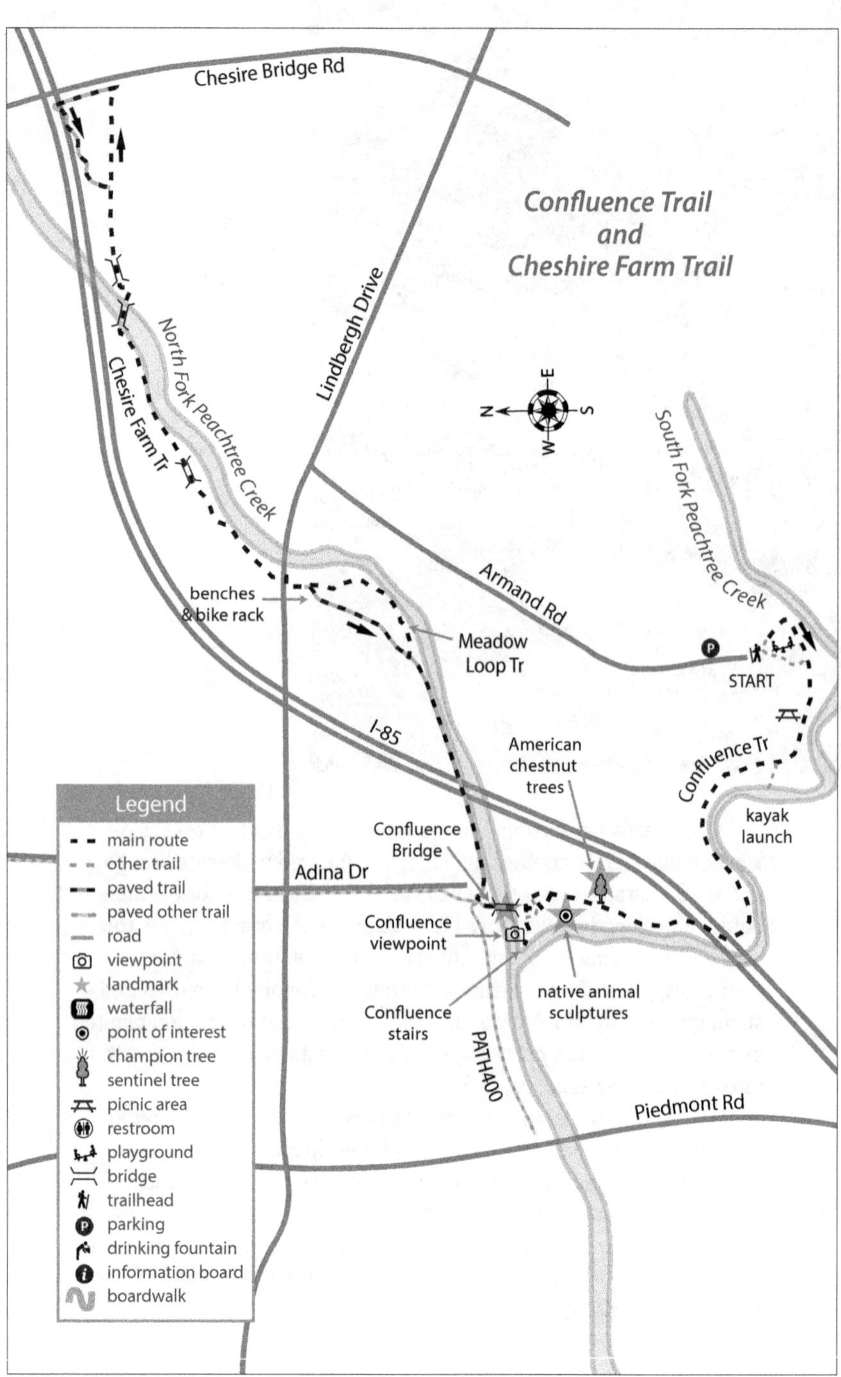

Chesire Bridge Rd
Confluence Trail
and
Cheshire Farm Trail
Lindbergh Drive
North Fork Peachtree Creek
Chesire Farm Tr
N
E
S
W
South Fork Peachtree Creek
Armand Rd
benches
& bike rack
Meadow
Loop Tr
START
I-85
American
chestnut
trees
Confluence Tr
kayak
launch
Confluence
Bridge
Adina Dr
Confluence
viewpoint
Confluence
stairs
native animal
sculptures
PATH400
Piedmont Rd
Legend
main route
other trail
paved trail
paved other trail
road
viewpoint
landmark
waterfall
point of interest
champion tree
sentinel tree
picnic area
restroom
playground
bridge
trailhead
parking
drinking fountain
information board
boardwalk

Cross the Confluence Bridge over North Fork Peachtree Creek to reach a paved multiuse path and junction near Adina Drive. Eventually, the path to the left will connect with the Beltline. Straight ahead, looking north along Adina Drive, you can connect to PATH400. Go right on the paved path that parallels the creek, then walk under multiple interstate bridges.

After emerging from under the bridges, you'll arrive at a junction with Meadow Loop Trail. Turn right to follow this dirt trail for 0.2 mile to reach a stone patio, benches, and a bike rack near Lindbergh Drive. Turn right and carefully cross Lindbergh Drive. From here, the trail surface is crushed gravel and is fairly eroded. It is passable on bicycle, but, unlike the previous paved trail, it is not good for wheelchairs or most strollers.

Hike 0.25 mile to a long bridge over North Fork Peachtree Creek under an I-85 on-ramp. After a steep downhill and crossing a smaller bridge, reach a junction in 0.1 mile with a concrete path on your left. Stay straight on the gravel path to reach Cheshire Bridge Road in 0.1 mile. Turn left onto the sidewalk along Cheshire Bridge Road. Just after reaching the interstate bridge, you'll see another trailhead on your left. Leave the sidewalk and hike this paved path back to the gravel trail and then turn right to retrace your steps back to Armand Park. The only alternative route on the way back is to hike the paved path after crossing Lindbergh Drive instead of the Meadow Loop Trail, which you've already hiked.

In 1.4 miles reach Armand Park to end your hike.

Piedmont Park has some of the best skyline views in the city.

Piedmont Park & Eastside Beltline

Piedmont Park is often called the Central Park of Atlanta. Not surprising, since its creators, the Olmsted Brothers, also designed Central Park in New York City. Though most people know Piedmont Park for its open lawns, which host concerts, art festivals, and outdoor movies, the forests of Piedmont Park have a special magic. This hike can introduce you to the natural areas of the park you may not be as familiar with.

HOW TO GET THERE

Driving Distance from Downtown Atlanta: 3 miles

Address: 1345 Piedmont Avenue NE, Atlanta, GA 30309

Nearest Interstate: I-75/I-85

Neighborhood: Midtown

Public Transit: MARTA 27 bus + 0.2-mile walk

Parking: Park in the SAGE parking deck (the deck is shared with guests of the Atlanta Botanical Garden, so be sure to check ahead for special events in Piedmont Park or the Atlanta Botanical Garden, when the deck will be very crowded)

HIKE DISTANCE

2.5-mile loop

DIFFICULTY

Overall: Easy to moderate

Navigation: Yellow signs on posts throughout the park

Terrain: Paved multiuse trails, some gravel paths, and a few dirt trails

Elevation Change: Mostly flat with a few minor hills

SAFETY

Usage ★★★★★

Visibility ★★★★★

Upkeep ★★★★★

Parking ★★★★★

HOURS

6:00 am to 11:00 pm

DOGS

Leashed dogs allowed

FACILITIES	• Toilets • Playgrounds, picnic areas, water fountains, info kiosks, sports fields, outdoor fitness equipment, dog park, restaurants, pool and splash park (summer only)
FEES & PERMITS	None
LAND MANAGER	City of Atlanta Parks & Recreation and Piedmont Park Conservancy

Landmarks

CHIMNEY SWIFT TOWER

Chimney swifts are migratory birds that roost upside down like bats in long hollow structures (like old chimneys and large hollow trees). Because suitable roosting spots can be hard to find, human-made swift towers like this one provide a safe haven for these special birds.

MAYOR'S MEMORY GROVE

A few yards from the Greystone Building is the Mayor's Memory Grove. Here you can see a list of the past mayors of the city and their terms of office and a tree planted in honor of each mayor.

STATE CHAMPION PIN OAK

- 158" circumference, 83' tall, 100' crown spread
- This pin oak was planted less than 100 years ago and thrives because of good growing conditions and little competition for sunlight. It's visible from the front entrance of the Greystone Building.

Hike Route

Start your hike at the bottom/ground level of the SAGE parking deck at the information kiosk and paved circle behind Magnolia Hall. If you are parked at a different level, you can take the elevator or stairs down to the bottom level to reach the Welcome Plaza.

Begin your hike by crossing the plaza down the stairs. Follow the yellow directional sign toward the dog park, taking a sharp left downhill. In 0.1 mile continue straight on the paved path through the tunnel under Evelyn Street.

After another 0.1 mile pass a ramp and staircase on your left that lead up to the Legacy Foundation and Grand Arbor (where you can also find toilets). Continue straight on the paved trail that continues

Chimney swift towers give migrating birds a place to rest.

along Clear Creek for another 0.2 mile before it intersects at Westminster Drive. Turn right and continue straight on the sidewalk through the roundabout, taking a right onto the Piedmont Commons loop. Immediately on your right is a chimney swift tower installed in partnership with the Birds Georgia. Along this route you'll find several interpretive signs developed by the Piedmont Park Conservancy that discuss watersheds, pollinators, native plants and animals, and pollution. Look for ways individual actions can contribute to a healthy ecosystem. Stay left at each junction to loop back, past beehives, to Westminster Drive.

Follow the path along Westminster Drive back uphill and take the first left onto the gravel path (soon to be paved) of the Eastside Beltline Trail. There are various art installations along this section of trail. In 0.3 mile carefully cross Evelyn Street and continue straight on the gravel trail. In another 0.2 mile walk through the Park Drive underpass, which is painted with a colorful mural. Immediately after passing under the bridge, turn right down the stairs and connect back to the paved Piedmont Park path near the dog park. Turn left and walk

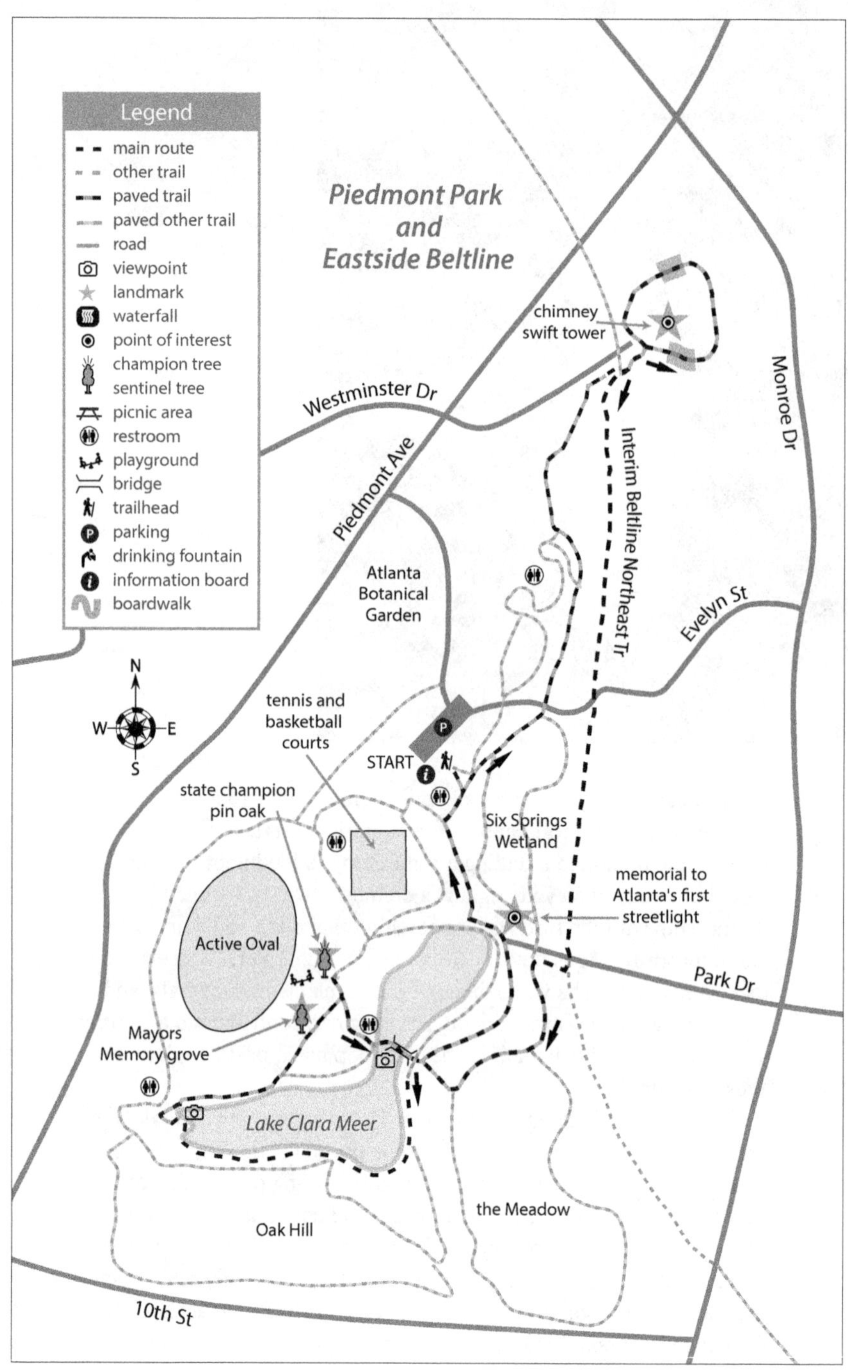
Legend
main route
other trail
paved trail
paved other trail
road
viewpoint
landmark
waterfall
point of interest
champion tree
sentinel tree
picnic area
restroom
playground
bridge
trailhead
parking
drinking fountain
information board
boardwalk
Piedmont Park and Eastside Beltline
N
W
E
S
chimney swift tower
Westminster Dr
Piedmont Ave
Monroe Dr
Interim Beltline Northeast Tr
Atlanta Botanical Garden
Evelyn St
tennis and basketball courts
START
state champion pin oak
Six Springs Wetland
memorial to Atlanta's first streetlight
Active Oval
Park Dr
Mayors Memory grove
Lake Clara Meer
the Meadow
Oak Hill
10th St

100 yards past the orchard and children's garden. Just beyond a flight of stairs on the right and the children's garden on the left, follow the path to the right as it curves around the Meadow and up the hill.

At the top of the hill curve right, then continue straight, across the main park road, toward a bridge over Lake Clara Meer. Just before crossing the bridge, take a sharp left and follow the small gravel path between the lakeshore and the main road. Look out across the lake for some of the city's best views of the Atlanta skyline. Shortly past a metal dogwood art installation take the path to the right, down to the water's edge, and continue on the compact gravel trail for 0.25 mile where the trail reaches the main dock of Lake Clara Meer below the historic visitor center. Walk around the circular path and continue up the far stairs. At the top of the stairs, turn right on the smaller sidewalk closest to the lake's edge. Follow this trail for 0.2 mile, staying to the left where it forks toward the historic Greystone Building and then going right toward the Greystone Building, playground, and swimming pool.

In 0.1 mile you will reach the Mayor's Memory Grove, which includes a monument to the past mayors of Atlanta and a tree planted in honor of each one. Walk toward the Greystone Building and you'll see the state champion pin oak on your left. The Greystone Building was a bathhouse in the late 1920s. Continue to the front of the Greystone Building and then take a sharp right to walk toward the bridge over Lake Clara Meer. On the way, you'll pass a playground on your right and toilets and a water fountain on your left.

Cross the bridge and turn left onto the park's asphalt main road. In 0.2 mile where the road forks, stay to the left, passing a memorial structure of Atlanta's first streetlight system made from the granite of Atlanta's first pavement. In 100 yards take a right and hike along a more narrow path, passing bocce ball courts on your left. When you reach a trail junction below Magnolia Hall, turn right and continue up the path, going left and then up the stairs to end your hike at the welcome kiosk near the parking deck.

A unique covered boardwalk helps hikers pass safely beneath a tall railroad trestle.

Tanyard Creek Park & Northside Beltline

The Eastside and Westside Beltlines have been developed for years and are lined with businesses, condos, and restaurants. But the Northside Beltline is still a hiker's destination. Though it is a paved urban trail that crosses three city parks between a golf course and residential neighborhoods, this hike is delightfully beautiful and serene. The route leads through a mature hardwood forest past an enormous champion white ash and parallels Tanyard Creek. If you want a longer walk, you can extend this hike by two miles on the Northside Beltline Trail around the Bobby Jones Golf Course.

HOW TO GET THERE	**Driving Distance from Downtown Atlanta:** 6 miles **Address:** 480 Collier Road NW, Atlanta, GA 30309 **Neighborhood:** Collier Hills **Nearest Interstate:** I-75 **Public Transit:** MARTA 110 bus + 0.6-mile walk **Parking:** Small paved parking lot off Collier Road at the intersection with Overbrook Drive or street parking off Walthall Drive
HIKE DISTANCE	2-mile out-and-back
DIFFICULTY	**Overall:** Easy **Navigation:** Wayfinding signage along route **Terrain:** Paved multiuse path **Elevation Change:** Mostly flat
SAFETY	**Usage** ★★★★★ **Visibility** ★★★★★ **Upkeep** ★★★★★ **Parking** ★★★☆☆
HOURS	6:00 am to 11:00 pm
DOGS	Leashed dogs allowed
FACILITIES	• No toilets • Trash cans, benches, playgrounds

FEES & PERMITS	None
LAND MANAGER	City of Atlanta Parks & Recreation and Beltline Foundation

Landmarks

SENTINEL SYCAMORE

Just off the right of the trail, this sycamore stands out not only for its size but also for its unusually curved trunk, leading to the obvious question: What caused the tree to grow in such a way?

STATE CHAMPION WHITE ASH

- 172" circumference, 129' tall, 56' crown spread
- This massive white ash stands less than a foot from the paved path and has a marker at its base. White ash is common, but an ash of this size is quite remarkable. It stands on an old homestead site that is now Louise G. Howard Park.

JUNIPER AND HACKBERRY

Find these two beautiful trees on the right of the trail between the golf course and the neighborhood. These two native trees produce a dark berry. Juniper berries are most widely used in the production of gin.

Hike Route

From the small parking lot, take the stairs down to the trailhead. There are several interpretive signs on your way down to the main path that detail the Battle of Peachtree Creek, which took place here. If you need a ramped entrance to the trail, you can start on Walthall Drive instead.

At the Beltline Trail turn right and immediately cross a bridge over a tributary of Tanyard Creek. Continue straight on the path for 0.1 mile before coming to a bridge on the left under power lines. There is a nice viewpoint of the creek here, but you're unlikely to see much wildlife due to the proximity to the road. Enjoy the view and then return to the path and continue the way you were going.

As you hike on you'll pass a playground surrounded by large trees. The trail curves left and over a bridge. There are small unofficial trails on either side of the bridge that you can use to get down to the creek, but be aware that this is an urban watershed, and you should avoid swimming or playing in the water.

This trail runs parallel to scenic Tanyard Creek.

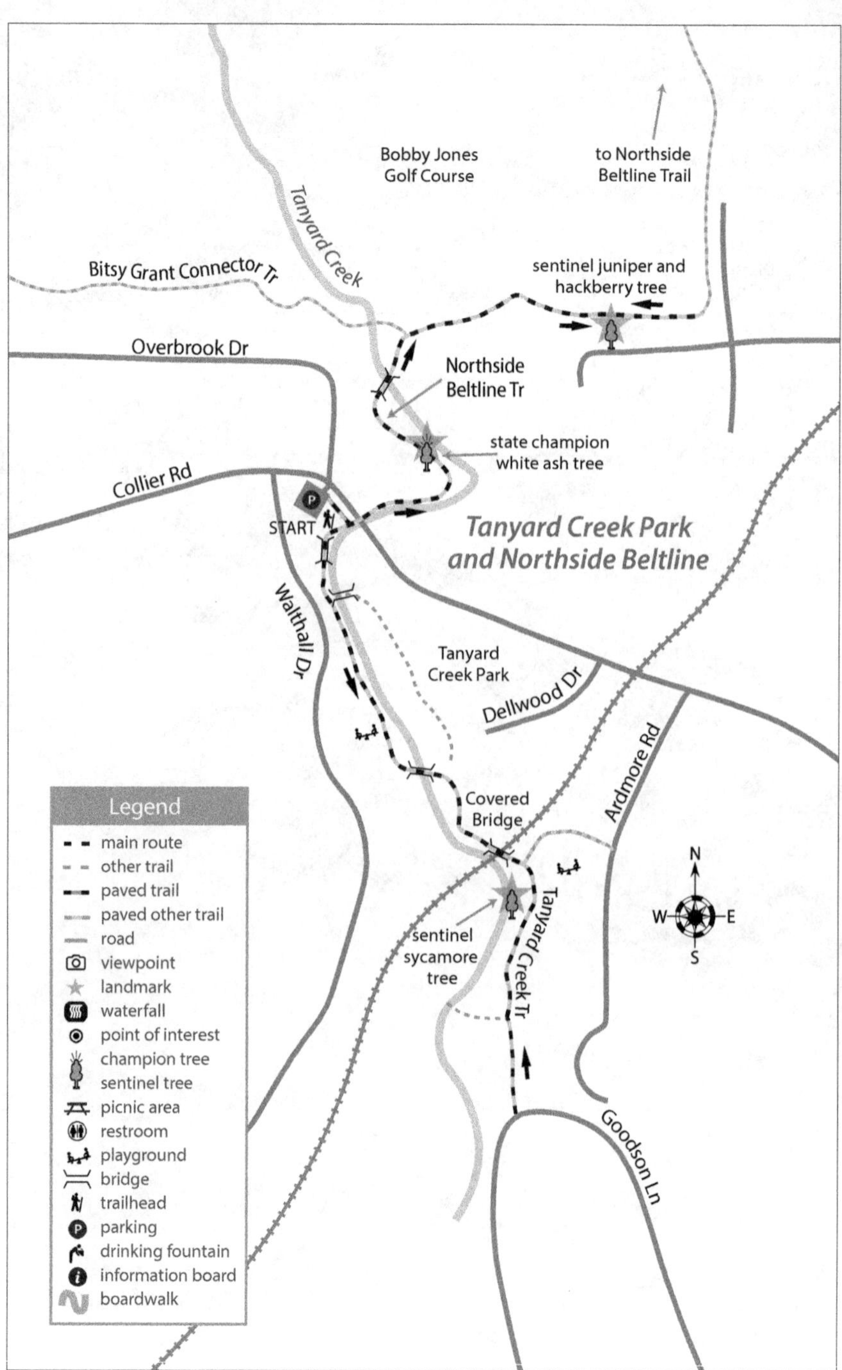

Bobby Jones
Golf Course
to Northside
Beltline Trail
Tanyard Creek
Bitsy Grant Connector Tr
sentinel juniper and
hackberry tree
Overbrook Dr
Northside
Beltline Tr
state champion
white ash tree
Collier Rd
START
Tanyard Creek Park
and Northside Beltline
Walthall Dr
Tanyard
Creek Park
Dellwood Dr
Ardmore Rd
Covered
Bridge
sentinel
sycamore
tree
Tanyard Creek Tr
Goodson Ln
N
W
E
S
Legend
main route
other trail
paved trail
paved other trail
road
viewpoint
landmark
waterfall
point of interest
champion tree
sentinel tree
picnic area
restroom
playground
bridge
trailhead
parking
drinking fountain
information board
boardwalk

Past the bridge 0.1 mile you'll reach a covered boardwalk that takes you under a railroad bridge. Immediately after exiting the covered boardwalk, you'll come to a junction near the Ardmore Park playground. Take the trail to the right, and in 100 yards you'll reach a sentinel sycamore, just off the right side of the trail.

After admiring the uniquely shaped tree, continue on the path for another 0.1 mile. The trail ends at stairs leading into a residential area. (Just before the stairs, an unofficial dirt trail leads to a creek monitoring station, where you can see a section of Tanyard Creek that has been channelized by concrete.) Turn around and retrace your steps back to where you began the hike. (On your way, just before crossing the bridge over Tanyard Creek, you could take an alternative route, which is to walk across the grassy field to the small viewpoint bridge where you stopped before.) Back where you started, instead of returning to the parking lot, continue straight beneath the Collier Road underpass.

Continue on the path, walking adjacent to a particularly scenic and rocky section of Tanyard Creek. In 0.15 mile the trail curves to the left and brings you to the 2010 state champion white ash. There's a small marker at the base of the tree.

In another 100 yards cross another bridge over Tanyard Creek. Pass a group of large boulders near a junction with the Northwest Beltline Connector to Bitsy Grant Tennis Center. Stay to the right to hike along the edge of the Bobby Jones Golf Course. In 0.1 mile on the right, just as the trail comes parallel with Golfview Road, look for a leaning juniper tree (also known as eastern red cedar) next to a giant hackberry tree, both of which are uniquely beautiful trees.

Continue on the path to where the trail intersects with North Colonial Homes Circle. Turn around here and retrace your steps 0.6 mile back to the parking lot to end your hike. If you want more hiking, continue straight on the Northside Beltline Trail for a two-mile loop around the golf course and through the Bitsy Grant Tennis Center, then back to your vehicle.

CHATTAHOOCHEE RIVER NATIONAL RECREATION AREA

The East Palisades trail is one of the best places to get sweeping views of the Chattahoochee.

East Palisades

This trail has gained popularity for its remarkable bamboo grove, a sought-after site for photo shoots on social media. But beyond its online presence, East Palisades is special for its stunning views of the Chattahoochee and ability to make you feel like you're in the mountains without leaving Atlanta's perimeter. The hike route passes through many ecological zones and has abundant wildlife and plant diversity—it's a hike not to miss.

HOW TO GET THERE	**Driving Distance from Downtown Atlanta:** 11 miles **Address:** 4058 Whitewater Creek Road NW, Atlanta, GA 30327 **Nearest Interstate:** I-75 **Neighborhood:** Mount Paran / Northside **Public Transit:** CobbLinc 50 bus + 3-mile walk to Indian Trail trailhead **Parking:** Gravel parking lot at the end of a National Park Service access road off Whitewater Creek Road
HIKE DISTANCE	4-mile loop
DIFFICULTY	**Overall:** Moderate to strenuous **Navigation:** Map posts at most junctions **Terrain:** Hard-packed dirt trails **Elevation Change:** Several extended ascents and descents
SAFETY	**Usage** ★★★★★ **Visibility** ★★★☆☆ **Upkeep** ★★★★☆ **Parking** ★★★★☆
HOURS	Dawn to dusk
DOGS	Leashed dogs allowed (many people use an area near the parking lot as an unofficial dog park, and you are likely to encounter many unleashed dogs at the beginning and along the first mile of the hike)

FACILITIES	• No toilets • Maps and trash cans
FEES & PERMITS	$5 daily fee—purchase at recreation.gov
LAND MANAGER	Chattahoochee River National Recreation Area—National Park Service

Landmarks

CITY CHAMPION RIVER BIRCH

- 103" circumference, 84' tall, 53' crown spread
- River birch (*Betula nigra*) is the only birch species commonly found in the metro area. It has bark that curls outward and must be near a permanent water source to survive. This tree is among the largest river birches inside the perimeter.

CITY CHAMPION PAWPAW

- 21" circumference, 37' tall, 11' crown spread
- No other tree native to North America produces a fruit as large as the pawpaw. The trees usually grow no higher than 15 or 20 feet but can produce a six-inch-long soft green fruit that people say tastes like the combination of a banana and a mango.

SENTINEL MOUNTAIN LAUREL

Though common to the North Georgia mountains, mountain laurel is more rare in Atlanta. It likes acidic rocky soils and steep slopes—exactly the habitat in the creek hollow at East Palisades. Visit in late spring, when the gorgeous pink-and-white flowers put on quite a show.

Hike Route

From the parking lot, begin your hike to the right at the map kiosk and immediately cross a bridge over the creek. Turn left at junction EP 1 and cross another bridge. In 0.2 mile cross a third bridge. In 0.1 mile you'll reach a large sycamore tree on the right. About 20 feet off the trail behind the sycamore is a city champion river birch.

In 0.2 mile cross a boardwalk and turn left at junction EP 2. Walk along the water's edge, and in 0.2 mile reach the city champion pawpaw tree just before junction EP 4. The tree is on your left, leaning over the water's edge. Depending on the time of year, you may see the green pod-like fruits developing. At junction EP 4 turn left.

The bamboo grove is a surprising and spectacular sight along the trail.

In less than 75 yards, turn right at junction EP 5 and hike up a steep hill. Turn left at the next junction (EP 6). The trail winds uphill for the next 0.35 mile. Continue straight at junction EP 8 halfway up the hill. In about 100 yards on the left you'll pass a large white oak along the ridgeline and continue on the trail as it curves to the right.

In 0.15 mile turn left at a junction (EP 10), then stay left at successive junctions. The trail descends a steep set of stairs to an overlook platform that provides nice views of the Chattahoochee. After taking in the view, continue along the trail (it's a right turn if you're facing the overlook), passing through a thicket of mountain laurel.

At the next junction (EP 14), stay straight. If you turn left, you will end up at the right place eventually, but the trail will take you down an incredibly steep hill that can be very difficult to navigate.

Hike 0.25 mile downhill to reach Cabin Creek. Cross a bridge on the left and pass several large sentinel mountain laurels. Stay left at junction EP 23 and hop across a small creek crossing. Walk uphill and to the left along the wider trail.

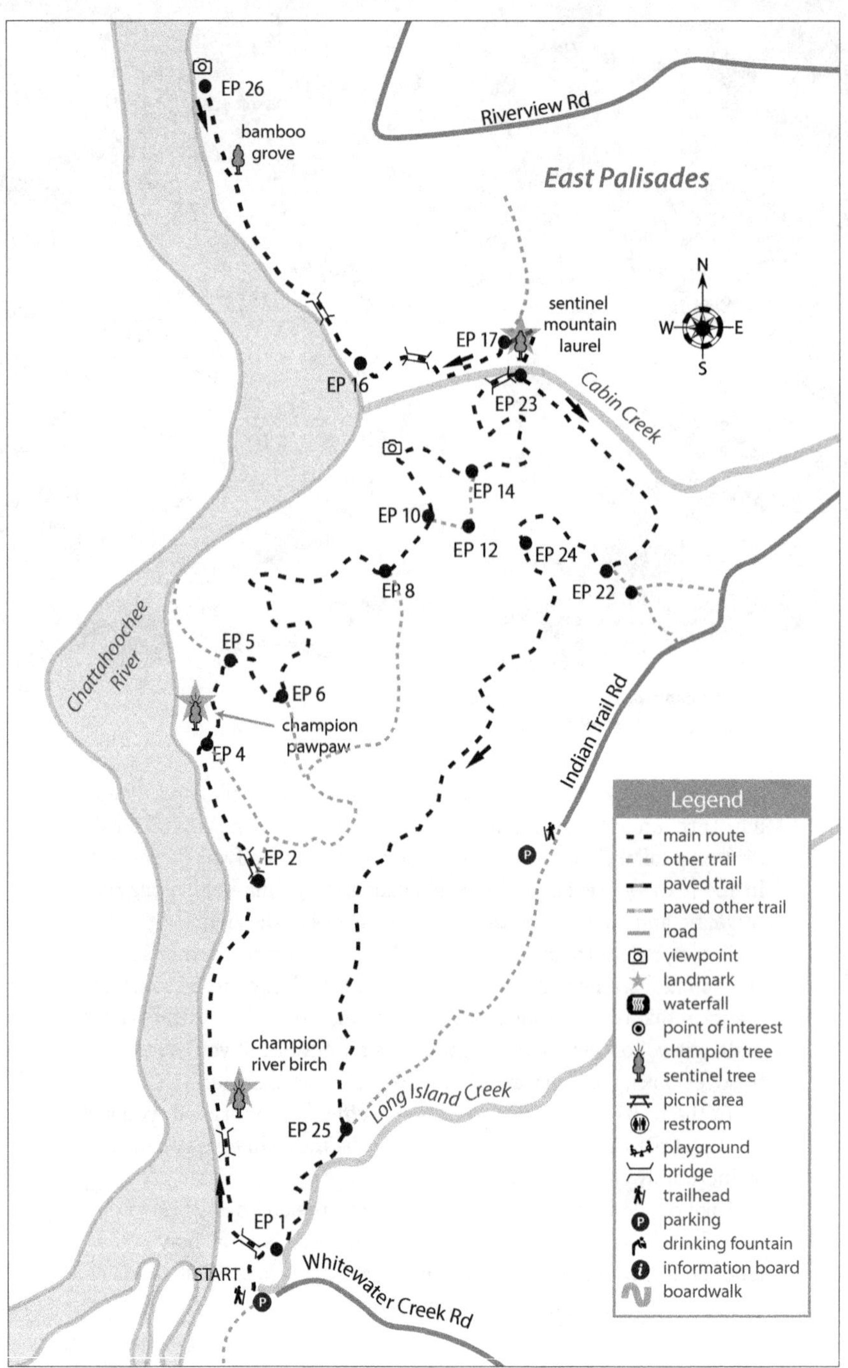

EP 26
bamboo grove
Riverview Rd
East Palisades
N
W
E
S
sentinel mountain laurel
EP 17
EP 16
EP 23
Cabin Creek
EP 14
EP 10
EP 12
EP 24
EP 8
EP 22
Chattahoochee River
EP 5
EP 6
champion pawpaw
EP 4
Indian Trail Rd
EP 2
champion river birch
Long Island Creek
EP 25
EP 1
START
Whitewater Creek Rd
Legend
main route
other trail
paved trail
paved other trail
road
viewpoint
landmark
waterfall
point of interest
champion tree
sentinel tree
picnic area
restroom
playground
bridge
trailhead
parking
drinking fountain
information board
boardwalk

Continue straight at the next junction (EP 17), then hike downhill to a bridge before reaching the foundation of an old building by the river's edge. Turn right and in 0.1 mile cross a bridge. Continue on the trail parallel to the Chattahoochee for another 0.2 mile to reach the bamboo grove. This grove has become a popular spot for photos and offers great views of the river.

Continue past the bamboo grove for 0.1 mile, following the trail up the rocks to a rocky viewpoint of the river. The trail leading up can be overgrown and steep, so be careful. The top of the rocks is a great place to have lunch or a snack and is also the turnaround point of this hike.

Return the way you came, passing the bamboo. At the old foundation, turn left. Continue the way you came until you reach the large wooden bridge over Cabin Creek by the sentinel mountain laurel. Cross the bridge and turn left at junction EP 23.

This small trail hugs the bank of the creek for 0.25 mile and then curves away from the creek to the right and uphill for 0.1 mile to reach a junction (EP 22) with a wider trail. Turn right, hiking uphill as the trail curves to the left. In 0.1 mile at the next junction (EP 24), stay to the left, taking the trail downhill.

In 0.6 mile after four small creek crossings you'll come to an interesting rock face on your left. In 0.2 mile at junction EP 25, go to the right. Follow this trail across a bridge and hike along Whitewater Creek for 0.1 mile to return to the larger bridge you crossed at the beginning of the hike. Cross the bridge and turn left to reach the parking area and finish your hike.

You'll quickly forget your proximity to the highway on this trail.

West Palisades

On beautiful warm weekends, Atlantans flock to the West Palisades unit of the Chattahoochee River National Recreation Area for hiking, swimming, and rafting. This trail includes a section of paved multi-use path, beautiful forest trails, and a swimming hole. Enjoy watching people "shooting the Hooch" in tubes and boats. Bring your swimsuit if you are brave enough to take a dip in the cold urban river water.

HOW TO GET THERE

Driving Distance from Downtown Atlanta: 11 miles
Address: 3444 Cobb Parkway, Atlanta, GA 30339
Neighborhood: Vinings
Nearest Interstate: I-75
Public Transit: MARTA 12 bus + 0.2-mile walk
Parking: Large paved parking lot

HIKE DISTANCE

4.5-mile lollipop loop

DIFFICULTY

Overall: Moderate to strenuous
Navigation: Map posts at most junctions
Terrain: Hard-packed dirt and gravel trails plus a section of paved trail
Elevation Change: Several extended ascents and descents

SAFETY

Usage ★★★★★
Visibility ★★★★☆
Upkeep ★★★★☆
Parking ★★★★★

HOURS

Dawn to dusk

DOGS

Leashed dogs allowed

FACILITIES

- Toilets
- Maps, garbage cans, water fountain, picnic tables

FEES & PERMITS

$5 daily fee—purchase at recreation.gov

LAND MANAGER	Chattahoochee River National Recreation Area—National Park Service

Landmarks

SENTINEL NORTHERN RED OAK

This tree at the river's edge is impressively large compared to its neighbors. Take note of the interesting structure of the tree: the base is quite thick, while the crown is quite small.

ROCK OUTCROP VIEWPOINT

This natural resting point is a great place to take a photo or experience the beauty of the Chattahoochee River. On hot summer days you may see people rafting, kayaking, or tubing down the river.

SENTINEL BEECH

This beech is one of the largest trees in the forest. Beech trees can tolerate a variety of growing conditions and are usually found near water.

Hike Route

Start your hike on the paved multiuse Rottenwood Creek Trail (WP 1) at the far end of the parking lot next to the large grassy field. Walk on the path for 0.5 mile under the I-75 bridge to a footbridge over Rottenwood Creek. After crossing the bridge, turn right at junction WP 2 onto a hard-packed dirt trail that parallels the Chattahoochee River.

In 0.1 mile pass a sentinel northern red oak on your right. Then in 0.2 mile reach a rock outcrop with a great view of the river. Continue past the outcrop for 0.1 mile over a footbridge that brings you to junction WP 5. Turn left and hike uphill for 0.2 mile to another junction (WP 4). Turn right and continue hiking uphill for 0.1 mile until the trail levels out at the top of the hill.

Hike along the ridge for 0.4 mile, continuing on the trail when it descends. At a junction (WP 6) at the bottom of the hill, turn right, following the blue blazes. Follow this trail for 0.2 mile, staying straight at subsequent unofficial junctions until the hill ascends slightly and connects with a wide dirt road (WP 8). Turn right onto the roadbed and follow the trail down a steep hill.

Pass two trail junctions (WP 9 and WP 15) on your way down the hill. When the roadbed splits at a grassy clearing, stay to the left to

Enjoy panoramic views of the Chattahoochee River.

reach restrooms and a trail junction (WP 11). Stay left after passing the bathhouse, following the trail for 0.2 mile to reach a sandy area and a nice spot for swimming, snacking, and/or taking in the views of the river. When you're ready, return the way you came. When you reach junction WP 11 near the restrooms, stay left to follow the trail parallel to the river. Continue hiking with the river on your left. At a junction (WP 10) in 100 yards, turn right and then immediately left back onto the wide paved road you hiked down previously.

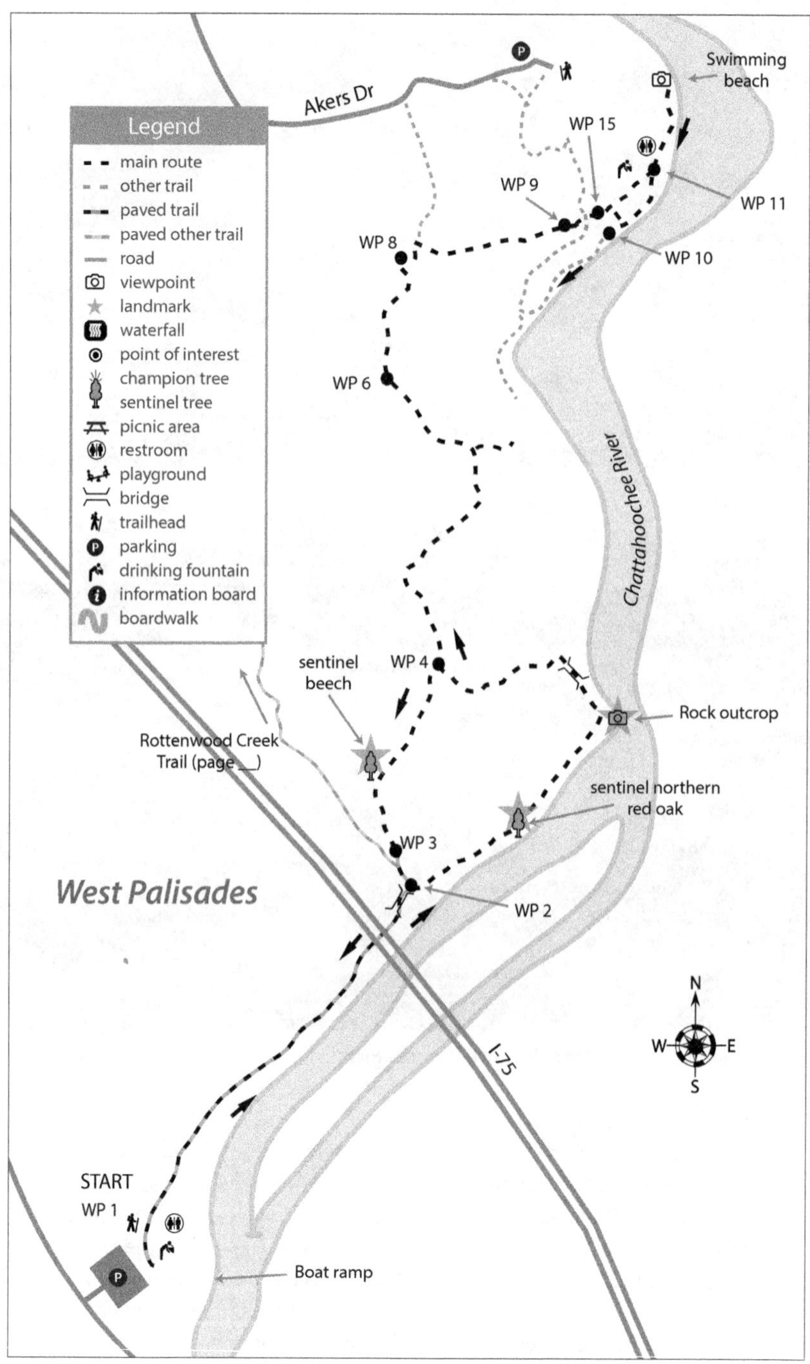

Akers Dr
Legend
main route
other trail
paved trail
paved other trail
road
viewpoint
landmark
waterfall
point of interest
champion tree
sentinel tree
picnic area
restroom
playground
bridge
trailhead
parking
drinking fountain
information board
boardwalk
Swimming beach
WP 15
WP 9
WP 11
WP 8
WP 10
WP 6
Chattahoochee River
sentinel beech
WP 4
Rock outcrop
Rottenwood Creek Trail (page ___)
sentinel northern red oak
WP 3
West Palisades
WP 2
N
W
E
S
I-75
START
WP 1
Boat ramp

In 0.1 mile turn left at the No Bikes signpost and continue back the way you came. In 0.2 mile turn left at junction WP 6 and hike back uphill. In 0.5 mile, at junction WP 4, stay to the right and continue hiking downhill, reaching a sentinel beech tree on your right in 0.15 mile. Continue on this trail until it intersects with Rottenwood Creek Trail at junction WP 3 and turn left onto the paved path. Take the trail over the bridge, under I-75, and back to the parking area to end your hike.

Enjoy beautiful creekside views along the trail.

Bob Callan Trail

As you traverse long sections of elevated path, you'll enjoy scenic views of Rottenwood Creek in the midst of the urban landscape of Cobb County. The highlight of this trail may be the rock outcrop creek viewpoint, a perfect place to appreciate the beauty of this urban creek. For those wanting a full day of adventure, this multiuse trail connects to the West Palisades (page 351) unit of the Chattahoochee River National Recreation Area via the Rottenwood Creek Trail (page 363) to the south.

HOW TO GET THERE	**Driving Distance from Downtown Atlanta:** 13 miles **Address:** 296 Interstate North Circle SE, Atlanta, GA 30339 **Neighborhood:** Cumberland **Nearest Interstate:** I-285 **Public Transit:** CobbLinc 10 bus + 1-mile walk **Parking:** Small paved parking lot
HIKE DISTANCE	2-mile out-and-back
DIFFICULTY	**Overall:** Easy to moderate **Navigation:** Map at trailhead; occasional wayfinding signage **Terrain:** Paved multiuse path **Elevation Change:** Minimal elevation change with a few minor hills
SAFETY	**Usage** ★★★★☆ **Visibility** ★★★★☆ **Upkeep** ★★★★★ **Parking** ★★★★☆
HOURS	Dawn to dusk
DOGS	Leashed dogs allowed
FACILITIES	• No toilets • Benches, picnic tables, trash cans

FEES & PERMITS	None
LAND MANAGER	Cobb County Parks & Recreation, Cumberland Trails

Landmarks

SENTINEL TULIP TREE

Tulip trees, commonly known as tulip poplars, are an American hardwood. They were often used by Native Americans and early European settlers to make dugout canoes. The Muscogee (Creek) traditionally used the bark of the tree to make baskets.

CREEK VIEWPOINT

The rock outcrop is easily accessed from the trail and is a beautiful spot to have a snack, read a book, or just admire the beauty of Rottenwood Creek.

SENTINEL BEECH TREE

This American beech is among the larger trees you'll pass along the hike. Female beech trees like this one produce a fruit called a beechnut that ripens and falls in autumn.

Hike Route

Start your hike from the map sign near the parking lot and take the trail to the left. Stay straight to enter a long elevated path parallel to Rottenwood Creek. In 0.25 mile, just after passing under the Windy Ridge Parkway bridge, you can find a sentinel tulip tree on the left side of the trail. Then pass picnic tables on the left, next to a large office building. Continue for another 0.25 mile to reach another long elevated path.

When the elevated path returns to ground level and the trail curves to the right, there's a rock outcrop to the right of the trail that's a nice spot to have a snack and watch the creek flow by. From here the trail continues curving between office buildings and the creek. Just as the trail curves left around a fenced building close to the trail, look to the right, just off the trail near the water's edge, for a sentinel beech tree.

In 0.1 mile you'll pass the remains of an old bridge leading to a residential area across the creek on the right. Although this trail is close to homes and businesses, it is still quiet and calm and hosts native plant species such as elderberry and muscadine.

The paved multiuse trail is great for hikers, bikers, strollers, and wheelchair users.

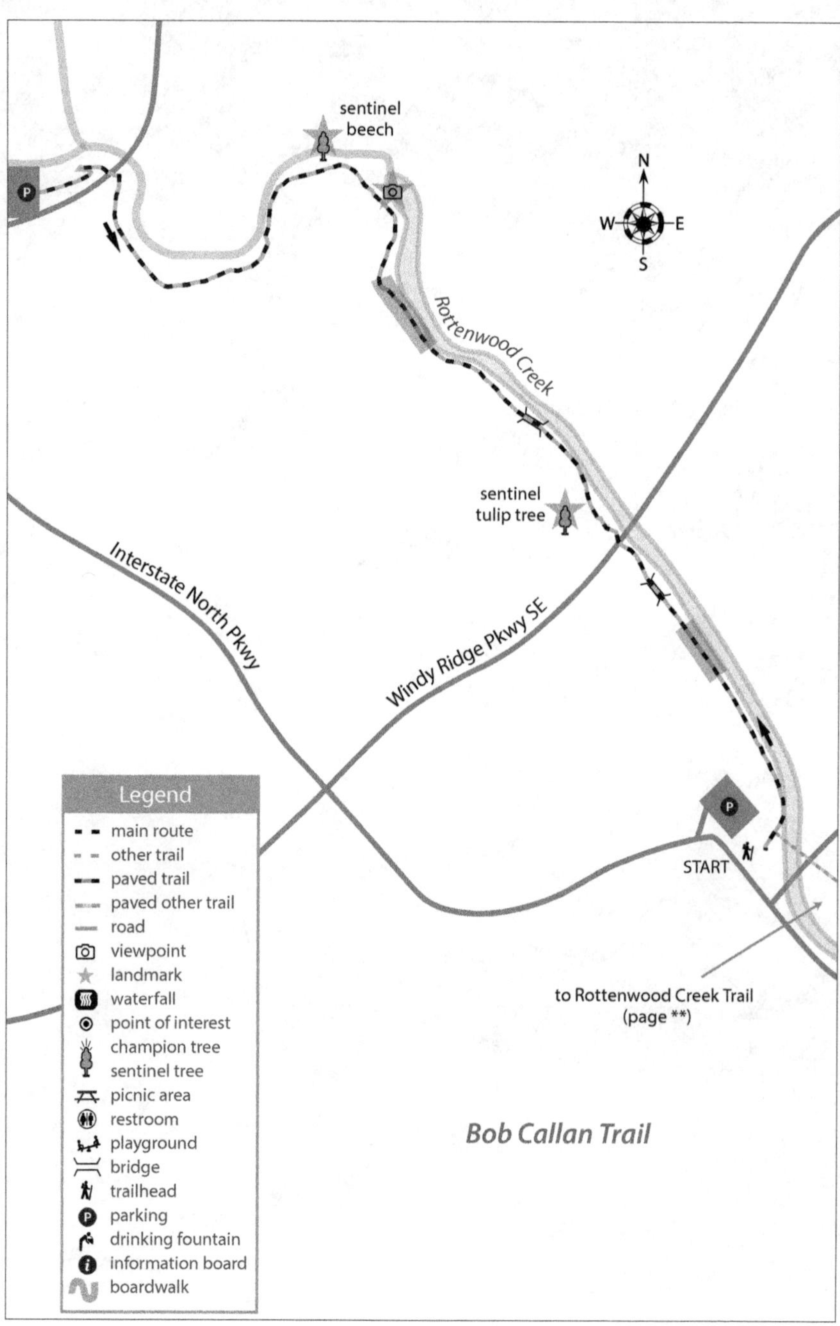
sentinel
beech
N
W
E
S
Rottenwood Creek
sentinel
tulip tree
Interstate North Pkwy
Windy Ridge Pkwy SE
Legend
main route
other trail
paved trail
paved other trail
road
viewpoint
landmark
waterfall
point of interest
champion tree
sentinel tree
picnic area
restroom
playground
bridge
trailhead
parking
drinking fountain
information board
boardwalk
START
to Rottenwood Creek Trail
(page **)
Bob Callan Trail

The trail passes under Interstate North Parkway in 0.2 mile. You'll then arrive at a boardwalk that curves up to the road and a private parking lot. Turn around here and retrace your steps 1 mile to complete your hike.

Hikers and bikers share the multiuse Rottenwood Creek Trail.

Rottenwood Creek Trail

Though the Rottenwood Creek Trail leads to the famous Chattahoochee River, its namesake creek is really the star of this hike. Rottenwood Creek cuts through a deep valley among boulders, rock outcrops, and hardwood forests. The route snakes under highway bridges only minutes from the Atlanta Braves' Truist Park, but this trail can transport you—both literally and figuratively—to a more quiet place. Want to extend your adventure? To the north, you can hike another mile on the Bob Callan Trail (page 357); to the south, the West Palisades trails (page 351) beckon; and to the east, Akers Mill Trail leads to Cochran Shoals (page 369).

HOW TO GET THERE

Driving Distance from Downtown Atlanta: 13 miles
Address: 296 Interstate North Circle SE, Atlanta, GA 30339
Neighborhood: Cumberland
Nearest Interstate: I-285
Public Transit: CobbLinc 10 bus + 1-mile walk
Parking: Small paved parking lot

HIKE DISTANCE

4-mile out-and-back

DIFFICULTY

Overall: Moderate
Navigation: Maps and trail information posted in several places; occasional wayfinding signage
Terrain: Paved multiuse path and boardwalk
Elevation Change: Much of this hike is flat, but there are several extended ascents and descents

SAFETY

Usage ★★★★☆
Visibility ★★★★☆
Upkeep ★★★★☆
Parking ★★★★☆

HOURS

Dawn to dusk

DOGS

Leashed dogs allowed

FACILITIES	• No toilets. Portable toilet at the Paces Mill trailhead • Benches, trash cans
FEES & PERMITS	None
LAND MANAGER	Cobb County Parks & Recreation and National Park Service

Landmarks

ROCK OUTCROP AND WATERFALL

The rocky ravine, outcrop, and waterfall are spectacular surprises underneath Cumberland Boulevard. The ravine's rock formations, the roar of the water, and the 8-foot cascade are hidden from drivers above but a treat for hikers like us!

A pedestrian bridge spans the gorge of scenic Rottenwood Creek.

HARDWOOD FOREST

As the trail climbs the ridge above Rottenwood Creek, to your left is a mature forest of hardwood trees. See if you can pick out chestnut oak, black gum, tulip tree (commonly known as tulip poplar), American beech, mockernut hickory, and more.

CHATTAHOOCHEE RIVER VIEWPOINT

At the confluence of Rottenwood Creek and the Chattahoochee River, there is a great view of the Palisades section of the river (upstream to the left) and the less scenic I-75 bridges (downstream to the right).

Hike Route

Start your hike from the map sign near the parking lot and take the trail to the right, across a repurposed road bridge across Rottenwood Creek. Just after crossing the bridge, there is a dirt trail that leads to an apartment complex, 0.15 mile away. It's not part of this hike route, but you might enjoy exploring it for beautiful creekside views. Walk past the bike rental station and turn right at the first junction to hike under the Interstate North Parkway bridge.

After passing underneath several I-285 bridges, come to an information sign and junction with Akers Mill Trail. (To the left, this trail leads 1 mile to the Cochran Shoals trailhead [page 369].) Stay straight here to continue on Rottenwood Creek Trail across a boardwalk adjacent to a parking lot. The trail passes under Cumberland Boulevard, curves left, then passes under Cumberland Boulevard again. Under this second road bridge, you'll find an amazing view of a giant rock outcrop and waterfall in the creek below.

Continue hiking across a steel pedestrian bridge and then uphill for 0.25 mile. As the trail ascends a ridge between Rottenwood Creek and Cumberland Boulevard, you can enjoy views of the forest canopy below you to the left, including oak, hickory, black gum, and tulip trees. After a steep uphill, the trail dips briefly, then climbs again to reach a high point near a power line pole and junction where you can access benches along Cumberland Boulevard.

Stay straight and descend the ridge on the curving trail for 0.5 mile past mile markers 1.14, 0.88, 0.87, and 0.76. Cross a wooden bridge and then curve left and over a steel bridge spanning Rottenwood Creek. At the far side of the bridge, the trail curves right onto a boardwalk. Hike 0.3 mile to enter the West Palisades unit of the Chattahoochee River National Recreation Area and reach a junction (WP 3) with a dirt trail on the left. Stay straight on the paved path to the

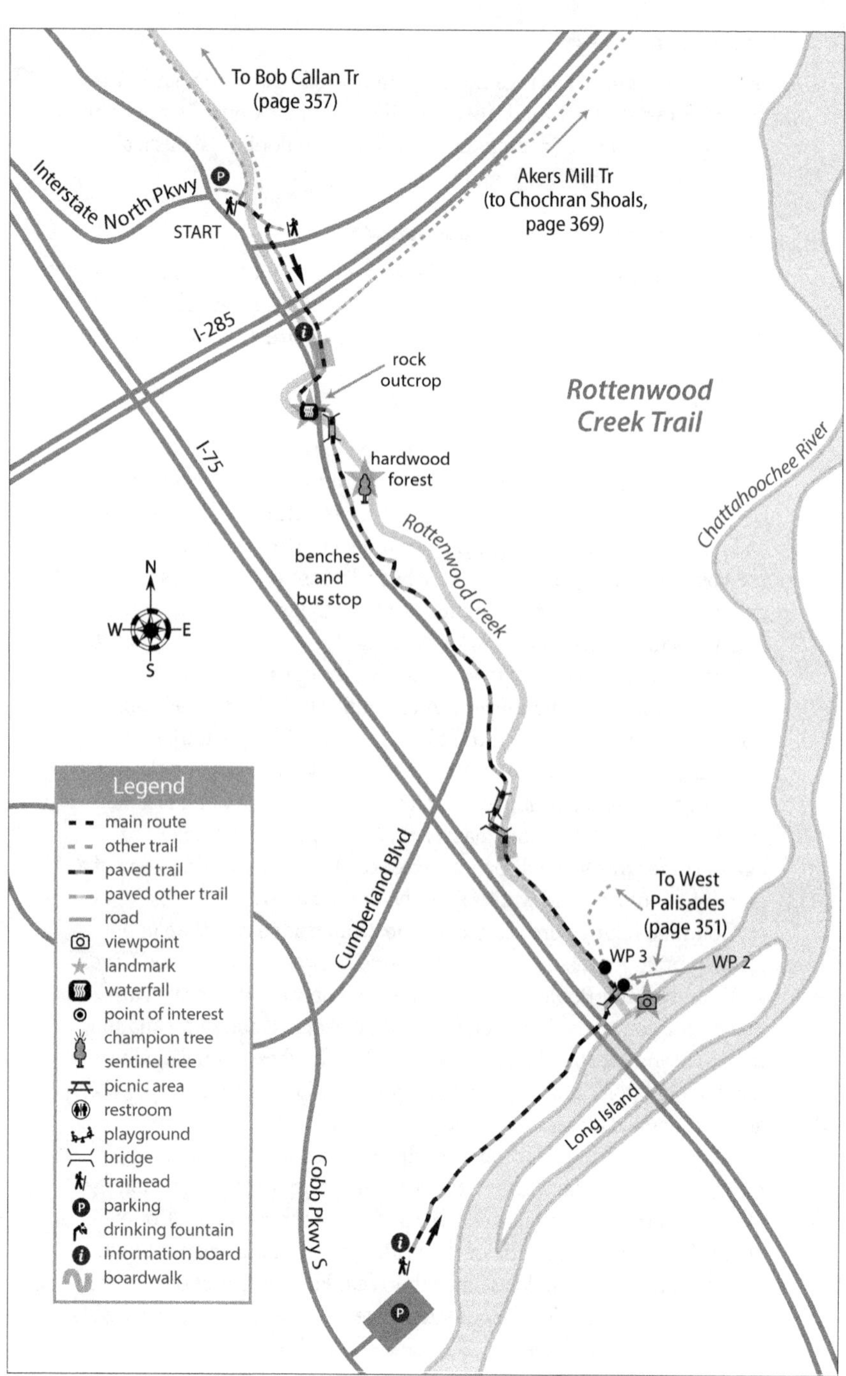

To Bob Callan Tr
(page 357)
Interstate North Pkwy
START
Akers Mill Tr
(to Chochran Shoals,
page 369)
I-285
rock
outcrop
Rottenwood
Creek Trail
hardwood
forest
I-75
Rottenwood Creek
Chattahoochee River
benches
and
bus stop
N
W
E
S
Legend
main route
other trail
paved trail
paved other trail
road
viewpoint
landmark
waterfall
point of interest
champion tree
sentinel tree
picnic area
restroom
playground
bridge
trailhead
parking
drinking fountain
information board
boardwalk
Cumberland Blvd
To West
Palisades
(page 351)
WP 3
WP 2
Long Island
Cobb Pkwy S

next junction (WP 2). To the left, you can hike the dirt trails of West Palisades (page 351) if you choose. Straight ahead is a great view of the Chattahoochee River. This hike turns right and stays on the paved path across another steel bridge over Rottenwood Creek.

Over the next 0.5 mile you'll hike under the I-75 bridge and walk parallel to the Chattahoochee River. There are many side trails to the left leading to the river's edge that are worth exploring here. When you reach the Paces Mill parking area, turn around and retrace your steps for 2 miles to complete your hike.

The flat section of trail along the Chattahoochee is popular among joggers and walkers.

Cochran Shoals

Used mostly for its flat jogging and walking paths along the river, the Cochran Shoals unit of the Chattahoochee River National Recreation Area is also home to miles of hiking and mountain biking trails. This route leads you through quiet Piedmont hollows, past small creeks, and along the edge of the Chattahoochee River. You can connect this loop with the Sope Creek hike (page 381) to make an epic 12-mile trek.

HOW TO GET THERE	**Driving Distance from Downtown Atlanta:** 13 miles **Address:** 2069 Eugene Gunby Road, Marietta, GA 30067 **Neighborhood:** Cumberland **Nearest Interstate:** I-75 **Public Transit:** MARTA 50 bus + 0.5-mile walk **Parking:** Large paved parking lot
HIKE DISTANCE	5.5-mile loop
DIFFICULTY	**Overall:** Moderate to strenuous **Navigation:** Trail map at trailhead, some blazes on trees, maps at most junctions **Terrain:** Hard-packed dirt trails, wide gravel trails **Elevation Change:** Rolling hills with several steep ascents and descents
SAFETY	**Usage** ★★★★★ **Visibility** ★★★★☆ **Upkeep** ★★★★☆ **Parking** ★★★★★
HOURS	Dawn to dusk
DOGS	Leashed dogs allowed
FACILITIES	• Toilets • Water fountain, dog waste station, bike rental, bike rack, picnic tables, trash cans

FEES & PERMITS	$5 daily fee—purchase at recreation.gov
LAND MANAGER	Chattahoochee River National Recreation Area—National Park Service

Landmarks

SENTINEL WHITE OAK

This leaning white oak on the right side of the trail is the largest tree in this area of the woods. Most of the Piedmont forests above the river have been logged many times. This tree began growing after the most recent logging, but its size and unique shape qualify it as a sentinel.

1800S-ERA GRAVESITE

Well preserved and maintained, this gravesite is an unexpected historical relic in the middle of the forest. The marked grave is for the Scribner family and Mary Andrews. The beautiful stone grave markers suggest they were a wealthy family.

SENTINEL WATER OAK

Located next to a bench and water fountain, this is the largest water oak in the park. Because it grows near an open area and has no competition for light, its trunk has grown thick, and its crown is rounded and full.

Hike Route

Start your hike at the payment kiosk at the far end of the parking lot. The hike begins on a very wide gravel path. In 0.1 mile on the left is a large rock shelter formation you can explore. On the main trail continue for 0.4 mile, cross a concrete bridge, and come to a junction (CS 21) with a smaller trail on the left. Turn left, pass the no bikes barrier and follow the trail along a boardwalk through wetlands. At the end of the boardwalk go left at junction CS 22. In 100 feet at the next junction (CS 23) go left and uphill. Follow this steep trail for 0.25 mile before the grade evens out on the top of the ridge, then hike another 0.25 mile.

Pass an unofficial junction on the left before coming to a clearing at junction CS 26. Turn left, pass through the no bikes barrier, and turn right immediately at the trail information sign. Cross through the clearing and then reenter the woods past another no bikes barrier.

An 1800s gravesite is an unexpected landmark in the middle of the park.

Take the trail steeply downhill and then across a small creek. In 0.15 mile, at a junction with a large beech tree, take a hard left and hike uphill. Stay left at the next junction (CS 27) and then pass a leaning sentinel white oak on the right in 100 yards.

In 0.1 mile the trail nears an enormous glass building. Bear right at junction CS 30 and hike along the edge of the property, getting a glimpse of the sculpture in the building's atrium. Then hike 0.20 mile more after the trail turns away from the building.

Stay straight at the first junction (CS 28) you come to. Turn left at the next junction (CS 29) and hike downhill. In 0.10 mile cross a suspension bridge and turn right at junction CS 31. Cross another bridge, then follow the trail for another 0.25 mile to come to a junction with a bridge on the right. Turn right and cross over the bridge. In 100 yards stay right at a junction leading to an apartment complex on the left before reaching the wide gravel shared use path.

Pass the no bikes barrier and turn left at junction CS 18. Continue on the gravel path for 0.25 mile, cross a bridge, and immediately turn left at junction CS 17 onto a small trail paralleling the creek. In 0.35

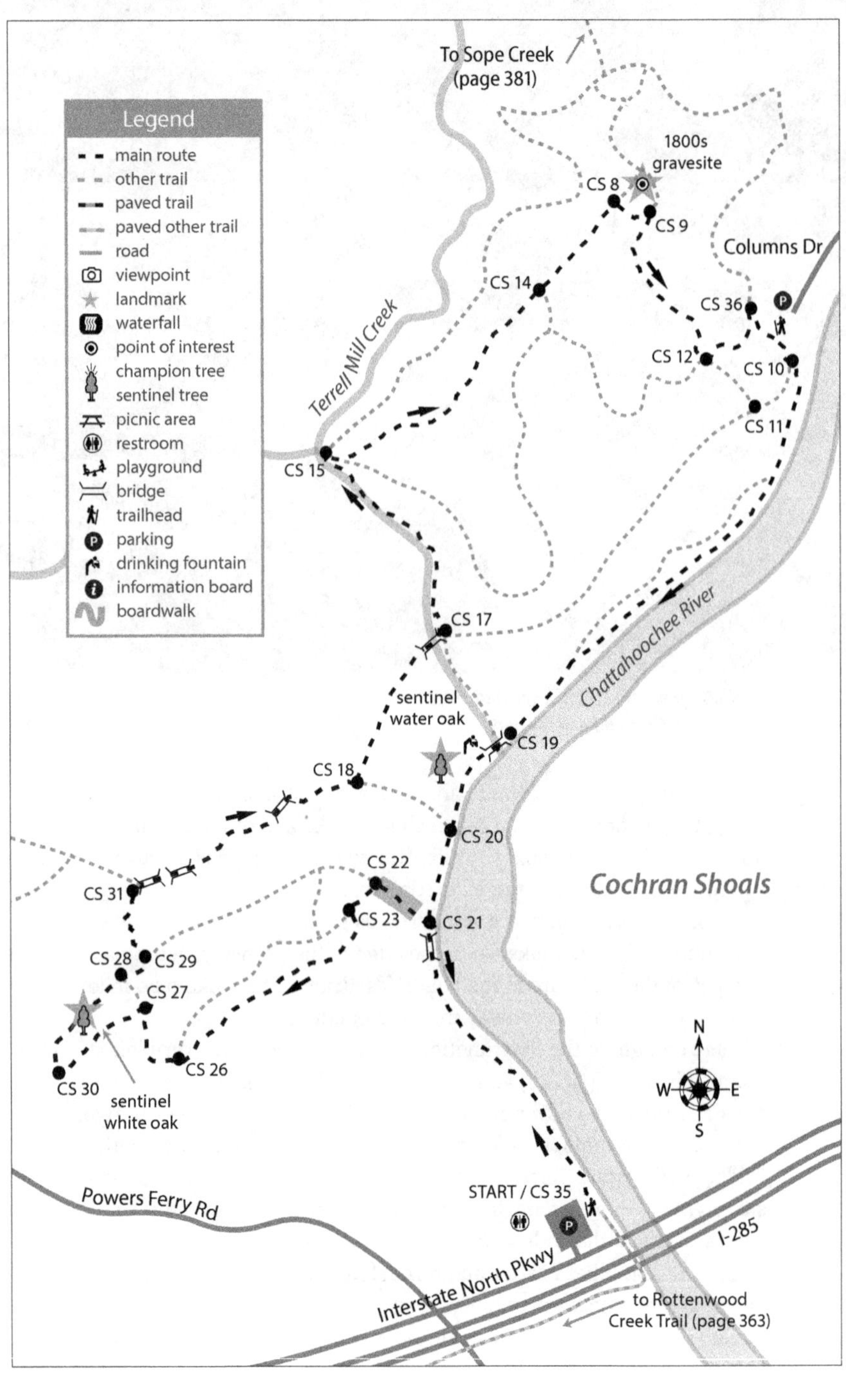

To Sope Creek (page 381)
Legend
main route
other trail
paved trail
paved other trail
road
viewpoint
landmark
waterfall
point of interest
champion tree
sentinel tree
picnic area
restroom
playground
bridge
trailhead
parking
drinking fountain
information board
boardwalk
1800s gravesite
CS 8
CS 9
Columns Dr
CS 14
CS 36
CS 12
CS 10
CS 11
Terrell Mill Creek
CS 15
CS 17
Chattahoochee River
sentinel water oak
CS 19
CS 18
CS 20
Cochran Shoals
CS 22
CS 31
CS 23
CS 21
CS 28
CS 29
CS 27
CS 26
CS 30
sentinel white oak
N
W
E
S
START / CS 35
Powers Ferry Rd
Interstate North Pkwy
I-285
to Rottenwood Creek Trail (page 363)

mile come to a junction with the bike trails. Facing the map post at junction CS 15, hike uphill on the trail directly behind you, crossing over the bike path and entering the trail through the no bikes barrier. Begin a long, steady, uphill climb.

After 0.35 mile stay straight at the next junction (CS 14). In 0.20 reach another junction (CS 8) and turn right. (If you stay straight here and at three subsequent junctions, you will eventually connect with the trail leading to Sope Creek [page 381].) This section of trail can be a bit overgrown in the summertime. Continue for 0.10 mile to reach a well-preserved gravesite from the 1800s and junction CS 9.

Turn right at the grave and hike downhill for 0.30 mile. At junction CS 12 stay straight and then turn left onto the wide gravel trail at junction CS 11. Follow the gravel trail to the north parking lot.

At the parking lot and junction CS 10, turn right and hike past the map and information kiosk and bike rentals. Stay to the right at the next junction and continue along the wide gravel trail that runs parallel to the Chattahoochee. In 0.2 mile, after passing a pole with reflective markers, turn left onto a small trail that is somewhat more secluded and peaceful and parallels the gravel path.

In 0.5 mile the smaller trail reconnects with the main gravel path. Merge and continue in the direction you have been going. Reach a junction (CS 19) near a bridge in 0.15 mile; there is a viewpoint platform on the left. Go straight across the bridge, immediately passing the sentinel white oak on the right behind the drinking fountain. Continue for another 0.15 mile to the next junction (CS 20) and viewpoint platform. Stay straight for 0.6 mile to return to the parking lot and finish your hike.

Great blue herons bask and hunt along the banks of the Chattahoochee.

Powers Island

Powers Island is one of the less crowded areas of the Chattahoochee River National Recreation Area. As an outpost for the Nantahala Outdoor Center, the parking lot also connects to a waterfront raft launch onto the Chattahoochee. The less traveled hiking trail provides a scenic hike on a loop along the edge of the river and across a densely forested ridge.

HOW TO GET THERE

Driving Distance from Downtown Atlanta: 7 miles
Address: 5450 Interstate North Parkway, Sandy Springs, GA 30328
Neighborhood: Sandy Springs
Nearest Interstate: I-285
Public Transit: MARTA 50 bus + 0.5-mile walk
Parking: Large paved parking lot

HIKE DISTANCE

2-mile loop

DIFFICULTY

Overall: Easy to moderate
Navigation: Trails marked by posts and maps at most junctions; map at trailhead; blue blazes
Terrain: Hard-packed dirt trails
Elevation Change: A couple significant ascents and descents but otherwise level

SAFETY

Usage ★★★☆☆
Visibility ★★★☆☆
Upkeep ★★★☆☆
Parking ★★★★☆

HOURS

Dawn to dusk

DOGS

Leashed dogs allowed

FACILITIES

- Toilets
- Water fountain, concessions, trash cans, dog waste station

FEES & PERMITS

$5 daily fee—purchase at recreation.gov

LAND MANAGER	Chattahoochee River National Recreation Area–National Park Service

Landmarks

SENTINEL WATER OAK

Pass an unusual water oak on your right, just before an unofficial trail junction on the right. Tree roots can be incredibly adaptable and strong, as demonstrated by this water oak growing around a boulder.

SENTINEL BEECH

This sentinel beech is midway up a long hill on the right side of the trail. Since this tree is located away from the trail, its smooth gray bark has been preserved from carvings.

SENTINEL SNAG

Though some may consider them an eyesore, snags (dead trees that are still standing) are an important resource in a forest. Even a dead tree can still provide food and shelter for a variety of birds, insects, reptiles, and mammals. This one was once a very large tree and is on the left side of a bridge.

Hike Route

Begin your hike at the far right corner of the parking lot at a map and information board, then enter the forest at a No Bikes sign. The first hundred yards have muscadines growing closely along the edge of the trail. In the summer you may also spot the delicate purple flowers of hog peanuts as you hike along the route. After 0.2 mile on the trail, look to your right to see a water oak growing on and around a boulder. Just after the tree is an unofficial trail on the right that leads up a small creek valley and then dead-ends at the edge of the park.

In 0.3 mile you will reach a map post at a junction. Go to the right, taking the trail as it goes uphill, immediately passing a giant white oak tree, and then coming to a patch of mountain laurel on your right. In 100 yards pass an unofficial trail leading up the ridge to your right. Continue for 0.15 mile, reaching a sentinel beech on the right just below the trail. Stay on this ridge, hiking uphill, for another 0.15 mile until the trail levels out at the top of the hill at a junction. (The trail to the right leads 100 yards steeply downhill to a private hiking trail only for the use of residents of 2100 Riveredge.)

A water oak grows around a boulder, a reminder that nature will find a way.

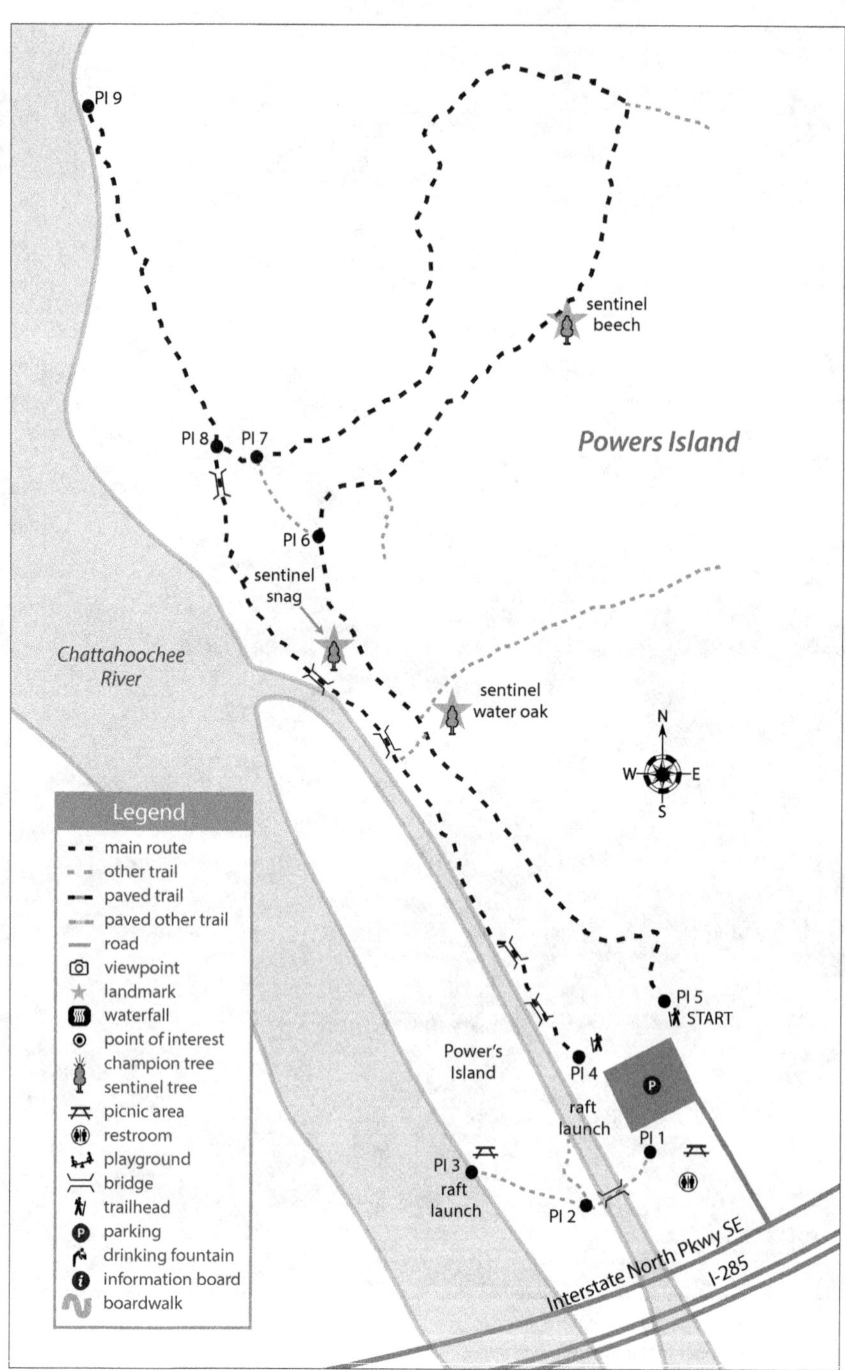
PI 9
sentinel beech
Powers Island
PI 8
PI 7
PI 6
sentinel snag
Chattahoochee River
sentinel water oak
N
W
E
S
Legend
main route
other trail
paved trail
paved other trail
road
viewpoint
landmark
waterfall
point of interest
champion tree
sentinel tree
picnic area
restroom
playground
bridge
trailhead
parking
drinking fountain
information board
boardwalk
PI 5
START
Power's Island
PI 4
raft launch
PI 1
PI 3
raft launch
PI 2
Interstate North Pkwy SE
I-285

Turn left and in less than 50 yards come to a large white oak on the left side of the trail. Continue hiking along the top of the ridge above a residential neighborhood before descending into the river valley. For 0.3 mile the trail continues generally downhill, passing buckeye, ferns, and native ginger before coming to a junction with a map post at junction PI 7.

Turn right and then immediately take another right at junction PI 8, passing under a fallen tree. Hike along the wide path along the Chattahoochee River, passing some nice large boulders for sitting or climbing in 0.1 mile on the right side of the trail. Just 100 yards past the boulders you'll enter a small bamboo forest. The bamboo forest continues for another 0.1 mile, passing a small stone foundation before ending at a map post (PI 9) and viewpoint of the river. From here, turn around and retrace your steps.

In 0.2 mile, when you reach junction PI 8, turn right, continuing to hike along the river's edge. In the summer, this narrow trail can be a bit overgrown. Cross a wooden bridge, then, while crossing a second bridge in 0.1 mile, look immediately on the left for a massive snag. Snags provide shelter and food for a variety of animals.

Continue hiking for 0.25 mile across three more bridges before turning left at junction PI 4 to reach the parking lot and ending your hike.

Explore the 150-year-old paper mill ruins.

Sope Creek

Sope Creek and the paper mill ruins along its banks provide impressive scenery along this hike, and Sibley Pond is a peaceful place to fish or bird-watch. If you're feeling up for a challenge, hike the Sope Creek loop to the Cochran Shoals loop (page 369) to create a 12-mile day hike. Be aware that this is also a popular route for mountain bikers, so be sure to follow the directional signage for hikers.

HOW TO GET THERE	**Driving Distance from Downtown Atlanta:** 18 miles **Address:** 3726 Paper Mill Road SE, Marietta, GA 30067 **Neighborhood:** Powers Park / East Cobb **Nearest Interstate:** I-75 **Public Transit:** CobbLinc 50 bus + 1.5-mile walk **Parking:** Paved parking lot
HIKE DISTANCE	4-mile loop
DIFFICULTY	**Overall:** Moderate **Navigation:** Maps at most trail junctions; some blazes on trees **Terrain:** Hard-packed dirt trails **Elevation Change:** Rolling hills with a few short but steep ascents and descents
SAFETY	**Usage** ★★★★★ **Visibility** ★★★★☆ **Upkeep** ★★★★☆ **Parking** ★★★★☆
HOURS	Dawn to dusk
DOGS	Leashed dogs allowed
FACILITIES	• No toilets • Picnic tables, trash can, dog waste station, water fountain
FEES & PERMITS	$5 daily fee—purchase at recreation.gov

LAND MANAGER Chattahoochee River National Recreation Area—National Park Service

---

Landmarks

SIBLEY POND

Soon after the start of your hike, you'll reach scenic Sibley Pond. The platform and open space here are utilized by park visitors for fishing and by park rangers for educational programming.

SOPE CREEK AND PAPER MILL RUINS VIEWPOINT

This rock outcrop near junction SC 6 is a great place to take a hiking break near the creek and to get a glimpse of the paper mill ruins. Have a snack and rehydrate while listening to the sounds of the flowing water.

PAPER MILL RUINS

The foundation of the paper mill ruins remains mostly intact. You can spend a few minutes exploring and walking through the structures. The mill produced paper used for Confederate currency and was destroyed by Union troops during the Civil War.

Hike Route

Most of the trails in the Sope Creek unit of the Chattahoochee River National Recreation Area were built for mountain biking. Hikers are welcome, but please be aware of and be courteous to bicyclists. Be sure to hike the *opposite* direction bikers are directed on the trailhead sign. These instructions are based on Friday directions: bikers ride clockwise (left), and hikers walk counterclockwise (right). Pay special attention while hiking uphill, because bikes may be coming downhill toward you at fast speeds. Always keep your eyes open and listen while hiking on trails shared with mountain bikers.

Start your hike by walking through the metal fence to the right of the map post (SC 1) to enter the wide gravel service road. Go straight past junction SC 2 and SC 15 to reach the Sibley Pond dam. After crossing the dam, go right at SC 14 to continue to loop around the pond.

In 0.15 mile cross a bridge and go left at SC 17. At the next junction (SC 18) in 0.1 mile, turn left. After another 0.1 mile, reach a junction (SC 19) with the wider bike trail. Pass through the no bikes barrier and turn right.

The banks of Sope Creek are a scenic spot for lunch or a snack.

Immediately after turning right, stay left at a junction with an unofficial trail on the right. Hike another 0.1 mile and stay right at junction SC 23 to stay on the bike trail (not left onto the hikers-only trail). Go left at the next junction in 0.1 mile.

In 0.4 mile you'll reach a junction (SC 24) with the trail on the right that leads to the Cochran Shoals (page 369) unit of the Chattahoochee River National Recreation Area. Continue left through an area with many young buckeye and beech trees as the trail parallels Fox Creek. In 0.3 mile go straight at junction SC 25 and cross a small footbridge.

In 0.25 mile cross another bridge and then go left and uphill across from an unofficial trail leading into an apartment complex. In 0.1 mile at the top of the hill, continue straight at junction SC 9. The trail parallels Sope Creek for 0.4 mile and this is a particularly secluded and scenic section of the hike. At the next junction (SC 8) turn right. In 0.1 mile go right at another junction (SC 7). In the next 0.2 mile, after crossing a creek near large boulders, stay to the right to reach another major junction. Turn right at SC 6 to take a short detour (100

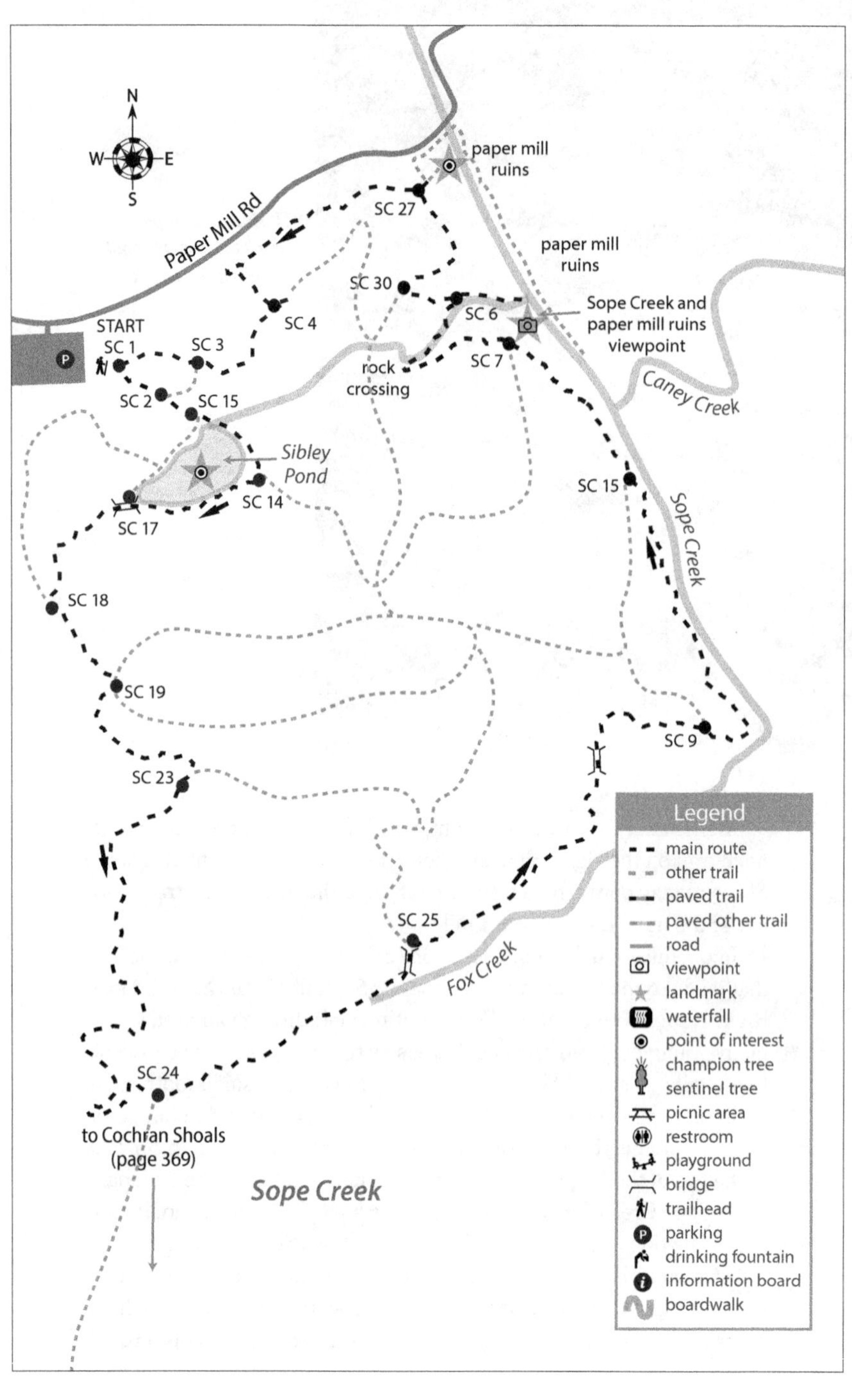
N
W
E
S
Paper Mill Rd
paper mill ruins
SC 27
paper mill ruins
SC 30
Sope Creek and paper mill ruins viewpoint
SC 6
SC 4
START
SC 1
SC 3
P
rock crossing
SC 7
Caney Creek
SC 2
SC 15
Sibley Pond
SC 15
SC 14
SC 17
Sope Creek
SC 18
SC 19
SC 9
SC 23
Legend
main route
other trail
paved trail
paved other trail
road
viewpoint
landmark
waterfall
point of interest
champion tree
sentinel tree
picnic area
restroom
playground
bridge
trailhead
parking
drinking fountain
information board
boardwalk
SC 25
Fox Creek
SC 24
to Cochran Shoals (page 369)
Sope Creek

yards) for a view of Sope Creek and a glimpse of the ruins. This is a very beautiful spot for a break or snack.

Retrace your steps past junction SC 6 and then take the right fork at the next junction (SC 30) in 50 feet. In 0.2 mile reach a junction (SC 26) with a large oak on the right that leads down to the mill ruins. Spend time exploring the ruins or sitting on the rocks along Sope Creek.

(To explore the optional spur to the ruins on the far side of Sope Creek, retrace your steps to the historical signpost and take the trail to the right leading toward the street. Cross the guardrail onto the sidewalk and cross the Paper Mill Road bridge over Sope Creek, immediately turning right onto a wide gravel path after the bridge. This path leads 0.3 mile to the ruins and Caney Creek. Retrace your route back to the other side of the creek and the historical sign.)

From the ruins and map post SC 27, return back uphill and go right. In 50 feet at the next junction (SC 26) go left. Turn right at the next two junctions (SC 4 and SC 3), following these hikers-only trails for 0.2 mile back to the parking lot to end your hike.

Large trees grow along the river's edge.

Johnson Ferry South

Though not as well used as its neighbor, Johnson Ferry North, this unit of the Chattahoochee River National Recreation Area offers a secluded picnic area and peaceful walking along the riverbank. The trail follows the path of an old farm road along the banks of the Chattahoochee. Large trees grow at the river's edge, and wild blackberries abound in the young forest that is quickly replacing the once cultivated fields.

HOW TO GET THERE

Driving Distance from Downtown Atlanta: 19 miles
Address: 4650 Columns Drive SE, Marietta, GA 30067
Neighborhood: Sandy Springs
Nearest Interstate: I-285
Public Transit: MARTA 87 bus + 2.5-mile walk
Parking: Gravel parking lot at the end of a gravel road off Columns Drive

HIKE DISTANCE

2-mile out-and-back

DIFFICULTY

Overall: Easy
Navigation: Map at trailhead
Terrain: Hard-packed dirt trail
Elevation Change: Minimal elevation change—very level

SAFETY

Usage ★★★☆☆
Visibility ★★★★☆
Upkeep ★★★★☆
Parking ★★★☆☆

HOURS

Dawn to dusk

DOGS

Leashed dogs allowed

FACILITIES

- No toilets
- Picnic pavilion, information board, dog waste station

FEES & PERMITS

$5 daily pass—can purchase at recreation.gov

LAND MANAGER

Chattahoochee River National Recreation Area—National Park Service

---

Landmarks

SENTINEL WATER OAKS

The farm that once existed on this site did not clear the large timber from the banks of the Chattahoochee. As a result, many older hardwood trees still remain, including these water oaks.

SENTINEL BLACK WALNUTS

Native black walnut trees produce nuts that are edible for animals and humans, but they are much harder to crack than the English walnuts we buy in the grocery stores. This grove of walnut trees to the right of the trail where the route curves left includes one of the largest of this species in the metro area.

RIVER VIEWPOINT

There are few rivers or creeks in Atlanta as scenic as the Chattahoochee, with its wide channel and tree-lined banks. Take a moment here to enjoy the view.

Hike Route

Start your hike facing the information signs near the parking area. Turn left onto the dirt trail that parallels the Chattahoochee River. In 100 feet on the right of the trail pass the first of several large sentinel water oaks. Just past the water oaks in 0.1 mile on the right is a small trail leading down to the river next to a large tree 20 feet off the trail.

Enjoy the serene hike along the Chattahoochee River and be on the lookout during the summer for wild blackberries growing on the edges of the trail. Hike the main path for an additional 0.5 mile. Just before the end, when the trail curves left, look on the right for three giant sentinel black walnut trees, which produce edible nuts. When the trail ends at Columns Drive, turn around and retrace your steps 0.6 mile to the parking area. Just as you reach the information board, take a small trail on the left that leads down to a closer view of the river. Return to the main trail and then hike left toward the large picnic pavilion.

Hike through the grassy field past the picnic pavilion and reenter the forest. Hike this trail for 0.3 mile to where it splits. The left fork leads to a great viewpoint at the river's edge. The right fork leads 50 feet to the end of the trail at map JS 2. Visit the river viewpoint and then turn around and retrace your steps back to the parking lot to finish your hike.

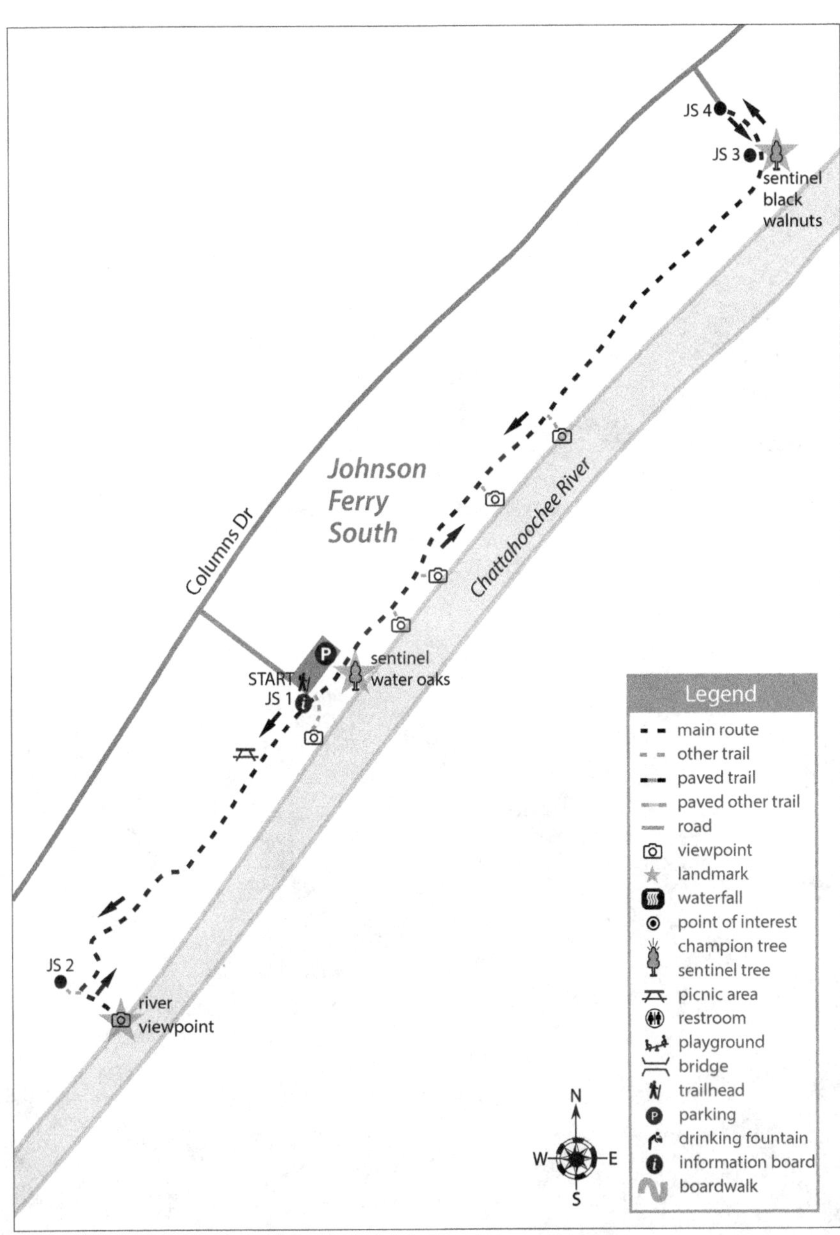
JS 4
JS 3
sentinel
black
walnuts
Johnson
Ferry
South
Columns Dr
Chattahoochee River
sentinel
water oaks
START
JS 1
JS 2
river
viewpoint
Legend
main route
other trail
paved trail
paved other trail
road
viewpoint
landmark
waterfall
point of interest
champion tree
sentinel tree
picnic area
restroom
playground
bridge
trailhead
parking
drinking fountain
information board
boardwalk
N
W
E
S

A field of native flowers shows bright colors in the summer.

Johnson Ferry North & Hyde Farm

This popular trail in the Chattahoochee River National Recreation Area provides a great place for a jog, a family outing, or an extended hike. Hikers can stroll along the riverbank, crisscross a rocky stream in a secluded hollow, and visit a historic farm. Leashed dogs will enjoy a quick splash in the creek on a hot summer day. And if you are feeling more adventurous, you can extend your hike upstream along the river for a great view of the Morgan Falls Dam.

HOW TO GET THERE	**Driving Distance from Downtown Atlanta:** 19 miles **Address:** 301 Johnson Ferry Road SE, Marietta, GA 30068 **Neighborhood:** Sandy Springs **Nearest Interstate:** I-285 **Public Transit:** MARTA 87 bus + 2-mile walk **Parking:** Large paved and gravel parking lots
HIKE DISTANCE	1.5-mile, 3.5-mile, or 5.5-mile loop
DIFFICULTY	**Overall:** Easy or moderate to strenuous, depending on the route **Navigation:** Occasional signage and map posts **Terrain:** Gravel and hard-packed dirt trails **Elevation Change:** Relatively flat with a few extended ascents and descents
SAFETY	**Usage** ★★★★☆ **Visibility** ★★★★☆ **Upkeep** ★★★★☆ **Parking** ★★★★★
HOURS	Dawn to dusk
DOGS	Leashed dogs allowed
FACILITIES	• Toilets • Water fountain, information kiosk, picnic areas, boat ramp
FEES & PERMITS	$5 daily fee—purchase at recreation.gov

LAND MANAGER Chattahoochee River National Recreation Area—National Park Service

Landmarks

ROCK OUTCROP CASCADE

The section of Mulberry Creek just upstream from junction JN 5 is very scenic. The water flows across an unusual rock outcrop with many cracks and fissures. If you choose to put your feet in the water, be careful, because the rocks can be slippery.

SENTINEL POST OAK

This giant tree near a community garden might be older than Hyde Farm. Its branches stretch wide and are laden with a special plant called resurrection fern that shrivels up and looks dead in dry weather but comes back to lush green life after rain.

MORGAN FALLS DAM VIEWPOINT

If you make it to this viewpoint, you've had a big adventure today. The dam was completed in 1904 and still produces hydroelectric power for Atlanta residents. It also helps control flooding. When the dam releases water, a giant waterfall erupts over its edge, making this spot one of the best views in the Atlanta area.

Hike Route

This hike has three options. Choose the options that best satisfy your appetite for adventure (and miles).

Begin your hike at the far left end of the gravel parking lot on a grassy trail between the fence and field. In 0.15 mile pass an interpretive sign about birds of the Chattahoochee, then reach junction JN 3 and turn left, immediately crossing a long boardwalk that leads into the forest. Stay right at the end of the boardwalk.

Hike for 0.5 mile through a mature forest and alongside several ponds and wetlands to reach junction JN 4 near mulberry creek. Go left. In 50 yards you'll reach junction JN 5. If you want to begin hiking back to the trailhead now, turn right and hike 0.1 mile to reach junction JN 6. If you want to continue your adventure and hike farther, continue below.

A long boardwalk at the entry to the forest is a prime spot to listen to frog calls.

ADVENTURE OPTION 1:
HIKE TO HYDE FARM (ADDS 2 MILES)

Junction JN 5 is where the National Park Service maintenance ends. To hike to Hyde Farm, stay straight and look for a beautiful cascade flowing through an unusual rock outcrop to your right. This trail continues for 0.75 mile, crossing the creek on rocks at least eight times. Just after a creek crossing with a blue Cobb County emergency location post, you'll reach a trail junction. Take the left fork.

Cross the creek one more time, then reach a junction near a footbridge built by an Eagle Scout. Turn right and cross the bridge, then hike uphill for 0.1 mile to reach a junction at the edge of a small lake. Continue straight along the ridge above the lake. The trail emerges from the forest into a power line clearing. Continue to circle the lake through the grass, passing multiple benches. When you reach Hyde Road, pass through the barrier and walk uphill to the right on the road through Cobb County Parks & Recreation facilities. You'll pass another barricade, then reach a fenced community garden and a

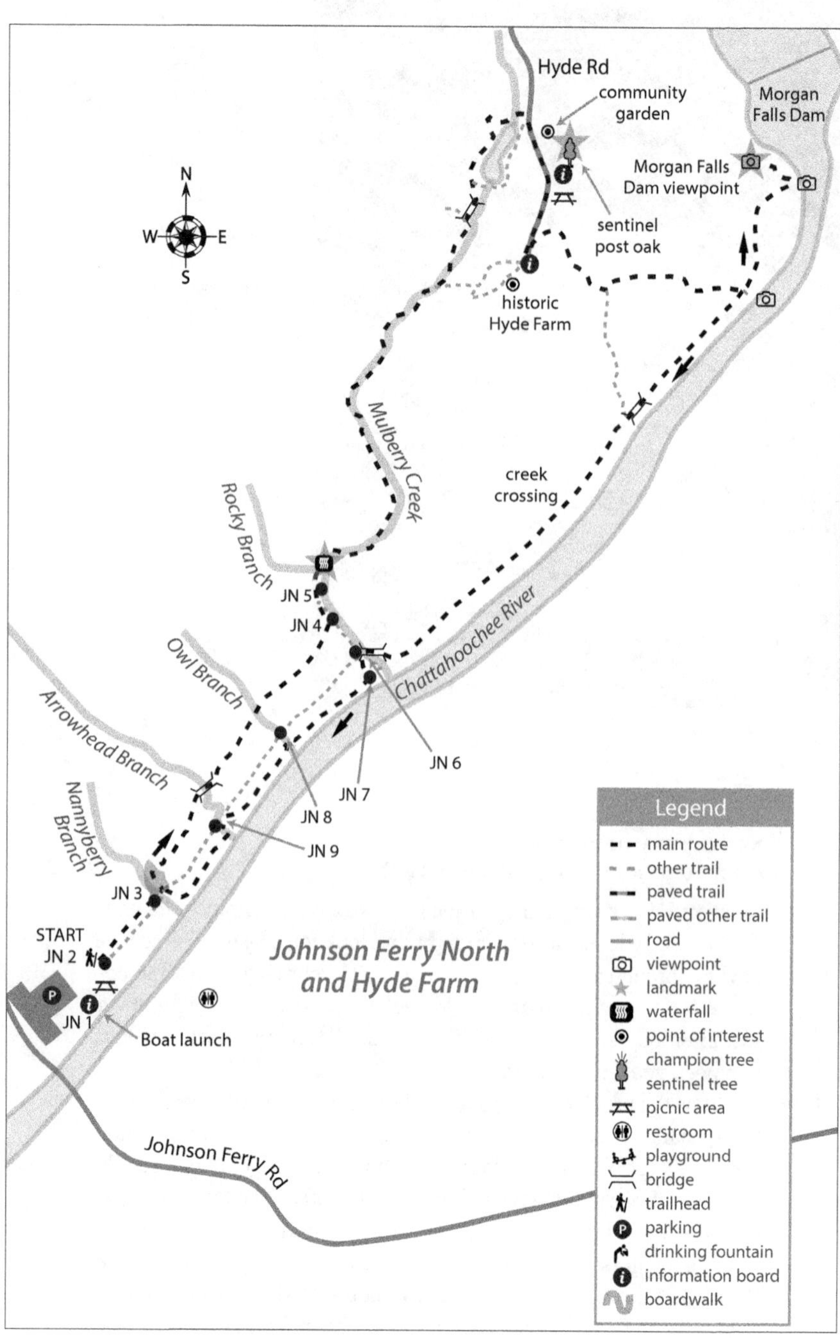

Hyde Rd
community garden
Morgan Falls Dam
Morgan Falls Dam viewpoint
sentinel post oak
historic Hyde Farm
Mulberry Creek
Rocky Branch
creek crossing
Chattahoochee River
Owl Branch
Arrowhead Branch
Nannyberry Branch
JN 1
START JN 2
JN 3
JN 4
JN 5
JN 6
JN 7
JN 8
JN 9
Boat launch
Johnson Ferry Rd
Johnson Ferry North and Hyde Farm
Legend
main route
other trail
paved trail
paved other trail
road
viewpoint
landmark
waterfall
point of interest
champion tree
sentinel tree
picnic area
restroom
playground
bridge
trailhead
parking
drinking fountain
information board
boardwalk

sentinel post oak tree with picnic tables under its branches. This is a good place for a midhike snack. Continue straight on Hyde Road to reach an information board near the historic farm.

If you want to begin hiking back to the trailhead now, face the information board and then turn right on the wide trail outside the split rail fence. Turn right at the next junction and hike downhill to the path along the creek that you hiked before, turn left, and hike 0.75 mile back to junction JN 5. If you want to extend your hike farther, continue below.

ADVENTURE OPTION 2: MORGAN FALLS DAM VIEWPOINT (ADDS 2 MILES)

Facing the information board at Hyde Farm, look for a trail behind you that runs parallel to the road and then curves to the right. Take this wide trail and hike downhill for 0.25 mile to reach a junction. Turn left and continue downhill. The trail narrows and passes through a clearing near private property. This next section of trail can be very overgrown. Walk 0.3 mile through a utilities clearing to reach a junction on the far side of the clearing. Turn left to hike 0.25 mile to two fantastic viewpoints of Morgan Falls Dam. After taking in the view, turn around and hike back to the junction in the clearing and continue straight, following the trail along the left edge of the clearing. This clearing contains sewer lines and a petroleum pipeline. Generally follow the raised concrete sewer access points.

Cross a concrete bridge over a creek in 0.3 mile, then pass a junction with a trail on the right that leads back uphill to Hyde Farm. Continue straight for 0.2 mile more. The trail then dips steeply downhill, crosses a creek, then heads steeply back up. After another 0.25 mile the clearing splits. Follow the trail along the left fork, then cross a concrete bridge that leads you back onto national recreation area land at junction JN 6.

It is here that these three hike routes join back together. From JN 6 hike toward the river into the forest to reach junction JN 7 in only about 100 yards. Turn right and hike 0.3 mile along the riverbank to reach junction JN 8 in the utility clearing. Turn left, cross a small creek, then turn left again onto a forested trail. Hike 0.2 mile until the trail emerges into the clearing again at JN 9. Cross another creek and turn left into the woods, then hike 0.2 mile to arrive back at the gravel parking lot to end your hike.

MORE TRAILS TO EXPLORE

While researching this guidebook we fell in love with so many more greenspaces than would fit on these pages. If you are looking for more adventure, we recommend you research and explore the following places.

Eastside

Avondale Lake
East Decatur Greenway
Frazier-Rowe Park
Glenn Creek Nature Preserve
Hidden Cove Park
Lenox-Wildwood Park
Little Creek Horse Farm & Park
Mary Scott Nature Park
Oakland Cemetery
Oldcastle Nature Trail at Marcus Autism Center
Shamrock Forest
Woodland Gardens

Southside

Brady Trail
Exchange Park
Grant Park
Intrenchment Creek Park
McDaniel Branch Wetlands
Skyhaven Quarry
Urban Food Forest at Browns Mill

Westside

Perkerson Park
Standing Peachtree Park
Whetstone Creek Trail

Northside

Atlanta History Center
Blackburn Park
Briarwood Park
Clear Creek Nature Preserve
Keswick Park
Lavista Park
Mountain Way Common
PATH400

ATLANTA'S CHAMPION TREES

Among the landmarks highlighted throughout this book are city and state champion trees. Trees Atlanta maintains the list of Atlanta's champion trees within the I-285 perimeter. All trees are nominated and identified by community members and then reviewed by trained volunteers.

A tree qualifies as an Atlanta champion tree if it is one of the three largest of its species inside the I-285 perimeter as measured by its circumference, height, and crown spread. Not all the trees listed below are along the hike routes in this book, but each tree can be found in its park using Trees Atlanta's champion tree list:

https://www.treesatlanta.org/atlantas-champion-trees/

* = tree mentioned specifically in this guidebook
† = state champion

Clyde Shepherd Nature Preserve

loblolly pine
southern red oak

Dearborn Park

red maple
northern red oak

Fernbank Forest

ironwood
bitternut hickory
pignut hickory
deodar cedar
eastern redbud
Japanese cedar†
American persimmon
spicebush
umbrella magnolia
dawn redwood
blackgum
sourwood
shortleaf pine
white pine
loblolly pine
black cherry
northern red oak
black oak
basswood
eastern hemlock*
winged elm

Frazer Forest & Deepdene Park

bitternut hickory
eastern red cedar
spicebush
sweetgum
shortleaf pine
northern red oak
rosebay rhododendron
basswood

Glenlake Park & Decatur Cemetery

American beech
pignut hickory*
Virginia pine*
American holly
eastern red cedar*
black locust
sassafras

Hahn Woods & Lullwater Preserve

devil's walking stick
ironwood
American beech
scarlet oak†
eastern hophornbeam
loblolly pine*
rusty blackhaw viburnum†

Kittredge Park

sassafras

Mason Mill Park

boxelder*
red maple*
river birch*
eastern red cedar
northern red oak

Mercer University Nature Trail

American holly*

Morningside Nature Preserve

loblolly pine

W.D. Thomson Park

basswood*

Zonolite Park & Herbert Taylor Park

silver maple*
bitternut hickory
pecan*
sugarberry

American persimmon
black walnut*
sweetgum*
tulip tree*
eastern cottonwood
black cherry*
scarlet oak
black oak
basswood

Freedom Park Trail

sugarberry

Connally Nature Park

white oak*†

Gresham Park & South River Trail

cherrybark oak

Lake Charlotte Nature Preserve

shagbark hickory

Cascade Springs Nature Preserve

ironwood
green ash
bigleaf magnolia*
sourwood*

Outdoor Activity Center

American beech*

Riverwalk Atlanta & Whittier Mill Park

silver maple*
pawpaw*
green ash
American sycamore
eastern cottonwood

Lionel Hampton Park & Beecher Hills Park

bitternut hickory*

Proctor Creek Greenway

northern red oak

Chastain Memorial Park

green ash*
white pine

Atlanta Memorial Park

river birch*
green ash*
Osage orange*
loblolly pine
water oak
bald cypress

Confluence Trail & Cheshire Farm Trail

American sycamore

Piedmont Park & Eastside Beltline

pin oak*†
black oak
black willow
winged elm

Tanyard Creek Park & Northside Beltline

American persimmon
white ash*†
Carolina silverbell

East Palisades

red maple
pawpaw*
river birch*
silverbell
chestnut oak
bladdernut

PHOTO CREDITS

All photos are by the authors except those on the following pages, for which the authors thank the photographers:

39	Marlene Goldman
42	Mary Ann Downey
156	Jessica Thompson
159	Paul Stevens

ABOUT THE AUTHORS

Jonah McDonald

Jonah McDonald arrived in Atlanta on foot over two decades ago. After completing his 2,172-mile southbound thru-hike on the Appalachian Trail, he put down roots in Atlanta. Today he serves as the DeKalb County park naturalist at Mason Mill Park. He published the first edition of *Hiking Atlanta's Hidden Forests: Intown and Out* in 2014. His second book, published in 2020, is titled *Secret Atlanta: A Guide to the Weird, Wonderful, and Obscure.*

Jonah is also a storyteller, television host, and tour guide. He loves exploring his city via bicycle or canoe or on foot and believes that there is a new story to learn and tell around every bend. When he's not already on an adventure, Jonah loves finding a new one. Connect with him at jonahmcdonald.com.

Zana Pouncey

Zana Pouncey is a native southerner and has lived in Atlanta for over 10 years. She loves city life with all her heart but is a passionate environmentalist at her core. Connecting people to nature is her calling. After graduating from Emory University with a degree in environmental science, Zana spent several years working in environmental advocacy and education for nonprofit organizations, including Trees Atlanta, Zoo Atlanta, and the Atlanta Botanical Garden. She has been awarded a Grosvenor Teacher Fellowship by the National Geographic Society, is on the board of the Atlanta Green Theater Alliance, has presented at environmental conferences and teacher workshops, and has written for National Geographic's Education blog.

Zana finds enjoyment in most outdoor activities and is partial to riding bikes and kayaking with her life partner, Matthew, as well as jogging, yoga, bird-watching from her porch, and gardening. She looks forward to the day her nieces and nephew are old enough to join her on hikes. Zana recently became a certified sound healing practitioner and aspires to become a certified herbalist.

She's incredibly grateful to be coauthor of the new edition of *Hiking Intown Atlanta's Hidden Forests.*